T0213009

Communications
in Computer and Information Science   743

Commenced Publication in 2007
Founding and Former Series Editors:
Alfredo Cuzzocrea, Orhun Kara, Dominik Ślęzak, and Xiaokang Yang

More information about this series at http://www.springer.com/series/7899

Enrique Cabello · Jorge Cardoso
André Ludwig · Leszek A. Maciaszek
Marten van Sinderen (Eds.)

Software Technologies

11th International Joint Conference, ICSOFT 2016
Lisbon, Portugal, July 24–26, 2016
Revised Selected Papers

 Springer

Editors
Enrique Cabello
Edifici Ampliación del Rectorado
Universidad Rey Juan Carlos
Madrid
Spain

Jorge Cardoso
Departamento de Engenharia Informática
Universidade de Coimbra
Coimbra
Portugal

André Ludwig
Kühne Logistics University – KLU
Hamburg
Germany

Leszek A. Maciaszek
Wroclaw University of Economics
Wroclaw
Poland

Marten van Sinderen
Information Systems Group
Enschede
The Netherlands

ISSN 1865-0929   ISSN 1865-0937 (electronic)
Communications in Computer and Information Science
ISBN 978-3-319-62568-3   ISBN 978-3-319-62569-0 (eBook)
DOI 10.1007/978-3-319-62569-0

Library of Congress Control Number: 2017945730

Printed on acid-free paper

This Springer imprint is published by Springer Nature
The registered company is Springer International Publishing AG
The registered company address is: Gewerbestrasse 11, 6330 Cham, Switzerland

Preface

The present book includes extended and revised versions of a set of selected papers from the 11th International Joint Conference on Software Technologies (ICSOFT 2016), held in Lisbon, Portugal, during 24–26 July, 2016.

ICSOFT 2016 received 84 paper submissions from 26 countries, of which 19% are included in this book. The papers were selected by the event chairs and their selection is based on a number of criteria that include the classifications and comments provided by the Program Committee members, the session chairs' assessment and also the program chairs' global view of all papers included in the technical program. The authors of selected papers were then invited to submit a revised and extended version of their papers having at least 30% innovative material.

The purpose of ICSOFT is to bring together researchers, engineers, and practitioners working in areas that are either related to new software paradigm trends or to mainstream software engineering and applications. ICSOFT is composed of two co-located conferences, each specialized in the aforementioned areas. Together, ICSOFT-EA and ICSOFT-PT aim at becoming a major meeting point for software engineers worldwide.

The papers selected to be included in this book contribute to the understanding of relevant trends of current research on software technologies, including:

– Modelling for mobile devices
– Software and system testing
– Model-driven software development
– Reengineering systems for multi-tenancy
– Embedded and real-time systems reconfiguration
– Domain-specific languages and modelling
– Software and systems quality
– Context-aware and dynamically adapting software systems

We would like to thank all the authors for their contributions and the reviewers who have helped ensure the quality of this publication.

February 2017

Enrique Cabello
Jorge Cardoso
André Ludwig
Leszek Maciaszek
Marten van Sinderen

Organization

Conference Chair

Enrique Cabello   Universidad Rey Juan Carlos, Spain

Program Co-chairs

ICSOFT-EA

Leszek Maciaszek   Wroclaw University of Economics, Poland and
Macquarie University, Sydney, Australia

ICSOFT-PT

Jorge Cardoso   University of Coimbra, Portugal and Huawei European
Research Center, Germany
André Ludwig   Kühne Logistics University, Germany
Marten van Sinderen   University of Twente, The Netherlands

ICSOFT-EA Program Committee

Markus Aleksy	ABB Corporate Research Center, Germany
Waleed Alsabhan	KACST, UK
Nicolas Anquetil	Inria and USTL, France
Jocelyn Armarego	Murdoch University, Australia
Bernhard Bauer	University of Augsburg, Germany
Fevzi Belli	Izmir Institute of Technology, Turkey
Jorge Bernardino	Polytechnic Institute of Coimbra, ISEC, Portugal
Mario Berón	Universidad Nacional de San Luis, Argentina
Andrea Burattin	University of Innsbruck, Austria
Dumitru Burdescu	University of Craiova, Romania
Fergal Mc Caffery	Dundalk Institute of Technology, Ireland
Antoni Lluís Mesquida Calafat	Universitat de les Illes Balears (UIB), Spain
Krzysztof Cetnarowicz	AGH, University of Science and Technology, Poland
Kung Chen	National Chengchi University, Taiwan
Marta Cimitile	Unitelma Sapienza, Italy
Rem Collier	University College Dublin, Ireland
António Miguel Rosado da Cruz	Instituto Politécnico de Viana do Castelo, Portugal

Lidia Cuesta	Universitat Politècnica de Catalunya, Spain
Aldo Dagnino	ABB Corporate Research, USA
Steven Demurjian	University of Connecticut, USA
Philippe Dugerdil	Geneva School of Business Administration, University of Applied Sciences of Western Switzerland, Switzerland
Maria Jose Escalona	University of Seville, Spain
João Faria	FEUP, University of Porto, Portugal
Cléver Ricardo Guareis de Farias	University of São Paulo, Brazil
Matthias Galster	University of Canterbury, New Zealand
Kehan Gao	Eastern Connecticut State University, USA
Hamza Gharsellaoui	Al-Jouf College of Technology, TVTC, Saudi Arabia
Paola Giannini	University of Piemonte Orientale, Italy
J. Paul Gibson	Mines-Telecom, Telecom SudParis, France
Hatim Hafiddi	INPT, Morocco
Slimane Hammoudi	ESEO, MODESTE, France
Jean Hauck	Universidade Federal de Santa Catarina, Brazil
Pedro Rangel Henriques	University of Minho, Portugal
Jose Luis Arciniegas Herrera	Universidad del Cauca, Colombia
Jose R. Hilera	University of Alcala, Spain
Jang-Eui Hong	Chungbuk National University, Korea, Republic of
Shihong Huang	Florida Atlantic University, USA
Zbigniew Huzar	University of Wroclaw, Poland
Ivan Ivanov	SUNY Empire State College, USA
Judit Jasz	University of Szeged, Hungary
Lingxiao Jiang	Singapore Management University, Singapore
Bo Nørregaard Jørgensen	University of Southern Denmark, Denmark
Sanpawat Kantabutra	Chiang Mai University, Thailand
Dimitris Karagiannis	University of Vienna, Austria
Carlos Kavka	ESTECO SpA, Italy
Mieczyslaw Kokar	Northeastern University, USA
Jitka Komarkova	University of Pardubice, Czech Republic
Jun Kong	North Dakota State University, USA
Martin Kropp	University of Applied Sciences Northwestern Switzerland, Switzerland
Rob Kusters	Eindhoven University of Technology and Open University of the Netherlands, The Netherlands
Giuseppe Lami	Consiglio Nazionale delle Ricerche, Italy
Konstantin Läufer	Loyola University Chicago, USA
David Lorenz	Open University, Israel
Ivan Lukovic	University of Novi Sad, Serbia
Ricardo J. Machado	Universidade do Minho, Portugal
Leszek Maciaszek	Wroclaw University of Economics, Poland and Macquarie University, Sydney, Australia

Dietmar Winkler	Vienna University of Technology, Austria
Murat Yilmaz	Çankaya University, Turkey
Elena Zucca	University of Genoa, Italy

ICSOFT-EA Additional Reviewers

Sharmistha Chatterjee	Florida Atlantic University, USA
Aritra Ghosh	Florida Atlantic University, USA
Carlos Salgado	Universidade do Minho, Portugal
Nikolaos Tantouris	University of Vienna, Austria
Michael Walch	University of Vienna, Austria

ICSOFT-PT Program Committee

Hafiz Farooq Ahmad	King Faisal University, Saudi Arabia
Markus Aleksy	ABB Corporate Research Center, Germany
Uwe Assmann	TU-Dresden, Germany
Colin Atkinson	University of Mannheim, Germany
Maurice H. ter Beek	ISTI-CNR, Pisa, Italy
Wolfgang Bein	University of Nevada, Las Vegas, USA
Fevzi Belli	Izmir Institute of Technology, Turkey
Jorge Bernardino	Polytechnic Institute of Coimbra, ISEC, Portugal
Marcello M. Bersani	Politecnico di Milano, Italy
Marcello Bonsangue	Leiden University, The Netherlands
Thomas Buchmann	University of Bayreuth, Germany
Dumitru Burdescu	University of Craiova, Romania
Nelio Cacho	Federal University of Rio Grande do Norte, Brazil
Fergal Mc Caffery	Dundalk Institute of Technology, Ireland
Gerardo Canfora	Rcost, Research Centre On Software Technology, Italy
Marta Cimitile	Unitelma Sapienza, Italy
Rem Collier	University College Dublin, Ireland
Agostino Cortesi	Università Ca' Foscari di Venezia, Italy
Sergiu Dascalu	University of Nevada, Reno, USA
Steven Demurjian	University of Connecticut, USA
Morgan Ericsson	Linnaeus University, Sweden
Maria Jose Escalona	University of Seville, Spain
Jean-Rémy Falleri	Bordeaux INP, France
João Faria	FEUP, University of Porto, Portugal
Cléver Ricardo Guareis de Farias	University of São Paulo, Brazil
Alain Finkel	École Normale Supérieure Cachan, France
Chiara Di Francescomarino	FBK-IRST, Italy
Kehan Gao	Eastern Connecticut State University, USA
Paola Giannini	University of Piemonte Orientale, Italy
J. Paul Gibson	Mines-Telecom, Telecom SudParis, France
Gregor Grambow	AristaFlow GmbH, Germany

Hatim Hafiddi	INPT, Morocco
Øystein Haugen	Østfold University College, Norway
Christian Heinlein	Aalen University, Germany
Jose Luis Arciniegas Herrera	Universidad del Cauca, Colombia
Jose R. Hilera	University of Alcala, Spain
Andreas Holzinger	Medical University Graz, Austria
Jang-Eui Hong	Chungbuk National University, Korea, Republic of
Milan Ignjatovic	Prosoftwarica GmbH, Switzerland
Ivan Ivanov	SUNY Empire State College, USA
Hermann Kaindl	Vienna University of Technology, Austria
Dimitris Karagiannis	University of Vienna, Austria
Dean Kelley	Minnesota State University, USA
Jun Kong	North Dakota State University, USA
Martin Kropp	University of Applied Sciences Northwestern Switzerland, Switzerland
Konstantin Läufer	Loyola University Chicago, USA
David Lorenz	Open University, Israel
Ahmad Kamran Malik	Quaid-i-Azam University, Pakistan
Eda Marchetti	ISTI-CNR, Italy
Manuel Mazzara	Innopolis University, Russian Federation
Greg Michaelson	Heriot-Watt University, UK
Marian Cristian Mihaescu	University of Craiova, Romania
Tommi Mikkonen	Institute of Software Systems, Tampere University of Technology, Finland
Dimitris Mitrakos	Aristotle University of Thessaloniki, Greece
Valérie Monfort	LAMIH Valenciennes UMR CNRS 8201, France
Mattia Monga	Università degli Studi di Milano, Italy
José Arturo Mora-Soto	Mathematics Research Center, Mexico
Claude Moulin	JRU CNRS Heudiasyc, University of Compiègne, France
Elena Navarro	University of Castilla-La Mancha, Spain
Paolo Nesi	University of Florence, Italy
Rory O'Connor	Dublin City University, Ireland
Claus Pahl	Free University of Bozen-Bolzano, Italy
Marcos Palacios	University of Oviedo, Spain
Jennifer Pérez	Universidad Politécnica de Madrid (UPM), Spain
Frantisek Plasil	Charles University in Prague, Czech Republic
Rosario Pugliese	Università di Firenze, Italy
Michel Reniers	Eindhoven University of Technology, The Netherlands
Carlos Rodriguez	University of Trento, Italy
Colette Rolland	Université de Paris 1 Panthèon Sorbonne, France
Carlos Rossi	Universidad de Málaga, Spain
Gustavo Rossi	Lifia, Argentina
Matteo Rossi	Politecnico di Milano, Italy

Gunter Saake	Institute of Technical and Business Information Systems, Germany
Francesca Saglietti	University of Erlangen-Nuremberg, Germany
Maria-Isabel Sanchez-Segura	Carlos III University of Madrid, Spain
Lionel Seinturier	University of Lille, France
Yeong-Tae Song	Towson University, USA
Hiroki Suguri	Miyagi University, Japan
Clemens Szyperski	Microsoft, USA
Carolyn L. Talcott	SRI International, USA
Dávid Tengeri	University of Szeged, Hungary
Chouki Tibermacine	LIRMM, CNRS and Montpellier University, France
Gianluigi Viscusi	EPFL Lausanne, Switzerland
Christiane Gresse von Wangenheim	UFSC, Federal University of Santa Catarina, Brazil
Dietmar Wikarski	FH Brandenburg University of Applied Sciences, Germany
Andreas Winter	Carl von Ossietzky University Oldenburg, Germany
Jinhui Yao	Xerox Research, USA
Jingyu Zhang	Macquarie University, Australia
Elena Zucca	University of Genoa, Italy

ICSOFT-PT Additional Reviewers

Dominik Bork	University of Vienna, Austria
Md Moinul Hossain	University of Nevada, Reno, USA
Lisa Palathingal	University of Nevada, Reno, USA
Larisa Safina	Innopolis University, Russian Federation

Invited Speakers

Uwe Assmann	TU-Dresden, Germany
Schahram Dustdar	Vienna University of Technology, Austria
Henry Muccini	University of L'Aquila, Italy

Contents

Software Engineering and Applications

Collaboration Viewpoint for Modeling Cross-Organizational Business Concerns

Ayalew Kassahun[✉] and Bedir Tekinerdogan

Information Technology Group, Wageningen University, Hollandseweg 1,
Wageningen, The Netherlands
{ayalew.kassahun, bedir.tekinerdogan}@wur.nl

Abstract. Organizations very often need to collaborate to achieve their business goals. Hereby it is important that the collaboration concerns are properly identified and reflected in their businesses. In practice, the business process design and architecture design are often carried out separately. This often leads to a misalignment between the business process and architecture design, a problem which becomes more severe when multiple collaborating organizations are involved. To address this problem, it is important to provide the proper design abstractions that can be used to detect and correct misalignments. To this end, we propose the architecture collaboration viewpoint that can be used by teams of business analysts and software architects when addressing business collaboration concerns. The collaboration viewpoint uses elements from business process and architecture viewpoints to provide new modeling artifacts for alignment. The design artefacts are mapping tables and workflow pattern diagrams that are used to identify misalignments and redesign the business processes. The viewpoint facilitates the communication between business analysts and architects. We illustrate the collaboration viewpoint for a food supply chain transparency system from a real industrial case study.

Keywords: Architecture viewpoint · Business collaboration · Collaboration viewpoint · Business process modeling · Workflow patterns

1 Introduction

Businesses today rarely operate in isolation but must collaborate with others in a coordinated fashion. To address collaboration concerns business analysts design business process models (BPMs) that integrate business activities across the collaborating organizations. BPMs have to be supported by underlying software systems, and therefore, BPMs will have a direct impact on the required software systems and the corresponding architectural design. Conversely, the architectural design imposes constraints on BPMs, and as a consequence, an inherent, mutual dependency exists between these two sets of designs.

Business collaboration involves BPMs that span multiple organizations – which we hereafter refer to as *business collaboration processes*. When realizing business collaboration processes multiple software systems need to be taken into account. As a result, the mutual alignment of BPMs and architectural designs becomes very

© Springer International Publishing AG 2017
E. Cabello et al. (Eds.): ICSOFT 2016, CCIS 743, pp. 3–21, 2017.
DOI: 10.1007/978-3-319-62569-0_1

cumbersome. We define the difficulties associated in aligning the two designs as *business collaboration concerns*.

The current practice addresses business process concerns and architectural concerns separately, and sequentially—first the BPMs are designed then the software architecture is designed using the BPM models as inputs. This approach is to an extent feasible if applied within the context of an individual organization. However, when dealing with multiple software systems from different organizations the approach becomes infeasible due to the mutual dependency between business process models and the software architecture.

To address the problem we studied the existing modelling approaches. At present, two distinct sets of viewpoints are used to address business collaboration concerns. Various architecture viewpoints are used for modelling the structure of software systems, which we hereafter referred to as *structural viewpoints*. Business process models and notations are used for modelling business processes and are hereafter referred to as *business process viewpoints*. The structural viewpoints do not directly address business process concerns. Likewise, the business process viewpoints do not consider architectural concerns. As a consequence, a business-IT alignment problem arises. The alignment problem has been discussed in the context of individual organizations (Avison et al. 2004; Hong-Mei 2008; Bartens et al. 2014; Aversano et al. 2016) but not in the context of business collaborations.

In this paper we introduce the *collaboration viewpoint* for addressing business collaboration concerns. In the collaboration viewpoint we use architectural and business process viewpoints to provide new kinds of models with the corresponding iterative design process for applying them. We introduce mapping tables and use workflow patterns as a means of identifying misalignment and redesigning the BPMs. The collaboration viewpoint is meant as means of enabling teamwork between software architects and business process analysts. The teamwork ensures that the business process and architecture views are well-aligned and feasible. We illustrate the viewpoint in real industrial case study for which a safety and quality transparency system for food supply chains is designed.

The remainder of this paper is organized as follows. Section 2 provides background information. Section 3 presents the case study used to demonstrate the collaboration viewpoint. Section 4 presents the collaboration viewpoint and a method for applying it. In Sect. 5 the viewpoint is applied to the case study. In Sect. 6 the related work is presented and in Sect. 7 concluding remarks are made.

2 Background

In this section we first discuss the background on software architecture, BPM, and workflow patterns.

2.1 Software Architecture

Software architecture defines the gross-level structure of a software system (ISO/IEC/IEEE 2011). Architecture modeling is important to enhance the understanding of the software system, support the communication among stakeholders, and guide the development process (Tekinerdogan 2014). A common practice to modeling architecture is using different architectural views that address the concerns of a specific group of stakeholders. Architectural views document the architectural design decisions from a specific viewpoint. That means, the designs documented in an architectural view follow the conventions, including models and notations, defined in the corresponding architectural viewpoint. From a given architectural viewpoint one or more architectural views can be designed (Clements et al. 2010; ISO/IEC/IEEE 2011).

In the literature, a number of viewpoints have been identified (Kruchten 1995; Hofmeister et al. 2000; Kruchten 2004; Lattanze 2008; Clements et al. 2010). The Views and Beyond (V&B) approach identifies three major viewpoints: *module, component-and-connector (C&C)*, and *allocation*. Module views deal with concerns related to implementation, such as, decomposition and generalization. The C&C and allocation viewpoints are structural viewpoints since they largely refer to the structure of the software system. The C&C views deal with the interaction structure, such as, data flow and message routing. The allocation viewpoint describes how software elements are allocated to the environment of the software system, such as, hardware or development team (Clements et al. 2010).

Recognizing that new viewpoints may be needed to address new kinds of concerns, the ISO/IEC 42010 standard for documenting software architecture (ISO/IEC/IEEE 2011) provides an extensible metamodel for defining new viewpoints.

2.2 BPM

A business process describes how the activities for achieving a particular business outcome are interrelated and how they are executed (Davenport and Short 1998). The process modelling approach has historically gained the attention of businesses when it was effectively used to address inefficiencies in functional organizations (Dumas et al. 2013). At its core, a BPM identifies the events of the business process and the series of activities that are triggered by them (Dumas et al. 2013). In practice, business processes are modeled by business analysts using visual modelling methods. The most prominent business processes modeling language is BPMN (Business Process Model and Notation) (ISO/IEC 2013). BPMs address business requirements, and as such, are inputs for the software architects as requirements that should to be addressed in the architectural design (The Open Group 2013).

2.3 Workflow Patterns

Workflow patterns are recurring problem-solution pairs that have been frequently used in business process modeling (Russell et al. 2006). In fact, BPMs can be viewed as being composed of workflow patterns. Since workflow patterns represent well-known problem-solution pairs, it is easier to describe, discuss and redesign a BPM by manipulating its constituent workflow patterns.

In the past, more than a hundred workflow patterns have been identified, categorized and cataloged (van der Aalst and ter Hofstede 2011). The most prominent categories are *control-flow*, *data-flow* and *resource-flow* workflow patterns (Van der Aalst et al. 2003). Control-flow patterns model the execution ordering of activities and are the basis for the patterns in the other categories. The data-flow patterns model how data flows along the flow of control. The resource-flow patterns model how work is assigned to resources (*e.g.* devices, people) following the flow of control. A short summary of workflow pattern categories and the workflow patterns in each category is provided in a previous publication (Kassahun and Tekinerdogan 2016).

3 Illustrative Case and Problem Statement

In this section we use a case study from the FIspace business collaboration research project (Verdouw et al. 2014) to illustrate collaboration concerns and describe the problem statement.

3.1 Case: Transparency in Food Supply Chains

A food supply chain network is a collaboration linkage of a series of food operators that transform agricultural input products into finished food products. The food operators involved include farmers, a series of food processors and distributors, and retailers. In addition, mandated by food regulations, various third-parties are involved to guarantee the safety and quality of food. In Europe, for instance, recurring food scandals and crises have led to regulations that mandate centralized animal registry systems (EC 2000; EC 2004; EC 2015) and procedures for tracking and tracing of food products (EC 2002; EC 2007; EC 2011). Guaranteeing the safety and quality of food requires, among other things, the smooth flow of transparency data. Transparency in food supply chains refers to the ability to track and trace input, intermediate and finished food products along the supply chain. A conceptual model of a food supply chain network is depicted in Fig. 1.

Transparency involves two basic business processes: *data capture* and *data query*. These business processes are implemented within the individual food operators (*internal transparency*) as well as across the supply chain (*external transparency*). A software system that realizes internal transparency is referred to as *Internal Transparency System (ITS)*; the integration of internal transparency systems that realizes external transparency is referred to as *External Transparency System (ETS)*. Recently, the GS1 system architecture is increasingly being adopted (GS1 2015) in realizing both internal and external transparency systems. The EPCIS (Electronic Product Code Information System) specification (EPCglobal 2014), which is part of the GS1 System Architecture, provides generic data models and interface definitions for both data capture and data query business processes.

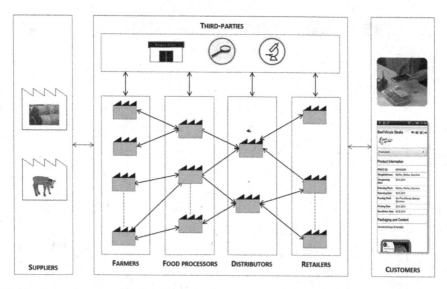

Fig. 1. A conceptual model of food supply chain networks. (Arrowed lines represent the flow of information through the network.).

We elaborate business collaboration concerns using the data query BPM depicted in Fig. 2. The BPM complies with the EPCIS specification, and is considered the preferred scenario. However, many food operators cannot support it. In the following, we first describe the BPM and then state the collaboration concern related to the model. The data query BPM is initiated when an end-user takes a food product—which can be input, semi-finished or end product—at a food operator and requests transparency data from the food operator's ITS. For the sake of simplicity we assume that each individual food product item has a unique ID and the ID is obtained by scanning the barcode of the product item. The end-user obtains transparency data using a barcode scanner or a smartphone application (*End-User App*). Upon scanning a barcode, the end-user app makes a query request and displays the transparency data returned. When the end-user scans a product item, the app requests transparency data from the food operator (indicated as *focal*). The ITS of the food operator determines where the product data reside. If the data reside locally it fetches the data from its own database; otherwise, it looks up the service address of the food operator (indicated as *partner*) that has the required data at a third-party discovery service. It then makes a query request to the partner food operator ITS, upon which the partner ITS returns the data it has about the item. Since the product may have passed through many food operators—and since transparency data about the ingredients are also part of the transparency data of a product item—this process is repeated until no more transparency data is desired or no more transparency data can be obtained. The focal and partner food operators are identical but drawn in two separate lanes to be able to show the interactions among the food operators clearly. Note, the focal food operator lane represents the one food operator that received the request from the end-user; the partner food operator lane represents all other food operators involved. After all data is gathered, the focal food operator sends the aggregated data to the app, which displays the data to the user.

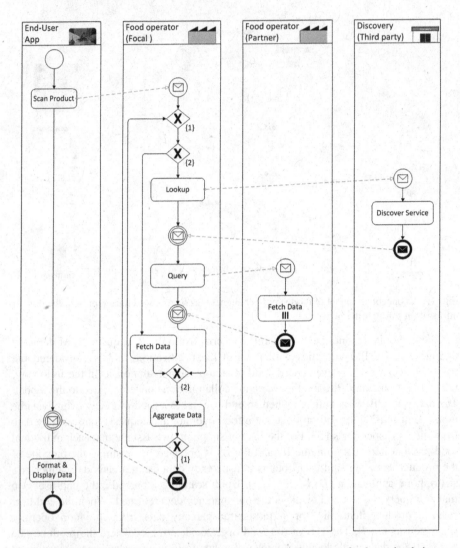

Fig. 2. A BPM showing how transparency data is queried across a food supply chain.

The BPM shown in Fig. 2 has to be implemented by all the four types of food operators shown in Fig. 1. The end-user app should also be provided by the food operators. However, in practice, many of the food operators do not support most of the activities the BPM and cannot provide end-user apps.

3.2   Problem Statement

In the previous sub-section we have described food supply chains and illustrated an inherent business collaboration concern they face regarding transparency. In the case study we identified a number of problems in aligning the BPMs representing the preferred scenario and the software systems that realistically can be realized by the collaborating partners. Specifically, we can define the following problems:

- *Difficulty in realizing business collaboration processes*

The elements of BPMs have to be supported by businesses depending on their roles. That is, process elements, such as, events, tasks and gateways have to be realized by architectural elements, such as, modules, components and nodes of the software systems that are distributed across many businesses. It turns out that the mapping of BPMs to the diverse software systems is not straightforward. For example, the BPM shown in Fig. 2 spans many food operators, many of which are, in practice, not capable of fulfilling all the steps. Particularly, many of the small food operators (mainly farmers) cannot afford to deploy the required software systems.

- *Lack of a common model for supporting the interaction between business analyst and architects*

Faced with the problem stated above business analysts and software architects from the various businesses come together to address the problem. However, the two stakeholder types use two separate sets of models hampering the communication between them. Business analysts use BPMs to define business processes. On the other hand, software architects use architecture viewpoints that mainly address concerns related to the structure of the software system. For the given case study, it was required early on to know which activities *can* be fulfilled by which food operators. Neither the business process models nor the software architecture views provide this information. A common model that depicts the business collaboration concerns (a model that maps elements of BPMs to elements of architectural design) would help to support the communication and the design rationale.

- *Early validation of the business process-architecture alignment is difficult*

Too often BPMs are validated after the software system is realized creating major risks. For example the BPM of Fig. 2 has an impact on the software components that need to be deployed at each food operator node. Given only this BPM and the corresponding architectural designs, it is not easy to validate that the two are aligned and feasible.

In light of the above obstacles we formulated the following general research question: How can we support software architects and business analysts to design BPMs and the corresponding software architecture as a team and minimize the mismatch between the two designs?

4   Collaboration Viewpoint

Adapting the template for documenting architecture viewpoints proposed in the ISO/IEC standard mentioned before we propose a collaboration viewpoint shown in Table 1. The key stakeholders for the viewpoint are identified as *software architects* and *business analysts*. In the collaboration viewpoint we adopt the BPMN modelling

Table 1. Collaboration viewpoint documentation guide.

Element	Description
Name	Collaboration Viewpoint
Stakeholders	• Business Analysts • Software Architects
Elements	• Elements of BPMN 2.0 • Elements from structural viewpoints (mainly Allocation and C&C) • Workflow patterns
Relations	• Maps to—BPMN models to collaborating partners • Maps to—structural models to collaborating partners • Maps to—BPMN models to workflow patterns
Properties and constraints	• Constraints as defined business process and structural viewpoints, and workflow patterns
Notation	• BPMN and notations used in structural viewpoint models • Tables for mapping model elements to collaborating partners: _Collaborating partners / BPMN Elements: Events … Activities … Gateways …_ _Collaborating partners / Structure Elements: Components … Nodes …_ • Tables for mapping workflow patterns to model elements • Workflow pattern diagram: (workflow pattern diagram element)
Relation to other views/viewpoints	BPMN 2.0 specification, workflow patterns catalogue, allocation and C&C viewpoints.
Examples	See section V

method to represent BPMs. BPMN is widely used among business analysts and is also easily understandable for software architects. BPMN models are used for three reasons. First, we use them to represent business collaboration. Second, we map BPMN elements to organizations in mapping tables so that we can reallocate them to a different organization during redesign. Third, we map fragments of BPMN models to workflow patterns so that we can redesign the business collaboration process based on well-understood patterns.

In addition to the business concerns the collaboration viewpoint uses elements of the *C&C* and *allocations* views. Hereby, we consider only the elements of the models of these structural views as modelling elements in the corresponding mapping table. The architectural elements we consider most relevant are *components* and *nodes*.

The mappings of business process and architectural elements are made using two tables shown in Table 1. The first table captures how business process elements are allocated across the collaborating partners; the second table captures how architectural elements are allocated across the collaborating partners. The tables are used for both redesign and validation purposes.

Workflow patterns are represented using a *workflow pattern diagram* which can also be represented as workflow mapping table. The workflow pattern diagram is a BPMN diagram on which the BPMN elements that belong to distinct workflow patterns are delineated using dashed-line blocks. To delineate the BPMN elements the BPM diagram will mostly require simplification. The creation and application of workflow pattern diagram is demonstrated in Sect. 5.

4.1   Method for Applying the Viewpoint

Figure 4 shows the method for applying the collaboration viewpoint. The method is started by business analysts; they first design the business collaboration models as BPMN models (step 1) and subsequently identify the relevant workflow patterns (step 2). The two steps are displayed sequentially but, in reality, they are intertwined. Next, in step 3, software architects model the structural views of the software architecture.

In step 4 the business analysts and the software architects work as a team to allocate elements of the BPMN and architectural views to collaborating partners using mapping tables. They use the workflow pattern diagrams to facilitate the allocation. In this step they identify misalignments and determine if redesign is required. If redesign is required the next (in step 5) they identify possible redesign business process elements, architectural elements and workflow patterns based on the insights gained from the mapping tables. In fact, the mapping tables are used reallocate elements. Then, either the entire process or part of it is repeated until no redesign is required. Finally (in step 6), the BPMs, the workflow pattern diagrams and the mapping tables are documented in collaboration views following the documentation outline proposed in the next sub section (Fig. 3).

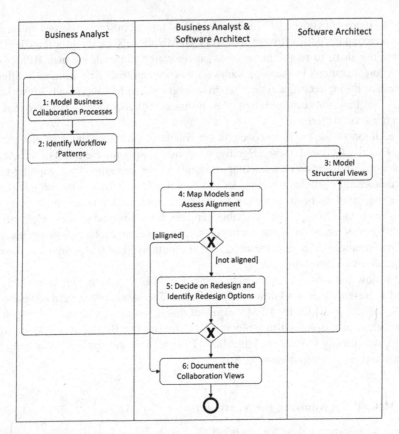

Fig. 3. A process diagram representing the process of modeling a collaboration view.

5   Applying the Collaboration Viewpoint

In this section we illustrate how the approach shown in Fig. 4 is applied in the real industrial case mentioned in Sect. 3. The first step of designing the BPMs is already demonstrated in the business collaboration model shown in Fig. 2. The second step is identifying the workflow patterns.

Figure 4 shows the main workflow patterns of the business collaboration model we identified, which are: *sequence (cf-1)*, *exclusive choice (cf-4)*, *simple merge (cf-5)*, *multiple instances without synchronization (cf-12)* and s*tructured loop (cf-21)*. A further analysis shows that the workflow patterns *cf-4 and cf-5* belong together. Similarly, the workflow patterns *cf-21 and cf-12* belong together. Therefore, we identify three workflow patterns, two of which are composite patterns.

The third step of the approach is to capture the existing software architecture that is already in place. For the sake of simplicity we distinguish between two major groups of food operators in terms of their existing software systems, *i.e.* their ITSs: *small food operator* (FO_{small}) and *large food operator* (FO_{large}), and a single *third party* (*3P*). Similarly, we identify three components of an ITS: a *data query component*, a *data*

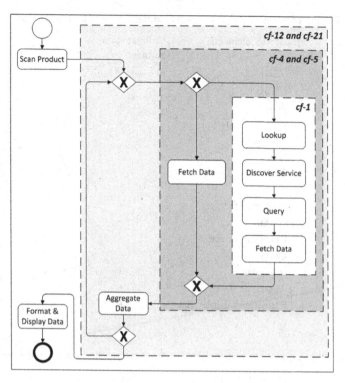

Fig. 4. A workflow pattern diagram of the query business collaboration process.

aggregator component and a *product data repository service*. In relation to the business collaboration process shown in Fig. 2 the data query component implements the *lookup* and *query* tasks and the 2nd XOR decision; the data aggregator component implements the aggregate data task and the 1st XOR decision; the data retrieval service implements the *fetch data* task.

The next step, step 4, is mapping the allocation of the elements of the business collaboration model and the architectural design to the collaborating partners. Table 2 shows how the BPM elements are allocated across the two types of food operators; Table 3 does the same but for architectural elements. The tables are interpreted as follows. A '+' sign in a cell implies that the business process or the architectural element is allocated to the corresponding collaboration partners and the collaboration partner indeed supports the element. For instance, the *scan product* task should be supported in *large food operator* nodes and it is indeed supported. A '−' sign implies that the business process or the architectural element is allocated to the collaboration partner but the collaboration partner fails to support the element. Using the above example, the *scan product* task should have been supported by *small food operator* nodes but it is not. An empty cell implies that the element is not relevant for the specific collaboration partner. A '~' sign implies that the business process or the architectural element is not allocated to the collaboration partner according to the models but in reality the collaboration partner supports the element. For instance, in the given supply

Table 2. Mapping of business process elements to the corresponding collaborating partners.

BPMN elements	Collaboration partners		
	FO_{small}	FO_{large}	3P
Events			
Start	–	+	~
End	–	+	~
Gateways			
XOR {1}	–	–	~
XOR {2}	–	–	
Tasks			
Scan product	–	+	~
Lookup	–	–	
Discover service	–	–	–
Query	–	–	
Fetch data	–	+	~
Aggregate data	–	+	~
Format and display data	–	+	~

Table 3. Mapping architectural elements to the corresponding collaborating partners.

Structural elements	Collaboration partners		
	FO_{small}	FO_{large}	3P
End–user app	–	+	~
Query component	–	–	
Data aggregator component	–	–	~
Product data repository service	–	+	~
Discovery service			+

chain a third party provides, for part of the supply chain, an end-user transparency app and transparency system that supports a number of tasks. An empty cell implies that the element is not relevant for the specific collaboration partner. Typically, these tables require knowledge of the state of affairs in all collaboration partners, which could be many, and it may require more fine-grained attributes than the simple +, –, ~ and *blank* entries. As shown in the table, it turns out that small food operators implement none of the required architectural elements adequately, large food operators provide only part, and a third party seems to fill the gap left by the food operators, albeit partly.

From Tables 2 and 3 it is clear that the desired business processes are not aligned with the existing architecture. The next step, step 5, is redesigning the business collaboration process by identifying better fitting workflow patterns, structural components and allocations. Obviously improved versions of Tables 2 and 3 are required. For instance, though small food operators do not fulfill the allocated tasks, it turned out that

Table 4. New allocation of architectural elements to collaborating partners.

Structural elements	Collaboration partners		
	FO_{small}	FO_{large}	3P
End-user app			+
Query component			
Data aggregator component			+
Product data repository service		+	+
Discovery service			+

they are, however, willing to (and usually do) delegate the tasks to a third party and pass the required transparency data to it that enables it to perform the delegated tasks. This is also consistent with some aspects of the food laws described in Sect. 3.1 that require centralized repositories of transparency data to be managed by third-parties or regulatory authorities.

In Table 4 we show the improved allocation of architectural elements that eliminates the misalignment identified in Table 3. (Similarly, a new allocation table for Table 2 can be produced but is not included for brevity.) The new allocation allows all food operators (small and large) to comply with the EPCIS specification by formalizing the roles that the third party was playing. However, it raises a new issue related to data capture. Because food operators have to pass transparency data to the third-party that enables it to perform the new tasks assigned to it, the data capture (which so far was local and trivial) now becomes a collaboration concern.

Now that we identified redesign options, we start a new iteration to improve the business collaboration model and associated software architecture. We start by rede-signing the workflow pattern diagram because the workflow patterns identified earlier seem to capture the fundamental essence of the query BPM and may not need substantial modifications. The BPM, on the other hand, may change substantially. In Fig. 5 we provide the improved workflow pattern diagram that contains the same three workflow patterns but in a slightly different configuration. The change in the configuration of the workflow patterns is a direct consequence of the new allocation. The details of the consequences of the new allocation are shown in the new BPM provided in Fig. 6. As in the previous business collaboration process the new business process is triggered by the end-user app but all query requests are always sent to the third party. Instead of all food operators, the new model involves only large food operators in the query business process. Small food operators no longer need to maintain their own transparency data and to support the fetch data task, because the third-party supports this task on their behalf. When these and other business process redesign issues are resolved the software architects (re)design the software architecture. Then new mapping tables are produced to see if there are any misalignments that have to be addressed.

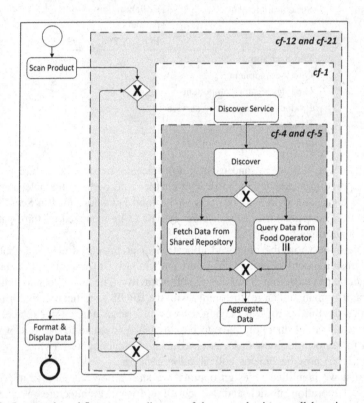

Fig. 5. Improved workflow pattern diagram of the query business collaboration process.

6   Related Work

The prominent way addressing business processes and software architecture concerns along with other concerns, such as general vision for the system, concerns related to technology, *etc.* in a consistent manner is to follow guidance provided by an enterprise architecture framework. The Zachman (Rational Software 2001) and TOGAF/ArchiMate (The Open Group 2013) frameworks are probably the most widely used and include the modeling of business processes and the designing of software architecture as part of the larger enterprise architecture. This framework use largely fixed categories of perspectives and concerns (*e.g.* vision, business concerns, software architecture concerns, *etc.*) Moreover, they follow a hierarchical conceptualization of models in which requirements cascade from vision, to BPMs, to software architecture and finally to technology architecture. A hierarchical approach suggests the use of elaborate methods to get the design at a higher hierarchical level before moving to the next. There are for instance extensive methods for analyzing the *as-is* BPMs and designing elaborate *to-be* BPMs (Sharp and McDermott 2009) before a large scale architectural design process commences. These approaches do not directly address

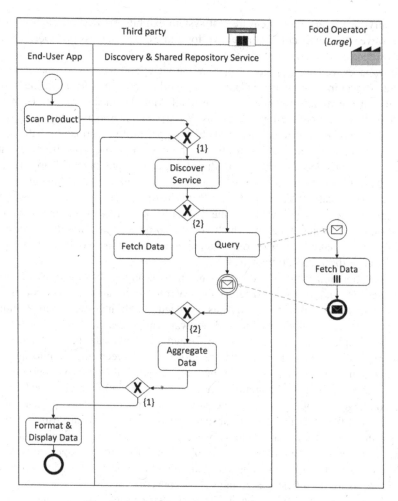

Fig. 6. Improved query business process model.

business collaboration concerns that often arise when different organizations are involved.

Business collaboration concerns could probably be addressed generically as cross cutting quality concerns across different viewpoints. In this respect business collaboration concerns could be viewed as concerns that cut across business process and architecture viewpoints. In this regard the concept of architectural perspectives is suggested that include a collection of activities, tactics and guidelines to be used across a number of the architectural views to address quality concerns (Woods and Rozanski 2005). In this context, Rozanski and Wood define several architectural perspectives for selected quality concerns such as security, performance, scalability, availability and evolution. In order to capture the system-wide quality concerns, each relevant perspective is applied to some or all views. In this way, the architectural views provide the description of the architecture, while the architectural perspectives can help to analyze and modify the architecture to ensure that system exhibits the desired quality properties. However, no architectural perspective for addressing business collaboration concerns has been addressed yet.

In this paper we have defined a collaboration viewpoint which is defined on top of structural viewpoints. Similarly, in our earlier work, we have considered the explicit modelling of viewpoints for quality concerns (Tekinerdogan and Sözer 2011) from viewpoints that address functional concerns. We have shown that quality concerns do not easily match the architectural elements that are primarily functional in nature. As a result, the communication and analysis of these quality concerns becomes more problematic in practice. We have introduced a general and practical approach for supporting architects to model quality concerns by extending the architectural viewpoints of the so-called V&B approach and illustrated the approach for defining recoverability and adaptability viewpoints (Sözer et al. 2013). In this paper we have focused on collaboration concerns which could also be seen as a non-functional concern. Like other quality concerns collaboration concerns require a dedicated viewpoint which we have discussed in this paper.

The collaboration viewpoint concerns the mutual alignment of BPMs and architectural designs and in this respect is closely related to architectural consistency analysis. Architecture consistency analysis has been mainly investigated in relation to consistency between software code and software architecture. Hereby, architecture consistency implies that the architecture design elements can be mapped to the implementation elements. In case the relationships between the architecture and implementation do not correspond then these are called architectural violations. If the relations that are present in the architecture are also found in the implementation then this is convergent relation. In case the architecture relation is not present in the implementation then this is called an absence relation. A successful design recovery technique that is used for architecture consistency checking is the reflexion modeling approach as proposed by Murphy et al. (Murphy et al. 2001). In this paper we have also focused on consistency of the architecture but now from a business model perspective in which we focused on business collaboration concerns.

In our earlier work (Tekinerdogan 2015), we have proposed to enhance existing reflexion modeling approaches using architecture viewpoints. We introduced the *architecture reflexion viewpoint* that can be used to define reflexion model for different architecture views. The viewpoint includes both a visual notation and a notation based on design structure matrices. The design structure reflexion matrices (DSRMs) that we have defined provide a complementary and succinct representation of the architecture and code for supporting qualitative and quantitative analysis, and likewise the refactoring of the architecture and code. For this we introduce the notion of *design structure reflexion matrices* (DSRM) and a generic reflexion modeling approach based on DSRMs.

In service-oriented architecture business collaboration concerns are addressed using choreography languages. In this respect recent research show that it is possible to automate the generation software from business processes choreography models (Autili et al. 2015). However, design heuristics for integrating misaligned business process and IT systems are largely missing.

7 Conclusion

The problem of business-IT alignment has been broadly addressed in the literature and several solutions have been provided for this. In this paper we have focused on the business process alignment with the architecture design. Further we have explicitly considered the alignment within the context of collaborating organizations. To this end we have identified three key collaboration concerns: ensuring that the BPMs are indeed supported by software components, ensuring that business analyst can communicate effectively with software architects in search of better design solutions, and validating the architecture with respect to the BPMs. The architecture collaboration viewpoint that we have proposed is novel from both the software architecture design perspective as well as the business process modeling perspective. We have shown that the viewpoint can support the communication among the business analysts and architects, and likewise help to align the business process models and the software architecture of the collaboration system. This has been justified by the application of the viewpoint to a real industrial case study on food supply chains. In our future work we will apply the viewpoint for other industrial cases.

References

Autili, M., Inverardi, P., Tivoli, M.: Automated synthesis of service choreographies. IEEE Softw. **32**(1), 50–57 (2015)

Aversano, L., Grasso, C., Tortorella, M.: Managing the alignment between business processes and software systems. Inf. Soft. Technol. **72**, 171–188 (2016)

Avison, D., Jones, J., Powell, P., Wilson, D.: Using and validating the strategic alignment model. J. Strateg. Inf. Syst. **13**(3), 223–246 (2004)

Bartens, Y., Schulte, F., Voss, S.: E-business IT governance revisited: an attempt towards outlining a novel bi-directional business/IT alignment in COBIT5. In: 2014 47th Hawaii International Conference on System Sciences (HICSS) (2014)

Clements, P., Bachmann, F., Bass, L., Garlan, D., Ivers, J., Little, R., Merson, P., Nord, R., Stafford, J.: Documenting Software Architectures: Views and Beyond. Addison-Wesley, Boston (2010)

Davenport, T.H., Short, J.E.: The new industrial engineering: information technology and business process redesign. IEEE Eng. Manage. Rev. **26**(3), 46–60 (1998)

Dumas, M., La Rosa, M., Mendling, J., Reijers, H.: Introduction to business process management. In: Dumas, M., La Rosa, M., Mendling, J., Reijers, H. (eds.) Fundamentals of Business Process Management, pp. 1–31. Springer, Heidelberg (2013)

EC: Regulation (EC) No 1760/2000 of the European Parliament and of the Council of 17 July 2000 establishing a system for the identification and registration of bovine animals and regarding the labelling of beef and beef productsand repealing Council Regulation (EC) No 820/97. Off. J. Eur. Communities **L204**, 1–10 (2000)

EC: Regulation (EC) No 178/2002 of the European Parliament and of the Council of 28 January 2002 laying down the general principles and requirements of food law, establishing the European Food Safety Authority and laying down procedures in matters of food safety. Off. J. Eur. Communities **L31**(1), 1–24 (2002)

EC: Regulation No. 911/2004 of 29 April 2004 implementing Regulation (EC) No 1760/2000 of the European Parliament and of the Council as regards eartags, passports and holding registers. Off. J. Eur. Union **L163**, 65–70 (2004)

EC: Factsheet: tracing food through the production and distribution chain to identify and address risks and protect public health, Brussels (2007)

EC: Commission Implementing Regulation (EU) No 931/2011 of 19 September 2011 on the traceability requirements set by Regulation (EC) No 178/2002 of the European Parliament and of the Council for food of animal origin. Off. J. Eur. Union **L242**, 1–2 (2011)

EC: Regulation (EU) No 2015/262 of 17 February 2015 laying down rules pursuant to Council Directives 90/427/EEC and 2009/156/EC as regards the methods for the identification of equidae (Equine Passport Regulation). Off. J Eur. Union **L59**, 51 (2015)

EPCglobal: EPC Information Services (EPCIS) Version 1.1 Specification. GS1 Standard Version 1.1, May 2014, Brussels, Belgium, GS1 AISBL (2014)

GS1: GS1 General Specifications, version 15, no 2, January 2015, GS1: 490 (2015)

Hofmeister, C., Nord, R., Soni, D.: Applied Software Architecture. Addison-Wesley Professional, Boca Raton (2000)

Hong-Mei, C.: Towards service engineering: service orientation and business-IT alignment. In: Proceedings of the 41st Annual Hawaii International Conference on System Sciences (2008)

ISO/IEC:. Information technology - Object Management Group Business Process Model and Notation. ISO/IEC 19510:2013 (2013)

ISO/IEC/IEEE: Systems and software engineering – architecture description. ISO/IEC/IEEE Standard 42010:2011 (2011)

Kassahun, A., Tekinerdogan, B.: Architecture viewpoint for modeling business collaboration concerns using workflow patterns. In: The 11th International Joint Conference on Software Technologies, Lisbon, 1: ICSOFT-EA, pp. 27–38 (2016)

Kruchten, P.: The Rational Unified Process: An Introduction. Addison-Wesley Professional, Boca Raton (2004)

Kruchten, P.B.: The 4 + 1 view model of architecture. IEEE Softw. **12**(6), 42–50 (1995)

Lattanze, A.J.: Architecting Software Intensive Systems: A Practitioners Guide. CRC Press, Boca Raton (2008)

Murphy, G.C., Notkin, D., Sullivan, K.J.: Software reflexion models: bridging the gap between design and implementation. IEEE Trans. Softw. Eng. **27**(4), 364–380 (2001)

Rational Software: The Zachman framework for enterprise architecture and rational best practices and products, a Rational Software White paper (2001). http://www.rational.com/

Russell, N., van der Aalst, W.M., Mulyar, N.: Workflow control-flow patterns: a revised view. BPM Center Report BPM-06-22 (2006)

Sharp, A., McDermott, P.: Workflow modeling: tools for process improvement and applications development. Artech House, Norwood (2009)

Sözer, H., Tekinerdoğan, B., Akşit, M.: Optimizing decomposition of software architecture for local recovery. Softw. Qual. J. **21**(2), 203–240 (2013)

Tekinerdogan, B.: Software architecture. In: Computing Handbook, Third edn., pp. 1–16. Chapman and Hall/CRC (2014)

Tekinerdogan, B.: Architectural drift analysis using design structure reflexion matrices. In: Sofware Quality Assurance in Large Scale and Complex Software-Intensive Systems, pp. 221–236. Elsevier (2015)

Tekinerdogan, B., Sözer, H.: Defining architectural viewpoints for quality concerns. In: Crnkovic, I., Gruhn, V., Book, M. (eds.) ECSA 2011. LNCS, vol. 6903, pp. 26–34. Springer, Heidelberg (2011). doi:10.1007/978-3-642-23798-0_3

The Open Group: ArchiMate 2.1 Specification (2013). http://pubs.opengroup.org/architecture/archimate2-doc/toc.html

van der Aalst, Wil., M.P., ter Hofstede, A.H.M.: Workflow Patterns (2011). http://www.workflowpatterns.com/. Accessed 23 Dec 2015

van der Aalst, W.M.P., ter Hofstede, A.H.M., Kiepuszewski, B., Barros, A.P.: Workflow patterns. Distrib. Parallel Databases **14**(1), 5–51 (2003)

Verdouw, C., Beulens, A., Wolfert, S.: Towards software mass customization for business collaboration. In: 2014 Annual SRII Global Conference (SRII) (2014)

Woods, E., Rozanski, N.: Using architectural perspectives. In: 5th Working IEEE/IFIP Conference on software architecture WICSA 2005 (2005)

A New Approach for Automatic Development of Reconfigurable Real-Time Systems

Wafa Lakhdhar[1(✉)], Rania Mzid[2,3], Mohamed Khalgui[1,5,6],
and Nicolas Treves[4]

[1] LISI Lab INSAT, INSAT Centre, University of Carthage,
Urbain Nord BP 676, Tunis, Tunisia
wafa.lakdhar@live.fr, khalgui.mohamed@gmail.com
[2] ISI, University Tunis-El Manar, 2 Rue Abourraihan Al Bayrouni,
Ariana, Tunisia
rania.mzid@gmail.com
[3] CES Lab ENIS, University of Sfax, B.P:w.3, Sfax, Tunisia
[4] CEDRIC Lab, CNAM, 292 rue Saint-Martin, Paris, France
[5] Systems Control Lab, Xidian University, August Bebel Str 70, Halle, China
nicolas.treves@cnam.fr
[6] School of Electrical and Information Engineering, Jinan University,
Zhuhai Campus, Zhuhai 519070, China

Abstract. In the industry, reconfigurable real-time systems are specified as a set of implementations and tasks with timing constraints. The reconfiguration allows to move from one implementation to another by adding/removing real-time tasks. Implementing those systems as threads generates a complex system code due to the large number of threads and the redundancy between the implementation sets. This paper shows an approach for software synthesis in reconfigurable uniprocessor real-time embedded systems. Starting from the specification to a program source code, this approach aims at minimizing the number of threads and the redundancy between the implementation sets while preserving the system feasibility. The proposed approach adopts Mixed Integer Linear Programming (MILP) techniques in the exploration phase in order to provide feasible and optimal task model. An optimal reconfigurable POSIX-based code of the system is manually generated as an output of this technique. An application to a case study and performance evaluation show the effectiveness of the proposed approach.

Keywords: Real-time system · Reconfigurable architecture · Timing constraints · Mixed Integer Linear Programming (MILP) · POSIX-based code

© Springer International Publishing AG 2017
E. Cabello et al. (Eds.): ICSOFT 2016, CCIS 743, pp. 22–44, 2017.
DOI: 10.1007/978-3-319-62569-0_2

NOMENCLATURE

U	Processor utilization
n	Number of thread
m	Number of implementation
Sys	System implementations set
imp_i	The ith implementation
F_i	The ith Function
T_{f_i}	The Period of the ith function
C_{f_i}	The WCET of the ith function
τ_i	The ith task
r_i	The release time of the ith task
T_i	The period of the ith task
C_i	The WCET of the ith task
D_i	The deadline of the ith task
P_i	The priority of the ith task
Rep_i	The Response time of the ith task
T_{reconf}	The reconfiguration time
T_{delete}	the spent time to delete a task
T_{creat}	the spent time to create a task
A	the number of deleted tasks
B	is the number of created tasks
Merge$_{ij}$	Merging Matrix
InitTask	Initial Task model
NewTask	New task model

1   Introduction

A real-time system is any system which has to respond to externally generated input stimuli within a finite and specified delay [1]. The development of real-time systems is not a trivial task because a failure can be critical for the safety of human beings [2]. The researchers are moving today toward proposing techniques for programming concurrent reconfigurable real-time systems. The reconfiguration refers to the architectural or behavioral modifications of a software system during its execution to meet user requirements [3]. The successful development of reconfigurable real-time systems greatly depends on low development costs and the respect of timing requirements. In fact, several approaches have been proposed to assist the designer in the synthesis of real-time systems at different levels of the development process. For real-time concerns, Cheddar tool [4] allows to model software architectures of real-time systems while ensuring the respect of real-time properties. To provide design-time guarantees on timing constraints, different scheduling methodologies can be used, such as earliest deadline first scheduling algorithm (EDF) which at each instant in time chooses for execution the currently-active job with the smallest deadline [5]. Indeed the authors in [6] propose the RT_Reconfiguration tool based on EDF scheduling to assist in designing a feasible reconfigurable real-time system using an agent-based approach. Among all priority driven policies, Rate Monotonic (RM) is a scheduling algorithm which was defined by Liu and Layland [7] where the priority of tasks is inversely proportional to their periods. The authors of [8] provide a method to drive the designer by producing a set of design solutions based on RM scheduling algorithm. In [9–11], the authors are interested in the optimization of deployment techniques from functional and platform models of real-time systems by using mixed integer linear programming (MILP). An MILP formulation is easily extensible, re-targetable to a different optimization metric and can easily accommodate additional constraints or legacy components [9]. The TASTE Toolset approach results from spin-off studies of the ASSERT project in order to propose innovative and pragmatic solutions to develop real-time systems using a language based on Simulink, SDL, ASN.1, C, and Ada [12]. There are many programming languages designed for the development of real-time systems such as POSIX (Portable Operating System Interface) [13]. The POSIX standard promotes portability of applications across different operating system platforms. The authors [14] use POSIX in the development of software for real-time and embedded systems.

The synthesis of a valid and optimal implementation model from a given specification is a crucial issue in the development of reconfigurable real-time applications. This synthesis consists in building the set of tasks implementing the applicative functions while meeting all related real-time constraints. The reconfiguration at the implementation level consists in adding/removing tasks or modifying their timing parameters to go from one implementation to another, which may require an additional time for reconfiguration. So that, the resulting implementation model should avoid redundancy between the different implementations to minimize the possible overhead.

In this paper, we present an approach toward an optimal implementation of reconfigurable uniprocessor real-time systems. The proposed approach aims to automatically produce a valid and optimal task model from a given specification. The task model consists of a set of tasks implementing the applicative functions that we assume independent and periodic. We assume also that assigning priorities to tasks is performed using rate monotonic algorithm RM [15]. The proposed approach is composed of three phases: the purpose of the first one is to produce an initial task model from the user specification. The second step aims to optimize this model by using mixed integer linear programming (MILP) techniques to generate a feasible and an optimal task model. The proposal considers timing constraints. As for metrics, we consider a multi-objective optimization which includes the minimization of the response time. Since there are many solvers handling MILP formulations, we use in this paper the CPLEX tool [16]. From this optimal model, the objective of the third phase is to produce a POSIX-based code for the considered application. The proposed approach is applied to a CCAS case study in order to show its applicability.

The paper is organized as follows. Section 2 gives an overview on related works. Section 3 provides the formalisation of approach. Section 4 explains in details the proposed approach to obtain a valid and optimal implementation model from the user specification. Section 5 illustrates the approach on the chosen case study and evaluates its efficiency. Finally, we summarize our work and discuss the future work in Sect. 6.

2   Related Works

In this section, we present the related works that deal with real-time systems and reconfigurable architectures.

2.1   Real-Time Scheduling

Several works deal with the synthesis problem of real-time systems. The correctness of such systems depends both on the logical result of the computation and the time when the results are produced [17]. Thus enforcing timeliness constraints is necessary to maintain correctness of a real-time system. In order to ensure a required real-time performance, the designer should predict the behaviour of a real-time system by ensuring that all the tasks meet their deadlines. Different classes of scheduling algorithms exist where each one is developed for a particular task model or an environment in which a real-time system operates. Among all priority driven policies, Rate Monotonic (RM) is a scheduling algorithm used in real-time operating systems. In the case of n synchronous, independent and periodic tasks such that their deadlines are equal to their periods, the processor utilization factor $U \leq \sum_{i=1}^{n} n(2^{\frac{1}{n}} - 1)$ is a necessary and sufficient condition for the RM-based scheduling of real-time tasks [18]. In the literature, many approaches such as [19–22] have been carried out in the area of schedulability analysis for meeting real-time requirements. In [23], the authors focus on worst-case execution by making conservative assumptions about the system. The authors of [22] use a combined offline and online scheduling technique. A worst-case execution time (WCET) schedule, which provides the ideal operating frequency and voltage schedule assuming that tasks require their worst-case computation time, is calculated offline. The online scheduler further reduces frequency and voltage when tasks use less than their requested computing quota, but can still provide deadline guarantees by ensuring all invocations complete no later than in the WCET schedule. Pillai and Shin [24] propose an optimal algorithm for computing the minimal speed that can make a task set schedulable. Chetto et al. [19] consider the effect of precedence constraints between tasks on the dynamic priority scheduling problem. That paper proposes an algorithm to accept or reject aperiodic tasks with precedence constraints to guarantee the timing behavior of the rest of the system's tasks. Liu et al. developed an algorithm PASS for real-time tasks with different priorities and deadlines. PASS considers the hard real-time tasks and the soft real-time tasks at the same time. The authors of [8,9,25–29] explore the use of constraint programming to solve scheduling problems, and presents several optimizations to speed up the search for a valid solution.

In [25], the authors propose a technique to minimize the number of tasks in a real-time system while satisfying timing constraints. The approach in [8] aims both to reduce the number of preemptions for minimizing timing overheads and to maximize the laxity of tasks in order to improve the schedulability of the design model. In [9], the authors propose a method for an optimized synthesis of AUTOSAR (Automotive Open System Architecture) which are architectures based on Mixed Integer Linear Programming (MILP) and GA (Genetic Algorithm). It takes into account three optimization objectives which are extensibility maximization, latency and tasks number minimization. In [30], the authors present Integer Linear Programming (ILP) for scheduling problem with dependent tasks in a multiprocessor homogeneous system. Jeannenot proposed in [31] a set of algorithms under periodic real-time tasks in a processor with dynamic variable speed to determine the suitable speeds execution for each task and minimize the total energy consumption.

2.2   Reconfiguration of Real-Time System

Nowadays, many research works have been proposed to develop reconfigurable systems. The authors in [6] propose an approach that deals with reconfigurable systems to be implemented with different tasks under deadline constraints according to user requirements. For that purpose, the authors define an agent-based architecture to check after any reconfiguration scenario the system's feasibility that can be affected when the tasks violate corresponding deadlines. In this case, the agent provide new parameters for infeasible tasks in order to re-obtain the system's feasibility. In [32], the authors describe a concurrent function block model to control the run-time reconfiguration process of a real-time holonic controller. They describe a real-time java implementation to support the function block-based real-time task execution and the run-time reconfigurability.

The authors in [33] propose a complete methodology to dynamically reconfigure tasks. They present an interesting experimentation showing the dynamic change by users of tasks without disturbing the whole system. The authors in [34] use the Real-time-UML as a meta-model between design models of tasks and their implementation models to support dynamic user-based reconfigurations of control systems. In [35], the authors aim to provide an automated development process from modelling to implementation for the dynamic software part of reconfigurable systems. TimeAdapt [36] is a development process for reconfigurable system design. It allows to specify reconfiguration actions, estimate whether their execution can be carried out within a given time bound and execute them in a timely manner. In the same context, the authors of [37] present an approach which deals with reconfiguration at different levels within the development process of distributed applications. They propose a model driven approach to help specifying and configuring reconfigurable systems.

2.3   Code Generation

There are some related approaches which generate complete real-time systems. In [12], the authors deliver an approach called TASTE to enable the generation of a complete real-time distributed system. This approach involves four phases: (i)The system modeling phase using formal techniques, (ii) The transformation phase, (iii) The feasibility analysis phase, and (vi) The code generation phase where the authors propose a new language based on existing and mature technologies such as Simulink, SDL, ASN.1, C, and Ada [1]. Barreto et al. [38] propose a software synthesis method for automatic generation of executable code from the formal model is performed. This approach is an extension of their previous work [39] which uses pre-runtime approach in order to find feasible schedules satisfying timing and power constraints. The authors in [40] provide a framework that allows designers to automatically generate, from a functional specification with dependency constraints described by the Prelude language, a set of real-time tasks that can be executed on a uniprocessor architecture.

Nowadays, there are many programming languages designed for the development of real-time systems. Among the most used real-time languages, we cite real-time java (RT-java) [41] formalized in June 2000. RT-java aims to support the programming of real-time codes from different directions used by other software development platforms. POSIX (Portable Operating System Interface) is a standard written in terms of the C programming language [13]. POSIX allows to create POSIX threads (pthreads [1]) by calling the *pthread_create* API function with different thread scheduling policies and priorities to meet different application requirements. POSIX defines three scheduling policies that can be used to schedule real-time applications [42]:

– SCHED_FIFO: FIFO order among entities of the same priority.
– SCHED_RR: Round robin order among entities of the same priority.
– SCHED_SS: Sporadic server scheduling, useful for scheduling aperiodic tasks.

As we assume that assigning priorities to tasks is performed using rate monotonic algorithm RM, we can implement it using POSIX primitives: At first we assign priorities to tasks in the usual way for RM (i.e. $P_i = \frac{1}{T_i}$). Then we query the range of allowed system priorities with:

sched_get_priority_min()

sched_get_priority_max()

After that we map task set onto system priorities. Finally we start tasks using assigned priorities and SCHED_FIFO.

This standard facilitates the application portability that is why we adopt it as a target language to implement a reconfigurable real-time system in the current paper.

The main contributions of this paper are four-fold. The first part consists in ensuring the respect of timing properties before the effective implementation of the real-time system (i.e. at the design level). Second, we are interested in the reconfiguration of real-time systems where the addition and removal of tasks are applied at run-time. Third, we propose a multi-optimization metric. Indeed, the proposed approach aims to minimize the reconfiguration time by avoiding a redundancy between the different implementations from one side. From the other side, it aims to minimize the response times of the real-time tasks in order to maintain the performance of the system. Finally, this work automatically generates a complete reconfigurable real-time system from the specification level by using the programming language POSIX. None of the existing works is solving all the four problems together.

3   System Formalization

In this section, we present a formal description of a reconfigurable uniprocessor system. We present in addition real-time prerequisites required to introduce the paper's contribution.

It is assumed in this work that a reconfigurable real time system Sys is defined as a set of implementations: $Sys = \{imp_1, imp_2 \ldots imp_m\}$. We denote by $Sys(t)$ the implementation defining the system at a particular time t (i.e. $Sys(t) = imp_i$). An implementation imp_i is composed of n tasks that we assume *independent* and *periodic* (i.e. $imp_i = \{\tau_1, \tau_2, \tau_3 \ldots \tau_n\}$). Each task τ_i executes a set of applicative functions $\tau_i = \{F_1, F_2, F_3 \ldots F_k\}$. A function F_i is characterized by static parameters $F_i = (T_{f_i}, C_{f_i})$ where T_{fi} is the activation period of the function F_i and C_{fi} is an estimation of its Worst Case Execution Time WCET. Note that these parameters are considered as inputs to the proposed approach and must be specified by the user. Each task τ_i is characterized by a set of real-time parameters $(r_i, T_i, C_i, D_i, P_i)$: its release time r_i, we assume that $r_i = 0$, its activation period T_i which is deducted from the activation periods of the functions implemented by this task, its capacity or worst case execution time C_i which is equal to the sum of the WCETs of the functions executed by this task, its deadline D_i we assume that $D_i = T_i$, the priority P_i, we assume that $P_i = 1/T_i$ since we adopt the Rate Monotonic (RM) priority assignment. The Fig. 1 depicts the task parameters:

Let U be the processor utilization factor defined by: $U = \sum_{i=1}^{n} \frac{C_i}{T_i}$. For timing verification, we perform in this paper Rate-Monotonic (RM) response time analysis based on the computation of an upper bound of the response time Rep_i of the different tasks constituting the task model. This analysis aims to verify whether these tasks complete their computations within the time limit specified by the real-time application i.e. the deadline ($Rep_i \leq D_i$) [18].

The reconfiguration scenario corresponds to adding/removing tasks or modifying timing parameters. Thus, we introduce the reconfiguration time T_{reconf} which refers to the time required to jump from one implementation to another according

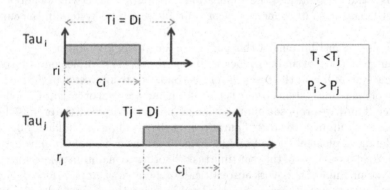

Fig. 1. Real-time task parameters.

to user requirements (i.e. reconfiguration conditions). This parameter is defined as follow:

$$T_{reconf} = A * T_{delete} + B * T_{creat}$$

where A is the number of deleted tasks, B is the number of created tasks, T_{delete} is the spent time to delete a task and T_{creat} is the spent time to create a task. We assume that the blanking time T_{delete} and creation time T_{creat} of all the tasks are equal for a considered platform (i.e. $T_{delete} = T_{creat}$). We denote by T_{cost} the spent time to create a task or to delete it (i.e. $T_{delete} = T_{creat} = T_{cost}$). Thus, the reconfiguration time is given as follow: $T_{reconf} = (A + B) * T_{cost}$.

4   Proposed Approach

In this section, we present an overview on our approach and detail the structure of different modules involved in this work.

4.1   Motivation and Definitions

We deliver an approach which automatically converts a high-level specification of a reconfigurable real-time system into an executable running on POSIX platform. The proposed approach aims to optimize the system code while meeting all related real-time constraints and avoiding any redundancy between the implementation sets. Figure 2 shows the process of the proposed approach. As entry, the designer provides the specification model which defines the reconfiguration conditions, the applicative functions that must be executed under a considered condition and the temporal parameters of each function. This model presents the input of the task generator step which aims to produce an initial task model. Then, the optimization step receives the generated model and proposes a valid and optimal task model. This model is finally converted into an executable program running under POSIX.

4.2   Task Generator

The first step consists in generating the initial task model. This stage considers the specification model as an input and aims to generate the initial task model which defines a possible implementation of the considered system. For each reconfiguration condition, this step generates an implementation and associates its appropriate functions. Then, for each generated implementation, it regroups the functions having the same period T_{fi} to be executed by one task τ_i. Since we assume that the release time $r_i = 0$ and $P_i = 1/T_i$, the task τ_i is characterized only by (T_i, C_i, D_i) where the period T_i corresponds to the period of the grouped functions, C_i is the sum of WCETs of the grouped functions and the deadline D_i of each task is equal to the corresponding period T_i.

Let us note that for the generation of this model, the optimization and real-time feasibility concerns are not considered. Algorithm 1 illustrates this

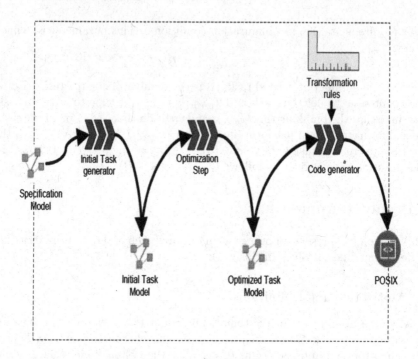

Fig. 2. Process overview.

generating step. The Initial task model can be generated with complexity $\mathcal{O}(N * M) + \mathcal{O}(P * M) = max(\mathcal{O}(N * M); \mathcal{O}(P * M))$, where N denotes the size of the conditions, M denotes the number of functions and P presents the number of implementations.

4.3   Task Model Optimization

This phase aims to produce a feasible and optimal implementation of the reconfigurable real-time system from the initial task model.

In order to avoid redundancy between the sets of implementation and reduce the number of tasks, this phase aims to merge the tasks belonging to different implementations but implementing the same functions and/or having close periods. For instance, let us consider two tasks $\tau_i \in imp_k$ and $\tau_j \in imp_l$. τ_i and τ_j are defined by a set of parameters: $\tau_i = (T_i, C_i, D_i)$ and $\tau_j = (T_j, C_j, D_j)$. These two tasks have close periods (i.e. $T_i = T_j + \delta t$) where δt is a constant defined by the user. We denote by τ_i' the task resulting from merging these two tasks which is characterized by

$$\tau_i'(T_i', C_i', D_i') = \begin{cases} T_i' = min(T_i, T_j) \\ C_i' = C_i + C_j \\ D_i' = min(D_i, D_j) \end{cases}$$

Algorithm 1. Task Generation

Input:
- F : Functions set
- ReconfCnd : Reconfiguration condition

Output:
- InitTask : Initial Task Model

1 **Notations:**
2 - Reconf_Cnd_Func: Correlation table between the reconfiguration conditions and the functions.
3 - imp : Implementation set
4 $nbr\_t \leftarrow 0$
5 $k \leftarrow 0$
6 /* Generation Of Implementations */
7 **for** $i \leftarrow 0$ **to** $SizeOf(ReconfCnd)$ **do**
8   **for** $j \leftarrow 0$ **to** $SizeOf(F)$ **do**
9   **if** $(F[j] \in Reconf\_Cnd\_Func[i])$ **then**
10             $imp[i][k] = F[j]$
11         $k + +;$

12 /* Generation Of Task Model */
13 **for** *each implementation* imp_i **do**
14   **for** *each function* F_j **do**
15   /* We create a task and we initialize its parameters with function F_j parameters */
16         $WcetOf(InitTask_{[nbr\_t]}) = WcetOf(F_j)$
17         $PeriodOf(InitTask_{[nbr\_t]}) = PeriodOf(F_j)$
18         $DeadlineOf(InitTask_{[nbr\_t]}) = DeadlineOf(F_j)$
19   **for** *each function* F_{j+1} **do**
20   /* We check if F_j and F_{j+1} have the same period and we evaluate if the result WCET is less than the task period to ensure the system feasibility */
21   **if** $PeriodOf(F_j) == PeriodOf(F_{j+1}))$ **then**
22   **if** $(WcetOf(F_j) + WcetOf(F_{j+1}) <= PeriodOf(InitTask_{[nbr\_t]}))$ **then**
23                     $WcetOf(InitTask_{[nbr\_t]}) = WcetOf(InitTask_{[nbr\_t]}) + WcetOf(F_{j+1})$
24     $nbr_t + +;$

25 **return** $InitTask$

Where T_i' corresponds to minimum of the two periods, C_i' is equal to the sum of their WCETs and the deadline D_i' of τ_i' is equal to the corresponding period T_i'. This approach allows to merge more than two tasks by optimizing other parameters like the sum of their response times. Thus, the considered problem is a combinatorial one, and the solution depends on many parameters. In order to implement properly the problem by taking into consideration the different constraints, we propose a MILP formulation of our problem. So we should define the objective function and the required constraints for parameters and variables.

Figure 3 shows an example to illustrate the scenario of reconfiguration which correspond to the transition from imp_1 to imp_2. The reconfiguration consists in removing τ_2, τ_3,τ_4 and adding τ_5, τ_6,τ_7, thus the reconfiguration time is defined as follows:

$$T_{reconf} = 3 * T_{delete} + 3 * T_{creat} = 6T_{cost}.$$

In order is to minimize the reconfiguration time T_{reconf}, tasks having close periods (or same period T in this example) must be merged (see Fig. 3). Consequently, after merging these tasks (i.e. τ_2 with τ_6, τ_3 with τ_7) T_{reconf} becomes:

$$T_{reconf} = 2 * T_{delete} + 2 * T_{creat} = 4T_{cost}$$

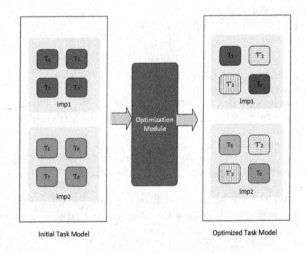

Fig. 3. Example of a reconfiguration scenario.

Definitions
Let m be the number of tasks in the initial model, let N be the number of tasks in the new task model, let s be the starting time which corresponds to effective starting time of each task. We denote by *InitTask* the initial task model which is a three column matrix where the first column presents the period T_i of task, the second one presents their WCETs C_i and the third column is their deadline D_i. *NewTask* is the resulting task model after merging the different tasks (i.e. optimized task model).

Objective Function

$$Maximize \sum_{i,j\in\{1,m\}} Merge_{ij} - \sum_{i,j\in\{1,m\}} Rep_{ij} \qquad (1)$$

This expression defines the objective function of our problem. Merge denotes a boolean variable used to mention whether two tasks τ_i and τ_j are merged. More in detail, $Merge_{ij}$ is equal to 1 if task $t_i \in imp_k$ and task $t_j \in imp_l$ are merged. The expression(1) aims to maximize the number of merged tasks and minimize the sum of response times of the different tasks constituting the task model.
In order to limit non meaningful merging situations, we define in addition the following constraints:

Merging Situation Constraints
The constraints (2) and (3) introduce the merging condition such as tow the tasks $\tau_i \in imp_k$ and $\tau_j \in imp_l$ will be merged if they have the same period.

$$\begin{array}{c} \forall i,j \in \{1 \ldots m\} \ et \ i \neq j, \\ if(InitTask[i,1] - InitTask[k,1]) = \delta t \quad then \quad Merge_{ij} = 1 \end{array} \tag{2}$$

$$\begin{array}{c} \forall i,j \in \{1 \ldots m\} \ et \ i \neq j, \\ if(InitTask[i,1] - InitTask[k,1]) \neq \delta t \quad then \quad Merge_{ij} = 0 \end{array} \tag{3}$$

The constraint (4) means that we have to maximize the number of merged tasks and thus minimize the number of tasks used in the task model. Indeed, this equation serves as a bound for the objective function (i.e. the number of merging operations).

$$N = m - \left(\sum_{i,j \in \{1 \ldots m\}} Merge_{ij} \right)/2 \tag{4}$$

Real-Time Constraints
NewTask is a three column matrix where the first column presents the periods of the new tasks computed by the constraint (5). The second column presents the WCETs of the tasks computed by the constraint (6) and the last column is the deadline presented by the constraint (7)

$$\forall k \in \{1 \ldots N\}, \forall i,j \in \{1 \ldots N\} : NewTask[k,1] = min(InitTask[i,1], InitTask[j,1]) \tag{5}$$

$$\begin{array}{c} NewTask[i,2] = (InitTask[i,2] + InitTask[j,2])Merge[i,j] + \\ (1 - Merge[i,j])InitTask[i,2] \end{array} \tag{6}$$

$$\forall i \in \{1 \ldots N\}, NewTask[i,3] = NewTask[i,1] \tag{7}$$

The constraint (8) verifies whether the new model meets the timing constraints.

$$U = \sum_{i=1}^{N} \frac{NewTask[i,2]}{NewTask[i,1]} \leq \sum_{i=1}^{N} N(2^{\frac{1}{N}} - 1) \tag{8}$$

Constraint (9) ensures that the response times Rep_i of the different tasks in the optimized model are lower or equal than their deadlines:

$$\forall i \in \{1 \ldots N\} Rep_i \leq NewTask[i,3] \tag{9}$$

Constraint (10) gives the computation formula of the response time Rep_i of task τ_i:

$$Rep_i = s[i] + NewTask[i, 2] \tag{10}$$

The response time Rep_i of a task τ_i is defined as the sum of its start time and its execution time.

$$\forall i \in \{1 \ldots N\} s[i] - s[j] >= NewTask[j, 2] \tag{11}$$

$$\forall i \in \{1 \ldots N\} s[j] - s[i] >= NewTask[i, 2] \tag{12}$$

To ensure a single executed task at any time, we should have either $s[i] - s[j] - NewTask[j, 2] >= 0$ or $s[j] - s[i] - NewTask[i, 2] >= 0$, for every pair of tasks t_i and t_j.

$$\forall i \in \{1 \ldots N\} s[i] <= r[i] \tag{13}$$

By respecting these constraints, the objective function will seek for the best way to merge tasks, so as to reduce the reconfiguration time while ensuring the respect of timing properties. The task model generated by the linear program will be interpreted by the code generator in order to generate a running program in POSIX.

4.4 Code Generator

The last step of our approach consists in building the executable application from the optimized task model. We generate a POSIX code on the basis of transformation rules. For each task in the optimized task model, the code generator implements a POSIX thread by using pthread. In addition, this step produces the controller code of the reconfigurable real-time system, which allow moving from implementation to another, following well-defined conditions (i.e. user requirements).

5 Case Study

In this section, we illustrate the proposed approach through a case study. The considered case study consists in a Car Collision Avoidance System (CCAS) [43]. Firstly, we present the CCAS specification. Then we apply the proposed approach using the suite of tools associated to an automatic construction of a feasible and optimal implementation of a reconfigurable real-time system.

5.1 CCAS Presentation

The Car Collision Avoidance System (CCAS) detects obstacles in front of the vehicle to which it is mounted and, if an imminent collision is detected, applies the brakes to slow the vehicle. To show the applicability of our approach, we consider in this paper a simplified version of this system. For clarity, several features of the system (CCAS) were omitted. Therefore, we only define two modes of operation:

(i) *Default mode:* represents a traditional use of CCAS,
(ii) *Economic mode:* represents a restrictive use of CCAS with safety requirements.

In the case where the economic mode must be enabled, the system jumps from the default mode to the secure one.

Default Mode: This mode is defined by five functions:

(i) F_1 (*ReadImage*): reads images from the input to the system from a radar,
(ii) F_2 (*Discrete Cosine Transformation: DCT*) moves the representation of the image from the spatial domain into the frequency domain
(iii) F_3 (*Quantization*): data in the frequency domain is selectively discarded to compress the image
(iv) F_4 (*InverseDCT*): moves the image back into the spatial domain
(v) F_5 (*Display*): displays the images for monitoring

The Figs. 4 and 5 present the overview of the CCAS system.

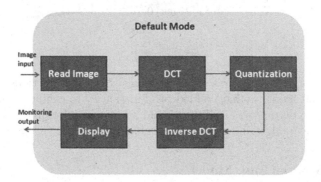

Fig. 4. CCAS overview in default mode.

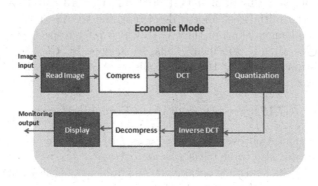

Fig. 5. CCAS overview in economic mode.

Table 1. CCAS specification in economic mode.

F_i	T_f	C_f
F_1	5 ms	1 ms
F_1'	5 ms	1 ms
F_2	5 ms	1 ms
F_3	15 ms	0.5 ms
F_4	15 ms	0.25 ms
F_4'	15 ms	0.25 ms
F_5	20 ms	2 ms

Table 2. CCAS specification in default mode.

F_i	T_f	C_f
F_1	5 ms	1 ms
F_2	5 ms	1 ms
F_3	15 ms	0.5 ms
F_4	15 ms	0.5 ms
F_5	20 ms	2 ms

Economic Mode: The economic Mode is defined by seven functions. Compared with the default mode, we have added two function F_1' to compress the received image and F_4' to decompress it. Tables 1 and 2 give a tabular presentation of the specification model describing the different functions of the CCAS system.

5.2   CCAS Initial Task Model

The second step consists in generating the implementations and their tasks from the specification model by applying Algorithm 1. Tables 3 and 4 give a tabular description of the initial task model describing the CCAS. This model shows two possible implementations of the CCAS which refer respectively to the two execution modes already specified. Thus, we denote by *CCASsys* the reconfigurable real-time system of the Car Collision Avoidance which defines two implementations:

$$CCASsys = \{DefaultMode, EconomicMode\}$$

The first implementation executes three tasks $DefaultMode = \{\tau_1, \tau_2, \tau_3\}$ and the second executes also three tasks $EconomicMode = \{\tau_4, \tau_5, \tau_6\}$. Each task is defined by the specific real-time parameters and implements the set of applicative functions having the same period.

Table 3. Tabular description of the initial task model of the CCAS in default mode.

Task	T_i (ms)	C_i (ms)	D_i (ms)	F_i
τ_1	5	3	5	$\{F_1, F_2\}$
τ_2	15	1	15	$\{F_3, F_4\}$
τ_3	20	2	20	$\{F_5\}$

Table 4. Tabular description of the initial task model of the CCAS in economic mode.

Task	T_i (ms)	C_i (ms)	D_i (ms)	F_i
τ_4	5	3	5	$\{F_1, F_1', F_2\}$
τ_5	15	1	15	$\{F_3, F_4, F_4'\}$
τ_6	20	2	20	$\{F_5\}$

5.3   CCAS Optimized Task Model

The third step corresponds to the generation of the optimized task model from the initial one. The objective of this step is to optimize the initial task model by minimizing the redundancy, the number of tasks and the response times of the different tasks. The merging matrix given by the task model optimization phase is given as follow:

$$Merge = \begin{pmatrix} 0\,0\,0\,0\,0\,0 \\ 0\,0\,0\,0\,1\,0 \\ 0\,0\,0\,0\,0\,1 \\ 0\,0\,0\,0\,0\,0 \\ 0\,1\,0\,0\,0\,0 \\ 0\,0\,1\,0\,0\,0 \end{pmatrix}$$

This matrix shows that the solution considered by the solver is the merge of τ_2 and τ_5 and the merge of τ_3 and τ_6. We note that tasks τ_1 and τ_4 are not merged by the solver even they have the same period because due to feasibility concerns (i.e. if the solver decide to merge τ_1 and τ_4, the resulting task will not meet its deadline). Tabular descriptions of task models generated by this phase are given in Tables 5 and 6.

Table 5. Tabular description of the optimized task model of the CCAS in default mode.

Task	T_i (ms)	C_i (ms)	D_i (ms)	Rep_i (ms)	Function
τ_1	5	3	5	7	F_1, F_2
τ_2'	15	2	15	10.7	F_3, F_4, F_4'
τ_3'	20	4	20	5.2	F_5

Table 6. Tabular description of the optimized task model of the CCAS in economic mode.

Task	T_i (ms)	C_i (ms)	D_i (ms)	Rep_i (ms)	Function
τ_1'	5	3	5	8	F_1, F_1', F_2
τ_2'	15	2	15	10.8	F_3, F_4, F_4'
τ_3'	20	4	20	5.3	F_5

After optimisation, the CCAS system consists also in two implementations but implementing different functions: $DefaultMode = \{\tau_1, \tau_2', \tau_3'\}$ and $Economic\text{-}Mode = \{\tau_1', \tau_2', \tau_3'\}$. We note that the number of tasks implementing the CCAS after optimization is only 4 tasks compared to 6 tasks in the initial task model. In addition, as we can see from Tables 5 and 6, the response times Rep_i of the different tasks are lower than their deadlines D_i and thus the timing constraints of the CCAS system are met. Figures 6 and 7 present the execution graphs of the tasks in the default mode and the economic mode of the CCAS system given by cheddar simulator [4]. These figures confirm that the system is feasible since all the tasks meet the related deadlines.

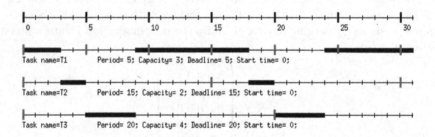

Fig. 6. Execution graph of CCAS tasks in default mode.

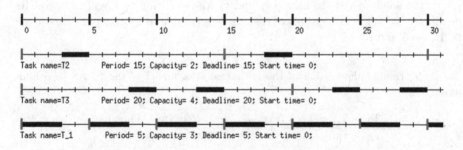

Fig. 7. Execution graph of CCAS tasks in economic mode.

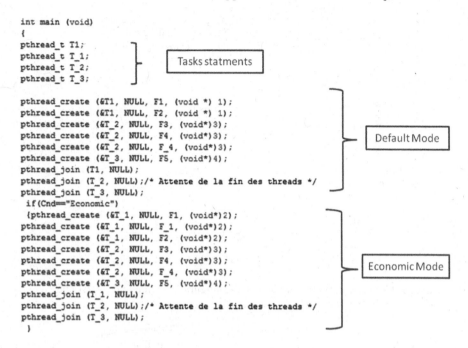

```
int main (void)
{
pthread_t T1;
pthread_t T_1;                    Tasks statments
pthread_t T_2;
pthread_t T_3;

pthread_create (&T1, NULL, F1, (void *) 1);
pthread_create (&T1, NULL, F2, (void *) 1);
pthread_create (&T_2, NULL, F3, (void*)3);
pthread_create (&T_2, NULL, F4, (void*)3);          Default Mode
pthread_create (&T_2, NULL, F_4, (void*)3);
pthread_create (&T_3, NULL, F5, (void*)4);
pthread_join (T1, NULL);
pthread_join (T_2, NULL);/* Attente de la fin des threads */
pthread_join (T_3, NULL);
  if (Cnd=="Economic")
  {pthread_create (&T_1, NULL, F1, (void*)2);
pthread_create (&T_1, NULL, F_1, (void*)2);
pthread_create (&T_1, NULL, F2, (void*)2);
pthread_create (&T_2, NULL, F3, (void*)3);
pthread_create (&T_2, NULL, F4, (void*)3);          Economic Mode
pthread_create (&T_2, NULL, F_4, (void*)3);
pthread_create (&T_3, NULL, F5, (void*)4);
pthread_join (T_1, NULL);
pthread_join (T_2, NULL);/* Attente de la fin des threads */
pthread_join (T_3, NULL);
  }
```

Fig. 8. Excerpt of the controller implementation.

5.4 Code Generation

The last step in our approach is the code generator. We generate a POSIX code from the optimized task model describing the CCAS. Figure 8 presents an excerpt of the controller POSIX code. The controller's role is to switch from one implementation to another under a considered condition. As shown in Fig. 8 if the variable "CND" is equal to "Economic" then the control executes the *EconomicMode* implementation else it executes the *DefaultMode*.

5.5 Performance Evaluation

The experiments are carried-out on Intel Core i5-4200U processor running at 1.6 GHz with 6 GB of cache memory. CPLEX is used as a MILP solver for the whole set of experiments. We evaluate the proposed approach by considering the CCAS system $CCASsys$ previously defined.

We denote by $T_{reconf_{initial}}$ the reconfiguration time in the initial task model of the CCAS and $T_{reconf_{Current}}$ the reconfiguration time in the optimized task one. These parameters are given as follow:

$$T_{reconf_{initial}} = 5 * T_{delete} + 6 * T_{creat} = 11 * T_{cost}$$

$$T_{reconf_{Current}} = 1 * T_{delete} + 2 * T_{creat} = 3 * T_{cost}$$

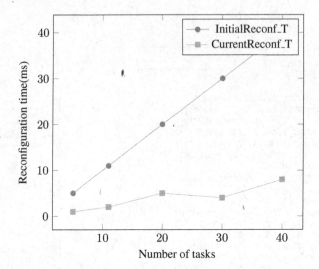

Fig. 9. Comparison between current reconfiguration time and initial one.

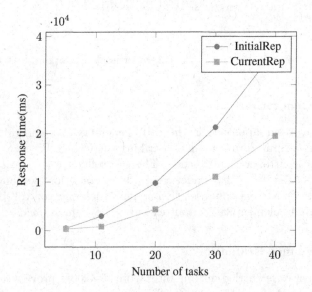

Fig. 10. Comparison between current response time and initial one.

We note that the proposed approach allows to reduce the reconfiguration time and thus improves the overall performance of the reconfigurable real-time system (CCAS). It minimizes also the sum of the response times of the considered tasks such as $Rep_{initial} = 3010$ ms and after optimization it becomes $Rep_{optimized} = 1920$ ms.

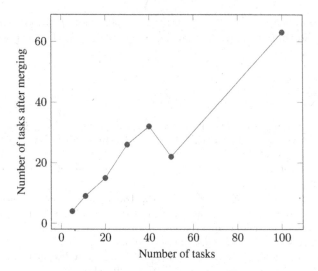

Fig. 11. Results of task merging.

In addition, we have randomly generated instances with 5 to 40 tasks. We compare the reconfiguration time and the sum of response times after optimization with the initial corresponding parameters. The numerical results are depicted in Figs. 9 and 10.

These figures show that the optimization of the reconfiguration and response times are clearer and more important for large scale reconfigurable real-time systems. In fact, when the number of tasks is more important, the optimisation phase will seek for solutions to merge tasks having the same periods while minimizing the response times of the different tasks. Such optimisation, reduce the reconfiguration time and guarantee the system feasibility. Figure 11 shows the number of tasks obtained after merging compared to the initial number of task. We compute average results by executing several times the linear program on randomly generated task sets. We observe from this figure that we are able to merge many tasks. Thus, we minimize the additional time overhead.

6   Conclusion

The contribution presented in this paper consists in a methodology that supports the development of reconfigurable real-time systems. By defining the specification such as reconfigurable conditions, functions and temporal constraints the approach generates as first step an initial task model. Then, this model will be optimized using MILP techniques to produce an optimized task model. Finally, our approach generates a POSIX-based code which describes the reconfigurable real-time system. We have evaluated the performance of the three-step approach. The numerical results show that the integer programming model allows to minimize the reconfiguration time and response times. As a future work, we aim to extend our approach by considering multiprocessor systems and other optimization metrics. So that we expect to evaluate scalability of the proposed method with an industrial example.

References

1. Burns, A., Wellings, A.: Real-Time Systems and Programming Languages: Ada, Real-Time Java and C/Real-Time POSIX, 4th edn. Addison-Wesley Educational Publishers Inc., USA (2009)
2. Cottet, F., Grolleau, E.: Systmes Temps Réel de Contrôle-Commande. Dunod, Paris (2005)
3. Polakovic, J., Mazare, S., Stefani, J.-B., David, P.-C.: Experience with safe dynamic reconfigurations in component-based embedded systems. In: Schmidt, H.W., Crnkovic, I., Heineman, G.T., Stafford, J.A. (eds.) CBSE 2007. LNCS, vol. 4608, pp. 242–257. Springer, Heidelberg (2007). doi:10.1007/978-3-540-73551-9_17
4. Singhoff, F., Legrand, J., Nana, L., Marcé, L.: Cheddar: a flexible real time scheduling framework. In: Proceedings of the ACM SIGADA International Conference, Atlanta. ACM (2004)
5. Baruah, S., Goossens, J.: Scheduling real-time tasks: Algorithms and complexity. Handb. Sched.: Algorithms Models Perform. Anal. **3** (2004)
6. Gharsellaoui, H., Gharbi, A., Khalgui, M., Ahmed, S.: Feasible automatic reconfigurations of real-time OS tasks. In: Handbook of Research on Industrial Informatics and Manufacturing Intelligence: Innovations and Solutions: Innovations and Solutions (2012)
7. Liu, C., Layland, J.: Scheduling algorithms for multiprogramming in a hard-real-time environment. J. ACM (JACM) **20**, 46–61 (1973)
8. Bouaziz, R., Lemarchand, L., Singhoff, F., Zalila, B., Jmaiel, M.: Architecture exploration of real-time systems based on multi-objective optimization. In: Proceedings of the 20th International Conference on Engineering of Complex Computer Systems (ICECCS), Gold Coast, QLD, pp. 1–10. IEEE (2015)
9. Mehiaoui, A., Wozniak, E., Tucci-Piergiovanni, S., Mraidha, C., Natale, M.D., Zeng, H., Babau, J., Lemarchand, L., Gerard, S.: A two-step optimization technique for functions placement, partitioning, and priority assignment in distributed systems. ACM SIGPLAN Not. **48**, 121–132 (2013)
10. Woźniak, E.: Model-based synthesis of distributed real-time automotive architectures. Ph.D. thesis, Université Paris Sud-Paris XI
11. Marinca, D., Minet, P., George, L.: Analysis of deadline assignment methods in distributed real-time systems. Comput. Commun. **27**, 1412–1423 (2004)
12. Pillai, P., Shin, K.: Taste-an open-source tool-chain for embedded system and software development. In: Proceedings of the Embedded Real Time Software and Systems Conference (ERTS), Toulouse, France (2012)
13. Lewine, D.: POSIX programmers guide. O'Reilly Media Inc., USA (1991)
14. Obenland, K.M.: The Use of Posix in Real-time Systems, Assessing its Effectiveness and Performance. The MITRE Corporation, McLean (2000)
15. Lehoczky, J., Sha, L., Ding, Y.: The rate monotonic scheduling algorithm: exact characterization and average case behavior. In: Proceedings of the Real Time Systems Symposium, pp. 166–171. IEEE (1989)
16. Ltkebohle, I.: IBM CPLEX Optimizer - United States (2016). http://www-01.ibm.com/software/commerce/optimization/cplex-optimizer/. Accessed 10 Apr 2016

17. Stankovic, J.: Misconceptions about real-time computing: a serious problem for next-generation systems. Computer **21**, 10–19 (1988)
18. Klein, M., Ralya, T., Pollak, B., Obenza, R., Harbour, M.G.: Analyzing complex systems. In: Klein, M., Ralya, T., Pollak, B., Obenza, R., Harbour, M.G. (eds.) Proceedings of Real-Time Analysis, pp. 535–578. Springer, US (1993)
19. Chetto, H., Silly, M., Bouchentouf, T.: Dynamic scheduling of real-time tasks under precedence constraints. Real-Time Syst. **2**, 181–194 (1991)
20. Swaminathan, V., Chakrabarty, K.: Real-time task scheduling for energy-aware embedded systems. J. Franklin Inst. **338**, 729–750 (2001)
21. Gruian, F.: Hard real-time scheduling for low-energy using stochastic data and DVS processors. In: Proceedings of the 2001 international symposium on Low power electronics and design, pp. 46–51. ACM (2001)
22. Krishna, C.M., Lee, Y.H.: Voltage-clock-scaling adaptive scheduling techniques for low power in hard real-time systems. IEEE Trans. Comput. **52**, 1586–1593 (2003)
23. Bini, E., Buttazzo, G.: A hyperbolic bound for the rate monotonic algorithm. In: Proceedings of the 13th Euromicro Conference on Real-Time Systems, Delft, pp. 59–66. IEEE (2001)
24. Pillai, P., Shin, K.: Real-time dynamic voltage scaling for low-power embedded operating systems. In: Proceedings of the 13th Euromicro Conference on Real-Time Systems, USA, pp. 59–66. ACM (2001)
25. Bertout, A., Forget, J., Olejnik, R.: Minimizing a real-time task set through task clustering. In: Proceedings of the 22nd International Conference on Real-Time Networks and Systems, p. 23, Versailles, France. ACM (2014)
26. Racu, R., Jersak, M., Ernst, R.: Applying sensitivity analysis in real-time distributed systems. In: 11th IEEE Real Time and Embedded Technology and Applications Symposium, pp. 160–169. IEEE (2005)
27. Pop, T., Eles, P., Peng, Z.: Design optimization of mixed time/event-triggered distributed embedded systems. In: Proceedings of the 1st IEEE/ACM/IFIP International Conference on Hardware/Software Codesign and System Synthesis, pp. 83–89. ACM (2003)
28. Aleti, A., Buhnova, B., Grunske, L., Koziolek, A., Meedeniya, I.: Software architecture optimization methods: a systematic literature review. IEEE Trans. Software Eng. **39**, 658–683 (2013)
29. Mraidha, C., Tucci-Piergiovanni, S., Gerard, S.: Optimum: a marte-based methodology for schedulability analysis at early design stages. ACM SIGSOFT Softw. Eng. Notes **36**, 1–8 (2011)
30. Hladik, P.-E., Cambazard, H., Déplanche, A.M., Jussien, N.: Solving a real-time allocation problem with constraint programming. Comput. Ind. Eng. **81**, 132–149 (2008)
31. Harbour, M.G.: Ordonnancement temps reel avec profilsvariables de consommation d'energie. In: Embedded Systems (2004)
32. Xu, Y., Brennan, R.W., Zhang, X., Norrie, H.: A reconfigurable concurrent function block model and its implementation in real-time java. Discret. Event Dynamic Syst. **9**, 263–279 (2002)
33. Rooker, M.N., Sünder, C., Strasser, T., Zoitl, A., Hummer, O., Ebenhofer, G.: Zero downtime reconfiguration of distributed automation systems: the ϵCEDAC approach. In: Mařík, V., Vyatkin, V., Colombo, A.W. (eds.) HoloMAS 2007. LNCS, vol. 4659, pp. 326–337. Springer, Heidelberg (2007). doi:10.1007/978-3-540-74481-8_31

34. Thramboulidis, K., Doukas, G., Frantzis, A.: Towards an implementation model for FB-based reconfigurable distributed control applications. In: IEEE International Symposium on Object-Oriented Real-Time Distributed Computing, pp. 193–200. IEEE (2007)
35. Krichen, F., Hamid, B., Zalila, B., Coulette, B.: Designing dynamic reconfiguration for distributed real time embedded systems. In: Proceedings of 10th Annual International Conference on New Technologies of Distributed Systems (NOTERE), Tozeur, Tunisia, pp. 249–254. IEEE (2010)
36. Guo, Y., Sierszecki, K., Angelov, C.A.: A reconfiguration mechanism for resource-constrained embedded systems, pp. 1315–1320. IEEE Computer Society, Washington, DC, USA (2008)
37. B. Hamid, A. Lanusse, A.R., Gérard, S.: Designing reconfigurable component systems with a model based approach. In: ARTIST Workshop on Adaptive and Reconfigurable Embedded Systems, Saint Louis, MO, USA, pp. 69–73 (2008)
38. Barreto, R., Neves, M., Oliveira Jr., M., Maciel, P., Tavares, E., Lima, R.: A formal software synthesis approach for embedded hard real-time systems. In: Proceedings of the 17th symposium on Integrated circuits and system design, pp. 163–168. ACM (2004)
39. Tavares, E., Barreto, R., Junior, M.O., Maciel, P., Neves, M., Lima, R.: An approach for pre-runtime scheduling in embedded hard real-time systems with power constraints. In: 16th Symposium on Computer Architecture and High Performance Computing, 2004, SBAC-PAD 2004, pp. 188–195. IEEE (2004)
40. Pagetti, C., Forget, J., Boniol, F., Cordovilla, M., Lesens, D.: Multi-task implementation of multi-periodic synchronous programs. Discret. Event Dyn. Syst. **21**, 307–338 (2011)
41. Binder, W., Hulaas, J.: Using bytecode instruction counting as portable cpu consumption metric. Electron. Notes Theoret. Comput. Sci. **153**, 57–77 (2006)
42. Harbour, M.G.: Real-time posix: an overview. In: VVConex 93 International Conference, Moscu. Citeseer (1993)
43. Brosse, E.: Marte-designer example-ccas - marte user manual (english) - modelio community forge (2011). https://forge.modelio.org/projects/marte-user-manual-english/wiki/marte-designer_example-CCAS. Accessed 1 Nov 2016

Testing Web Services with Model-Based Mutation

Faezeh Siavashi[1(✉)], Junaid Iqbal[1], Dragos Truscan[1], and Jüri Vain[2]

[1] Faculty of Science and Engineering, Åbo Akademi University, Åbo, Finland
{faezeh.siavashi,junaid.iqbal,dragos.truscan}@abo.fi
[2] Department of Computer Science, Tallinn University of Technology,
Tallinn, Estonia
juri.vain@ttu.ee

Abstract. One way of evaluating the robustness of a web service is to test it against invalid inputs. We introduce a model-based mutation technique which automatically generates faulty test inputs. From the specification of a Web service, a test model is designed using UPPAAL Timed Automata and the conformance between the model and the implementation is validated via online model-based testing with the UPPAAL TRON tool. A set of mutation operators is applied to the test model in order to generate mutant test models. We validate all generated mutants via verification rules and select those that are executable and introduce proper mutations. We employ bisimulation as a tool for detecting and eliminating equivalent mutants, that is those mutants which have identical input-output behavior with the original test model. The resulting mutants are used for online test generation against the service implementation in order to check whether the latter allows for unspecified behavior. We discuss tool support and present an experiment of applying our method for a case study of a blog web service with real-life properties. The experiment shows that the proposed approach of mutating the specifications is effective in detecting errors both in the system functionality and in the test model.

Keywords: Web service · Model-based mutation testing · UPPAAL · TRON · Bisimulation of UPPAAL Timed Automata

1 Introduction

Software applications that support machine-to-machine interactions over the Internet have heavily increased the role of web services. One main characteristic of web services is that they are accessed via clearly defined interfaces over the standard HTTP protocol. This kind of systems should be robust against erroneous inputs. This means that one needs to ensure that the web service implementation is tested with respect not only to its expected behavior, but also to its unexpected behavior. The former can be checked by running test cases derived from the specification, whereas the latter can be done via robustness testing, by executing invalid inputs.

© Springer International Publishing AG 2017
E. Cabello et al. (Eds.): ICSOFT 2016, CCIS 743, pp. 45–67, 2017.
DOI: 10.1007/978-3-319-62569-0_3

When defining test inputs, the model-based specifications are preferred over manually written test scripts since the machine can verify the correctness of the models and automatically generate the test inputs from them. Moreover, test generation from models enables systematic construction of extensive test cases.

One way to create invalid test inputs is using *specification mutation*, where a set of well-defined mutation operators generate syntactic changes to the specifications and produce specification mutants. Although originally the mutations have been applied directly to source code, it has also been extended also to specification languages [1]. When applied to modeling languages, mutation used to create the models that generate invalid scenarios as test cases, which then are executed against the implementation under test (IUT). If the IUT conforms to the mutated specification (i.e., the IUT accepts an unspecified sequence of inputs), it means that its behavior is inconsistent with its original specification and it may have unspecified or incorrect behavior.

In this work, we propose a tool-supported approach for robustness testing of web service using UPPAAL Timed Automata (UTA). The conformance between the model and the IUT is first checked via UPPAAL TRON, an online conformance testing tool which supports both test generation and test execution. As a first contribution, we introduce a test generation method, which derives mutants from the specification and executes them via online testing. We use a selection of mutation operators that are previously defined in the literature and adapt them for the online testing process targeted in this work.

As a second contribution, in our method, we add verification properties to mutated model segments to ensure reachability of the mutated elements at runtime. If a mutant does not satisfy the verification properties, it cannot be used for online testing, hence, we eliminate it. Furthermore, to ensure that the mutated part will be executed during the testing process, we monitor whether the mutated elements are reached during test execution.

As a third contribution, we provide an approach for detecting and eliminating equivalent mutants, that is those mutant models which exhibit identical timed input-output behavior with the original test model, even if the two models are syntactically different. For this purpose, we verify the timed bisimilarity of the corresponding UPPAAL timed automata models.

As a forth contribution, we empirically evaluate which of the existing mutation operators for UPPAAL timed automata are effective for online testing of web services. For this purpose, we define two formulas to measure the efficiency of mutation operators as well as their fault detection rate.

Parts of this work have been originally presented in [2]. In this version, we extend previous work as follows: we provide a method for detecting equivalent mutants, we discuss tool support for the entire approach, we address a larger set of mutation operators, we use a different case study to complement the previous results and we provide a more detailed analysis of the results.

The remainder of this paper is organized as follows: In Sect. 2, we briefly revisit the background concepts behind UPPAAL timed automata, conformance testing with TRON, and specification mutation analysis. Section 3 details the steps of our approach and its tool support. The case study and the experiments used to validate our approach are presented in Sect. 4. The results are discussed in Sect. 4.6 and possible improvements are suggested in Sect. 6. Threats to validity of the proposed method are discussed in Sect. 7. We review the literature for related work in Sect. 8. Finally, we conclude our study and present future work in Sect. 9.

2   Background

We first review the UPPAAL tool set and we introduce the conformance testing with UPPAAL TRON , then we elaborate on the concept of specification mutation testing.

2.1   UPPAAL Timed Automata (UTA)

UPPAAL is a model-checker tool for modeling, simulation, and verification of real-time systems using an extended version of timed automata called UPPAAL timed automata (UTA) [3]. A timed automaton is a state machine with locations, actions, and clocks.

In UPPAAL, a system is designed as a network of several such timed-automata called processes working in parallel. A process can be executed individually or in sync with another process. Synchronization of two processes is possible by using input/output actions (denoted as "!" for emitting and "?" for receiving synchronizations, respectively). The processes consist of locations and edges. The state of the system can be shown by the locations of all processes, their clock value intervals, and their variable values. The edges between locations represent state transitions including clock resets. UPPAAL is extended further with global and local to some process variables that can be of type *integer, boolean, clock* and arrays of those.

Edges can be constrained by predicates (over the clocks or variables) known as *guards*, which defines when the corresponding edge is enabled. State transitions are specified on edges as variable updates. A location can be restricted over the clock invariants, which specify how long the system can stay in that location. If there is more than one enabled edge at a time, then one of them will be randomly selected. This gives more freedom to represent non-deterministic behaviour, especially in systems with random discrete events [4].

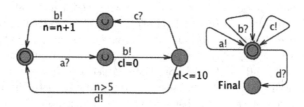

Fig. 1. Example of an UTA model [2].

An example of a UTA model consisting of two timed automata is shown in Fig. 1. The communication between automata is modeled using channel synchronizations (e.g., a, b, c, d) and variables (e.g., n). Time is modeled via the clock variable cl.

The UPPAAL model-checker uses a simplified version of TCTL [5], which enables to exhaustively verify the models w.r.t their specifications. The query language consists of state formulae and path formulae. State formulae (φ) is an expression that describes the properties of an individual state while path formulae can be used to specify which properties (like reachability, safety, and liveness) hold over a given path [6].

If there is a state in the model that has no enabled outgoing transitions, then the model is said to be in a deadlock. A $\Box$ *not deadlock* query, can be used to verify that for all paths in the model, there is no deadlock state.

The safety property checks that "something bad will never happen". In UPPAAL it can be expressed in the form $A \Box \varphi$ (φ should be true in all reachable states) and $E \Box \varphi$ (there should exist a maximal path such that φ is always true).

The liveness property determines that "something will eventually happen" and it is shown by $A \Diamond \varphi$ (φ is eventually satisfied) and $\varphi \rightsquigarrow \phi$ (whenever φ is satisfied, then eventually ϕ will be satisfied).

Reachability properties validate the basic behavior of the model by checking whether a certain property is possible in the model with the given paths. The reachability can be expressed in the form of $E \Diamond \varphi$ (there is a path from the initial state, such that φ is eventually satisfied along that path).

2.2 Online Model-Based Testing

Model-Based Testing (MBT) [3] is an approach which uses behavioral models of the system under test to generate tests. Based on how tests are generated and executed, there are two distinct approaches of MBT: offline and online testing. In *offline testing*, the complete test scenarios and test oracle are created before the test execution, whereas online testing is a combination of test generation and execution: only one test input at a time is generated and executed, then the next test input is generated based on the previous test output [7]. This continues until the test termination criteria are satisfied or an error occurs.

In this study, we use the online testing tool UPPAAL TRON, which is an input/output conformance testing tool for testing real-time systems based on the *rtioco* conformance relation [8]. In TRON, the UTA model is divided in two partitions: a system partition and an environment partition, and the communication between the two is observed against the inputs and outputs of the IUT. Test stimuli are selected randomly from the enabled test inputs. A *test adapter* is used for converting abstract test cases to concrete inputs to the IUT and for converting concrete outputs into abstract outputs represented in the model. Via *online testing*, the state-explosion problem is reduced because only a portion of the state space is needed to be calculated and stored at each step. Also, the non-determinism of systems can be simulated on-the-fly by random selection of the test inputs.

The result of online testing with TRON can be *passed*, *failed*, or *inconclusive*. An inconclusive test result means that the environment model cannot progress since the IUT output is unexpected or timeout occurred when waiting for test output.

2.3 Specification Mutation Analysis

Specification mutation analysis is an approach used to design tests to evaluate the correctness and consistency of the specification or of the program [1]. When the mutation analysis is applied to the specification, a set of *mutation operators* create slightly altered versions (mutants) of the specification. The tests will be generated from the mutated specification and used to assess whether the IUT is accepting the tests. The following types of mutants are defined in the literature [9]:

- **Killed:** the tests generated from a mutant specification fail against the implementation, under the precondition that the tests generated from the original specification have passed.
- **Alive:** all test cases generated from the mutant pass against the IUT. Alive mutants can be divided into two sub-types:
- **Equivalent:** The mutant manifests the same behavior as the original model, even if they are syntactically different.
- **Non-equivalent:** The mutant does not have the same behavior as the original model, however, all tests generated from the mutant pass against the IUT. These mutants indicate that the implementation is too permissive and is not able to detect the invalid inputs.

3 Method

In this section, a method which combines specification mutation testing and online model-based testing is presented. The outcome of the method is to generate and identify *non-equivalent alive mutants* which are used to show that there might be some inconsistencies between the specification and the implementation. The collected mutants are subject to further investigation to identify whether the source of the problem is in the specification or in the implementation. Figure 2 illustrates an overview of the method including six main phases (separated by dashed lines), as follows:

3.1 Design and Conformance Testing

From the given specifications of a system, e.g., a web service, a test model is designed. The test model consists of two partitions: the system under test and

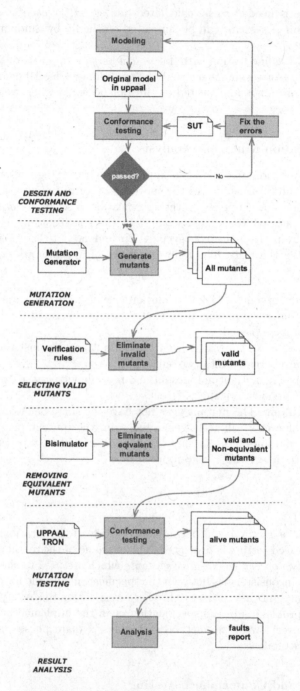

Fig. 2. Model-based mutation testing approach.

its environment. The former models the activities that a typical user performs against the web service, while the latter models how the system should respond to user activities. For instance, a flight booking server receives different HTTP requests (such as searching, checking in, etc.) and returns the corresponding HTTP responses. For each request and response, two edges are specified in the model. It should be noted that, failure responses are not modeled since adding all possible failure response types might make the model too complex.

In order to ensure that the model is correctly designed according to the specification, we verify it via model-checking. Deadlockfreeness and reachability properties are two common and essential properties that the model should satisfy. These properties ensure that the model can be used later on for online testing.

The test adapter is implemented to convert the observable test interface I/O actions into HTTP messages and vice-versa. The adapter is also used to check the status codes of different HTTP responses, before forwarding them to the tester. The TRON testing tool orchestrates the communications between the test model and the IUT, and check the I/O conformance between the two. During the online testing, the expected behavior of the IUT is validated and possible modeling errors or implementation bugs are resolved.

3.2   Mutation Generation

From a verified test model various modified versions are created. Each modified version of the original model is called *mutant model* (or simply *mutant*). Test generated from mutants will also exhibit a mutated behaviors compared to the original ones.

Mutation operators implement the rules that create systematic mutation of a given context. They are uniquely defined for a specific modeling language. For example, different modeling languages (UML, Petri Nets, UPPAAL, etc.) have different mutation operators. Mutation operators for UTA have been previously defined by Aboutrab et al. [10] and by Aichernig et al. [11], as summarized in Table 1. As one may notice, the two sets of operators are mostly similar in purpose, however they differ in the restrictions that are employed in each element. For instance, for a guard, three mutation operators (RTC, WTC and STC) are defined by Aboutrab et al., while, all three definitions are covered in one mutation operator (μCG) in the work of Aichernig et al.

Mutation operators that are used in this paper are selected from this list, combining the definition of the similar mutation operators in both studies. Only one of the mutation operators (sink location) was not selected in this study, since it will produce higher order mutations which are beyond the scope of this work.

We have restricted some of the operators to make them suitable for online testing with TRON. As we mentioned earlier, the IUT and its environment (user, or other systems) are specified in separate automata and they communicate via synchronization channels and global variables. All channels between the model of the system and its environment and the variables attached to those channels are observable by TRON. Based on the type of the input or output, TRON controls which action can be executed at a given time. Therefore, if there are multiple

Table 1. Mutation operators of timed-automata, [2].

Mutated elements	Aichering et al. [11]	Aboutrab et al. [10]	Informal definition
Guard	Change Guard (μCG)	Restricting Timing Constraints (RTC)	Restricts, expands or alters guards
		Widening Timing Constraints (WTC)	
		Shifting Timing constraints (STC)	
	Negate guard (μCg)	-	Guard will be replaced by its negation
Invariant	Change invariant (μCi)	-	Restricts, expands or change value of invariants
Clock	Invert reset (μIr)	Resetting a Clock (RC)	Removes or adds clock resets
		Not-Resetting a Clock (NRC)	
Action	Change action (μCa)	Exchanging Input Actions (EIA)	Changes names of actions
		Exchanging Output Action (EOA)	
	Change source (μCs)	-	Changes source location of actions
	Change target (μCt)	Transferring Destination Locations (TDL)	Changes target locations of actions
Location	Sink location (μSl)	-	Makes a new locations and changes targets of all actions to the new location

processes in the model and some of the synchronizations among them are not defined in the IUT, then they cannot be observed by TRQN. Thus, they will not be mutated either. It should be noted that in this study, only the system under test (SUT) partition is mutated and we limit our approach to partitions with only one timed automaton process.

Additionally, the mutation operator for changing the name of the actions (i.e. μCa) is only applied on input actions in the SUT model. The reason behind this is that the implementation of the web service is a black box and thus we cannot change them. The requests (inputs actions), on the other hand, come from outside of the SUT and can be manipulated. We select EIA mutation operator that will be effective since the sequence of requests will be mutated, whereas mutating the output actions does not make a suitable mutation.

Finally, the direction of synchronizations will not be changed (i.e., switching "?" to "!") since the requests from the environment are modeled as input actions ("?") and changing them into output actions indicates that the requests will be changed into responses, which is not applicable in web services. The web service is the receiver of the requests from the user and not the sender of the requests.

The mutation operators adapted from Table 1 and used in this paper are presented in the following.

1. **Change Name of Input Action (CNI).** This operator is same as EIA, which replaces the name of an input action (denoted by "?") with the name of other actions. Thus, the expected sequence of the inputs to the implementation will be different.
2. **Change Target (CT).** This operator is similar to TDL and μCT. As it name suggests, it changes the target of an interface action to other location. This operator can break the flow of test inputs and violate the state of the IUT. Both input and output actions can be mutated by this operator.
3. **Change Source (CS).** This operator is similar to μCS defined in [11] changes the source location of an action to other locations. Similar to CT, this operator gives a different I/O sequence.
4. **Change Guard (CG).** For this operator, we followed the definition of μCG, which changes the clock constants in guards by a random value. It is effective for mutating the enabling condition of an action.
5. **Negate Guard (NG).** It is the same operator as μNG which negates the guards and may cause some paths of the test model to become unreachable.
6. **Change Invariant (CI).** Similar to μCI, it shifts values of the invariants to a different range, extending or restricting the constraints of the model. It can cause actions fire earlier (or later) than expected by original model.
7. **Invert Reset (IR).** This operator is same as μIR which deletes the resetting of the clock and moves it to one action before or after. It means that the resetting is shifted one edge earlier or later.

Figure 3 shows the mutants of a model and corresponding mutants using the above operators. In our approach, we only apply first order mutation. That is, a mutant model contains only one mutated segment based on a single operator.

3.3   Selecting Valid Mutants

In the context of this paper, we define a valid mutant as one which can be executed by TRON and in which the mutated part is reachable. To this end, we verify if all mutations are reachable and deadlock free.

In UPPAAL, the reachability property is defined for locations and the valuations of variable sets. When an action is mutated, we define the reachability property for the target location of that action. For instance, in Fig. 3(b), the input action a? is mutated into c?, hence, the reachability for this mutation should be defined for its target location (i.e., l). For example, in Fig. 3(b), we have $E \diamond l$, which verifies if that the mutation can be reached and executed.

Nevertheless, for CT and CS that change target and source of actions, the above reachability is not suitable. Thus, we add an alternative method to define reachability in these circumstances. For a mutated action, we add a *trap variable* update [12] on its edge. The initial value of the variable is set to **false**. The variable will be updated to **true** whenever the mutated action is executed, and

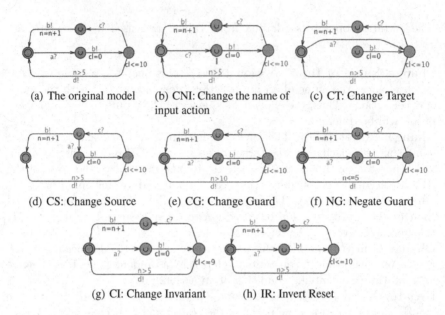

(a) The original model

(b) CNI: Change the name of input action

(c) CT: Change Target

(d) CS: Change Source

(e) CG: Change Guard

(f) NG: Negate Guard

(g) CI: Change Invariant

(h) IR: Invert Reset

Fig. 3. A model with examples of mutants generated by the selected mutation operators [2].

so the reachability can be achieved by checking if the variable eventually will be set to true ($E \diamond trap$).

One can use trap variables to ensure that the mutation part of the model will be reached during the test execution as well. In the case that the minimum repetitive execution of mutation is needed the boolean trap variable should be replaced by an integer counter variable *count* and the reachability condition with $E \diamond count >= const$. Those models that pass the verification process are considered as *valid mutants* and can be executed against the IUT.

Beside reachability, the deadlock-freeness property will also be verified. The deadlock freeness property can be expressed as $A\square$ *not deadlock*, which indicates that for all existing path in the model there is no deadlock.

Early validation of the mutants reduces the number of final valid mutants by eliminating false negatives which cause semantic and syntactic errors.

3.4   Detecting and Removing Equivalent Mutants

In order to detect those mutants which have equivalent observable input-output behavior we employ bisimulation relation checks. Intuitively, two UTA are *bisimilar* if they accept the same timed language, i.e., they perform exactly the same observable action transitions and if they reach bisimilar states. In other words, each of the systems cannot be distinguished from the other by an external observer. Bisimulation relation is symmetric. Bisimulation for timed automata has been originally introduced by [13] and shown in [14] to be decidable for parallel timed processes. In order to observe bisimilarity between the original model and one of its mutants, we follow these steps:

1. we compose a new UTA model containing both the original and a mutant model,
2. we add additional, side-effect free, synchronization channels between the models for the observable actions,
3. we verify that the complete model never deadlocks on all possible paths.

The mutants selected after the validation step described in Sect. 3.3 were examined for their bisimilarity.

Figure 4 depicts an example of a bisimulation model used to detect bisimilarity between two models. The observable channels and shared variables between environment and the SUT partition of the mutant process are renamed (using the *BISIM_* prefix) and added as a counterpart to observe the bisimilarity. A committed location between each channel and its counterpart to ensure that both observable actions take place at the same time. Thus, the deviation of the behavior of either process results in a deadlock which violates the condition of bisimilarity. The non-bisimilar models are good candidates for mutation testing due to their erroneous behavior. All mutants which are found to be bisimilar with the original model are considered equivalent, and consequently, are eliminated.

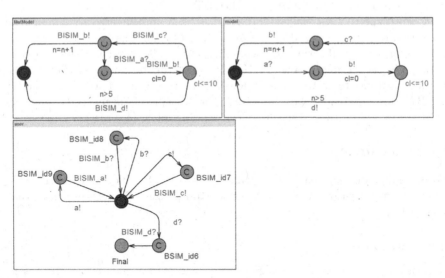

Fig. 4. UTA containing an original process (*model*), a mutated process (*MutModel*), and a shared environment process (*user*).

3.5   Mutation Testing

Each valid mutant model is executed in a testing session with UPPAAL TRON. The verdict of an online testing session with TRON can be *passed*, *failed*, or *inconclusive.* In TRON, an inconclusive verdict indicates that either the observed output from the IUT is not valid, or there is an unacceptable delay in receiving responses from the IUT. We consider that the mutants that generate inconclusive test cases exhibit different behavior than the original model and thus they are considered as *killed.* When executing the mutants we assume implicitly that these test runs are exhaustive w.r.t. the mutation, i.e. all mutations injected are also covered by these test runs.

3.6   Result Analysis

The last phase of our method is to evaluate the results by reasoning about the unexpected behaviors that the IUT shows during test execution. The focus of the analysis is on the non-equivalent mutants, which generate different invalid test inputs, thus, these test inputs are manually evaluated to find the correlations between them and the actual faulty behaviors.

3.7   Tool Support

Tool support has been implemented to automate several of the activities discussed in the previous section. The UPPAAL tool set is used for modeling and verification of the original model. Then the TRON tool and a test adapter is implemented to interface TRON with the IUT.

A prototype tool set, called *MuUTA*, has been implemented to support the generation of mutants based on the selected mutation operators, to automatically perform the verification of reachability and deadlock-freeness rules for each mutant via the *verifyta* utility of UPPAAL and run bisimulation checks. The tool also instantiates a test session for each mutant using TRON test adapter and IUT and eliminates those mutants that are killed. All generated mutants are stored based on their status in corresponding folders for further analysis.

4   Experiment

We exemplify our approach using the case study of a blog web service. We define the specifications of the web service and present different use cases that are satisfied.

4.1   Case Study

The case study represents a blog website that is implemented in REpresentational State Transfer (REST) [15] architectural style. The web service provides functionality for creating a user account, posting new articles, commenting, deleting/editing posts and comments, managing the user profile, etc. similar to other social networks. These main characteristics of a sample blog web service include authorization of users to access to features of the web service. The web service is implemented in Python using Flask web developing micro framework [16]. Figure 5 shows a use case diagram of the blog web service. Each use case is detailed below:

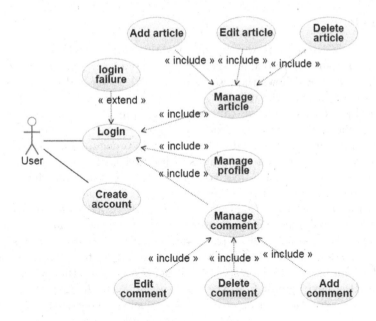

Fig. 5. Use case diagram of blog web service.

- **Create New Profile.** A new user can create a unique profile in blog service in order to use the features of the web service. It includes inserting a valid (and unique) username and a password.
- **Log In.** A user is able to log in with registered username and password. No two usernames are similar.
- **Manage Profile.** A signed up user can have access to his profile for further settings.
- **Delete Profile.** A user can delete his profile. This action logs him out from the blog as well as removes all of his posts and comments.
- **Post New Article.** A user can post new articles. Each article has a title and body.
- **View Articles.** Both user and reader (blog reader) are able to search throughout the blog and read the posted articles.
- **Comment Articles.** A user can comment on articles of the blog.
- **Edit/Delete Articles.** A user, who is owner of an article can edit/delete it.
- **Edit/Delete Comments.** An owner of the article can manage his comments.
- **Idle User.** There is a timer in the blog which checks whether a user is idle for more than 10 min. If so, then the service will automatically logs out the user.

4.2 Model

From the above descriptions, we have specified the system as a UTA model which consists of two automata: one for the blog web service and one for the environment (user). Figure 6 shows the models of the case study and the interactions between the service and the users.

From the specifications, we can define some use case scenarios which are designed in the model as well. For example, the above specification of edit/delete an article is designed in the model accordingly. In order to delete/edit an article, in the user and blog automata are synchronized as follows: the user sends a request *logged_in*, which is received in the blog by the same channel. The response from the blog will be either *loged_in* which changes the state of the model to the next location (id46 in blog) or *login_failed* which returns it to the initial location. This synchronization will continue by *manage_ar* (getting an specific article), which will be responded by either *access_ar* (access to the article) or *access_denied* (does not allow to have access to the article, or the article does not exists). If the response channel is *access_ar*, then there are two options for the next request from the user: *edit_ar* and *delete_ar* which will be responded by *edited_ar* and *deleted_ar* respectively. Similarly, the rest of the specifications are designed as UTA models as described above.

The model is verified before using it for test generation for deadlock-freeness and that the requirements are satisfied. For example, to ensure that editing article is possible we define a global boolean variable (e.g. a) and update its value to TRUE on *edited_ar*. Then we define a reachability property like $E \Diamond a == true$ which, if satisfied, indicates that there is at least a path in which a will be eventually true.

4.3 Generating Valid Mutants

In this experiment, we mutate the blog automaton (Fig. 6(a)) to generate mutated models. The total time for generation and validation of all mutants took 246 s on a Windows 7 Enterprise 64-bit operating system, Intel quad-core CPU and 16 GB RAM. In total, the generator provided 1019 mutants, of which 470 mutants were valid (i.e., passed the verification properties). As the numbers suggest, early verification of the mutants is helpful in having only mutants applicable for testing and thus, reducing the time of the test execution. The majority of the valid mutants, 300, were generated by the CS operator, in contrast with 102 valid mutants provided by CNI and 32 by CT. All generated mutants by IR and NG passed the validation process, and other mutation operators have a small share of valid mutants.

4.4 Detecting and Removing Equivalent Mutants

After performing equivalence checking, a number of 31 mutants were eliminated as being bisimulation equivalent. We eliminated them from the valid mutants,

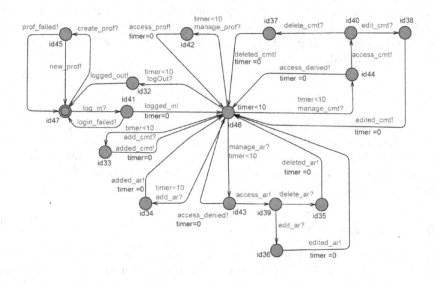

(a)

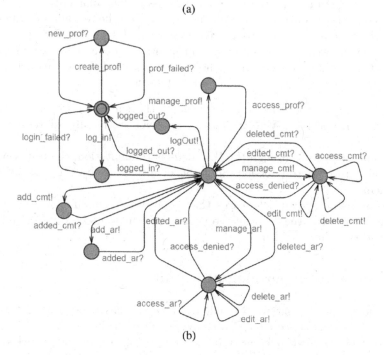

(b)

Fig. 6. Behavioral model of blog: (a) blog service, (b) blog user.

resulting a number of 439 valid non-equivalent mutants. The equivalence detection process took 286 s. Obviously, none of the mutants generated by CS, CT, CG and CNI were equivalent since they change the trace of the mutant which is clearly different than the original one. Only one mutant from NG is remained as valid non-equivalent. All mutants generated by IR and NG were equivalent and thus were eliminated.

4.5 Mutation Testing

We execute each mutant with TRON against the implementation of the blog web service. Each test session is set for 180 s in sequence, and we check that the mutated state is covered by the test and is also covered at runtime. It took roughly 8 h to execute the 439 non-equivalent mutants of which 436 have been killed.

4.6 Results Analysis

The resulting 33 alive mutants have been used for further analysis. In this step, we are interested in understanding why the tests generated from each alive mutant did not fail against the IUT. The process is done manually.

We detected 3 inconsistencies in the test model and the test adapter while no error in the code. In contrast, to the results presented in the previous paper [2], where the errors were detected on the implementation of the IUT, in this paper the detected errors were localized in the test adapter and the test model only.

The inconsistencies that are found are as follows:

- Mutation in some of alive mutants change the timing of which could not be killed by the IUT. Mutants by CG and NG are mainly addressing this inconsistency.
- For some mutants, although the IUT detects the mutation, the test adapter does not stop the test session. Some of alive mutants by CT revealed this problem.
- Some mutants generate the cases that regardless their difference from the original test cases, they are not erroneous. Alive mutants by CS, CN and CT revealed the same problem.

5   Analysis of Experimental Results

One of the questions that we wanted to answer in this paper was about the efficiency of the mutation operators used in our approach. Table 2 summarizes the results of the method at different steps, while Fig. 7 shows the 100% stacked bar chart showing the ratio of different types of mutants for different operators. For instance, IR and NG have the highest percentage of valid mutants in proportion to their generated mutants, however, majority of them were eliminated by the equivalence detection. The valid mutants in CS and CNI are more than half of

Table 2. Result of mutation testing.

Name	Generated	Valid	Non-equivalent	Alive
CNI	132	102	102	1
CT	420	32	32	8
CS	420	300	300	19
CG	12	4	4	4
NG	16	16	1	1
CI	3	0	0	0
IR	16	16	0	0
Total	1019	470	439	33

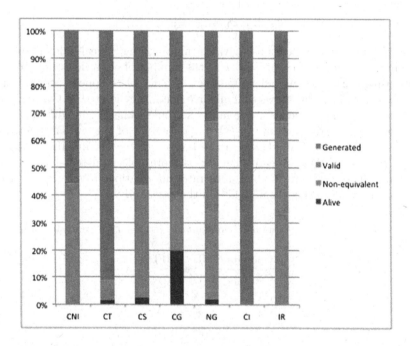

Fig. 7. The proportion of the result of each mutation operator and the total result of testing.

their generated mutants and none of them were equivalent. Small proportion of generated mutants in CT and CG are valid and no valid mutant is generated by CI.

Two formulas were defined previously for the efficiency of mutation operators showing how many of the mutants reveal the faults [2]. By calculating the number of equivalent mutants we can calculate the mutation efficiency for each mutation operator as follows:

Mutation Efficiency: For each mutation operator, we calculate how many mutants are alive. We calculate the efficiency of each mutation operator in generating alive mutants:

$$ME_i = \frac{A_i}{V_i} \,, \tag{1}$$

where A is the number of alive mutants, V is the number of valid non-equivalent mutants of the mutation operator i.

Mutation Fault Detection: Since after finding a fault in each category, we discard the rest of them, the formula for fault detection will be applied based on the categories. For each category that shows a fault, we score the corresponding operators. For each operator, we measure the mutation fault detection with following formula:

$$MFD_i = \frac{NE_i}{T_i - E_i} \,, \tag{2}$$

where NE is the number of non-equivalent mutants that reveal hidden faults, T is the number of total mutants and E is the number of equivalent mutants.

By using Formula 1, we calculated the efficiency of the operators that have alive mutants. The result shows that all alive mutants generated by CG remained alive, however, none of them shows a fault and thus CG has 0% in fault detection. A quarter of generated mutants by CT and only 6.3% of the mutants generated by CS were efficient. While CS is in the bottom of the list in ME, it has the highest rank in MFD. It means that CS is more able to detect faults in the model and the test adapter. Table 3 illustrates information on how the mutation operators are able to show some faults in the case study.

Table 3. Mutation efficiency and mutation fault detection for the suggested operators.

Operators	ME	MFD
CNI	~1%	0.7%
CT	25%	1.6%
CS	6.3%	2.3%
CG	100%	0%
NG	6.2%	0%

6 Discussion

Some improvements can reduce the test execution time while increasing the probability of finding faults. The results of mutation testing from this study and the previous one [2] indicate that an intelligent choice of the mutation operators can attain high mutation efficiency scores while reducing the time of testing. For instance, the mutations generated by IR, NG and CG were not effective, thus either they should be changed to stronger operators or simply not considered.

Another improvement could be done in the process of fault detection. Redundant work is done on detecting the same faults. This extra effort can be reduced by categorizing the alive mutants in such a way that all mutations of a certain location or action in the model will be in a single category. As soon as any of the mutants in a category detects a fault, then the rest of the mutants on that group can be eliminated from the fault detection analysis. The idea behind this is that the locations and actions in a model represent actual states of the system under test and if there is a state which contains a fault, then any mutant from that state may be able to reveal that fault. However, more experiments are needed to show the correctness of this test effort reduction technique.

The main downside of model-based mutation testing comes from MBT: the process of designing models from the specification, verifying them and writing the test adapter (to translate model-level test inputs into acceptable test script for the IUT and vice versa) is time consuming. However, once the above artifacts are created, the model-based mutation testing process could be automated to a large extent. Also reusing existing models from development process would help in reducing the effort as it is often the case in regression testing. Moreover, the new method of equivalence detection helped us to reduce the number of alive mutants into half. The mutation testing does not add any overhead into MBT. The mutation generator tool automatically generates correct and valid mutations and thus, it reduces the mutant generation time.

Finally, the process of result analysis is manual and for large-scale systems, it is tedious. But some degree of tool support could be provided via TRON2UPPAAL backtracing tool described in [17]. This tool allows one to load a test execution trace generated from TRON and load it in the UPPAAL simulator for visualization and step-wise debugging.

7   Threats to Validity

There are two main threats related to our study. One is related to the mutation operators. Despite the fact that we have followed the systematically and formally defined mutation operators and implemented them in our study, there might be some more effective mutation operators or combinations of operators that we have missed. We argue that the current number of mutation operators provides a large number of mutants which can provide faulty test inputs which are close to the accepted inputs.

The other threat is that the results are strongly related to the test model and to the case study used. Different test designers can specify the same system in various ways which may provide different results of mutation testing. Perhaps having a systematic modeling approach specifically for web services (if there is any) would resolve such threat.

More extensive studies are needed in order to investigate how the specification mutation can be applied in larger case studies preferably industrial-sized web services. Besides, more experiment on larger scales would be helpful in finding whether there is any correlation between certain mutation operators and the real faults in design and implementation of web services.

8   Related Work

A comprehensive analysis is done on all available mutation testing method presenting the current state of the art in this field and the open challenges [18].

Lee and Offutt [19] introduced an Interaction specification Model which formalize the interactions among Web components. They defined a set of mutation operators for XML data model in order to mutate the inputs of the Web components. Li et al. [20] presented mutation testing methods using XML schema to create invalid inputs. Mutation testing is extended to XML-based specification languages for Web services. Lee et al. presented an ontology based mutation operators on OWL-S, which is an XML-based language for specifying semantics of web services [21]. They mutate semantics of the specifications of their case study such as data mutation, condition mutation, etc. Wang and Huang presented a mutation testing approach based on OWL-S to validate the requirements of web services [22]. Also, Dominguez et al. presented a mutation generator tool for WS-BPEL.

We discuss those that are most similar to our approach. Work has been done on using model checking techniques for validation and verification of web servicesWSC. There are two studies that review the literature on testing Web services [23, 24]. Starting from specification languages for modeling Web services, researchers perform simulation, verification and test generation using model checking tools. Most of the works use model checking for specification and verification and only one group use the models for the test generation as well.

Using TA models for mutation testing has been mostly studied on a real-time and embedded system. In [10, 11] mutation operators for TA are presented. Aboutrab et al. proposed a set of mutation operators for timed automata to empirically compare priority-based testing with other testing approaches [10]. However, in their approach, the generation of mutations is done manually. Aichernig et al. presented model-based mutation testing real-time system using UPPAAL [11]. The mutation operators that are defined in their work are more detailed and some of them are implemented as mutation bounded model-checking and incremental SMT solving. They showed that using mutations for timed automata has potential on debugging and revealing the unexpected behavior of the IUT.

We applied/modified the mutation operators of TA presented by these studies for testing the robustness of web servicesWSC. Similar to [11], we apply mutations on non-deterministic models, however, in their work, they use only the UTA model of the IUT and do not consider the environment. In our approach, however, each mutant is a closed model communicating with its environment. We check deadlockfreeness and reachability in order to reduce the number of invalid mutants. Also, we use different verification and test generation processes.

There are some works that target UTA as the specification language for Web services. In most of the works, the authors transformed the specification that is defined in their selected languages into UTA and then they investigated its properties. For instance, in [25], the specification of a web serviceWSC is defined initially in the form of UML and then transformed into UTA for an online testing purpose. In [26], Cambronero et al. verify web services by the UPPAAL tool for validation and verification of their described system that is transformed from WS-CDL into a network of TA. In [27], Diaz et al. also provide a translation from WS-BPEL to UTA. Time properties are specified in WS-BPEL and translated to UTA. However, requirements are not traced explicitly, while verification and testing are not discussed.

9 Conclusions and Future Work

The popularity of web services has significantly increased in recent years and as a consequence their robustness and reliability have become more important. One way of testing robustness of such dynamic systems is to check their behavior against invalid and stressful environment. In this paper, a model-based mutation testing method is presented using the UPPAAL TA for assessing the robustness of web services.

The method includes six steps, starting with designing a test model via UPPAAL TA and executing online conformance testing with UPPAAL-TRONagainst the implementation of the service, continuing with the generation of mutant test models based on a selection of mutation operators and with eliminating invalid and equivalent mutants. Then, the IUT is tested against each mutant, and the mutants which result in a failure are considered killed and eliminated. Finally, the results of the mutation testing are evaluated manually, by investigating the alive mutants, in order to reveal potential faults in the test model or in the IUT.

In this paper, we evaluated the presented method by experimenting Blog System as a case study. The web service is implemented in REST architectural style and with timing constraints. The results showed that from a total 1019 generated mutants, 470 were found to be valid mutants, that were usable for testing and from 33 alive mutants, three different errors in the test model were uncovered. Combined with the previous results on a different case study, in which several faults were uncovered in the implementation, it shows the our approach has the potential to detect faults not found otherwise via functional testing. One improvement compared to the previous work of the paper is in the automatic detection of equivalent mutants, which was previously done manually and which now allowed us to reduce the number of mutants.

There are some research directions that would certainly improve the current method. From the two different case studies of web services, we have achieved some useful information for reducing the testing effort specially in larger scale use cases. Automation of this process of the approach reduces the errors and increases the scalability of the target applications.

For future work, we plan to run more experiments and evaluate a larger set of mutation operators. We also plan to make the mutation process more efficient by applying more mutation selection and mutation reduction techniques and by running different processes in parallel.

References

1. Budd, T.A., Gopal, A.S.: Program testing by specification mutation. Comput. Lang. **10**, 63–73 (1985)
2. Siavashi, F., Truscan, D., Vain, J.: On mutating UPPAAL timed automata to assess robustness of web services. In: Maciaszek, L., Cardoso, J., Ludwig, A., Sinderen, M.V., Cabello, E. (eds.) Proceedings of the 11th International Joint Conference on Software Technologies, vol. 1, pp. 15–26. SCITEPRESS-Science and Technology Publications (2016)
3. Utting, M., Pretschner, A., Legeard, B.: A taxonomy of model-based testing approaches. Softw. Test. Verif. Reliab. **22**, 297–312 (2012)
4. Hessel, A., Larsen, K.G., Mikucionis, M., Nielsen, B., Pettersson, P., Skou, A.: Testing real-time systems using UPPAAL. In: Hierons, R.M., Bowen, J.P., Harman, M. (eds.) Formal Methods and Testing. LNCS, vol. 4949, pp. 77–117. Springer, Heidelberg (2008). doi:10.1007/978-3-540-78917-8_3
5. Alur, R., et al.: Model-checking for real-time systems. In: Proceedings of Fifth Annual IEEE Symposium on e Logic in Computer Science, LICS 1990, pp. 414–425. IEEE (1990)
6. Behrmann, G., David, A., Larsen, K.G.: A tutorial on UPPAAL. In: Bernardo, M., Corradini, F. (eds.) SFM-RT 2004. LNCS, vol. 3185, pp. 200–236. Springer, Heidelberg (2004). doi:10.1007/978-3-540-30080-9_7
7. Larsen, K.G., Mikucionis, M., Nielsen, B.: Online testing of real-time systems using UPPAAL. In: Grabowski, J., Nielsen, B. (eds.) FATES 2004. LNCS, vol. 3395, pp. 79–94. Springer, Heidelberg (2005). doi:10.1007/978-3-540-31848-4_6
8. Larsen, K., et al.: Testing real-time embedded software using UPPAAL-TRON: an industrial case study. In: Proceedings of the 5th ACM International Conference on Embedded Software, pp. 299–306. ACM (2005)
9. Belli, F., et al.: Model-based mutation testing approach and case studies. Sci. Comput. Program. **120**, 25–48 (2016)
10. Aboutrab, M., et al.: Specification mutation analysis for validating timed testing approaches based on timed automata. In: 36th Annual IEEE Computer Software and Applications Conference, COMPSAC 2012, Izmir, Turkey, 16–20 July 2012, pp. 660–669 (2012)
11. Aichernig, B.K., Lorber, F., Ničković, D.: Time for mutants — model-based mutation testing with timed automata. In: Veanes, M., Viganò, L. (eds.) TAP 2013. LNCS, vol. 7942, pp. 20–38. Springer, Heidelberg (2013). doi:10.1007/978-3-642-38916-0_2
12. Gargantini, A., Heitmeyer, C.: Using model checking to generate tests from requirements specifications. In: Nierstrasz, O., Lemoine, M. (eds.) ESEC/SIGSOFT FSE -1999. LNCS, vol. 1687, pp. 146–162. Springer, Heidelberg (1999). doi:10.1007/3-540-48166-4_10
13. Bengtsson, J., Yi, W.: Timed automata: semantics, algorithms and tools. In: Desel, J., Reisig, W., Rozenberg, G. (eds.) ACPN 2003. LNCS, vol. 3098, pp. 87–124. Springer, Heidelberg (2004). doi:10.1007/978-3-540-27755-2_3
14. Čerāns, K.: Decidability of bisimulation equivalences for parallel timer processes. In: Bochmann, G., Probst, D.K. (eds.) CAV 1992. LNCS, vol. 663, pp. 302–315. Springer, Heidelberg (1993). doi:10.1007/3-540-56496-9_24
15. Richardson, L., Ruby, S.: RESTful Web Services. O'Reilly, Sebastopol (2008)
16. Grinberg, M.: Flask Web Development: Developing Web Applications with Python. O'Reilly Media, Inc., Sebastopol (2014)

17. Iqbal, J., Truscan, D., Vain, J., Porres, I.: TRON2UPPAAL backtracer tool from TRON logs to UPPAAL traces. Technical report 1138, Turku Centre for Computer Science (2015)
18. Jia, Y., Harman, M.: An analysis and survey of the development of mutation testing. IEEE Trans. Softw. Eng. **37**, 649–678 (2011)
19. Lee, S.C., Offutt, J.: Generating test cases for XML-based web component interactions using mutation analysis. In: Proceedings of 12th International Symposium on Software Reliability Engineering, ISSRE 2001, pp. 200–209 (2001)
20. Li, J.H., Dai, G.X., Li, H.H.: Mutation analysis for testing finite state machines. In: Second International Symposium on Electronic Commerce and Security, ISECS 2009, vol. 1, pp. 620–624. IEEE (2009)
21. Lee, S., et al.: Automatic mutation testing and simulation on OWL-S specified web services. In: 41st Annual Simulation Symposium, ANSS 2008, pp. 149–156 (2008)
22. Wang, R., Huang, N.: Requirement model-based mutation testing for web service. In: 4th International Conference on Next Generation Web Services Practices, NWESP 2008, pp. 71–76 (2008)
23. Rusli, H.M., et al.: Testing web services composition: a mapping study. In: Communications of the IBIMA 2011, pp. 34–48 (2007)
24. Bozkurt, M., et al.: Testing web services: a survey. Department of Computer Science, King's College London, Technical report TR-10-01 (2010)
25. Rauf, I., Siavashi, F., Truscan, D., Porres, I.: An integrated approach for designing and validating REST web service compositions. In: Monfort, V., Krempels, K.H. (eds.) 10th International Conference on Web Information Systems and Technologies, vol. 1, pp. 104–115. SCITEPRESS Digital Library (2014)
26. Cambronero, M.E., et al.: Validation and verification of web services choreographies by using timed automata. J. Logic Algebraic Program. **80**, 25–49 (2011)
27. Díaz, G., et al.: Model checking techniques applied to the design of web services. CLEI Electron. J. **10**, 5–11 (2007)

Software Product Line Test Suite Reduction with Constraint Optimization

Mats Carlsson[1]([✉]), Arnaud Gotlieb[2], and Dusica Marijan[2]

[1] RISE SICS, P.O. Box 1263, 164 29 Kista, Sweden
mats.carlsson@ri.se
[2] Simula Research Laboratory, P.O. Box 134, 1325 Lysaker, Norway
{arnaud,dusica}@simula.no

Abstract. In many cases, Software Product Line Testing (SPLT) targets only the selection of test cases which cover product features or feature interactions. However, higher testing efficiency can be achieved through the selection of test cases with improved fault-revealing capabilities. By associating each test case a priority-value representing (or aggregating) different criteria, such as importance (in terms of fault discovered in previous test campaigns), duration or cost, it becomes possible to select a feature-covering test suite with improved capabilities. A crucial objective in SPLT then becomes to identify a test suite that optimizes reaching a specific goal (lower test duration or cost), while preserving full feature coverage.

In this article, we revisit this problem with a new approach based on constraint optimization with the NVALUE and GLOBALCARDINALITY constraints and a sophisticated search heuristic. These constraints enforce the coverage of all features through the computation of max flows in a network flow representing the coverage relation. The computed max flows represent possible solutions which are further processed in order to determine the solution that optimizes the given objective function, e.g., the smallest test execution costs.

Our approach is implemented in a tool called FLOWER/C and experimentally evaluated on both randomly generated instances and standard benchmarks. Comparing FLOWER/C with MINISAT+ and CPLEX, state-of-the-art tools for constraint optimization, we show that our approach is competitive with both tools on random instances and benchmarks. Our results show that MINISAT+ is not competitive at all, whereas when the priority-value of each test case is uniformly set to 1, that FLOWER/C approaches CPLEX in performance. We compare four different models of FLOWER/C, using different global constraints, and the one mixing different constraints shows the best performance with high reduction rates. These results open the door to an industrial adoption of the proposed technology.

Keywords: Test suite reduction · Test suite optimization · Software product line testing · Feature coverage

© Springer International Publishing AG 2017
E. Cabello et al. (Eds.): ICSOFT 2016, CCIS 743, pp. 68–87, 2017.
DOI: 10.1007/978-3-319-62569-0_4

1   Introduction

1.1   Context

Testing a software product line entails at least the selection of a test suite which covers all the features of the product line. Indeed, even if it may not guarantee that each product would behave correctly, ensuring that each feature is tested at least once is a minimum requirement of Software Product Line Testing (SPLT) [1,2]. However, among the various test suites which cover all the features, some have higher fault-revealing capabilities than other, some have reduced overall execution time or energy consumption properties [3]. Dealing with different criteria when selecting a feature-covering test suite is thus important. Yet, at the same time, the budget allocated to the testing phase is usually limited and reducing the number of test cases while maintaining the quality of the process is challenging. For example, selecting a feature-covering test suite which minimizes its total execution time is desirable for testing some product lines which are developed in continuous delivery mode [4]. Similarly, if the execution of each test case is associated to a cost (because the execution requires access to cloud resources under some service level agreement), then there is a challenge in selecting a subset of test cases which can minimize this cost. Of course, ideally one would like to deal with all the criteria (feature coverage, execution time, energy consumption, . . .) at the same time in an optimization process [5]. Unfortunately, this approach cannot offer strong guarantee on the coverage of features or reachability of a global minimum, which is often not acceptable for validation engineers. Thus, there is room for approaches which offer guarantees in terms of feature coverage and optimize individually some criterion such as test execution time or energy consumption.

1.2   Existing Results

Test suite reduction has received considerable attention in the last two decades. Briefly, we can distinguish greedy techniques [6–8], search-based testing techniques [5,9], and exact approaches [3,10–13]. Test suite reduction should not be confused with test selection and generation for software product lines which has also received considerable attention these last years [2].

Greedy techniques for test suite reduction are usually based on variations of Chvátal's algorithm [14], which selects first a test case covering the most features and iterates until all features are covered. In the 90's, [15] proposed a technique which approximates the computation of minimum-cardinality hitting sets. This work was further refined with different variable orderings [16,17]. More recently, [7] introduced the delayed-greedy technique, which exploits implications among test cases and features to further refine the reduced test suite. The technique starts by removing test cases covering the features already covered by other test cases. Then, it removes test features which are not in the minimized feature set, and finally it determines a minimized test suite from the remaining test cases by using a greedy approach. Jeffrey and Gupta extended this approach by retaining test cases which improve a fault-detection capability of the test suite [8]. The technique uses additional coverage information of test cases to selectively keep additional test cases in the reduced suites that are redundant with respect to the testing criteria used for the suite. Comparing to [15], the approach produces bigger solutions, but with higher fault detection effectiveness.

One shortcoming of greedy algorithms is that they only approximate true global optima without providing any guarantee of test suite reduction. Search-based testing techniques have been used for test suite reduction through the exploitation of meta-heuristics. [18] explores classical evolutionary techniques such as hill-climbing, simulated annealing, or weight-based genetic algorithms for (multi-objective) test suite reduction. By comparing 10 different algorithms for different criteria in [5], it is observed that random-weighted multi-objective optimization is the most efficient approach. However, by assigning weights at random, this approach is unfortunately not able to place priority over the various objectives. Other algorithms based on meta-heuristics are examined in [9].

All these techniques can scale up to problems having a large number of test cases and features but they cannot explore the overall search space and thus they cannot guarantee global optimality. On the contrary, exact approaches, which are based either on Boolean satisfiability or Integer Linear Programming (ILP) can reach true global minima. The best-known approach for exact test suite minimization is implemented in MINTS [10]. It extends a technique originally proposed in [19] for bi-criteria test suite minimization. MINTS can be interfaced with either MINISAT+ (pseudo-Boolean) or CPLEX (ILP). It has been used to perform test suite reduction for various criteria including energy consumption on mobile devices [3]. Similar exact techniques have also been designed to handle fault localization [12]. Generally speaking, the theoretical limitation of exact approaches is the possible early combinatorial explosion to determine the global optimum, which exposes these techniques to serious limitations even for small problems. In the context of feature covering for software product lines, an approach based on SAT solving has been proposed in [20]. In this approach, test suite reduction is encoded as a Boolean formula that is evaluated by a SAT solver. An hybrid method based on ILP and search, called DILP, is proposed in [11] where a lower bound for the minimum is computed and a search for finding a smaller test suite close to this bound is performed. Recently, another ILP-based approach is proposed in [21] to set up upper limits on the loss of fault-detection capability in the test suite. In [22], Monthuy *et al.* proposed a constraint called SC for the set covering problem. They created a propagator for SC by using a lower bound based on an ILP relaxation. Finally, [13] introduced an approach for test suite reduction based on the computation of maximum flows in a network flow. This theoretical study was further refined in [23] where a comparison of different constraint models was given, but there was no multi-objective test suite optimization.

In this article, we propose a new approach of feature-based test suite reduction in software product line testing. Starting from an existing test suite covering a set of features of a software product line, our approach selects a subset of test cases which still covers all the features, but also minimizes one additional criterion which is given under the form of sum of priorities over test cases. This is an exact approach based on two abstractions from Constraint Programming: the NVALUE [24] and GLOBALCARDINALITY [25, 26] global constraints. These constraints enforce the link between test cases and features while constraining the cardinality of the subset of features each test case has to cover. By combining these tools with a sophisticated search heuristics, our approach creates a constraint optimization model which is able to compete with the best known approaches for test suite reduction, namely MINISAT+ and CPLEX.

Associating a number to each test case is convenient to establish priorities when selecting test cases. Indeed, such a priority-value can represent or aggregate different notions such as execution time, code coverage, energy-consumption [3], fault-detection capabilities [12] and so on. Using these priorities, feature-based test suite reduction reduces to the problem of selecting a subset of test cases such that all the feature are covered and the sum of test case priorities is minimized. Feature-based test suite reduction generalizes the classical test suite reduction problem which consists in finding a subset of minimal cardinality, covering all the features. Indeed, feature-based test suite reduction where all test case have the same priority reduces to size minimization of the test suite. We shall call this the *uniform* case. However, solving feature-based test suite reduction is hard as it requires in the worst case to examine a search tree composed of all the possible subsets of test cases. For a test suite composed of N cases, there are 2^N such subsets where N typically ranges from a few tens to thousands, which makes exhaustive search intractable.

1.3   Contributions

The work presented in this article is built on top of previously-reached research results. In 2014, we initially proposed a simple single-criterion constraint optimization model for test suite reduction based on the search of max-flows in a network flow representing the problem [13]. This simple model was refined by using more sophisticated constraint optimization models in [23] which also reported preliminary experimental results. The present article is an extended version of [27], where we addressed software product line test suite reduction with Constraint Programming. The conference paper presented three constraint optimization models based on two abstractions from Constraint Programming, namely the NVALUE and GLOBALCARDINALITY global constraints for performing test suite reduction optimization in the context of SPLT. These models also featured a dedicated search heuristic for finding an optimal test suite in a very efficient way. The present article extends the proposed approach by introducing yet another constraint optimization model, by defining precise presolving rules and a greedy algorithm for obtaining initial upper bounds. It also extends the evaluation of the conference paper to standard benchmarks, and discusses the industrial application of the described methods and tool. According to our knowledge, this is the first time a test suite minimization approach based on advanced

Constraint Optimization techniques is proposed in the context of SPLT. These constraint optimization models have been put at work to select test suites on both randomly-generated instances of the problem and also classical benchmarks.

1.4   Outline

The next section introduces the necessary background material to understand the rest of the article. Section 3 presents our approach to the feature-based test suite reduction problem. Section 4 details our implementation and experimental results. Section 5 discusses the industrial application of our methods and tool, while Sect. 6 discusses related work. Finally, Sect. 7 concludes the article.

2   Background

This section introduces the problem of feature-based test suite reduction and briefly reviews the notion of global constraints. It also presents the NVALUE and GLOBALCARDINALITY global constraints.

2.1   Feature-Based Test Suite Reduction

Feature-based Test Suite Reduction (FTSR) aims to select a subset of test cases out of a test suite which maximizes the sum of its *priorities*, or dually minimizes the sum of its *costs*, while retaining its coverage of product features. In the following, we will speak about costs rather than priorities.

Formally, a FTSR problem is defined by an initial test suite $T = \{t_1, \ldots, t_m\}$, each test case being associated a cost $c(t_i)$, a set of n product features $F = \{f_1, \ldots, f_n\}$ and a function $cov : F \mapsto 2^T$ mapping each feature to the subset of test cases which cover it. Each feature is covered by at least one test case, i.e., $\forall i \in \{1, \ldots, n\}, |cov(f_i)| > 0$. An example with 5 test cases and 5 features is given in Table 1, where the value given in the table denotes the cost of the test case. Given T, F, c, and cov, a FTSR problem aims at finding a subset of test cases such that every feature is covered at least once, and the total cost of the selected test cases is minimized.

Table 1. An example of a feature-based test suite reduction problem.

	f_1	f_2	f_3	f_4	f_5
t_a	2	2	-	-	-
t_b	1	-	1	-	-
t_c	-	3	3	-	3
t_d	-	-	-	2	2
t_e	-	-	-	1	-

Definition 1 (Feature-based Test Suite Reduction (FTSR)). *A FTSR instance is a quadruple* (T, F, c, cov) *where* T *is a set of* m *test cases* $\{t_1, \ldots, t_m\}$ *along with their costs* $c(t_i)$, F *is a set of* n *product features* $\{f_1, \ldots, f_n\}$, $cov :$ $F \mapsto 2^T$ *is a coverage function mapping each feature to the subset of test cases that cover it. An optimal solution to FTSR is a subset* $T' \subseteq T$ *such that for each* $f_i \in F$, *there exists* $t_j \in T'$ *such that* $t_j \in cov(f_i)$ *and* $\sum_{t_j \in T'} c(t_j)$ *is minimized.*

A labeled bipartite graph can be used to encode any FTSR problem, with edges denoting the function cov and labels denoting c, the costs over the test cases, as shown in Fig. 1. Note that the costs are associated to the test cases and not to the features. In fact, in feature-based test suite reduction, all the features must be covered at least once, and so it is pointless to define costs over features. As an extension, it is possible to consider for each test case different costs for covering the features but this complicates the problem without bringing much benefit as it is too complex for validation engineers to manage complex priority sets. Note also that the optimal solution shown in Fig. 1 is not unique. For example, $\{t_a, t_b, t_d\}$ covers all the features and also has $Cost = 5$. When all the costs are the same, then the FTSR problem reduces to the problem of finding a subset of minimal size.

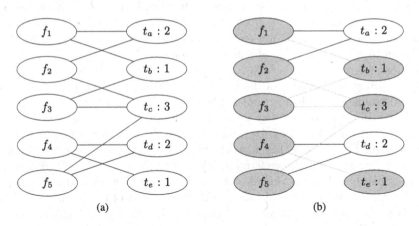

Fig. 1. FTSR as a labeled bipartite graph (a) and an optimal ($Cost = 5$) solution (b).

2.2   Global Constraints

Constraint Programming is a declarative paradigm where instructions are replaced by constraints over variables which take their values in a variation domain [28]. In this context, any constraint enforces a symbolic relation among a subset of variables, which are known only by their type or their domain. Formally speaking, a *domain variable* V is a logical variable with an associated domain $D(V) \subset \mathbb{Z}$ which encodes all possible labels for that variable. In the rest of the article, upper-case letters or capitalized words will denote domain variables, while lower-case letters or words will denote constant values. For example, let the domain variable $COLOR$ take its value in the domain $\{\texttt{black}, \texttt{blank}, \texttt{blue}, \texttt{red}, \texttt{yellow}\}$ which is encoded as 1..5, and let the constraint PRIMARYCOLOR($COLOR$) enforce $COLOR$ to be $\texttt{blue}$, $\texttt{red}$, or $\texttt{yellow}$, but not $\texttt{black}$ or $\texttt{blank}$. We say that $3, 4$ and 5 *satisfy* PRIMARYCOLOR and that $1, 2$ are *inconsistent* with respect to the constraint. In the rest of the article, we will use $a..b$ to denote $\{a, a+1, \ldots, b-1, b\}$ and $\{a, b\}$ to denote the set composed only of a and b. Note that in our context, we consider only finite domains, i.e., domains containing a finite number of distinct values.

A constraint program is composed of both regular instructions and constraints over domain variables. Interestingly, constraints come with filtering algorithms which can eliminate some inconsistent values. For example, let the constraint SAMECOLOR($COLOR_1$, $COLOR_2$) enforce $COLOR_1$ and $COLOR_2$ to take the same color. Suppose that the variable $COLOR_1$ has domain $\{\texttt{blue}, \texttt{red}, \texttt{yellow}\}$ and that $COLOR_2$ has domain $\{\texttt{blank}, \texttt{blue}, \texttt{red}\}$, then the constraint prunes both domains to $\{\texttt{blue}, \texttt{red}\}$, because all other values are inconsistent with the constraint SAMECOLOR. Among the possible types of constraints, we have *simple constraints*, which include domain, arithmetical and logical operators, and *global constraints* [29]. The constraints PRIMARYCOLOR and SAMECOLOR are simple constraints as they can be encoded with a domain and an equality operators. A *global constraint* is a relation which holds over a non-fixed number of variables and typically implements a dedicated filtering algorithm. A typical example of global constraint is NVALUE($N, (V_1, \ldots, V_m)$), introduced in [24], where $N, V_1, \ldots, V_m$ are domain variables and the constraint enforces the number of distinct values in $V_1, \ldots, V_m$ to be equal to N. This constraint is useful in several application areas to solve tasks assignment and time-tabling problems. For example, suppose that N is a domain variable with domain 1..2 and $FLAG_1, FLAG_2, FLAG_3$ are three domain variables with domains $FLAG_1 \in \{\texttt{blue}, \texttt{blank}\}$, $FLAG_2 \in \{\texttt{yellow}, \texttt{blank}, \texttt{black}\}$ and $FLAG_3 \in \{\texttt{red}\}$, then the constraint NVALUE($N, (FLAG_1, FLAG_2, FLAG_3)$) can significantly reduce the domains of its variables. In fact, the value 1 is inconsistent with the constraint and can thus be filtered out of the domain of N, as there is no intersection between the domains of $FLAG_1$ and $FLAG_3$. It means that, if there is a solution of the constraint, it should contain at least two distinct values, constraining N to be equal to 2. In addition, the domains of $FLAG_1$ and $FLAG_2$ have only a single value in their intersection ($\texttt{blank}$), meaning that they can only take this value and all the other values are inconsistent. So, in conclusion, the constraint NVALUE($N, (FLAG_1, FLAG_2, FLAG_3)$) is solved and $N = 2$, $FLAG_1 = FLAG_2 = \texttt{blank}$ and $FLAG_3 = \texttt{red}$. Of course, this is a favorable case, whereas other instances may lead to pruning only some of the inconsistent assignments and are able to solve the constraint. In this case, a search procedure must be launched in order to eventually find a solution. This search procedure selects an unassigned variable and will try to assign it a value from its current domain. The process is repeated until all the unassigned variables become instantiated or a contradiction is detected. In the latter case, the process backtracks and makes another value choice. This process is parametrized by a search heuristic which selects the variable and the value to be assigned first.

In our framework, we will use a powerful global constraint, which can be seen as an extension of NVALUE: the GLOBALCARDINALITY constraint or GCC for short [25]. The $GCC(T, d, O)$ constraint, where $T = (T_1, \ldots, T_n)$ is a vector of domain variables, $d = (d_1, \ldots, d_m)$ is a vector of distinct integers, and $O = (O_1, \ldots, O_m)$ is a vector of domain variables. $GCC(T, d, O)$ holds if and only if for each $i \in 1..m$ the number of occurrences of d_i in T is O_i. The O_i variables are called the *occurrence variables* of the constraint. The filtering algorithm associated to GCC is based on the computation of max-flows in a network flow. The time complexity of the algorithm by Quimper *et al.* [26] is $O(n^2 + nm)$, and so GCC can be exploited for filtering inconsistent values in polynomial time.

3   Feature-Based Test Suite Reduction Through Global Constraints

In this section, we show how constraint optimization models based on NVALUE and GCC can encode the Feature-based Test Suite Reduction problem. These encodings are explained in Sect. 3.1, while Sect. 3.3 introduces dedicated search heuristics to deal with priority-based test case selection.

3.1   Constraint Optimization Models for FTSR

The FTSR problem can be encoded with the following scheme: each feature f_i can be associated with a domain variable F_i with domain $D(F_i) = \{j \mid$ test case t_j covers $f_i\}$. So, for example, the problem reported in Table 1 can be encoded as follows: $F_1 \in \{1, 2\}, F_2 \in \{1, 3\}, F_3 \in \{2, 3\}, F_4 \in \{4, 5\}, F_5 \in \{4\}$.

In Fig. 2, we show four constraint optimization models of a given a FTSR problem (F, T, c, cov):

Generic. This is the generic model for priority-based test case selection, where the explicit objective is to minimize the total cost of the selected test cases.

Altcost. This is also a model for the generic, non-uniform case, but uses an objective function that is based on a sum over the features instead of over the test cases. The ith term in the sum is $c(F_i) \times X_i$ where $c(F_i)$ denotes the cost-value associated to the case selected to cover F_i and X_i denotes a Boolean variable. The term $c(F_i) \times X_i$ is nonzero if F_i is assigned to a test case not covering any previous feature, and zero otherwise. Note that in the uniform case, the expression $c(F_i) \times X_i$ simplifies to X_i.

NValue. This model for the uniform case exploits the NVALUE constraint, since the objective can be simplified to minimizing the number of selected test cases.

Mixt. This model, also for the uniform case, is equivalent to the NVALUE model, but additionally uses a GCC constraint for counting the occurrences of test cases.

In these models, $(F_1, \ldots, F_n)$ and $(O_1, \ldots, O_m)$ are decision variables, whereas the Boolean variables $B_1, \ldots, B_m$ are local variables introduced to establish the link with the costs. $B_i = 1$ corresponds to test case t_i being selected.

GENERIC	Minimize
	$Cost$
	s.t.
	$GCC((F_1, \ldots, F_n), (1, \ldots, m), (O_1, \ldots, O_m)),$
	$B_i \equiv (O_i > 0),$ $\forall i \in 1..m$
	$Cost = \sum_{i \in 1..m} c(i) \times B_i.$
ALTCOST	Minimize
	$Cost$
	s.t.
	$GCC((F_1, \ldots, F_n), (1, \ldots, m), (O_1, \ldots, O_m)),$
	$X_1 = 1,$
	$X_i \equiv (F_1 \neq F_i \wedge \cdots \wedge F_{i-1} \neq F_i),$ $\forall i \in 2..n$
	$Cost = \sum_{i \in 1..n} c(F_i) \times X_i.$
NVALUE	Minimize
	N
	s.t.
	$NVALUE(N, (F_1, \ldots, F_n)).$
MIXT	Minimize
	N
	s.t.
	$GCC((F_1, \ldots, F_n), (1, \ldots, m), (O_1, \ldots, O_m)),$
	$NVALUE(N, (F_1, \ldots, F_n)).$

Fig. 2. Four constraint optimization models for solving FTSR where the domain variables O_i denote the number of times test case i is selected to cover any feature in $F_1, \ldots, F_n$, B_i are Boolean variables denoting the selection of test case i, and X_i are Boolean variables, true if and only if feature i introduces a new test case into the solution.

The objective of the models is to minimize $Cost$, the total cost of the selected test cases. The models can be solved by searching the space composed of the possible choices for the decision variables. It is worth noting that this allows us to branch either on the choice of features or on the choice of test cases, except in NVALUE.

Note that even if the models given in Fig. 2 solve the FTSR problem, they include a search within a search space of exponential size $O(d^n)$ where d is the size of the largest domain among the feature variables. This does not come as a surprise as the feature covering problem is a variant of the set covering problem, which is NP-hard [10].

3.2 Search Heuristics

Search heuristics consist of both a variable-selection strategy and a value-assignment strategy, both of which relate to the finite domain variables used in the constraint optimization model. Regarding variable selection, a first idea is to use the *first-fail principle* in the models of Fig. 2, which first selects a variable representing a feature that is covered by the least number of test cases. As all the features have to be covered, it means that those test cases are most likely to be selected. However, this strategy ignores the selection of the test case having the smallest cost or the test cases covering the most features, which would be very interesting for our FTSR problem. Regarding value selection, it is also possible to define a special heuristic for our problem.

3.3 A FTSR-Dedicated Heuristic

Unlike static variable selection heuristics used in greedy algorithms such as, for example, the selection of variables based on the number of features they cover, our strategy is more dynamic and the ordering is revised at each step of the selection process. As shown in Algorithm 1, our strategy is similar in spirit to Chvátal's greedy algorithm. It selects first the occurrence variable O_i associated to the test case t_i that finds the best compromise between cost and feature coverage (line 2), then the search forks into a forward branch and a backtrack branch. In forward execution, all features that can be are covered by t_i by assigning O_i to its maximal value (line 4). On backtracking, t_i is removed from the available test cases by assigning O_i to zero (line 5). The search iterates until all features have been covered. As shown in our experimental results, this FTSR-dedicated heuristic is a very powerful method for solving the FTSR problem. Consequently, we use it for all models except NVALUE, for which we use *first-fail*, because that model does not have occurrence variables.

4   Implementation and Results

We implemented the constraint optimization models and search heuristics described above in a tool called FLOWER/C. The tool is implemented in SICStus Prolog [30] and utilizes its `clpfd` library, which is a constraint solver for finite domains [31]. It reads a file which contains the data about test cases, covered features, costs, execution time, etc. and processes these data by constructing a dedicated constraint optimization model. Solving the model requires an implementation of the search heuristics and an input format tuned for preprocessing. These steps are encoded in SICStus Prolog 4.3.2 and a runtime is embedded into a tool with a GUI, in order to ease the future industrial adoption of the tool.

PROCEDURE FTSR($(F_1, \ldots, F_n), (O_1, \ldots, O_m), c$)
1: **while** not all O_i variables have been fixed **do**
2:     $i \leftarrow i'$ that maximizes $|D(O_{i'})|/c(i')$
3:     **switch** (execution direction)
4:     **case** forward: $O_i \leftarrow \max(D(O_i))$ {fix all possible F_j variables to i}
5:     **case** backward: $O_i \leftarrow 0$ {prune i from all possible F_j variables}
6:     **end switch**
7: **end while**

Algorithm 1. The FTSR-dedicated search procedure.

Our experiments include comparisons with IBM Cplex Optimizer 12.2, running on a single thread, and MiniSat+ 1.0. The experiments were run on a quad core 2.8 GHz Intel desktop with 8 MB cache per core, running Ubuntu Linux (using only one processor core).

We performed experiments on both random instances of FTSR and standard set covering instances benchmarks that were used in the literature. For random problems, we created a generator of FTSR instances, which takes several parameters as inputs such as the number of features, the number of test cases along with their associated costs, and the density of the relation cov which is expressed as the probability of any $t_j \in cov(f_i)$. We generated nine random datasets as shown in Table 2. As standard benchmarks, we used 80 instances from OR-Library[1]. 70 of these instances have non-uniform costs and were originally used in [32,33]. Their number of features ranges from 50 to 400 and the number of test cases from 500 to 4000. Ten of the instances have uniform costs and were originally used in [34]. Their number of features ranges from 240 to 28160 and the number of test cases from 192 to 11264. Finally, we used 16 real-world crew scheduling instances that were used in [35]. Fourteen of them come from American Airlines, and two are bus driver scheduling problems. The number of features ranges from 105 to 681 and the number of test cases from 2241 to 9524.

Table 2. Random datasets used in the experiments.

	SD1	SD2	SD3	SD4	TD1	TD2	TD3	TD4	TD5
Features	100	100	100	100	250	500	1000	1000	1000
Test cases	300	300	300	300	500	5000	5000	5000	7000
Density	0.015	0.020	0.025	0.030	0.04	0.02	0.01	0.005	0.01
Instances	20	20	20	20	50	50	50	50	50

All instances are presolved before test suite minimization. Presolving consists in applying the following three steps until nothing more can be deleted. Similar rules can be found in [36]:

- If there are two test cases $\{t_i, t_j\} \in T$ such that $\{f \mid t_i \in cov(f)\} \subseteq \{f \mid t_j \in cov(f)\}$ and $c(t_i) \geq c(t_j)$, then t_i is subsumed by t_j and can be deleted from the instance.
- If there are two features $\{f_i, f_j\} \in F$ such that $cov(f_j) \subseteq cov(f_i)$, then f_i is subsumed by f_j and can be deleted from the instance.
- If there is a feature f with a single covering test case t, then f is pre-assigned to t, and t and f as well as all other features that can be covered by t are deleted from the instance.

We then compute with an adapted version of Chvátal's greedy algorithm (see Algorithm 2) a first solution to the presolved instance and supply its cost C_{greedy} as an upper bound to the optimization solver in all our experiments.

---

[1] http://people.brunel.ac.uk/~mastjjb/jeb/orlib/scpinfo.html.

In our results, we present the *reduction rate* as the ratio $\frac{C_{\text{solver}}}{C_{\text{greedy}}}$, where C_{solver} is the best cost found by the optimization solver in the given experiment. The figures contain box plots with the first and third quartiles at the ends of the box, the median indicated by a thick horizontal line in the interior of the box, and the maximum and minimum at the ends of the whiskers.

PROCEDURE Chvátal$((V, E), c) :$ (cost, solution)
1: $(C, S) \leftarrow (0, \emptyset)$
2: **while** $E \neq \emptyset$ **do**
3:      $t' \leftarrow t$ that maximizes $|\{f \mid (f, t) \in E\}|/c(t)$
4:      $(C, S) \leftarrow (C + c(t'), S \cup \{t'\})$
5:      $F \leftarrow \{f \mid (f, t') \in E\}$
6:      $E \leftarrow \{(f, t) \mid (f, t) \in E \wedge f \notin F\}$
7: **end while**
8: **return** (C, S)

Algorithm 2. Adapted version of Chvátal's greedy algorithm applied to bipartite graph $G = (V, E)$ and cost function c.

4.1   Comparison of the Various CP Models

Figure 3 contains a comparison of the CPU time used to solve instances of FTSR for the four CP models for the uniform case used in our implementation FLOWER/C. We measured the time taken to find a global optimum of the constraint optimization models. In this experiment, we used datasets SD1–SD4. A time-out of 300 seconds was used in order to keep reasonable time for the results analysis.

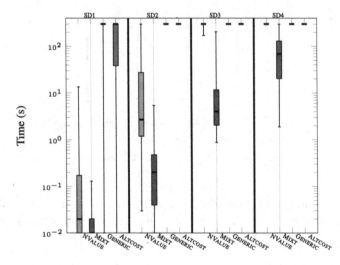

Fig. 3. Comparison of CPU time for FLOWER/C with four different CP models to find a global optimal value (time-out = 300 s).

We observe that both GENERIC and ALTCOST time out on datasets SD2, SD3 and SD4, but ALTCOST outperforms GENERIC on dataset SD1. We also see that MIXT outperforms all other models, with NVALUE as the runner-up.

Comparing the CPU time taken by the four models is obviously interesting but it may hide differences in terms of reduction rates obtained in a given amount of time. This is the objective of the following experiment.

4.2   Comparison of the Reduction Rate

Figure 4 shows the test suite reduction rate after 30 s of computation. In this experiment, the NVALUE model is the least effective one and in fact is never able to achieve any reduction. This is likely explained by the use of the FTSR-dedicated heuristic enabled by the GCC constraint, which significantly reduces the search effort required to solve the problem. We also observe that ALTCOST significantly outperforms GENERIC, where the latter achieves significant reduction on dataset TD1 only. We speculate that the reason why ALTCOST outperforms GENERIC lies in the cost function: the former cost function is a sum over the n features, whereas the latter cost function is a sum over the m test cases, and usually $n << m$.

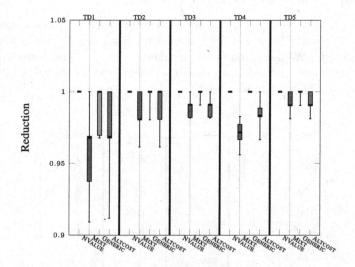

Fig. 4. Comparison of reduction rate for the CP models (time-out = 30 s).

Despite the interest of comparing constraint optimization models using similar techniques based on global constraints, it is equally important to compare Constraint Programming techniques with other approaches.

4.3 Evaluation of FLOWER/C Against Other Approaches

In the next experiment, we compared our implementation, FLOWER/C using the MIXT model, with MINISAT+ and CPLEX on randomly-generated instances.

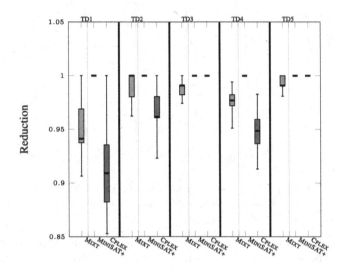

Fig. 5. Comparison of reduction rate of FLOWER/C (Mixt), MINISAT+, and CPLEX on random instances with unit costs (time-out = 60 s).

Figure 5 shows the results of experiments when considering the reduction rate achieved by all the three approaches in 60 s of CPU time. In this experiment, cost 1 is used for all test cases. We observe that for three of the datasets, CPLEX outperforms the other solvers, whereas for TD3 and TD5, MIXT is able to reduce the test suite but CPLEX is not. This is because CPLEX does not find any solution within the given time contract, whereas MIXT does. If its own preprocessing is switched off, CPLEX is unable to find any solutions for TD2 and TD4 either. It is also worth noting that MINISAT+ is never able to achieve any reduction. This does not come as a big surprise, since the FTSR problem has a simple formulation in terms of integer linear program which are better solved with an ILP solver than with a pseudo-Boolean one.

In the experiment reported in Fig. 6, we used a variant of datasets TD1–TD5 with a random cost value for each test case between 1 and 100. This time CPLEX outperformed the other solvers, whereas ALTCOST was somewhat more effective than GENERIC. Once again, MINISAT+ is never able to achieve any reduction.

4.4 Evaluation on Set-Covering Instances

In this experiment, we compared the reduction rate on the 70 non-uniform and the 10 uniform instances from OR-library, as well as the 16 non-uniform crew scheduling problems. The comparison is shown in Fig. 7. For the uniform case,

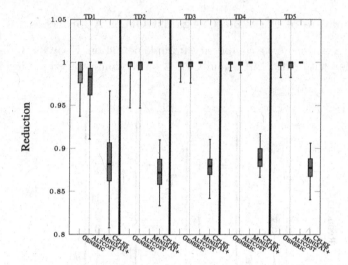

Fig. 6. Comparison of reduction rate of GENERIC, ALTCOST, MiniSAT+, and CPLEX on random instances with non-uniform costs (time-out = 60 s).

CPLEX is able to achieve reduction for three out of ten instances, whereas for six instances, no solution is found within the time contract. MIXT is able to achieve reduction for three out of ten instances, and MiniSAT+ on two. For the non-uniform OR-library instances, CPLEX outperforms the other solvers, achieving reduction for 64 instances out of 70, and ALTCOST performing slightly better than GENERIC. MiniSAT+ is not able to achieve any reduction on these instances. The picture is similar for the crew scheduling instances.

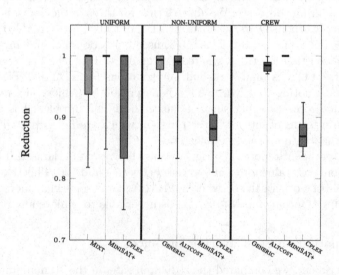

Fig. 7. Comparison of reduction rate on set-covering problems (time-out = 60s).

5 Application in an Industrial Setting

In collaboration with an industry partner, the proposed approach has been applied to the testing of large-scale communication software. In this domain, there are high requirements for software quality, as well as hard requirements for the duration of the overall testing activities. The software is developed following a continuous integration practice, which implies that there is only a limited amount of time available for testing after a commit has been made to the common codebase. In addition, not all the test cases that are related to the change are considered equal in terms of importance. The ones that are testing more critical functionality have higher priority in execution. Test engineers have been dealing with the problem of large test suites mainly manually, making a tradeoff between the size and the quality of test suites. As the size and complexity of the software started increasing, more test cases were developed covering the new functionality, which made the manual process of test selection highly non-scalable. To help solve this problem, we proposed the test suite reduction approach discussed in this article. The approach was applied in testing of one software release in a two-step process. First, for the given software change, after the code was committed to the codebase, test engineers identified a set of related test cases out of the overall test database. Afterwards, we analyzed the selected candidate test set and located the features, representing software functionality, covered by the test set. This information was the basis for the mapping between features and test cases needed by the proposed test reduction approach. The initial results of the experimentation show that the approach has high potential for effort reduction in this application domain. Currently, we are preparing to apply the approach for testing new software releases, in a process that will run in parallel with the current industry practice. These experiments will enable us to perform a systematic and thorough evaluation of the effectiveness of the approach based on several metrics, such as time reduction, or fault detection effectiveness increase.

6 Related Work

In this section, we analyze our approach FLOWER/C based on Constraint Programming and global constraints with other approaches for feature-based test suite reduction. Different techniques have been proposed to minimize the number of test cases in the context of feature coverage. Among these approaches, Combinatorial Interaction Testing (CIT) [37] is the most important. As observed by Kuhn in [38], software defects are often due to the interactions of only a small number of parameters of features. A simple case of CIT, widely used by validation engineers, is one-way or pairwise testing. One-way testing aims at covering each feature at least once while pairwise testing aims at covering all the interactions between two features [37]. Some of the best algorithms used to generate all combinatorial interactions have been implemented in commercialized tools, such as AETG [37], TConfig and so on. Even if these tools have demonstrated their potential for industrial adoption, they do not guarantee the reach of global minima when it comes to find the smallest subset of test cases such that all features are covered at least once. Moreover, they hardly take into account costs and other criteria (test execution time, code coverage, etc.) when selecting test cases.

More recently, some authors have proposed to use constraint solvers to generate test cases such that all one-way or pairwise feature interactions are covered. CIT can been tuned for the coverage of feature interactions with SAT-solving as shown in [39]. [40] proposes to convert variability models (used to represent all the features of a software product line) in Alloy declarative programs, so that an underlying SAT-solver can be used to generate test cases. Despite its novelty, this approach does not scale well because it is based on a generate-and-test paradigm. More precisely, it proposes a candidate test case and test whether it covers remaining uncovered features or not. Moreover, it represents the coverage relation with Boolean variables, which may lead to a combinatorial explosion in the problem representation. Unlike this approach, FLOWER/C represents the problem in a radically different way by associating a finite domain to each variable associated to a test case. This representation is efficient as it allows us to save much space. Furthermore, using global constraints, FLOWER/C can prune the search space by eliminating in advance possible choices of test cases which would lead to non-optimal feasible solutions. [41] proposes to use a greedy algorithm for solving the problem. Another greedy algorithm coupled with clever heuristics is proposed in [42]. Although this approach allows validation engineers to deal with large industrial case studies, it is not easily comparable to FLOWER/C as it uses heuristics and does not guarantee to reach global minima.

7 Conclusion

In the context of software product line testing, this article addresses the Feature-based Test Suite Reduction problem which aims at minimizing a test suite where costs are assigned to the test cases, while preserving the coverage of tested features. It introduces FLOWER/C, a tool based on global constraints and a dedicated search heuristics to solve this problem. The tool is evaluated on both random instances and standard benchmarks of the problem and the results showed that Constraint Programming with global constraints achieves good results in terms of reduction rate. Among the four Constraint Programming models with different global constraints which are compared, we show that a mixture of NVALUE and GCC achieves the best result. Interestingly, these results show that Constraint Programming is competitive with other test suite optimization approaches.

The main perspective of this work includes the deployment of this technique and its industrial adoption. Even if the preliminary results reported in this article need to be further refined and extended, we believe that they are sufficiently convincing to industrialize the technology. For that purpose, its integration within an existing software development chain needs to be understood. In particular, handling meta-data about test cases such as duration, priority and code-coverage needs a proper instrumentation and the implementation or usage of specific monitoring tools to capture the required information.

Acknowledgement. We are grateful to Marius Liaeen from Cisco Systems, Norway and Alexandre Petillon for their participation to the discussion and initial work related to the approach described in the article. This work is partly supported by the Research Council of Norway (RCN) through the research-based innovation center Certus, under the SFI program.

References

1. Johansen, M.F., Haugen, Ø., Fleurey, F.: Properties of realistic feature models make combinatorial testing of product lines feasible. In: Whittle, J., Clark, T., Kühne, T. (eds.) MODELS 2011. LNCS, vol. 6981, pp. 638–652. Springer, Heidelberg (2011). doi:10.1007/978-3-642-24485-8_47
2. Henard, C., Papadakis, M., Perrouin, G., Klein, J., Traon, Y.L.: Multi-objective test generation for software product lines. In: 17th International Software Product Line Conference, SPLC 2013, pp. 62–71 (2013)
3. Li, D., Jin, Y., Sahin, C., Clause, J., Halfond, W.G.J.: Integrated energy-directed test suite optimization. In: International Symposium on Software Testing and Analysis, ISSTA 2014, San Jose, CA, USA, 21–26 July 2014, pp. 339–350 (2014)
4. Stolberg, S.: Enabling agile testing through continuous integration. In: Agile Conference, AGILE 2009, pp. 369–374. IEEE (2009)
5. Wang, S., Ali, S., Gotlieb, A.: Cost-effective test suite minimization in product lines using search techniques. J. Syst. Softw. **103**, 370–391 (2015)
6. Rothermel, G., Harrold, M.J., Ronne, J., Hong, C.: Empirical studies of test-suite reduction. Soft. Test. Verif. Reliab. **12**, 219–249 (2002)
7. Tallam, S., Gupta, N.: A concept analysis inspired greedy algorithm for test suite minimization. In: 6th Workshop on Program Analysis for Software Tools and Engineering (PASTE 2005), pp. 35–42 (2005)
8. Jeffrey, D., Gupta, N.: Test suite reduction with selective redundancy. In: 21st International Confernce on Software Maintenance, pp. 549–558 (2005)
9. Ferrer, J., Kruse, P.M., Chicano, F., Alba, E.: Search based algorithms for test sequence generation in functional testing. Inf. Softw. Technol. **58**, 419–432 (2015)
10. Hsu, H.Y., Orso, A.: MINTS: a general framework and tool for supporting test-suite minimization. In: 31st International Conference on Software Engineering (ICSE 2009), pp. 419–429 (2009)
11. Chen, Z., Zhang, X., Xu, B.: A degraded ILP approach for test suite reduction. In: 20th International Conference on Software Engineering and Knowledge Engineering (2008)
12. Campos, J., Riboira, A., Perez, A., Abreu, R.: GZoltar: an eclipse plug-in for testing and debugging. In: IEEE/ACM International Conference on Automated Software Engineering, ASE 2012, pp. 378–381 (2012)
13. Gotlieb, A., Marijan, D.: FLOWER: optimal test suite reduction as a network maximum flow. In: Proceedings of International Symposium on Software Testing and Analysis (ISSTA 2014), San José, CA, USA (2014)
14. Chvátal, V.: A greedy heuristic for the set-covering problem. Math. Oper. Res. **4**(3), 233–235 (1979)

15. Harrold, M.J., Gupta, R., Soffa, M.L.: A methodology for controlling the size of a test suite. ACM TOSEM **2**, 270–285 (1993)
16. Offutt, A.J., Pan, J., Voas, J.M.: Procedures for reducing the size of coverage-based test sets. In: 12th International Conference on Testing Computer Software (1995)
17. Agrawal, H.: Efficient coverage testing using global dominator graphs. In: Workshop on Program Analysis for Software Tools and Engineering (PASTE 1999) (1999)
18. Wang, S., Ali, S., Gotlieb, A.: Minimizing test suites in software product lines using weight-based genetic algorithms. In: Genetic and Evolutionary Computation Conference (GECCO 2013), Amsterdam, The Netherlands (2013)
19. Black, J., Melachrinoudis, E., Kaeli, D.: Bi-criteria models for all-uses test suite reduction. In: 26th International Conference on Software Engineering, pp. 106–115 (2004)
20. Uzuncaova, E., Khurshid, S., Batory, D.: Incremental test generation for software product lines. IEEE Trans. Soft. Eng. **36**, 309–322 (2010)
21. Hao, D., Zhang, L., Wu, X., Mei, H., Rothermel, G.: On-demand test suite reduction. In: International Conference on Software Engineering, pp. 738–748 (2012)
22. Mouthuy, S., Deville, Y., Dooms, G.: Global constraint for the set covering problem. In: Journées Francophones de Programmation par Contraintes, pp. 183–192 (2007)
23. Gotlieb, A., Carlsson, M., Liaeen, M., Marijan, D., Petillon, A.: Automated regression testing using constraint programming. In: Proceedings of Innovative Applications of Artificial Intelligence (IAAI 2016), Phoenix, AZ, USA (2016)
24. Pachet, F., Roy, P.: Automatic generation of music programs. In: Jaffar, J. (ed.) CP 1999. LNCS, vol. 1713, pp. 331–345. Springer, Heidelberg (1999). doi:10.1007/978-3-540-48085-3_24
25. Régin, J.C.: Generalized arc consistency for global cardinality constraint. In: 13th International Conference on Artificial Intelligence (AAAI 1996), pp. 209–215 (1996)
26. Quimper, C.-G., López-Ortiz, A., Beek, P., Golynski, A.: Improved algorithms for the global cardinality constraint. In: Wallace, M. (ed.) CP 2004. LNCS, vol. 3258, pp. 542–556. Springer, Heidelberg (2004). doi:10.1007/978-3-540-30201-8_40
27. Gotlieb, A., Carlsson, M., Marijan, D., Petillon, A.: A new approach to feature-based test suite reduction in software product line testing. In: Maciaszek, L.A., Cardoso, J.S., Ludwig, A., van Sinderen, M., Cabello, E. (eds.) 11th International Joint Conference on Software Technologies (ICSOFT 2016), pp. 48–58. SciTePress (2016)
28. Rossi, F., Beek, P.V., Walsh, T.: Handbook of Constraint Programming (Foundations of Artificial Intelligence). Elsevier Science Inc., New York (2006)
29. Régin, J.C.: Global constraints: a survey. In: van Hentenryck, P., Milano, M. (eds.) Hybrid Optimization, pp. 63–134. Springer, Heidelberg (2011). doi:10.1007/978-1-4419-1644-0_3
30. Carlsson, M., et al.: SICStus Prolog User's Manual. Swedish Institute of Computer Science. Release 4.3.0 edn. (2014). ISBN 91-630-3648-7
31. Carlsson, M., Ottosson, G., Carlson, B.: An open-ended finite domain constraint solver. In: Glaser, H., Hartel, P., Kuchen, H. (eds.) PLILP 1997. LNCS, vol. 1292, pp. 191–206. Springer, Heidelberg (1997). doi:10.1007/BFb0033845
32. Beasley, J.E.: An algorithm for set covering problem. Eur. J. Oper. Res. **31**, 85–93 (1987)
33. Beasley, J.E.: A lagrangian heuristic for set-covering problems. Naval Res. Logist. (NRL) **37**, 151–164 (1990)
34. Grossman, T., Wool, A.: Computational experience with approximation algorithms for the set covering problem. Eur. J. Oper. Res. **101**, 81–92 (1997)

35. Caprara, A., Fischetti, M., Toth, P.: A heuristic method for the set covering problem. Oper. Res. **47**, 730–743 (1999)
36. Eén, N., Biere, A.: Effective preprocessing in SAT through variable and clause elimination. In: Bacchus, F., Walsh, T. (eds.) SAT 2005. LNCS, vol. 3569, pp. 61–75. Springer, Heidelberg (2005). doi:10.1007/11499107_5
37. Cohen, D.M., Dalal, S.R., Fredman, M.L., Patton, G.C.: The AETG system: an approach to testing based on combinatorial design. IEEE Trans. Softw. Eng. **23**, 437–444 (1997)
38. Kuhn, D.R., Wallace, D.R., Gallo, A.M.: Software fault interactions and implications for software testing. IEEE Trans. Softw. Eng. **30**, 418–421 (2004)
39. Mendonca, M., Wasowski, A., Czarnecki, K.: SAT-based analysis of feature models is easy. In: 13th International Software Product Line Conference, SPLC 2009, pp. 231–240. Carnegie Mellon University, Pittsburgh (2009)
40. Perrouin, G., Oster, S., Sen, S., Klein, J., Baudry, B., Traon, Y.L.: Pairwise testing for software product lines: comparison of two approaches. Software Qual. J. **20**, 605–643 (2012)
41. Oster, S., Markert, F., Ritter, P.: Automated incremental pairwise testing of software product lines. In: Bosch, J., Lee, J. (eds.) SPLC 2010. LNCS, vol. 6287, pp. 196–210. Springer, Heidelberg (2010). doi:10.1007/978-3-642-15579-6_14
42. Johansen, M.F., Haugen, Ø., Fleurey, F.: An algorithm for generating *t*-wise covering arrays from large feature models. In: 16th International Software Product Line Conference, SPLC 2012, pp. 46–55. ACM, New York (2012)

A Survey on Testing Distributed and Heterogeneous Systems: The State of the Practice

Bruno Lima[1,2(✉)] and João Pascoal Faria[1,2]

[1] INESC TEC, FEUP Campus, Rua Dr. Roberto Frias, s/n,
4200-465 Porto, Portugal
{bruno.lima,jpf}@fe.up.pt
[2] Faculty of Engineering, University of Porto,
Rua Dr. Roberto Frias, s/n, 4200-465 Porto, Portugal

Abstract. Distributed and heterogeneous systems (DHS), running over interconnected mobile and cloud-based platforms, are used in a growing number of domains for provisioning end-to-end services to users. Testing DHS is particularly important and challenging, with little support being provided by current tools. In order to assess the current state of the practice regarding the testing of DHS and identify opportunities and priorities for research and innovation initiatives, we conducted an exploratory survey that was responded by 147 software testing professionals that attended industry-oriented software testing conferences. The survey allowed us to assess the relevance of DHS in software testing practice, the most important features to be tested in DHS, the current status of test automation and tool sourcing for testing DHS, and the most desired features in test automation solutions for DHS. Some follow up interviews allowed us to further investigate drivers and barriers for DHS test automation. We expect that the results presented in the paper are of interest to researchers, tool vendors and service providers in this field.

Keywords: Software testing · Distributed systems · Heterogeneous systems · Systems of systems · State of the practice

1 Introduction

Due to the increasing ubiquity, complexity, criticality and need for assurance of software-based systems [3], testing is a fundamental lifecycle activity, with a huge economic impact if not performed adequately [16]. Such trends, combined with the needs for shorter delivery times and reduced costs, demand for the continuous improvement of software testing methods and tools, in order to make testing activities more effective and efficient.

Nowadays software is not more like simple applications but has evolved to large and complex system of systems [4]. A system of systems consists of a set

© Springer International Publishing AG 2017
E. Cabello et al. (Eds.): ICSOFT 2016, CCIS 743, pp. 88–107, 2017.
DOI: 10.1007/978-3-319-62569-0_5

of small independent systems that together form a new system. The system of systems can be a combination of hardware components (sensors, mobile devices, servers, etc.) and software systems used to create big systems or ecosystems that can offer multiple different services. Currently, systems of systems capture a great interest from the software engineering research community. These type of systems are present in different domains like e-health [1] or transportation [17].

Testing these distributed and heterogeneous software systems or systems of systems, running over interconnected mobile and cloud-based platforms, is particularly important and challenging. Some of the challenges are: the difficulty to test the system as a whole due to the number and diversity of individual components; the difficulty to coordinate and synchronize the test participants and interactions, due to the distributed nature of the system; the difficulty to test the components individually, because of the dependencies on other components. Because of that, the attention from the research community increased, however, the issues addressed and solutions proposed have been primarily evaluated from the academic perspective, and not the viewpoint of the practitioner.

Hence, the main objective of this paper is to explore the viewpoint of practitioners with respect to the testing of distributed and heterogeneous systems (DHS), in order to assess the current state of the practice and identify opportunities and priorities for research and innovation initiatives. For that purpose, we conducted an exploratory survey that was responded by 147 software testing professionals that attended industry-oriented software testing conferences, and present the main results in this paper. Besides introductory questions for characterizing the respondents and contextualizing their responses, the survey contained several questions with the aim of assessing the practical relevance of testing DHS, the importance of testing several features of DHS, the current level of test automation and tool sourcing, and the desired features in test automation solutions for DHS. We expect that the results presented in the paper are of interest to researchers, tool vendors and service providers in the software testing field.

This paper extends our previous conference paper [11] with detailed explanations and new sections about background and test automation obstacles.

The rest of the paper is organized as follows: Sect. 2 presents some background on software testing concepts and terminology used in the survey. Section 3 presents the research method used to conduct the survey. Section 4 presents the results, which are further discussed in Sect. 5. Section 6 presents the conclusions of follow up interviews to further investigate drivers and barriers for DHS test automation. Section 7 describes the related work. Section 8 concludes the paper and points out future work.

2   Background

In this section it is presented some background on software testing concepts and terminology used in the survey.

2.1   Test Levels

There are different levels during the software testing process [2]. Typically the levels considered are: unit testing, integration testing, system testing and acceptance testing.

Unit testing is the testing of individual hardware or software units or groups of related units [7]. The goal of unit testing is to isolate each part of the program and show that individual parts are correct in terms of requirements and functionality.

In the case of a distributed and heterogeneous system comprising a set of interconnected components running on different machines or execution environments, unit testing usually refers to the testing of individual components. In automated testing, if a component under test calls other components, such components need to be simulated by test stubs (see definition of test stub in the next section).

Integration testing is the testing in which software and/or hardware components are combined and tested to evaluate the interaction between them [7].

In the case of integration testing of a distributed and heterogeneous system, besides checking the interactions of system components with the environment (users or external systems), it is also useful to check the interactions between components of the system, to improve fault detection and localization. Checking such interactions may be challenging, because of observability limitations.

System testing is the testing conducted on a complete, integrated system to evaluate the system's compliance with specified requirements [7]. System testing is concerned mainly with testing the interactions of the system with the environment (users or external systems), and evaluating extra-functional properties.

In the case of a distributed and heterogeneous system, interactions with the environment (users or external systems) typically occur at multiple locations. In automated testing, coordinating the test components that simulate those users or external systems is specially challenging, because of their distributed nature.

Acceptance testing is the formal testing conducted to determine whether or not a system satisfies its acceptance criteria and to enable a customer, a user, or other authorized entity to determine whether or not to accept the system [7].

2.2   Test Harness

In software testing, a test harness is a collection of software and test data configured to test a program unit by running it under varying conditions and monitoring its behavior and outputs.

As shown in the Fig. 1, there are typically three main test components in a test harness: test driver, test stub and test monitor. The test drivers are responsible for calling the target code, simulating calling units or a user. In automatic testing they are also responsible for the implementation of test cases and procedures. The test stubs simulate modules, units or systems called by the target code; normally mock objects are used for this purpose. The test monitor is responsible to collect all the informations (or interactions) sent and received by the component under test. This information is important for fault diagnosis.

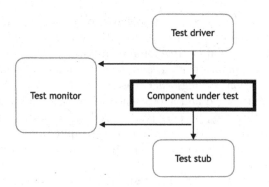

Fig. 1. Test harness.

2.3   Testing Methods

Software testing methods are traditionally divided into white-box testing [14], gray-box testing [12] and black-box testing [5].

In white-box testing, the internals of the system under test (SUT) are all visible. As a consequence, the knowledge about these internal matters can be used to create tests. Furthermore, white-box testing is not restricted to the detection of failures, but is also able to detect errors. Failures occur when there exist discrepancies between the specification and the behavior of the system. Errors are unexpected errors that occur while running the test. [13] Advantages are tests of higher quality because of the knowledge about system internals; however, there is also a big disadvantage, because looking into all aspects of a program requires a high effort.

In black-box testing, the SUT internal content is hidden from the tester. The tester only has knowledge about possible input and output values. The black-box testing only allows to test input-output functionality (functional testing). As an advantage, this technique is close to realistic conditions. One important disadvantage is the lack of internal information, which could be useful to generate tests, because sometimes it is necessary to know the content to test boundary values, that are normally responsible for failures.

In gray-box testing the advantages of both previous techniques are combined. The test design is realized at white-box level but the tests are executed at black-box level. For the tester, this has the advantage of having access to the SUT internal information while designing tests; however, the tests are executed under realistic conditions, where only failures are detected. Gray-box testing techniques are used for commercial model-based testing (MBT), where, e.g., the test model contains information about the internal structure of the SUT, but the SUT internal matters themselves are not accessible (e.g. for reasons of non-disclosure).

2.4   Test Automation

Several testing activities can be automated, with varying costs and benefits [15].

The testing activity that is most commonly automated is test execution. This requires that test cases are implemented as executable test scripts, test classes, etc. Support test components may also have to be developed, to act as test drivers, test monitors or test stubs. Automatic test execution is important to reduce the cost of regression testing, support iterative development approaches, enable load and performance testing, and avoid human errors that are common in manual test execution, among other reasons.

In the case of distributed and heterogeneous systems, automated test execution is specially challenging, because of the need to support multiple platforms and the need to coordinate the injection of test inputs and the monitoring of test outputs at distributed points, and very few testing frameworks exist for such systems [10].

Test coverage analysis is another testing activity that is commonly automated, usually in connection with automated test execution. Test coverage analysis is specially important in white-box testing, to determine parts of the code that are not being properly exercised, and help identifying additional test cases for increasing coverage.

Test case generation is usually performed manually. However, model-based testing (MBT) methods and tools have attracted increasing attention from industry, because of the ability to automatically generate test cases from system models. Based on behavioral models of the SUT, MBT tools are able to generate *abstract test cases*, which can be subsequently translated into *concrete test cases* ready for execution, based on mapping information between the model and the implementation.

In the case of distributed and heterogeneous systems, automated test case generation is specially challenging, because of the difficulty of modeling several characteristics inherent to such systems, such as timing aspects, concurrency aspects, and non-determinism, among other features, with very limited support provided by current MBT tools.

3   Research Method and Scope

The research method used in this work is the explanatory survey. Explanatory surveys aim at making explanatory claims about the population. For example, when studying how developers use a certain inspection technique [18].

3.1   Goal

The main goal of this work is to explore the testing of DHS from the point of view of industry practitioners, in order to assess the current state of the practice and identify opportunities and priorities for research and innovation initiatives.

More precisely, we aim at responding to the following research questions:

- **RQ1:** How relevant are DHS in the software testing practice?
- **RQ2:** What are the most important features to be tested in DHS?
- **RQ3:** What is the current status of test automation and tool sourcing for testing DHS?
- **RQ4:** What are the most desired features in test automation solutions for DHS?

3.2   Survey Distribution and Sampling

Since our main goal was to collect the point of view of industry practitioners that were involved in the testing of DHS, we shared the survey to the participants of two industry-oriented conferences in the software testing area: TESTING Portugal 2015[1] and User Conference on Advanced Automated Testing (UCAAT) 2015[2]. In total we distributed 250 surveys and we obtained 167 answers. From these 167 answers, only 147 were complete and valid. Most of the invalid answers were related with respondents that did not complete the survey.

3.3   Survey Organization

The survey was composed of two main parts. The first part was an introduction, where we explained the goal of the survey and define the term "Distributed and Heterogeneous Systems" in the context of this survey. In the context of this survey we define a Distributed and Heterogeneous System as a set of small independent systems that together form a new distributed system, combining hardware components and software systems, possibly involving mobile and cloud-based platforms.

The second part of the questions is divided in three different groups. The first group is related with the professional characterization of the participants. The second group contains questions about the company characterization. The last group contains the questions related with the testing of DHS and the main research questions underlying the survey.

4   Results

4.1   Participants Characterization

Before drawing conclusions on the main questions of this survey it is important to realize the profile of the survey participants. The results show that most of the people (70%) that responded this survey work in software testing, verification & validation and 41% are in the current position for more than five years (see Fig. 2).

Regarding the experience in software testing, the results show (see Fig. 3) that the majority of the survey participants have more than 5 years of experience in software testing in general and 40% have more than 5 years of experience with DHS.

4.2   Company Characterization

The companies surveyed worked in a large range of industry sectors. The results represented in Fig. 4 identify more than 10 different industry sectors.

---

[1] http://www.cvent.com/events/testing-portugal-2015/event-summary-a1a41d7f0867 4008b58e43454bb9f54a.aspx.

[2] http://www.etsi.org/news-events/events/868-2015-etsi-ucaat.

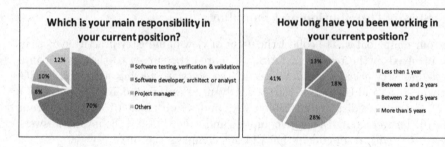

Fig. 2. Current position and time in current position [11].

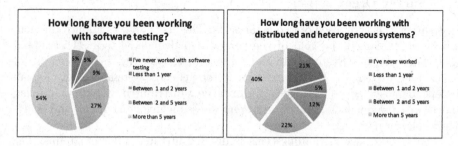

Fig. 3. Time in software testing [11].

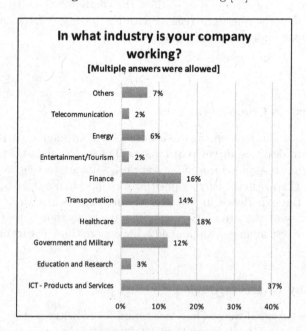

Fig. 4. Industry sectors [11].

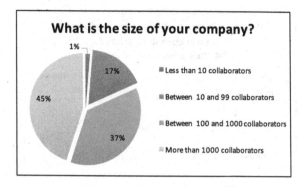

Fig. 5. Company size [11].

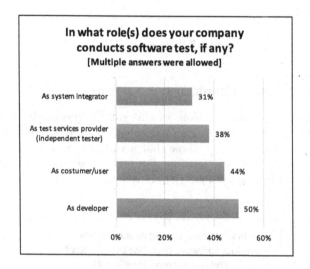

Fig. 6. Company roles [11].

We also analyzed the size of the companies according to their number of collaborators. Most of the companies are large companies, 37% have between 100 and 1,000 collaborators and 45% have more than 1,000 collaborators (Fig. 5).

The answers to 'In what role(s) does your company conducts software test, if any?' show that half of the companies performs tests to the software developed by themselves (Fig. 6).

Regarding the types of test levels performed, we realize from the answers (Fig. 7) that the unit testing level is the less performed and the other three levels (integration, system and acceptance) are performed with the same frequency.

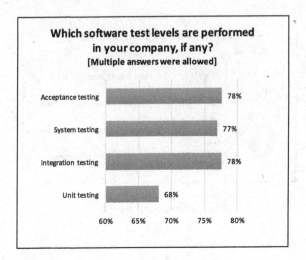

Fig. 7. Test levels [11].

4.3 Distributed and Heterogeneous Systems Testing

Focusing now on the main questions of this survey, specifically related to the testing of DHS, the answers to 'In what role(s) does your company conducts software test (for DHS), if any?' show that a vast majority of 90% of the companies (all but 10%) conducts tests for DHS in at least one role, with 42% of the companies performing tests for DHS developed by themselves (Fig. 8).

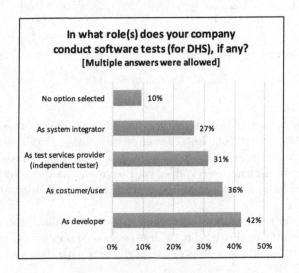

Fig. 8. Test roles DHS [11].

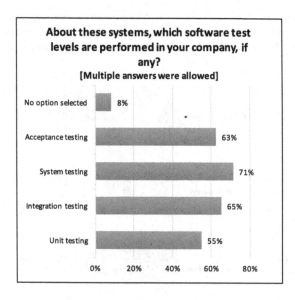

Fig. 9. Test levels DHS [11].

We also tried to understand what kinds of levels are most commonly used in the testing of such systems. Regarding the responses obtained (Fig. 9), there is a higher emphasis on system testing (71%) followed by integration testing (65%). Only 8% of the respondents did not mention any test level for DHS.

Regarding the most important features that need to be tested in DHS, the results in Fig. 10 show that the feature that was considered the most important to be tested was 'Interactions between components of the system' (with 76% of responses high or very high), followed by 'Interactions between the system and the environment' (71%) and 'Multiple platforms' (66%). All the features have been considered of 'very high' or 'high' importance by a majority of respondents (50% or more).

Regarding the level of test automation for DHS, the results presented in Fig. 11 show that 75% of the tests follow some automated process, however only 16% are fully automatic, which is lower than the 25% who claim to perform only manual testing.

For people who responded that there is at least some automatic process, we asked what kind of tool they use. With this question we can understand the level of effort required to automate the testing process. Looking at the results (Fig. 12) we realize that only 31% use a commercial tool to automate the process, and the majority, 69%, use a tool developed in-house, reusable or not in different SUTs.

Regarding the desired features of a test automation solution for DHS, the results presented in Fig. 13 show that the most important features (based in the percentage of responses high or very high) in an automated testing tool for DHS are 'Support for automatic test case execution' (75%) and 'Support for multiple platforms' (71%).

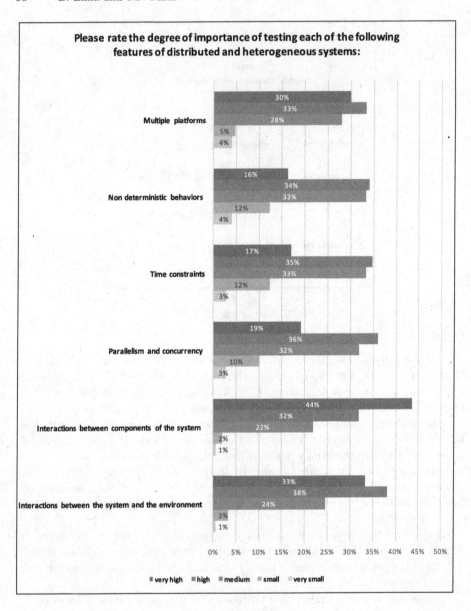

Fig. 10. Features.

As a possible solution to test DHS, we asked the participants in this survey if they would find useful a tool to test these systems that use only a model of interactions (UML sequence diagram) as an entry model. The results (Fig. 14) show that 86% consider useful a tool with these characteristics.

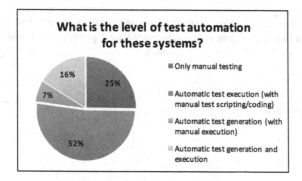

Fig. 11. Automation level [11].

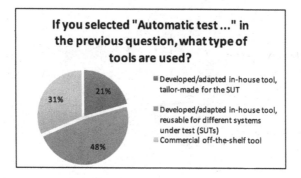

Fig. 12. Automation tool [11].

4.4   Multivariate Analysis

For questions specifically related to the opinion of the participants, a multivariate analysis was held with the aim to determine whether the participants' responses depend on their current function (Software testing, verification & validation versus all the others).

The results of the chi-square test for independence show that there is no statistically significant association (for a 95% significance level) between the current function (Software testing, verification & validation versus all others) and the answers to the questions shown in Figs. 10, 13 or 14.

5   Discussion

5.1   Relevance of Respondents

The results presented in the previous section show that this survey met the original purpose with regard to their target audience, since 70% of respondents' primary responsibility is related to 'Software testing, verification & validation'. With regard to their experience, the results showed that they are not only people

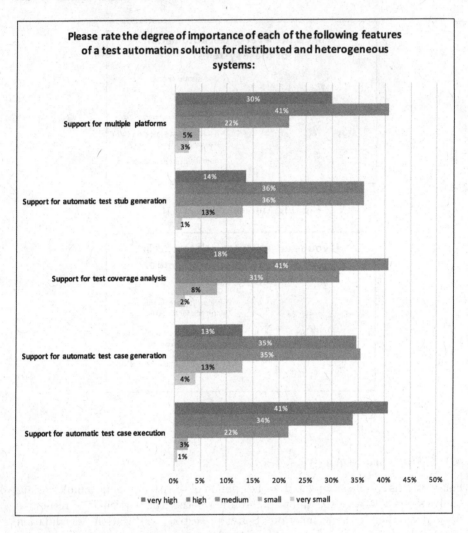

Fig. 13. Tool features.

who are mostly in their current position for several years, as work with software testing in general and specifically with DHS. With respect to the type of companies, the results show that this survey covers companies with diverse activity sectors and also large companies (45% have more than 1000 collaborators) which provides a great support to the conclusions reached.

Concerning the main conclusions we can draw from the results, they are next organized according to the initial research questions.

5.2   RQ1: How Relevant Are DHS in the Software Testing Practice?

The results (Fig. 8) show that a vast majority of approximately 90% of the companies surveyed (all with software testing activities in general) conducts

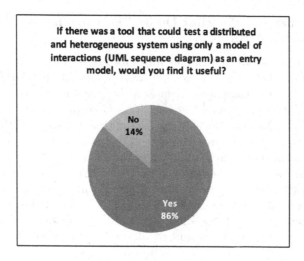

Fig. 14. New tool [11].

tests for DHS, in at least one role and at least one test level, hence confirming the high relevance of DHS in software testing practice.

5.3   RQ2: What Are the Most Important Features to Be Tested in DHS?

Regarding the most important features that need to be tested in DHS, the results in Fig. 10 show that the feature that was considered the most important to be tested was 'Interactions between components of the system' (with 76% of responses high or very high), followed by 'Interactions between the system and the environment' (71%) and 'Multiple platforms' (66%).

Nevertheless, all the features inquired were considered of high or very high importance by a majority of respondents (50% or more).

5.4   RQ3: What Is the Current Status of Test Automation and Tool Sourcing for Testing DHS?

The results show that the current level of test automation for DHS is still very low, and there is large room for improvement, since 25% of companies in the survey claim that they only perform manual tests, against only 16% who claim to test DHS with a full automatic process.

If we look for companies that have some type of automation in its testing process, we realize that the automation process is requiring a high effort in the creation/adaptation of own tools, because only 31% of companies claim to use a commercial tool to test these types of systems.

5.5   RQ4: What Are the Most Desired Features in Test Automation Solutions for DHS?

Regarding the conclusions that can be drawn for future work, particularly at the level of creating tools that can reduce the effort required to test DHS, looking at Fig. 13, we realize that companies identify as key aspects of a tool to test such systems the ability to automate test execution (75% of responses with high or very high importancte) and the support for multiple platforms (71%).

Nevertheless, all the features inquired were considered of medium, high or very high importance by a large majority of respondents (83% or more).

The comparison of the degree of importance attributed to automatic test case execution (96% of the responses mentioning a medium, high or very high importance in Fig. 13) with the current status (78% of companies applying automatic text execution in Fig. 11), show that there is a significant gap yet to be filled between the current status and the desired status of automatic test case execution.

The gap is even bigger regarding automatic test case generation, with 83% of the responses mentioning a medium, high or very high importance in Fig. 13, and only 23% of the companies currently applying automatic text generation in Fig. 11.

We realized even by the Fig. 14, that companies are highly receptive to a test tool that has only a model of interactions as an input model for automatic test case generation and execution.

6   Case Based Analysis of Test Automation Obstacles

In order to analyze the drivers and barriers for DHS test automation in companies, we conducted follow-up interviews with some survey respondents. For the interviews we selected a sample of survey respondents from companies with different sizes (in terms of number of employees) and different test automation strategies.

6.1   Case A

Company A is a small company that develops software for external customers. The company performs manual tests on the software they develop. The justifications given by this company for only performing manual testing are:

- the low economic capacity to purchase commercial testing tools. Small companies and startups have limited budgets that have to be managed with many limitations and focusing on the rapid development of their products, leaving aside investments on test tools;
- the lack of human resources (in terms of availability and expertise) to allocate to test automation tasks. This type of company usually has a small number of employees, so all end up taking on various tasks. As the main focus is the rapid development of products, the use of any testing tool that requires additional learning time is immediately discarded;

– if they adopted a test automation solution, it would be costly to maintain automated test cases because of constant changes of product requirements and features, implying frequent changes in the test cases and test harness.

6.2   Case B

Company B is a large company that develops software for government and military areas. This company uses automation for test execution but still uses a manual process for test case generation (i.e., the creation of test scripts). For test automation, the company uses tools developed in-house, based on open-source frameworks. The justification given for not resorting to commercial tools is mainly due to the high costs charged by suppliers of these tools, often requiring the purchase of extra plug-ins for any additional feature needed.

Besides that reason, the following justifications were given for using tools developed in-house:

– to maintain knowledge within the company. Large companies prefer to develop their own tools because they are often unwilling to share information about their products with commercial tool vendors. For this reason they make use of open source tools that can be easily modified by the experts of the test area of the company itself;
– to be able to make adjustments to the tools more quickly, not being dependent on any vendor. Commercial tools leave companies dependent on their manufacturer, so large companies prefer to develop their own testing tools, since in the current market conditions it is increasingly important to have a quick reaction capability to modify the software.

With regard to manual test generation, the following justifications were given by the representative of the company for not using any automation process:

– the software developed by the company has very specific features that might be difficult to address with existing test generation tools;
– the lack of knowledge of company staff with regard to the creation of models needed as input for test case generation and the subsequent generation of test cases (this is one aspect that the company intends to improve in the near future).

6.3   Case C

Company C is a small to medium company that provides consulting services in the area of software testing. Most automation solutions that the company proposes and implements for its customers are related with test execution (and not test generation).

The reasons given for this have to do mainly with:

– the difficulty to automatically generate test cases;

- customers have no system model;
- the creation of system models requires a great effort;
- the system being tested is in a state of constant evolution and therefore not worth the effort in automatic test generating (or event automatic test execution).

As regards the tools that this company suggests to their customers for test execution automation, in most cases they recommend commercial testing tools. According to the representative of this company, this choice happens due to the following reasons:

- commercial tools are "ready to use";
- commercial tools do not require that the company has specialized human resources to adapt the test tool.

However, when the client has know-how in the test area, this company also indicates open source solutions that, in spite of requiring more maintenance, end up giving more flexibility and of course greater freedom to their users.

6.4   Synthesis

Analyzing the answers we have come to the conclusion that there are still several barriers and obstacles that prevent companies from adopting a fully automated test process.

Regarding the reasons for not adopting an automated test execution approach, we conclude that the main reasons are:

- cost of commercial testing tools (A);
- lack of human resources (availability and expertise) (A);
- frequent changes in the software under test (A, C).

For companies that have some level of automation in the testing tasks, the choice between commercial tools and in-house tools (usually based on open source tools) depends essentially on the type of company, since although the commercial tools are referred in the interviews as "ready to use" facilitating in this way the test automation process, they have several drawbacks, namely:

- are expensive, especially if extra functionalities and/or platforms are required (B);
- create too much dependence from vendors, and reduce flexibility for extensions and adaptations (B, C);
- know-how related with test automation is kept outside the company (B).

Regarding the reasons for choosing between a manual versus an automated test generation approach (with automatic test generation from models), we found:

- lack of human resources (availability and/or expertise) (A, B);
- frequent changes in the software under test (A, B, C);
- lack of system models (B, C);
- effort required for the creation of system models (B, C).

7   Related Work

We only found in literature one survey [6] that discuss some aspects related to the testing of heterogeneous systems. The survey conducted by [6] explored the testing of heterogeneous systems with respect to the usage and perceived usefulness of testing techniques used for heterogeneous systems from the point of view of industry practitioners in the context of practitioners involved in heterogeneous system development reporting their experience on heterogeneous system testing. For achieving this goal the authors tried to answer two research questions:

- RQ1: Which testing techniques are used to evaluate heterogeneous systems?
- RQ2: How do practitioners perceive the identified techniques with respect to a set of outcome variables?

The authors concluded that the most frequently used technique is exploratory manual testing, followed by combinatorial and search-based testing, and that the most positively perceived technique for testing heterogeneous systems was manual exploratory testing. Our work has a different objective of the survey conducted by Ghazi. The Ghazi main goal was to identify testing techniques, our aim is to understand how distributed systems and heterogeneous are tested in companies realizing which test levels are performed and which are the automation levels for testing these systems. The Ghazi survey also involved a much smaller number of participants (27).

As regards the general software testing in the literature there are many surveys, however as the main aim of our work is to analyze the state of practice, we analyze surveys carried out in the industry by recognized standardization bodies as ISTQB [8]. The most recent survey of this organization [9] conducted over more than 3,000 people from 89 countries, although it has a different purpose of our work because is related to the software test in general, provides results that meet the results presented in this article, namely that there are still significant improvement opportunities in test automation (was considered in this study the area with highest improvement potential).

8   Conclusions

In order to assess the current state of the practice regarding the testing of DHS and identify opportunities and priorities for research and innovation initiatives, we conducted an exploratory survey that was responded by 147 software testing professionals that attended industry-oriented software testing conferences.

The survey allowed us to confirm the high relevance of DHS in software testing practice, confirm and prioritize the relevance of testing features characteristics of DHS, confirm the existence of a significant gap between the current and the desired status of test automation for DHS, and confirm and prioritize the relevance of test automation features for DHS. The survey results indicated a limited adoption of complete test automation processes by companies.

For better understanding what are the obstacles that companies face for not adopting complete test automation approaches, we conducted follow-up interviews with companies of different sizes and testing approaches. The conclusions drawn from the interviews allowed us to identify some common obstacles, such as the cost of acquisition and difficulty of adaptation of test automation tools, the cost of test suite maintenance (namely with frequent changes in the software under test), and the effort and expertise required for the creation of system models needed as input for automatic test suite generation. We expect that the results presented in the paper are of interest to researchers, tool vendors and service providers in this field.

As future work, we intend to develop techniques and tools to support the automatic test generation and execution of test cases for DHS, addressing some of the obstacles previously identified, namely by using UML sequence diagrams as input for test generation to simplify the description of the SUT.

Acknowledgements. This research work was performed in scope of the project NanoSTIMA. Project "NanoSTIMA: Macro-to-Nano Human Sensing: Towards Integrated Multimodal Health Monitoring and Analytics/NORTE-01-0145-FEDER-000016" is financed by the North Portugal Regional Operational Programme (NORTE 2020), under the PORTUGAL 2020 Partnership Agreement, and through the European Regional Development Fund (ERDF).

References

1. AAL4ALL: Ambient Assisted Living For All (2015). http://www.aal4all.org
2. Beizer, B.: Software Testing Techniques. Dreamtech Press (2003)
3. Boehm, B.: Some future software engineering opportunities and challenges. In: Nanz, S. (ed.) The Future of Software Engineering, pp. 1–32. Springer, Heidelberg (2011). doi:10.1007/978-3-642-15187-3_1
4. DoD: systems engineering guide for systems of systems. Technical report, Office of the Deputy Under Secretary of Defense for Acquisition and Technology, Systems and Software Engineering Version 1.0 (2008)
5. Edwards, S.H.: A framework for practical, automated black-box testing of component-based software. Softw. Test. Verification Reliab. **11**(2), 97–111 (2001)
6. Ghazi, A.N., Petersen, K., Börstler, J.: Heterogeneous systems testing techniques: an exploratory survey. In: Winkler, D., Biffl, S., Bergsmann, J. (eds.) SWQD 2015. LNBIP, vol. 200, pp. 67–85. Springer, Cham (2015). doi:10.1007/978-3-319-13251-8_5
7. IEEE: IEEE Standard Glossary of Software Engineering Terminology. IEEE Std 610.12-1990, pp. 1–84, December 1990
8. ISTQB: International Software Testing Qualifications Board, March 2016. http://www.istqb.org/
9. ISTQB: ISTQB worldwide software testing practices report 2015–2016. Technical report (2016). http://www.istqb.org/references/surveys/istqb-worldwide-software-testing-practices-report-2015-2016.html
10. Lima, B., Faria, J.P.: Automated testing of distributed and heterogeneous systems based on UML sequence diagrams. In: Lorenz, P., Cardoso, J., Maciaszek, L.A., Sinderen, M. (eds.) ICSOFT 2015. CCIS, vol. 586, pp. 380–396. Springer, Cham (2016). doi:10.1007/978-3-319-30142-6_21

11. Lima, B., Faria, J.P.: Testing distributed and heterogeneous systems: state of the practice. In: Proceedings of the 11th International Joint Conference on Software Technologies - Volume 1: ICSOFT-EA, pp. 69–78 (2016)

12. Linzhang, W., Jiesong, Y., Xiaofeng, Y., Jun, H., Xuandong, L., Guo, Z.: Generating test cases from UML activity diagram based on gray-box method. In: 11th Asia-Pacific Software Engineering Conference, pp. 284–291. IEEE (2004)

13. Mills, H.D., Dyer, M., Linger, R.C.: Cleanroom software engineering (1987)

14. Ostrand, T.: White-box testing. In: Encyclopedia of Software Engineering (2002)

15. Ramler, R., Wolfmaier, K.: Economic perspectives in test automation: balancing automated and manual testing with opportunity cost. In: Proceedings of the 2006 International Workshop on Automation of Software Test, AST 2006, NY, USA, pp. 85–91. ACM, New York (2006). http://doi.acm.org/10.1145/1138929.1138946

16. Tassey, G.: The Economic impacts of inadequate infrastructure for software testing. Technical report, National Institute of Standards and Technology (2002)

17. Torens, C., Ebrecht, L.: RemoteTest: a framework for testing distributed systems. In: 2010 Fifth International Conference on Software Engineering Advances (ICSEA), pp. 441–446, August 2010

18. Wohlin, C., Höst, M., Henningsson, K.: Empirical research methods in software engineering. In: Conradi, R., Wang, A.I. (eds.) Empirical Methods and Studies in Software Engineering, pp. 7–23. Springer, Heidelberg (2003)

Model-Based Recovery and Adaptation Connectors: Design and Experimentation

Emad Albassam, Hassan Gomaa$^{(\boxtimes)}$, and Daniel A. Menascé

Department of Computer Science, George Mason University, Fairfax, VA, USA
{ealbassa, hgomaa, menasce}@gmu.edu

Abstract. This paper describes the design of model-based Recovery and Adaptation Connectors (RAC) that handle recovery and adaptation concerns of services in service-oriented architectures. When a service needs to be dynamically adapted, RAC ensures that the service first transitions to a quiescent state before it is replaced with a new service. When a service recovers from a run-time failure, RAC ensures that transactions that have been interrupted due to service failure are aborted and then restarted with the recovered service. Thus, RAC ensures that no transactions are lost due to dynamic service adaptation or failure. The design of the RAC is based on the autonomic computing MAPE-K loop model and handles both stateless and stateful services. Our approach has been validated through experimentation of planned failure and adaptation scenarios.

Keywords: Self-adaptation · Self-configuration · Self-healing · Dynamic · Software adaptation · Autonomic computing · Component recovery · Recovery patterns · Adaptation patterns · Mape-K loop model · Recovery connectors · Adaptation connectors · State machines

1 Introduction

Service-oriented architectures (SOA) are a well-known approach for building increasingly complex software systems from independently developed services. SOAs often run in environments that are evolving and subject to failures. Thus, these systems need to be capable of self-configuring and self-healing autonomously without human intervention.

Previous papers prescribed adaptation connectors and showed how these connectors can be used to adapt service-oriented software systems at run-time [1–3]. This paper describes the concept of recovery and adaptation patterns and how a model-based Recovery and Adaptation Connector (RAC) can integrate self-healing and self-configuration capabilities so that a service or coordinator in SOA can be dynamically replaced or removed after original deployment or recovered after a run-time failure.

In this paper, we describe how the design of the RAC, which was previously shown to handle adaptation and recovery concerns of stateless services [4], can be extended to handle adaptation and recovery of stateful services with both idempotent and non-idempotent operations [5]. The RAC design is based on the MAPE-K loop model [6]. The monitoring activity notifies the RAC of service failures. The analysis activity identifies the transactions interrupted due to service failure. The planning activity

© Springer International Publishing AG 2017
E. Cabello et al. (Eds.): ICSOFT 2016, CCIS 743, pp. 108–131, 2017.
DOI: 10.1007/978-3-319-62569-0_6

determines the procedure to recover interrupted transactions. The execution activity performs the recovery actions and restores any failed transactions.

The rest of this paper is organized as follows. Section 2 highlights key concepts and assumptions. Section 3 discusses the design of RACs. Section 4 shows how the RAC design can be extended to handle stateful services. Section 5 describes how RACs can be used in different SOA patterns. Section 6 discusses experimentation of RAC. Section 7 discusses related work. Finally, Sect. 8 concludes the paper and discusses future work.

2 Key Concepts

This section describes the key concepts for providing a systematic and reusable approach for self-healing and self-configuration of CBSAs [7].

Autonomic Control. Manual management of large and complex software systems is difficult and costly. Such manual systems could be automated by providing the following autonomic properties: self-healing, self-configuration, self-optimization, and self-protection [6]. The MAPE-K loop model is widely used to implement autonomic controllers and consists of four activities (monitoring, analysis, planning, and execution) that operate on a knowledge-base of the system. We use the general MAPE-K loop model to support self-healing and self-configuration of autonomic services.

Recovery and Adaptation Connectors (RACs). RACs are used to separate adaptation and recovery concerns from service concerns so that a service can be dynamically adapted and recovered from failures.

Recovery Patterns. A recovery pattern defines how components in an architectural pattern can be dynamically relocated and recovered to a consistent state after a component has failed.

Adaptation Patterns. A software adaptation pattern defines how a set of components that make up an architectural pattern dynamically cooperate to change the software configuration to a new configuration [3].

Message-based Transactions. A transaction in CBSAs is defined by Kramer and Magee as an information exchange between multiple components through messages [9] while a transaction in transactional processing systems is defined as an atomic unit of work [5]. We combine these two definitions as: a transaction is an information exchange between two or more components through messages such that either all messages in a transaction are eventually exchanged or none of them are.

We make the following assumptions in this paper:

- Only one component can fail permanently at a time based on the fail-stop failure model [10] in which components do not send any erroneous messages but simply cease functioning when they fail. Furthermore, we assume that failures are not caused by malicious attacks.

- Message delivery uses a reliable network transport protocol.
- Recovery and adaptation connectors do not fail.
- Clocks are synchronized among all nodes.

3 Recovery and Adaptation Connectors

This section describes the design of the basic structure of a RAC for SOAs. We assume that there are multiple clients and a single service that processes multiple client requests concurrently. The service responds to each request from the client. The RAC manages transactions between a client and a service that comprise either single request/response messages or a dialog. Section 5 shows how the same RAC design can handle adaptation and recovery in other, more complex architectural patterns.

3.1 Design of RAC

RAC (Fig. 1) behaves as a proxy for the service by receiving requests from clients and then forwarding these requests to the service. The RAC also receives responses from the service, which are then forwarded to requesting clients.

To ensure safe adaptation at run-time and recoverability of service failures, the RAC must keep track of the transactions that the service is currently engaged in and must maintain messages (i.e., requests and responses) that pass through it so that these messages can be held during adaptation and can be recovered when the service fails.

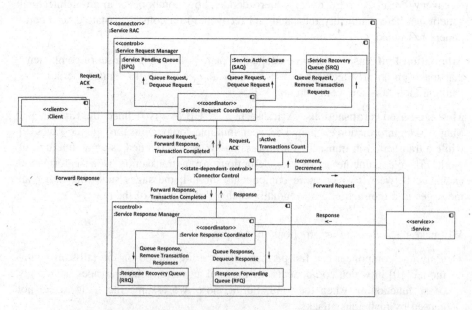

Fig. 1. Design of RAC showing messages during normal execution [4].

RAC has a control object (Connector Control in Fig. 1) that handles sending messages to and receiving responses from application components, and also handles adaptation and recovery concerns of the service. To facilitate maintenance of application messages, requests and responses are stored by the RAC in queues located at the Service Request Manager and the Service Response Manager (Fig. 1), respectively. Each manager is provided with a coordinator component for controlling the queues it manages. The goal of these coordinators is to separate the concerns of queue management from adaptation and recovery concerns handled by Connector Control.

3.2   Service Request Manager

Every request sent by a client to a service passes through the Service Request Coordinator (Fig. 1). The Service Request Coordinator maintains the following three queues for storing client requests based on the status of these requests:

Service Pending Queue (SPQ). The SPQ stores client requests received by the RAC but that have not yet been forwarded to the service. The purpose of this queue is to buffer requests for the service so that any requests received by the RAC while the service is being dynamically adapted or is in the failed state are preserved until the service becomes active again. Thus, the SPQ ensures that no requests to the service are lost due to dynamic adaptation or recovery.

Service Active Queue (SAQ). This queue stores client requests that have been forwarded to the service but do not have corresponding service responses at the RAC, either because the service is still processing the request and has not generated the corresponding response yet or because the service response was lost due to service failure.

The RAC uses this queue to determine pending requests that must be processed by the service first before the service can be dynamically adapted. Furthermore, the RAC uses this queue to recover requests that were lost by the service (due to service failure) before the corresponding responses of these requests are received by the RAC.

Service Recovery Queue (SRQ). This queue stores client requests that have corresponding service responses at the RAC. This queue ensures that previous requests of each dialog that the service is currently engaged in are preserved so that these dialogs can also be recovered in case they were interrupted due to service failure.

3.3   Service Response Manager

Responses sent by the service are received by the Service Response Coordinator (Fig. 1). The Service Response Coordinator maintains two queues for storing responses:

Response Forwarding Queue (RFQ). This queue stores service responses that have been received by the RAC but have not yet been forwarded to the requesting client.

Response Recovery Queue (RRQ). This queue stores service responses after they have been forwarded to the requesting clients. This queue ensures that a service response that has been forwarded by the RAC to the requesting client cannot be lost due to client failure. In this case, when the RAC receives a duplicate request from a recovered client, the corresponding response is obtained from the RRQ and forwarded to the recovered client, without requiring the service to process the request again.

3.4 Connector Control State Machine

Connector Control (Fig. 1) is a state-dependent control component that handles recovery and adaptation of the service by tracking its current state. While the service is active, Connector Control keeps track of whether the service is currently engaged in any transactions with its clients so that it can base its adaptation and recovery decisions accordingly.

The Connector Control state machine (Fig. 2) consists of two orthogonal state machines (STMs). Integrated Adaptation and Recovery is the orthogonal STM that handles service adaption and recovery. The Message Queue Management STM is responsible for notifying the Service Request Coordinator and the Service Response Coordinator when a client acknowledges the completion of a transaction to enable these coordinators to remove the messages of this transaction from their queues.

The orthogonal integrated adaptation and recovery state machine (Fig. 3) consists of three composite states: (1) Active, which defines behaviour during normal service execution, (2) Adapting, which defines behaviour during dynamic service adaptation, and (3) Recovering, which defines behaviour during recovery.

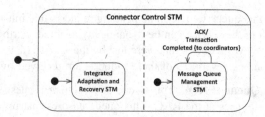

Fig. 2. State machine executed by Connector Control [4].

Normal Service Execution. Initially, Connector Control is in the Waiting for Request state (Fig. 3) indicating that the service is currently not engaged in any transactions with its clients. When Connector Control receives a client request, it forwards the request to the service, increments the number of active transactions that the service is currently engaged in, and transitions to the Processing state. While in the Processing state, Connector Control forwards requests to the service and forwards responses to requesting clients. Connector Control remains in the Processing state as long as the service is engaged in one or more transactions. Furthermore, Connector Control increments the number of active transactions when it forwards a request that initiates a

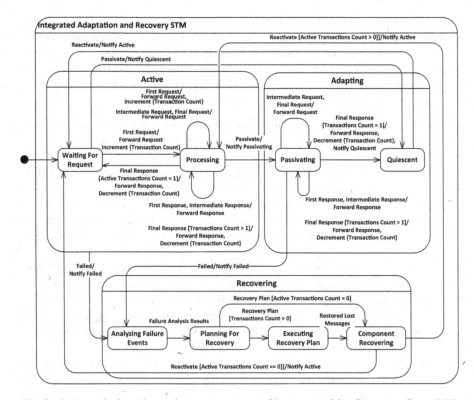

Fig. 3. Integrated adaptation and recovery state machine executed by Connector Control [4].

new transaction with the service and decrements this number when it receives the final response of a transaction from the service. At this time, Connector Control forwards that final response of the final transaction to the requesting client and transitions back to the Waiting for Request state.

Dynamic Service Adaptation. In order to safely adapt the service at run-time, the service must be in a quiescent state [9] in which it is not involved in any transactions and will not receive any new transactions from its clients. At this point, the service can be removed or replaced at run-time after it has sent the final response of every transaction it is currently engaged in. In the Passivating state, Connector Control must not forward any requests that initiate new transactions with the service, so that the service can eventually transition to the quiescent state where it can be safely adapted.

If Connector Control receives the Passivate command from Change Management [9] while it is in the Waiting for Request state (Fig. 3), then the service is not engaged in any transactions with its clients. It thus transitions immediately to the Quiescent state, and notifies the Service Request Coordinator that the service is quiescent so that it holds all requests it receives from clients in the SPQ. On the other hand, if Connector Control receives the Passivate command while it is in the Processing state, then the service is engaged in one or more transactions with its clients. In this case, Connector

Control transitions to the Passivating state, where the service completes existing transactions. While in the Passivating state, Connector Control forwards intermediate requests it receives to the service and forwards service responses it receives to requesting clients. Eventually, when all active transactions are completed, Connector Control notifies the Service Request Coordinator that the service is transitioning to the Quiescent State where the service can be safely adapted.

Service Recovery. While the service is in the recovering state, Connector Control must not forward any requests and must ensure that all failed transactions are restarted when the service is recovered.

Recovering a service from failure is handled by the connector using the MAPE-K loop model for self-healing and self-configuration, as explained next.

The monitoring activity of MAPE-K notifies the RAC of the service failure. When Connector Control receives a failure notification, it notifies the Service Requests Coordinator of the failure and then transitions to Analyzing Failure Events state (Fig. 3).

The Analyzing Failure Events state corresponds to the analysis activity of MAPE-K where the RAC identifies all transactions that were interrupted due to service failure. The RAC determines that a transaction has failed if either the SAQ or SRQ contain a request that initiates a transaction with the service but neither the RFQ nor the RRQ contains a response that completes that transaction. When failure analysis is completed, Connector Control transitions to the Planning for Recovery state.

The Planning for Recovery state corresponds to the planning activity of MAPE-K where the RAC determines the recovery plan for the failed transactions. The plan identifies which requests must be resent to the recovered service so that failed trans-actions are restarted at the recovered service. The recovery plan is determined by executing the following recovery policy:

- First, the RAC forwards previous requests of every failed dialog that the service was engaged in before it failed. These requests are recovered from the SRQ and are forwarded sequentially in the same order they were processed before service failure to ensure that the recovered service also processes these requests in that order.
- Second, the RAC forwards the requests of failed transactions queued in the SAQ, which contains pending requests that were lost by the failed service before the RAC received the responses to these requests. Note that at this step, if a request that is being forwarded is of a dialog, then (from the previous step) the service must have already received all previous requests of this dialog.
- Third, the RAC forwards all requests in the SPQ, which are new requests that have been received while the service is in the recovering state, to the recovered service.

The Executing Recovery Plan state corresponds to the execution activity of MAPE-K where the RAC restores all requests that must be resent to the recovered service by moving these requests from the SRQ and SAQ to the SPQ, as specified in the recovery plan. When all requests are restored, Connector Control transitions to the Component Recovering state in which the connector waits until the service is relocated and instantiated by Change Management, and then has its connection with the recovered service established. Eventually, when Connector Control receives the

Reactive command, Connector Control transitions to the Active State and notifies the Service Request Coordinator that the service is active so that Service Request Coordinator resumes sending requests queued in the SPQ to Connector Control.

3.5   Service Request Coordinator STM

Based on the discussion in the previous section, the Service Request Coordinator must forward to Connector Control certain types of client requests based on the current state of the service, as shown in Fig. 4. While the service is active (Fig. 4), the Service Request Coordinator forwards all client requests it receives to Connector Control and also queues these requests in the SPQ.

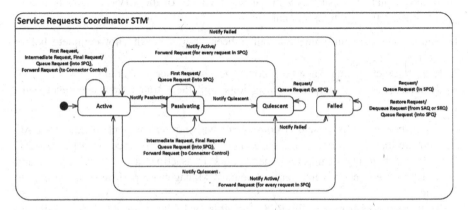

Fig. 4. State Machine executed by Service Request Coordinator [4].

When the Service Request Coordinator is notified that the service is passivating, it transitions to the Passivating state. The behavior of the Service Requests Coordinator while in this state is similar to its behavior in the Active state with one exception: in the Passivating state, the Service Request Coordinator does not forward to Connector Control any requests that initiate a new transaction with the service, and instead, queues such requests in the SPQ. Eventually, the Service Request Coordinator is notified that the service has become quiescent, causing the Service Request Coordinator to transition to the Quiescent state. While in the Quiescent state, the Service Request Coordinator does not forward any requests to Connector Control and instead queues them in the SPQ. Finally, when service adaptation is completed, the Service Request Coordinator receives a notification that the service is active, causing the Service Request Coordinator to transition to the Active state and to forward all requests queued in the SPQ to Connector Control.

When service failures occur, the Service Request Coordinator transitions to the Failed state. While in the Failed state, the Service Request Coordinator holds all client requests it receives in the SPQ. The Service Request Coordinator may also receive messages from the execution activity of MAPE-K to restore any client requests that were lost due to service failure. As a result, the Service Request Coordinator moves these requests from the SRQ and the SAQ to the head of the SPQ so that these requests are resent to the recovered service. Finally, when the service is recovered, the Service Request Coordinator forwards all requests stored in the SPQ and then transitions back to the Active state.

4 Handling Adaptation and Recovery of Stateful Services

This section discusses extending the design of the RAC in Sect. 3 to handle recovery and adaptation of *stateful* services with both idempotent and non-idempotent operations. It is assumed that the state of the stateful service is maintained by a transactional processing system that supports committing, aborting, and preparing transactions [5]. The transactional processing system handles recovery of the service's state to a consistent state by using a transactional log to:

1. Undo all transactions that have either been aborted or did not complete before service failure.
2. Redo transactions that have been committed before service failure.
3. Restore the state of prepared transactions until these transactions are either committed or aborted.

Since the service is a stateful component with non-idempotent operations, RAC must ensure that the service processes a client request exactly once. That is, the RAC must ensure that (1) committing the client's transaction at the service side and (2) updating the queues at the Service Request Manager are performed as an atomic operation.

To achieve this behavior, the RAC forwards each client request to the service by initiating a distributed transaction using the Two-Phase Commit (2PC) protocol [5]. In this approach, Connector Control of the RAC acts as the coordinator of the distributed transaction while the service and the Service Request Coordinator act as participants of this distributed transaction, as explained next.

During normal execution, when there are no failures, the interaction between the RAC and the service is as follows (Fig. 5):

1. When Connector Control of the service RAC (not shown in Fig. 5) receives a client request, it forwards the client request to the service in a 2PC transaction. This request corresponds to the Prepare To Commit message in the 2PC protocol. Connector Control also forwards this request to the Service Request Coordinator, which is a second participant of this 2PC transaction. As a result, the Service Request Coordinator prepares to commit the client request by moving this request from the Service Pending Queue to the Service Active Queue and then acknowledges preparing the transaction to Connector Control.
2. The service prepares to commit the client request and then sends the response to the RAC. The service response corresponds to the Ready To Commit message in the 2PC protocol.

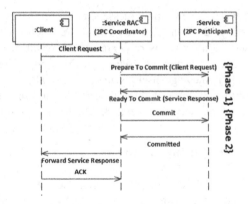

Fig. 5. Handling stateful services using two-phase commit.

3. Connector Control then sends the Commit message to both the service and the Service Request Coordinator. The Service Request Coordinator then commits the transaction by moving the client request from the Service Active Queue to the Service Recovery Queue and then acknowledges committing the transaction to Connector Control.
4. The service commits the prepared transaction and then sends the Committed message to the RAC which completes this 2PC transaction.
5. The RAC forwards the service response to the requesting client.

In this pattern, the service can be dynamically removed or replaced after it has completed all 2PC transactions that it is currently engaged in. When the RAC is notified of a service failure by the monitoring activity, it determines a recovery action for each distributed transaction it has initiated with the service as follows:

- If the RAC has forwarded a client request to the service but the service failure occurred during phase 1 of the 2PC transaction, the RAC restores the client request by moving it from the Service Active Queue to the Service Pending Queue. When the service is recovered, the RAC instructs the recovered service to abort this transaction so that the recovered service aborts the transaction if it has previously been prepared to commit. Note that if the service failed before preparing to commit the transaction, it ignores the Abort message from the RAC. Since the client request is stored back in the Service Pending Queue, then the RAC eventually restarts this transaction with the recovered service.
- If the RAC has received a service response from the service but has not yet forwarded the Commit message to the service (i.e., service failure occurred before initiating phase 2 of the 2PC transaction), then the service must have prepared to commit this transaction before it failed. As a result, the RAC sends the Commit message to the service after it has recovered so that it commits this transaction. When the recovered service commits the transaction, it sends the Committed message to RAC which completes this transaction.

- If the RAC has forwarded the Commit message to the service but the service failure occurred during phase 2 of the 2PC transaction, the RAC resends the Commit message to the service after it has recovered. As a result, the recovered service commits the prepared transaction and sends the Committed message to the RAC. Note that the Commit message itself is idempotent. That is, if the service has committed the transaction before failure, then receiving a duplicate Commit message causes the recovered service to send the Committed message to the RAC.

5   Recovery and Adaptation Patterns

This section describes how the RAC design shown in the previous section can be used to handle adaptation and recovery of components in other architectural patterns [1].

5.1   Asynchronous Message Communication with Callback

Typical client/service communication uses the Synchronous Message Communication with Reply pattern, in which the client sends a message to the service and waits for a response. In the Asynchronous Message Communication with Callback pattern (Fig. 6), a client sends an asynchronous request to the service but can continue executing and receive the service response later. The request sent by the client contains a callback handle that the service uses when it finishes processing the client request so that it can send the response back to the client. A client in this pattern does not send another request to the service until it receives a response to the previous request.

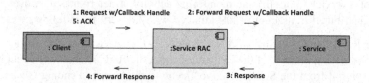

Fig. 6. Asynchronous message communication with callback handle pattern.

Since in this pattern, a client sends one request at a time to the service, the RAC (shown in Fig. 1) handles requests and responses for this pattern in the same way as for synchronous communication with reply. Thus, although the client behaviour is different, the service behaviour is not. For this reason, the adaptation and recovery for the Asynchronous Message Communication with Callback pattern is handled in the same way as described in Sects. 3 and 4.

5.2   Service Registration

In service-oriented architectures, a service registers its name, location and service description with a broker, which acts as an intermediary between the clients and the

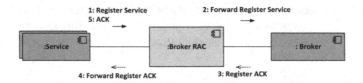

Fig. 7. Service registration pattern.

service. In the Service Registration pattern (Fig. 7), the service initiates a transaction with the broker by sending it a registration request containing the service information. The broker then registers the service and sends an acknowledgement to the service. The service can also re-register with the broker if it moves its location, which requires another transaction between the service and the broker.

From the adaptation and recovery point of view, this pattern can be treated as a client that communicates with a service using the Synchronous Message Communication with Reply pattern. Thus, the adaptation and recovery patterns for this architectural pattern are exactly the same as described in Sects. 3 and 4.

5.3   Broker Handle

After the service has registered with the broker, clients use the broker to locate the service. In the Broker Handle pattern (Fig. 8), a client sends a request to the broker to obtain the service's handle. The broker then sends a response to the client containing the service's handle as a parameter. The client then uses the service's handle to interact with the service.

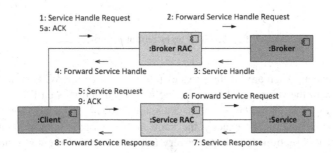

Fig. 8. Broker handle pattern.

In this pattern, a client initiates two sequential transactions by first initiating a transaction with the broker to obtain the service's handle and then by initiating a transaction with the service using the service's callback handle. As a result, these transactions can fail and be recovered independently of each other.

A broker is adapted after it has completed all the requests it has received, including brokering requests from clients requesting a handle and service requests for registration. New requests are held up until the broker has been relocated. In the case of a broker failure, all requests it is dealing with are aborted and only restarted when the broker has been relocated and instantiated. Both adaptation and recovery are carried out as described in Sects. 3 and 4.

5.4   Service-Oriented Architectures

In service-oriented architectures (SOAs), the goal is to increase loose coupling between services so that instead of services depending on each other, coordinators are provided for situations where multiple services need to be accessed, and access to them needs to be coordinated and/or sequenced (see Fig. 9). We consider that the coordinator may interact with the services sequentially and/or concurrently and that the interaction between the coordinator and the multiple services involves a compound transaction that can be broken down into an atomic, independent transaction between the coordinator and each service, as described in the next subsection.

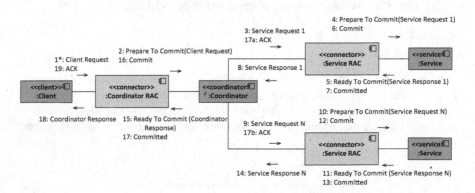

Fig. 9. SOA architectural pattern.

In this pattern, when any of the services fail, the service's RAC restarts each failed transaction with the service without affecting other transactions that the coordinator is currently engaged in with other services. Thus, the recovery and adaptation patterns for services in this pattern are exactly the same as discussed in Sects. 3 and 4. The remainder of this section describes recovery and adaptation of the coordinator.

For coordinators, we assume the general case in which the coordinator is a stateful component. Therefore, the Coordinator RAC must forward client requests to the Coordinator in 2PC transactions using the same approach described Sect. 4 so that updating the Coordinator RAC's queues and updating the Coordinator's internal state is an atomic operation. Therefore, the Coordinator RAC coordinates the 2PC transaction it initiates with the Coordinator while the Coordinator coordinates access to the services. The behavior of the Coordinator RAC and the Coordinator is as follows:

1. When the Coordinator RAC receives a client request (message 1 (m1) in Fig. 9), it forwards this client request to the coordinator in a 2PC transaction (m2). This message corresponds to the Prepare to Commit message in the 2PC protocol.
2. When the Coordinator receives the client request, it initiates a compound transaction, which consists of initiating a constituent atomic transaction with each service.
3. When the Coordinator receives responses from all services (m8 and m14), it prepares to commit the compound transaction it has initiated in the previous step and then sends its response (m15) to the Coordinator RAC. This response corresponds to the Ready To Commit message for the 2PC transaction initiated in step 1.
4. The Coordinator RAC then sends the Commit message (m16) to the Coordinator.
5. The Coordinator then commits the previously prepared compound transaction, sends ACK messages to the service RACs so that these connectors can safely remove messages for this transaction from their queues, and then sends Committed (m17) to the Coordinator RAC. At this point, the 2PC transaction between the Coordinator's RAC and the Coordinator is completed.
6. The Coordinator's RAC sends the Coordinator's response to the client (m18).

Adaptation and Recovery of Coordinators. In the case of a client interacting with a coordinator, if the coordinator needs to be adapted, then the client request needs to be completed before adaptation. This means that the entire 2PC transaction between the Coordinator RAC and the Coordinator must complete before adaptation can take place, since completion of this 2PC transaction ensures that the last compound transaction initiated by the coordinator is also completed.

In the case of coordinator failure, when the coordinator is recovered, the recovered coordinator must abort the last compound transaction it initiated, if this compound transaction has not been prepared to commit before failure. Since the interaction between the coordinator's RAC and the coordinator involves a 2PC transaction, then the coordinator's RAC executes similar recovery actions to those described in Sect. 4 to recover this 2PC transaction in case it failed, as follows:

- If the Coordinator RAC has forwarded a client request to the Coordinator but the coordinator failure occurred during phase 1 of the 2PC transaction, the coordinator RAC saves the client request by moving it from the Coordinator Active Queue to the Coordinator Pending Queue. When the coordinator is recovered, the coordinator RAC instructs the recovered coordinator to abort this transaction so that the recovered coordinator aborts the compound transaction, even if it has been prepared to commit. Since the client request is stored in the Coordinator Pending Queue, then eventually the coordinator's RAC restarts this transaction with the recovered coordinator. Since transactions to coordinators can be restarted, a recovered coordinator may send duplicate requests to Service RACs. These Service RACs detect and discard duplicate requests by comparing message sequence numbers of incoming messages with previously received messages. Furthermore, if responses of duplicate requests are queued in the Response Recovery Queue (RRQ), then these service RACs resend these responses to the recovered coordinator. Note that from Fig. 9, a service RAC does not discard a service response for any transaction until it receives an ACK message from the coordinator that initiated this transaction.

Because a coordinator sends ACK messages to service RACs only after it has committed the compound transaction it initiated, this ensures that a service RAC can always recover responses of the duplicate requests it receives from recovered coordinators. Note that if a Service RAC does not maintain in its RRQ the response of a duplicate request, the service RAC forwards the response to the coordinator after it receives this response from the service.

- If the coordinator RAC has received a ready to commit response from the coordinator but has not yet sent the Commit message to the coordinator (i.e., a coordinator failure occurred before initiating phase 2 of the 2PC transaction), the coordinator must have prepared to commit this distributed transaction before it failed. As a result, the coordinator's RAC sends the Commit message to the recovered coordinator for this distributed transaction so that it commits this transaction. When the recovered coordinator commits the transaction, it sends the Committed message to the coordinator RAC, which completes this transaction.
- If the coordinator RAC has forwarded the Commit message to the coordinator but has not yet received the Committed message (i.e., a coordinator failure occurred during phase 2 of the 2PC transaction), the coordinator's RAC resends the Commit message to the recovered coordinator. As a result, the recovered coordinator commits the prepared transaction, sends ACK messages to the service RACs, and then sends the Committed message to the coordinator's RAC.

6 Validation

The design of the RAC has been validated through experiments based on the Online Shopping System case study [1], which is an example of a service-oriented architecture. In this case study, customers can request to purchase items from suppliers. Several services are involved to carry out purchase requests such as the Customer Account Service, Delivery Order Service, Catalog Service, and Credit Card Service. Therefore, coordinators are used to facilitate integration of these services.

In these experiments, each component and RAC was implemented in Java and has a separate thread of control. In addition, Java Sockets were used for message delivery. The implemented architecture runs on a cluster consisting of 30 nodes. Thus, both components and RACs are concurrent and distributed in these experiments. In addition, we used MySQL as a transactional processing system that provides the Two Phase Commit interface for coordinator and service components. Each component uses this interface to actually prepare, commit, and abort the messages it receives from its RAC. The use of MySQL at each component was made out of expedience. In practice, one would implement 2PC without requiring all the complexity of a full Database Management System (DBMS) (Fig. 10).

6.1 Service Failure Scenario

The service failure scenario demonstrates the ability of the service RAC to recover failed transactions. In this scenario, the Delivery Order Service (DOS) is concurrently processing four transactions, which are in different states at the time of failure, as

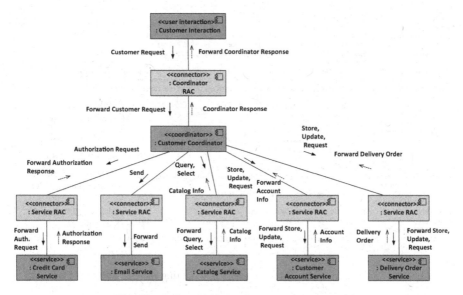

Fig. 10. Online Shopping System case study [1].

described below. This experiment validates the failure recovery scenarios described in Sect. 4. The execution trace (Fig. 11) indicates that DOS fails while it is engaged in four transactions as follows:

- Transaction t1: this transaction failed after the Service RAC has sent the Prepare to Commit message to the service but before this RAC has received the Ready To Commit message from the service. Note that in this case, the service could have failed either (1) before preparing to commit this transaction, (2) after preparing to commit the transaction but before sending Ready To Commit to the RAC, or (3) after sending Ready To Commit to the RAC such that this response was lost due to service failure. Although these three cases are not distinguishable from the RAC's point of view, the RAC executes the same recovery actions to recover these cases.

- Transaction t2: this transaction failed after the service RAC has received the Ready To Commit message from the service but before this RAC has forwarded the Commit message to the service.

- Transaction t3: this transaction failed after the RAC has sent the Commit message to the service but before receiving the Committed message from the service. Therefore, the service could have failed either (1) before committing this transaction, (2) after committing the transaction but before sending Committed to the RAC, or (3) after sending Committed to the RAC such that this response was lost due to service failure. Although these three cases are not distinguishable from the RAC's point of view, the RAC executes the same recovery actions to recover these cases.

- Transaction t4: this transaction failed after the service RAC has received the Committed message from the service.

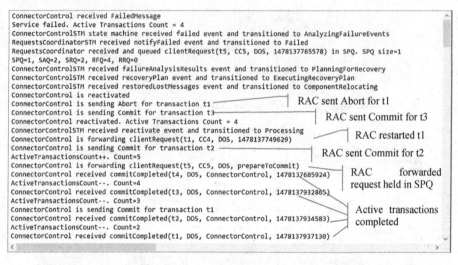

Fig. 11. Fragment of the execution trace of RAC during planned failure scenario.

In addition to these four transactions, the RAC received a fifth transaction (t5) after it was notified by the monitoring activity of service failure. Upon arrival, the request t5 is held by the RAC in the SPQ. In this scenario, the execution trace (Fig. 11) indicates that the content of the RAC's queues is as follows:

The SPQ contains one request that was held due to service failure:

– Request(t5, CC5, DOS) where t5 is the identifier of the transaction, CC5 is the identifier of the message sender, and DOS is the identifier of the message recipient.

The SAQ contains two prepare to commit requests that have been forwarded to the service:

– Request(t2, CC1, DOS)
– Request(t1, CC4, DOS)

The SRQ contains two commit requests as follows:

– Request(t4, CC2, DOS)
– Request(t3, CC3, DOS)

The RFQ contains four received responses:

– ReadyToCommit(t2, DOS, CC1)
– ReadyToCommit(t4, DOS, CC2)
– Committed(t4, DOS, ConnectorControl)
– ReadyToCommit(t3, DOS, CC3)

RRQ does not indicate any responses that have been forwarded to clients.

During the analysis activity which is handled in the Analyzing Failure Events state (Fig. 3), the execution log indicates that the RAC determined a status for each of these active transactions as follows:

- For transaction t1, the RAC determined the status of this transaction as *Preparing*, since the SAQ contains the Prepare To Commit request to the service but neither the RFQ nor the RRQ contain the Ready To Commit response for this transaction.
- For transaction t2, the RAC determined the status of this transaction as *Prepared*, since the SAQ contains the Prepare To Commit request to the service and the RFQ contains the Ready To Commit response for this transaction.
- For transaction t3, the RAC determined the status of this transaction as *Committing*, since the SRQ contains the Commit request for this transaction but neither the RFQ nor the RRQ queues contain the Committed response for this transaction.
- For transaction t4, the RAC determined the status of this transaction as *Committed*, since the SRQ contains the Commit request to the service for this transaction and the RFQ contains a Committed response for this transaction.

During the planning activity which is handled in the Planning for Recovery state (Fig. 3), the RAC determined recovery actions for each active transaction as follows:

- For transaction t1, since this transaction failed while being prepared to commit by the service during the first phase of 2PC, the recovery actions determined by the RAC for this transaction after service recovery were (1) to abort this transaction with the service and then (2) to restart this transaction with the recovered service.
- For transaction t2, since this transaction failed after being prepared to commit by the service, the RAC will eventually send the Commit message for this transaction when the service has recovered.
- For transaction t3, since the service failed while committing this transaction, the recovery action determined by the RAC for this transaction was to resend the Commit message to the recovered service.
- Transaction t4 does not require any recovery actions since it was completed before service failure.

During the execution phase which is handled in the Executing Recovery Plan state (Fig. 3), the service RAC restored the requests of the transactions that must be restarted with the recovered service by moving these requests from the SAQ to the head of SPQ. In this scenario, only transaction t1 needs to be restarted with the recovered service. Therefore, the execution log indicates that this message is moved from the SAQ to the SPQ. The content of SPQ after restoration is:

- Prepare(t1, CC4, DOS) //recovered request which was restored from the SAQ
- Prepare(t5, CC5, DOS) //request held in the SPQ due to service failure

When the RAC is reactivated after the service has recovered, the execution trace indicates that the RAC aborted and then restarted transaction t1 with the recovered service, (2) requested the recovered service to commit transactions t2 and t3, and (3) forwarded transaction t5 which was previously held in the SPQ due to service failure.

The execution trace indicates that service execution resumed normally and that all active transactions were eventually committed.

6.2   Service Adaptation Scenario

To illustrate the behavior of the service RAC during adaptation, we use an adaptation scenario that involves adapting the DOS. This experiment validates the adaptation scenario described in Sect. 4. In this scenario, the DOS is concurrently processing four transactions, which are in different states at the time of adaptation, as described below. In this scenario, the service RAC received the Passivate command from an external Change Manager (which oversees the adaptation process) [9] while the service is engaged in the following four active transactions:

- Transactions t1 and t2: service passivation is requested after the Service RAC has sent the Prepare To Commit messages for these transactions to the service but before this RAC has received the Ready To Commit responses from the service.
- Transactions t3 and t4: service passivation is requested after the service RAC has sent the Commit messages for these transactions to the service but before it has received the Committed responses from the service.

When service adaptation is requested, the content of the RAC queues are as follows:
The SPQ does not contain any requests held by the service RAC.
The SAQ contains two prepare to commit requests sent to the service:

- Request(t1, CC3, DOS)
- Request(t2, CC2, DOS)

The SRQ contains two commit requests sent to the service:

- Request(t3, CC4, DOS)
- Request(t4, CC1, DOS)

The RFQ contains two service responses as follows:

- ReadyToCommit(t3, DOS, CC4)
- ReadyToCommit(t4, DOS, CC1)

The RRQ does not indicate any responses that have been forwarded to clients.

As a result of passivation, the execution trace indicates that the service RAC transitioned into the Passivating state (Fig. 3) where it permitted these four active transactions to gradually terminate. While in Passivating state, a new request was received and queued by the Service RAC into the SPQ. After the service completed all active transactions, the execution trace indicates that the Service RAC transitioned to the Quiescent state (Fig. 3) at which time the service was dynamically replaced. During the adapting state, further requests are received and queued by RAC. After adaptation is completed, the service RAC received the reactivate command. As a result, the RAC transitioned to the Active state and forwarded all queued requests in its SPQ to the service. At this point, normal execution is resumed between RAC and the service (Fig. 12).

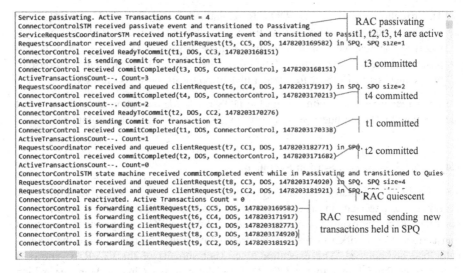

Fig. 12. Fragment of the execution trace of RAC during planned adaptation scenario.

6.3 Coordinator Recovery Scenario

The coordinator failure scenario demonstrates the ability of the coordinator RAC to recover failed transactions. In this scenario, the Customer Coordinator (CC) fails while processing one transaction from Customer Interaction (CI). Furthermore, failure of CC occurred after the CC has initiated the following three sequential transactions:

1. Before failure, the CC initiated a transaction with the Customer Account Service (CAS) and received the response of this transaction from this service.
2. Before failure, the CC initiated a transaction with the Credit Card Service (CCS) and received the response of this transaction from this service.
3. Before failure, the CC initiated a transaction with the DOS. However, the CC failed before receiving the response of this transaction from this service.

In this recovery scenario, the execution trace (not shown due to space limitation) indicates that when the CC has recovered, the coordinator RAC (1) instructed the recovered CC to abort the CI transaction and then (2) restarted this transaction with the recovered CC. Furthermore, the execution trace of the CAS RAC, CCS RAC, and DOS RAC indicate that these RACs received duplicate requests from the recovered CC. The RAC of each of these services reacted to these duplicate requests as follows:

1. The execution trace of the CAS RAC indicates that this RAC discarded the duplicate request and sent back to the recovered CC the response of this request using its Response Recovery Queue (RRQ).
2. The execution trace of the CCS RAC indicates that this RAC discarded this duplicate request and sent back to the recovered CC the response of this request using its Response Recovery Queue (RRQ).

3. The execution trace of the DOS RAC indicates that this RAC discarded the duplicate request. The execution trace also showed that this RAC has not yet received the response of the original request from the DOS (i.e., DOS is still processing the original request). Therefore when this RAC received the response of this request from DOS, it forwarded that response to the recovered CC.

After receiving the response from the DOS RAC, the execution trace showed that the recovered CC continued working on this transaction until it has completed.

6.4 Coordinator Adaptation Scenario

The coordinator adaptation scenario is an experiment to validate the adaptation of the coordinator as described in Sect. 5. In this scenario, the CC RAC received the passivate command from the external Change Manager while the CC is preparing to commit a transaction. As described in Sect. 5, the transaction must complete before the coordinator can be replaced. The execution trace (not shown) of the CC RAC shows a Passivate command sent to the CC RAC by the external Change Manager, which results in the CC RAC transitioning from Processing state to Passivating state. When the transaction ended with the sending of the coordinator response to the client, the state machine transitioned to the Quiescent state. While the CC RAC is in quiescent state, it received and queued a new transaction from the CI in the Coordinator Pending Queue.

After replacing CC, the CC RAC received the reactivate message from the external Change Manager and then transitioned from the Quiescent to the Waiting for Request state. When the Request Coordinator of the CC RAC is also reactivated, which caused it to transition from the Quiescent state to the Active state, it forwarded the queued transaction to Connector Control. Connector Control then transitioned to Processing state and handled this transaction normally as described in Sect. 5.

7 Related Work

Approaches to self-healing, self-configuration, and autonomic systems have been the subject of many recent studies. However, the focus of most of these studies has been on centralized approaches [11]. Nonetheless, decentralized approaches are more applicable to SOAs due to high autonomy, loose coupling, and heterogeneity of services. One challenge with decentralized approaches, however, is carrying out adaptation with only partial knowledge of the system [12]. In this research, we consider that none of the nodes has a complete view of the transactions exchanged between application components. Instead, knowledge of transactions is distributed among multiple RACs to increase decentralization such that each RAC maintains only knowledge of transactions to its component. As a result, a RAC can handle adaptation and recovery concerns of its component independently of other RACs.

A survey of self-healing systems [13] states that a core problem in these systems is the integration of the self-healing property with other self-* properties. This paper tackles this problem by investigating how self-healing and self-configuration approaches, which are described next, can be integrated with the help of a RAC.

In the area of self-configuration and dynamic software adaptation, prior work by Kramer and Magee investigated how a component must transition to a quiescent state before it can be safely adapted [9]. Based on this quiescence property, it is possible to define adaptation patterns for various architectural patterns. For instance, Gomaa et al. defined several adaptation patterns for SOAs including patterns for different types of service coordination and distributed transactions [2, 3, 8]. In addition, Ramirez et al. discussed various reconfiguration patterns for self-adaptive systems [14]. The use of connectors for reconfiguring service connections without affecting application execution was proposed by Li et al. [15].

Self-healing is a broad concept that includes a wide range of different approaches including reactive and proactive [16] self-healing that target different types of problems such as software aging and transient faults [17], performance degradation [18], and software faults [19]. Due to the wide spectrum of prior works done in the area of self-healing, we highlight some of the prior works that focus on self-healing in service-oriented architectures that are capable of handling fail-stop failures. Interested readers can refer to existing, more extensive self-healing surveys for other approaches (e.g., [13]). In the area of self-healing for SOAs, Danilecki et al. suggest a tailored rollback recovery protocol for the distinctive characteristics of SOAs [20]. Their approach consists of requesting the service for available checkpoints and then instructing the service to roll back to a consisting state using one of these checkpoints. In this paper, we assume that services cannot be queried for checkpoints. However, we assume that services are transactional [5]. Therefore, recovery is done on a transaction-by-transaction basis. Prior works also investigated extending BPEL with self-healing capabilities [21, 22]. Angarita et al. investigated multiple recovery strategies for recovering web services including retry, replication, and checkpointing [23]. Salatge et al. suggest the use of fault-tolerance connectors to increase service dependability in SOAs [24]. However, none of these works considered integrating self-configuration, by driving the service state to a quiescent state, with self-healing capabilities. Platform-dependent self-healing approaches are also possible. For instance, Candea et al. investigated expanding JBoss application services with self-healing capabilities [25]. In this paper, we consider platform-independent design of RACs.

Compared to the above approaches, the focus of this paper is to investigate the problem of integrating adaptation and recovery patterns for SOAs, which is an area that has received little attention in the literature. Furthermore, we consider embedding adaptation and recovery state machines in connectors rather than application components to achieve higher degrees of reuse and separation of concerns.

8 Conclusions

This paper described recovery and adaptation patterns for various SOA patterns. To increase reuse of these patterns, we developed an integrated recovery and adaptation state machine and embedded this state machine into a Recovery and Adaptation connector (RAC), so that recovery and adaptation concerns are separated from service and coordination concerns. To increase decentralization of our approach, we designed each RAC so that it can handle recovery and adaptation of its component autonomously and independently of other RACs.

The contributions of this paper are (1) the design of the RAC and (2) the experimentation results of the RAC design, which show the ability of the RAC to handle adaptation and recovery of both services and coordinators under different failure and adaptation scenarios.

The focus of this paper has been on recovery of transactions and architecture adaptation. We are currently investigating how the recovery of components can be further automated using DeSARM [26], a decentralized software architecture discovery mechanism. Furthermore, we are working on extending the RAC design so that it can also handle recovery and adaptation of components in asynchronous architectural patterns, such as the master/slave and control patterns, in which the RAC does not receive responses from its component. Future work also includes handling concurrent node failures and tolerating failures of RACs using replication techniques. In addition, we are investigating recovery of distributed transactions that involve updates at more than one service. Finally, we are considering the design of a universal RAC that is capable of handling recovery and adaptation of components in different architectural patterns and formally proving recovery and adaptation properties of the RAC.

Acknowledgments. This work is partially supported by the AFOSR award FA9550-16-1-0030.

References

1. Gomaa, H.: Software Modeling and Design: UML, Use Cases, Patterns, and Software Architectures. Cambridge University Press, Cambridge (2011)
2. Gomaa, H., Hashimoto, K., Kim, M., Malek, S., Menascé, D.A.: Software adaptation patterns for service-oriented architectures. In: Proceedings of the 2010 ACM Symposium on Applied Computing, pp. 462–469. ACM, New York (2010)
3. Gomaa, H., Hashimoto, K.: Dynamic self-adaptation for distributed service-oriented transactions. In: Proceedings of the 7th International Symposium on Software Engineering for Adaptive and Self-Managing Systems. IEEE Press, Piscataway (2012)
4. Albassam, E., Gomaa, H., Menascé, D.A.: Model-based recovery connectors for self-adaptation and self-healing. In: Maciaszek, L.A., Cardoso, J.S., Ludwig, A., van Sinderen, M., Cabello, E. (eds.) Proc of the 11th International Joint Conference on Software Technologies (ICSOFT 2016) - ICSOFT-EA, Lisbon, Portugal, 24–26 July 2016, vol. 1. SciTePress (2016)
5. Bernstein, P.A., Newcomer, E.: Principles of Transaction Processing, 2nd edn. Morgan Kaufmann, Burlington (2009)
6. Kephart, J.O., Chess, D.M.: The vision of autonomic computing. Computer. **36**, 41–50 (2003)
7. Taylor, R.N., Medvidovic, N., Dashofy, E.M.: Software Architecture: Foundations, Theory, and Practice. Wiley, Hoboken (2009)

8. Gomaa, H., Hussein, M.: Software reconfiguration patterns for dynamic evolution of software architectures. In: Fourth Working IEEE/IFIP Conference on Software Architecture (2004)
9. Kramer, J., Magee, J.: The evolving philosophers problem: dynamic change management. IEEE Trans. Softw. Eng. **16**, 1293–1306 (1990)
10. Avizienis, A., Laprie, J.-C., Randell, B., Landwehr, C.: Basic concepts and taxonomy of dependable and secure computing. IEEE Trans. Dependable Secure Comput. **1**, 11–33 (2004)
11. Lemos, R., Giese, H., et al.: Software engineering for self-adaptive systems: a second research roadmap. In: Lemos, R., Giese, H., Müller, Hausi A., Shaw, M. (eds.) Software Engineering for Self-Adaptive Systems II. LNCS, vol. 7475, pp. 1–32. Springer, Heidelberg (2013). doi:10.1007/978-3-642-35813-5_1
12. Krupitzer, C., Roth, F.M., VanSyckel, S., Schiele, G., Becker, C.: A survey on engineering approaches for self-adaptive systems. Pervasive Mob. Comput. **17**, 184–206 (2015)
13. Schneider, C., Barker, A., Dobson, S.: A survey of self-healing systems frameworks. Softw. Pract. Exp. **45**, 1375–1398 (2015)
14. Ramirez, A.J., Cheng, B.H.C.: Design patterns for developing dynamically adaptive systems. In: Proceedings of the 2010 ICSE Workshop on Software Engineering for Adaptive and Self-Managing Systems, pp. 49–58. ACM, New York (2010)
15. Li, G., Han, Y., Zhao, Z., Wang, J., Wagner, R.M.: Facilitating dynamic service compositions by adaptable service connectors. Int. J. Web Serv. Res. **3**, 68–84 (2006)
16. Huebscher, M.C., McCann, J.A.: A survey of autonomic computing-degrees, models, and applications. ACM Comput. Surv. **40**, 7:1–7:28 (2008)
17. Silva, L.M., Alonso, J., Torres, J.: Using Virtualization to Improve Software Rejuvenation. IEEE Trans. Comput. **58**, 1525–1538 (2009)
18. Magalhães, J.P., Silva, L.M.: SHÕWA: a self-healing framework for web-based applications. ACM Trans. Auton. Adapt. Syst. **10**, 4:1–428 (2015)
19. Bruning, S., Weissleder, S., Malek, M.: A fault taxonomy for service-oriented architecture. In: 10th IEEE High Assurance Systems Engineering Symposium, HASE 2007 (2007)
20. Danilecki, A., Holenko, M., Kobusińska, A., Szychowiak, M., Zierhoffer, P.: Applying message logging to support fault-tolerance of SOA systems. Found. Comput. Decis. Sci. **38**, 145–158 (2013)
21. Subramanian, S., Thiran, P., Narendra, N.C., Mostefaoui, G.K., Maamar, Z.: On the Enhancement of BPEL engines for self-healing composite web services. In: International Symposium on Applications and the Internet. SAINT 2008, pp. 33–39 (2008)
22. Modafferi, S., Conforti, E.: Methods for enabling recovery actions in Ws-BPEL. In: Meersman, R., Tari, Z. (eds.) OTM 2006. LNCS, vol. 4275, pp. 219–236. Springer, Heidelberg (2006). doi:10.1007/11914853_14
23. Angarita, R., Rukoz, M., Cardinale, Y.: Modeling dynamic recovery strategy for composite web services execution. World Wide Web **19**, 89–109 (2016)
24. Salatge, N., Fabre, J.-C.: Fault tolerance connectors for unreliable web services. In: 37th IEEE/IFIP International Conference on Dependable Systems and Networks (2007)
25. Candea, G., Kiciman, E., Zhang, S., Fox, A., Keyani, P., Fox, O.: JAGR: An Autonomous Self-Recovering Application Server (2003)
26. Porter, J., Menasce, D., Gomaa, H.: DeSARM: a decentralized software architecture discovery mechanism for distributed systems. In: Presented at the 11th International Workshop on Models@run.time (MODELS 2016), Saint-Malo, France, 4 October 2016

Supporting Visual Data Exploration via Interactive Constraints

Wendy Lucas[✉] and Taylor Gordon

Bentley University, Waltham, MA, USA
{wlucas, Gordon_taylor}@bentley.edu

Abstract. This work aims to bridge the gap between the goals of the users of information visualization systems and the techniques that are currently available to them for interacting with force-directed layouts. We propose that the benefits from applying positional constraints to graphical objects extend beyond their typical use in network graphs. In particular, a constraint-based approach can be an effective means for aiding users in exploring multivariate data that, by its nature, is difficult to present effectively. Providing easy to use and understand slider components for specifying the strength of constraints applied in a layout gives users the ability to subtly control graphic object positioning. Objects can be filtered and automatically grouped based on the value of one or more properties, with each property representing a different data variable. Applying different constraint strengths to these groups provides an effective means for identifying commonalities and patterns in multivariate data.

Keywords: Force-directed layouts · Interactive data exploration · Constraint specification · Multivariate data

1 Introduction

Constraint-based approaches to graph layouts are most frequently applied to network diagrams. Typically, the goal is to generate aesthetically pleasing layouts that aid users in identifying and exploring relationships between nodes and node groupings. Force-directed algorithms help to minimize the crossing of links while clustering related nodes together. The resulting graphs support many data exploration activities, such as identifying authorities and hubs in a network community [2] or finding patterns and anomalies [3].

This type of approach is not usually applied, however, in those cases where the locations of the individual graphical objects representing the data being visualized also convey meaning. One issue is that a force-directed layout is continuously in motion and will not necessarily be in the same configuration each time it is rendered. Furthermore, user interactions can also affect the layout in indeterminate ways. Thus, while the positions of graphic objects in a force-directly layout can be useful in discovering relationships between elements, it is less helpful in revealing information about the underlying data properties represented by a particular graphical object.

Another issue with applying constraint-based approaches to layouts beyond network graphs is the limited means available to users for controlling the outcome. The

© Springer International Publishing AG 2017
E. Cabello et al. (Eds.): ICSOFT 2016, CCIS 743, pp. 132–152, 2017.
DOI: 10.1007/978-3-319-62569-0_7

most common means available for interacting with objects in a force-directed layout include:

- Dragging on a node or node grouping. This can affect not only the positions of the objects with which the user interacts, but potentially all other objects in the layout. Thus, users cannot know with any certainty the effects their interactions will have on the layout.
- Jiggling a node. A quick back and forth motion applied to a node can be helpful for untangling links that have crossed but can also cause unpredictable changes in the layout.

It is the algorithm underlying the layout, rather than the user, that ultimately determines the configuration of the nodes and links that are typically being represented. Such algorithms often model nodes as charged particles that repel each other, with links acting as dampened springs that pull related nodes together [4]. The position of each node is then calculated to maintain an equilibrium that minimizes the overall kinetic energy in the graph.

In most cases, the user will know little if anything about the algorithm that is controlling a force-directed layout. The varying ways in which forces may be exerted on the graphical components in the layout are also not obvious. While it may be possible to configure the strengths of the forces being applied programmatically, it is unlikely that the typical user will have the skills and knowledge to do so. Sophisticated users can add their own widgets for manipulating layouts, but this is also not an option for the majority of users who do not have that expertise [5].

The motivation for the work presented here is based on the premise that force-directed layouts should not be limited primarily to network diagrams; rather, users should be able to apply force-based constraints to any graphic object in any type of layout. In layouts involving multivariate data (i.e., datasets containing more than three variables), such constraint-based approaches can be particularly beneficial for supporting exploration and presentation activities.

In order to make a constraint-based approach to visualization accessible to everyone, mechanisms that are intuitive and easy to use are needed that allow the user to:

- Manipulate the strength of the constraints applied to all graphic objects in the layout.
- Form groups of graphic objects based on user-specified criteria and apply different constraint strengths to each group.
- Exert control over the constraint-solving process so that the user can interact with objects in a layout without interference.
- Return a layout to its pre-constrained state, regardless of any changes that may have occurred to that layout due to the constraint-solving process and/or user manipulation.

We contend that, if users can apply constraint-based approaches to layouts beyond network graphs and are able to subtly manipulate object positioning, a door will be opened into new and unanticipated ways for exploring and interacting with data. Providing additional tools for object selection, grouping, and filtering serves to further empower users in data exploration and presentation activities. Supporting user creativity is an emerging and important direction for computing research and development [6].

The approach described in this paper is built upon a declarative language that enables the specification of visual layouts by tying graphical objects to data values via a scaling function [7]. The actual placement of objects is influenced by the strengths of the constraints applied to them in conjunction with user manipulation. The language specification currently supports the following five constraint types, as noted in [1]: equality, approximate equality (henceforth referred to as near), non-overlap, and horizontal and vertical alignment.

The language has been implemented in a proof-of-concept information visualization (Infovis) prototype. In addition to interacting with graphical objects via standard mouse movements, the user can manipulate slider components in the interface to control the strength of the constraints being exerted on those objects. An earlier version of the language and prototype were used in an initial empirical study with eleven participants. It demonstrated the usefulness of the slider-based approach to controlling the layout of a force-directed tree graph that was subjected to conflicting constraints [8].

This paper is an expanded version of [1], in which we demonstrated the application of constraints in visual layouts that were not limited to network graphs. The controls that were introduced in [1] allow the user to:

- Pause and resume the constraint solving process. This leaves the user free to explore the underlying properties represented by the graphic objects without the risk of making inadvertent changes to the layout.
- Apply a bounding box constraint to confine graphic objects to a specified area.
- Use a free-form "lasso" tool to add graphic objects to a group.
- Manipulate the strength of the constraints being applied to the graphic objects in a group, either while the constraint-solving process is running or when it has been paused.

We introduce here the means for filtering graphic objects based on the values of one or more data attributes. If the user so chooses, those objects can be automatically grouped together. After the user applies a filter, the color intensity of non-selected objects decreases, so they fade into the background while the selected objects stand out. Thus, users can easily identify objects with particular characteristics.

If the user chooses the automatic grouping option, then the filtered objects appear in a grouping box, just as if they had been selected with the lasso tool mentioned above. Alternatively, filters can be applied after groups have been formed in order to identify previously unspecified property values that objects both within and outside of groups may have in common.

The ability to manipulate the strength of the constraints applied to a filtered group can be used to declutter a presentation; discover patterns and other shared characteristics amongst objects in the group; and visually differentiate between those objects and others in the layout with different attribute values. Objects can be easily removed from groupings and constraints on their positions can be reset to restore the original layout.

In the next section of this paper, we discuss related work. We then present the visual interface and demonstrate by example the mechanisms provided for specifying constraint strengths, grouping graphic objects, and filtering objects based on attribute values. This is followed by application examples that highlight the benefits of our proposed approach. We conclude by summarizing the contributions of this work and discussing directions for future research.

2   Related Work

Earlier research that laid the groundwork for the approach presented here for user control of positional constraints include [9–11]. GLIDE [9] is an interactive tool for drawing small graphs, where node positioning is governed by "macro" constraints (or Visual Organization Features) such as alignment, sequential placement, even spacing, etc. The constraint-based authoring tool described in [10] focuses on large networks. It allows the author to manipulate similar constraints as those supported by GLIDE, but also provides two higher-level styling tools that automatically generate placement constraints. The author can then modify the layout by removing some or all of those constraints. Dunnart [11], another constraint-based authoring tool, supports horizontal and vertical alignment and distribution constraints; horizontal and vertical sequencing constraints; and an "anchor" tool for fixing the position of one or more objects. The author can also manipulate sliders to change parameters of a goal function that measures the quality of a layout, such as the minimum separation between nodes connected by directed edges.

A primary difference between the above approaches and the one described in this article is that the former focus solely on network layouts. While the use of sliders in Dunnart is similar to our use here for controlling the strength of the constraints that govern object positioning, no mechanism exists in Dunnart for selecting particular objects and limiting changes in parameter values to only those objects.

More typically, sliders are used in dynamic queries for narrowing the range of data points to be selected [12, 13]. They are one of a number of widgets that provide users of commercial visualization tools, such as Tableau, Spotfire, and QlikView, with the means for filtering ordinal, quantitative, and temporal data [14].

While filtering alone does not provide users with control over graphic object positioning, it does reveal those items with shared attribute values. It is one of the three steps in Shneiderman's Information Seeking Mantra [15]: *Overview first, zoom and filter, then details-on-demand*. These capabilities allow users to explore visualizations that have already been rendered in accordance with a predefined layout.

According to Yi et al. [12], the intent of interaction in information visualization can be categorized as: *select* (mark something of interest), *explore* (show something else), *reconfigure* (show a different arrangement), *encode* (show a different representation), *abstract/elaborate* (show more or less detail), *filter* (show something conditionally) and *connect* (show related items). Thus, users may choose a different representation or arrangement for their data and can apply filters for showing only those items that have particular property values. They cannot, however, control their placement within the selected representation.

A less commonly used interaction technique that does affect positioning is referred to as the "jitter" operation, which allows the user to apply jitter to items in a visualization. Those items will then randomly shift by a small spatial increment, thus revealing other items that may have previously been hidden. This operation is supported in Spotfire [16]. In our approach, increasing the strength of a non-overlap constraint while keeping objects close to their original positions by maintaining the near constraint will achieve the same result.

The Dust & Magnet (DnM) multivariate information visualization technique [17] has the most in common with our approach, in that user interactions affect not only the selection but also the positioning of items with particular attribute values. DnM is based on a magnet metaphor, in which data items are visualized as specks of iron that move when the user manipulates "magnets" representing data attributes. As the user drags a magnet across the screen, all dust particles with matching attribute values are attracted to it. More than one magnet can be added to the screen, so even though the user can manipulate only one magnet at a time, each particle can be attracted toward multiple magnets simultaneously. The influence, or magnitude, of a magnet is controllable by a slider. Magnets can also repel dust particles, with another slider controlling the repellent threshold. The user can also change the size or color of a dust particle to reflect attribute values.

The approach described in this paper allows the user to vary the strength of positional constraints applied to all and/or selected graphic objects in a layout. Groups of objects can be formed based on shared attribute values, and different constraints can be specified for each group. Thus, the user is able to manipulate a presentation to highlight different properties of the data, as represented by visual attributes. In addition, layouts are not limited to one particular type of graph, as demonstrated in this paper. The constraint-solving process can also be paused to allow further exploration of the current configuration, and constraints can be reset to return a graph to its original layout. The flexibility of this approach and the control it gives to users over object positioning differentiate it from the other work described here.

3 Applying and Manipulating Constraints

In this section, we describe the prototype Infovis interface and the controls it provides for specifying the strength of the constraints that can be enforced on a layout. We demonstrate by example how the user can explore the datasets represented by graphic objects via constraint manipulation and filtering. Lastly, we show how the user can group objects by either selecting them with a lasso tool or by adding a filter on their data properties. A different set of constraint strengths can then be applied to each grouping, thereby highlighting relationships and patterns in the data being represented.

3.1 Interface Components

The Infovis prototype is comprised of three detachable panels: a coding window, a canvas, and a panel for controlling constraints. The coding window is where users can create, edit, and run programs written in the language described in [7]. The output from running that code is rendered in the canvas. A specification for visualizing Anscombe's quartet [18] and the resulting layout are shown in Fig. 1.

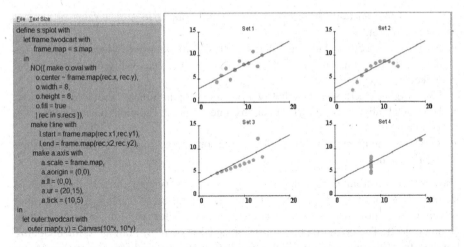

Fig. 1. Interface panels in Infovis prototype include a coding window and a canvas where the visualization is rendered.

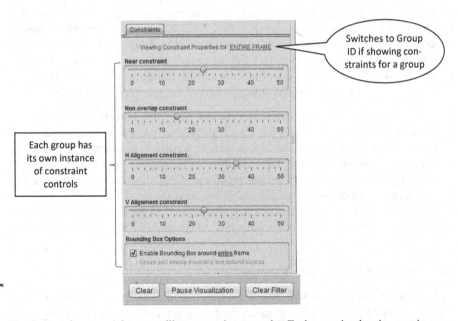

Fig. 2. Interface panel for controlling constraint strengths. Each grouping has its own instance of slider values. The bottom of the interface includes the buttons for clearing the drawing canvas shown in Fig. 1, for pausing the constraint-solving process, and for clearing any filters that have been applied.

The third panel has controls for manipulating constraint strengths, as shown in Fig. 2. The five positional constraints identified earlier in this paper that have been implemented in the language specification are defined as follows [1]:

- Equality (=): anchors the position of a graphic object to a data value or another graphic object.
- Near (~): specifies that a graphic object should be within close proximity (as defined in the constraint resolution algorithm) of a data value or another visual object.
- Non-overlap (NO): specifies that two or more graphic objects should not overlap.
- Horizontal alignment (HAlign): aligns one or more graphic objects along the x-dimension.
- Vertical alignment (VAlign): aligns one or more graphic objects along the y-dimension.

The equality constraint is not controllable by a slider, as its strength is absolute. Each of the other four constraints is unenforced when its slider is set to 0 and is at its maximum value when its slider is set to 50. There are also controls for specifying a bounding box around objects. The bounding box constraint is either on or off. In Fig. 2, the bounding box constraint around the entire frame (i.e., the drawing canvas shown in Fig. 1) has been selected. The constraints exerted on the objects to keep them within the frame will counteract the positional constraints that may be pushing them outward.

If a user creates a grouping of objects, as described in the next section, and then clicks anywhere in that group, the panel in Fig. 2 will be updated to show the values of the constraints applied to the objects in that group. The heading will also change to identify the group (such as Group 1). Clicking anywhere in the canvas outside of the group will reset the constraints panel to showing the values for the overall frame.

There are three buttons located at the bottom of the interface (see Fig. 2):

- *Clear* terminates the visualization process and clears the drawing canvas.
- *Pause Visualization* suspends the constraint-solving process. The user can then interact with the objects in the layout without having to counteract the forces in effect on those objects. The label on this button toggles between pausing and resuming the visualization. Clicking on *Resume Visualization* will reactivate the constraints in accordance with the values specified by the sliders.
- *Clear Filter* removes any filters that have been specified for selecting objects in the visualization based on their underlying data values, as described in the next section.

3.2 Constraint Specification Example

In specifying a visual layout with the Infovis language, data attributes from the datasets being represented are tied to the visual attributes of graphic objects. An example of this is shown in Fig. 3, where the attributes of graphic objects called points and ellipses have been tied to values selected by queries to a database. A point is represented in this language by intersecting horizontal and vertical lines. Both points and ellipses are defined by center x and y coordinates, widths, heights, and colors. A built-in scale called the Canvas maps data values to positions in the drawing area. In the code shown in Fig. 3, the mapping is one-to-one for each x and y coordinate. Since the widths and heights of the ellipses are tied to the same data property, they will be rendered as circles.

```
let circles = {make s:ellipse with
        s.center ~ Canvas(rec.x, rec.y),
        s.width = rec.z,
        s.height = rec.z,
        s.color = ColorMap(rec.color),
        s.fill = true
      | rec in SQL("select x, y, z, color from table1")}
in
   let points = {make p:point with
           p.center ~ Canvas(rec.a, rec.b),
           p.width = rec.c,
           p.height = rec.c,
           p.color = ColorMap(rec.color)
        | rec in SQL("select a, b, c, color from table2")}
   in
      NO(points),NO(circles),NO(points, circles),
      VAlign(points),VAlign(circles),VAlign(points, circles),
      HAlign(points),HAlign(circles),HAlign(points, circles);
```

Fig. 3. Specification for a scatterplot using circle and point objects, with non-overlap, horizontal alignment, and vertical alignment constraints applied to the positions of sets of circles, sets of points, and sets of circles and points.

The equality (=) and near ($\sim$) constraints can be specified between two values, such as attribute values of two different objects or an attribute value and a scaled data value. The other constraints in Fig. 3 are non-overlap (NO), vertical alignment (VAlign) and horizontal alignment (HAlign). They can be specified between two or more objects and between two sets of objects. In the above specification, a point cannot overlap with any other point, a circle cannot overlap with any other circle, and points and circles cannot overlap with each other.

The near constraints will pull each circle and point toward their coordinate values. At the same time, the non-overlap constraints will push each circle away from other circles, each point away from other points, and each circle and point away from all objects of the other type. Horizontal alignment and vertical alignment constraints will conflict with each other and may also conflict with the near and non-overlap constraints.

When the visualization process is initiated, all of the constraint sliders are set to 0, so there are no conflicts. The user can then choose which constraints to apply, and at what strength levels. Individual graphic objects can also be moved by the user, which can aid the constraint resolution process. In addition, the user can pause the process, reposition any objects, and then resume it.

Figure 4 shows the output from executing the code in Fig. 3. In the image on the left, the equality constraint is the only one being enforced, with the near constraint acting like an equality constraint since no other forces are in effect. The x-y coordinates that determine the initial, center position of the circle and point objects are, in many cases, in close proximity, so there is a great deal of overlap.

In the image in the middle of Fig. 4, the near and non-overlap constraint sliders have been manipulated. The near constraint, which has a higher precedence in the constraint-solving algorithm, was adjusted slightly upward from the zero position to a

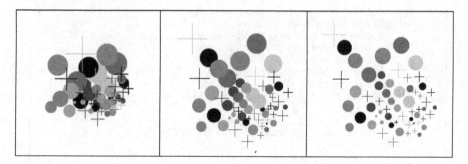

Fig. 4. In the left image, only the equality constraint is being enforced. In the middle image, the near constraint and the non-overlap constraint are enforced. In the right image, the near constraint is lessened and the non-overlap constraint is strengthened.

value of 2. The non-overlap constraint was adjusted to a value of 15. The graphic objects have moved out from their initial positions but are in the same general pattern. There is still, however, some overlap, but it is possible to see all of the objects, including those that were entirely hidden before.

For the image on the right in Fig. 4, the non-overlap constraint was increased to 20. Now all of the objects are clearly visible in their entirety. This makes it easier to double-click on any object in the layout, which will open its property window. The properties of the object, and the values retrieved from the database that were assigned to those properties, will be listed. The graphic properties typically include an x and y coordinate, width, and height. For objects represented by geometric shapes, such as ellipses and rectangles, an area property is also defined.

To return objects in a layout to their original position, the user can simple set the near constraint slider to its maximum value and set all other sliders to zero.

Filtering and Grouping Objects

Constraints can also be applied to groups of objects. The constraints specified for a group will override those specified for the entire frame. For example, if the near constraint slider is set to 40 for the objects in the frame but to five for the objects in a group, then the latter will be the strength of the constraint applied to objects in the grouping.

There are two ways that groups can be created. One is by filtering objects in a layout based on specified property values and then automatically adding all filtered objects to a group. The other is by using a lasso tool to select objects to be grouped together. Following are descriptions of each of these approaches.

Grouping Objects via Filtering. Filters can be specified for highlighting objects whose properties are tied to one value, one or more values, or a range of values, depending on the property type. For example, a data range can be specified for a numeric property, while multiple options can be selected for a shape or color property. Right-clicking anywhere on the canvas will open the Filter window, as shown in Fig. 5. After applying a filter, the color intensity of all graphic objects that do not meet the selection criteria will fade, leaving those that do meet the criteria easy to identify, as shown in the

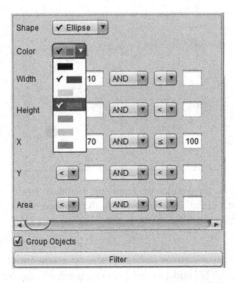

Fig. 5. Filter window in which Shape has been set to Point or Ellipse (dropdown menu not shown), Color to red or blue, Width to above 10, and X to between 70 and 100, inclusive. (Color figure online)

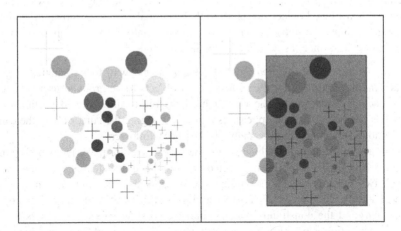

Fig. 6. Left image shows results of applying filter shown in Fig. 5 to rightmost layout in Fig. 4. Right image shows same filter applied with the Group Objects option selected. (Color figure online)

left image in Fig. 6. If the user selects the Group Objects option in the Filter window, then the filtered objects will be added to a group, as shown in the right image in Fig. 6.

When an object in a group is clicked on, the background of the grouping box becomes light blue (see right image in Fig. 6). The constraints panel will also change to show the set of constraints applied to the objects in the selected group. While the constraints specified for the entire frame will still be applied to all objects, the constraints specified for the group will take precedence.

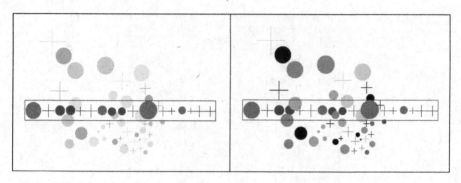

Fig. 7. Left image shows the results of removing the near constraint and enforcing the non-overlap and horizontal alignment constraints on the grouped objects in Fig. 6. Right image shows the same layout after the filter has been removed.

In generating the images shown in Fig. 7, the near constraint was set to zero, the non-overlap constraint to 27, and the horizontal alignment constraint to 50 for objects in the group. Clicking on any object that has not been grouped clears the background of the grouping box and switches the constraints panel to showing the values that have been set for the frame.

Removing filtering by clicking the Clear Filter button (see Fig. 2) causes the color intensity of non-filtered objects to return to their original values, as shown in the image on the right in Fig. 7. Objects can be removed individually from a group, or all objects can be removed at once, as described later in this section.

Grouping Objects with a Lasso Tool. Filtering is one way to automatically group objects. Another option is for the user to select objects to be grouped using a "lasso" tool. To activate this option, the user right-clicks on an unpopulated portion of the frame. The mouse cursor then appears as a lasso. Dragging the cursor along the canvas leaves a dotted trail showing the path that has been followed.

As the user selects graphic objects with the mouse, a color mask is applied to those objects to show they have been selected. When the user releases the mouse after selecting two or more objects, a pop-up window appears. The user is then given the option of adding the selected objects to a group, in which case a grouping box appears around them and the constraints panel is updated to show the set of sliders for that group. If that option is not chosen, the color masking is removed from any objects that had been selected.

To make the selection process easier, the user can pause the visualization by clicking on the Pause button shown in Fig. 2. Once the selection has been completed, clicking that button again will cause the visualization to resume.

In the image shown on the left in Fig. 8, the user has first moved the objects in the group created with filtering (identified as Group 1) to the bottom of the canvas. Since the horizontal alignment is in effect, all of the objects in that group move together when any one of them is dragged. The user then used the lasso tool to randomly select and group objects. This grouping is identified as Group 2.

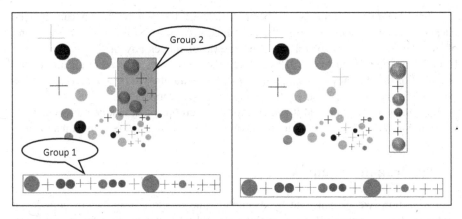

Fig. 8. Left image shows results of dragging Group 1 below other objects in the layout and then selecting and grouping other miscellaneous objects into Group 2. Right image shows results of removing the near constraint and enforcing the non-overlap and vertical alignment constraints on the objects in Group 2.

The right image in Fig. 8 shows the outcome of setting the near constraint to zero, the non-overlap constraint to 11, and the vertical alignment constraint to 39 for the objects in Group 2. The user has also dragged the objects in this group to the right side of the canvas.

To remove an object from a grouping, the user must first pause the visualization and then right-click on the object. The grouping box will be highlighted in blue, and a recycle bin icon will appear under the selected object, as shown in the left image in Fig. 9. Clicking the 'X' on the bin will delete the object from the group. The user can then select more objects for removal. Alternatively, the user can double-click on any item in a group. A pop-up window will then appear, giving the user the option of removing all objects from a group. This option was applied to the objects in Group 1, with the results shown in the right image in Fig. 9.

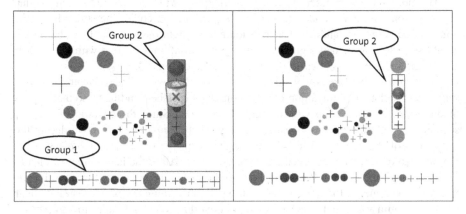

Fig. 9. Left image shows objects being removed one at a time. In right image, some objects remain in Group 2, while Group 1 has been entirely removed. (Color figure online)

When the removal process has been completed, the resume button can then be clicked. The layout will remain in the current configuration until the user changes any of the constraint sliders set for the entire frame or moves any of the objects in the layout. Any slight adjustment will reinforce the constraints applied to all ungrouped objects. For those in any remaining groups, the constraints will be enforced so long as no other constraints specified for the group take precedence.

To return a visualization to its initial layout, all groups must first be removed. Then the near constraint should be set to its maximum value and all other constraints to zero.

4 Application Examples

In this section, we demonstrate by example some of the advantages of applying a constraint-based approach to data exploration and presentation. Our focus here is on multivariate data, in which each variable is represented by a different visual property.

4.1 Flow Map

A classic example of visualizing multivariate data is Charles Minard's famous depiction of Napoleon's March on Moscow (parts of this example were also used in [1]). We consider here the portion of the map that focuses on the route of troop movement on the March to and from Moscow. In Minard's depiction, a flow map was used to represent both locations and the flow of objects between locations. He used approximate geography to show troop movements, with line segments for the legs of the journey. The width of those segments indicated the number of surviving troops and the color indicated the direction of troop movement.

The top image in Fig. 10 shows the troop movement portion of the map generated with the Infovis prototype. Constraint strengths are all set to zero, so labels appear at their specified locations. Some of these labels are not readable, as they overlap with each other and/or line segments in the map.

To address the first issue of labels overlapping with each other, a non-overlap constraint on labels was added to the graph specification code. The strengths of the non-overlap constraint and the near constraint were both then adjusted, so that labels would stay close to their designated locations but would not overlap with each other. The resulting layout is shown in the middle image of Fig. 10.

While more labels are now visible, some are still hidden by line segments. The next step was to add an additional non-overlap constraint on labels and lines, so that objects of one type cannot overlap with objects of the other. Since the position of the line segments is set with equality constraints, only labels are allowed to move during the constraint-solving process. The bottom image of Fig. 10 shows the layout when the non-overlap constraint is enforced on labels and lines. All of the labels are now clearly visible, though they are no longer as close to the locations they were marking. Labels can easily be returned to their correct positions by increasing the near constraint slider to its maximum value and decreasing the non-overlap constraint slider to zero.

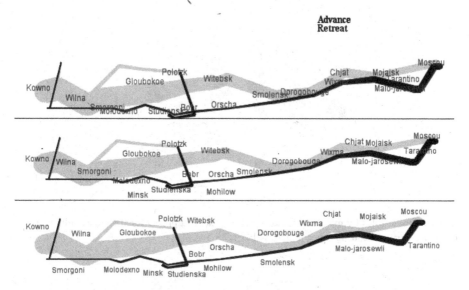

Fig. 10. The top image uses data from Minard's map of Napolean's March on Moscow to depict troop movement. No constraints are applied. In the middle image, non-overlap constraints are enforced on labels. In the bottom image, non-overlap constraints are enforced on labels and on labels and lines.

4.2   Plot of Sales Data

In this next example, we consider a plot of randomly generated monthly sales data over a six month time period. Monthly sales figures by sales territory and by sales person are represented by circular objects. The center of each circle indicates the month (x-coordinate) and dollar value of sales in 100k units (y-coordinate). The area of each circle is proportional to the sales volume, while its color indicates the sales territory, with NE for northeast, NW for northwest, C for central, SE for southeast, and SW for southwest. Each circle is also labeled with the initials of the sales manager for that territory during that time period. Figure 11 shows the initial plot of this data (a similar plot using the same data appears in [1].

It is evident that some of the objects representing monthly sales data in Fig. 11 are not visible, based on the overlapping values for certain data labels. Enforcing the non-overlap constraint on all circular objects reveals those that were hidden, as shown in Fig. 12. The repositioning of the affected objects, however, has made it very difficult to determine which circles go with which month and sales values.

Before applying non-overlap constraints, it would be helpful to filter the data so that we can explore a portion of it at a time. As a first step, the user sets a filter to select the data from months one and two, the results of which are shown in Fig. 13. The lasso tool is then used to create two groups of data, one for each case where there are overlapping circles. Horizontal and non-overlap constraint strengths are then increased for those groups. The results are shown in the image on the left of Fig. 14, while the image on the right shows the layout after the groupings have been removed.

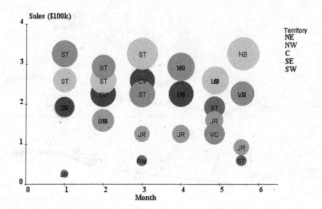

Fig. 11. Dollar sales by month by territory, with circle area proportional to sales volume, color indicating territory, and manager initials as labels.

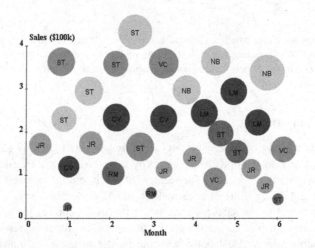

Fig. 12. The layout from Fig. 11 with the non-overlap constraint enforced on circular objects.

It is now possible to read the labels and discern the relative sizes of all the sales data for months one and two (right-clicking on any of the circles reveals the actual attribute values). A similar process can be followed for presenting and exploring all of the sales data represented in this plot.

The layout can always be returned to its original configuration by removing any filters and groupings and setting the near constraint slider to its maximum value.

4.3   Scatterplot of Patient Data

This last example involves a scatterplot for examining relationships between age, gender, body mass index (BMI) and hemoglobin A1c (HbA1c), which identifies average plasma glucose concentration. Elevated levels of HbA1c characterize diabetes.

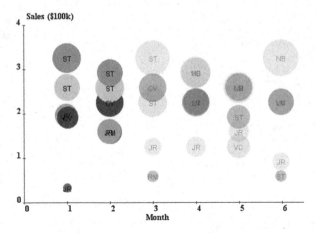

Fig. 13. The layout from Fig. 11 with a filter applied to months one and two.

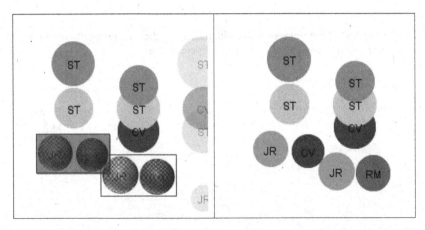

Fig. 14. The left image shows two groups, one for each of the overlapping circles representing sales in months one and two, respectively. Horizontal and non-overlap constraints have been enforced on those groups. In the image on the right, the groupings have been removed.

In the scatterplot in Fig. 15, there are 70 rectangular objects. Each of these is associated with an individual patient using randomly generated data. The center of each rectangle indicates the patient's age (x-coordinate) and HbA1c measure (y-coordinate), the area represents the BMI, and the color represents gender, with red for female and blue for male. Half of the patients are identified as male and half as female. All are between 20 and 40 years in age.

It is difficult at this point to identify any patterns or relationships in the data. As a first step, applying filters and automatically grouping the results can be used to stratify the patients into different risk levels. In Fig. 16, a filter has been applied to identify

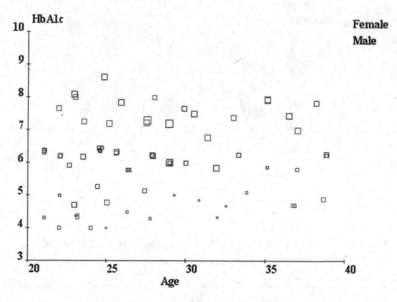

Fig. 15. Scatterplot of HbA1c versus Age, with the area of the rectangular objects proportional to BMI and their color indicating gender. (Color figure online)

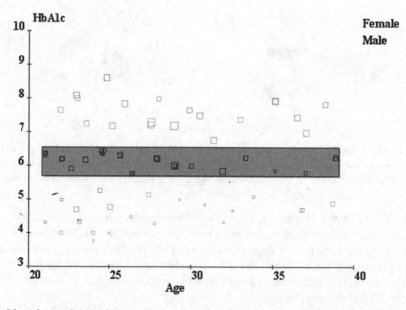

Fig. 16. After applying a filter to the plot shown in Fig. 15 that limits HbA1c to values between 5.7 and 6.4, inclusive, and automatically grouping the results. (Color figure online)

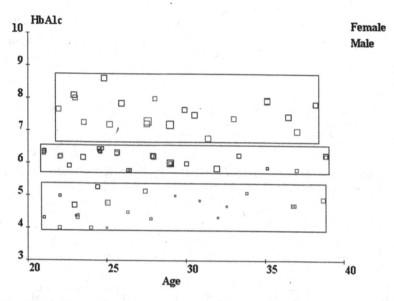

Fig. 17. After adding additional filters and groupings. The top group contains rectangles associated with HbA1c levels of 6.5 and higher (diabetes), the middle group with levels between 5.7 and 6.4, inclusive (pre-diabetes), and the bottom group with levels at or below 5.6 (normal).

patients whose HbA1c level places them in the prediabetes category (ranging from 5.7 to 6.4), and the results have been automatically grouped.

After removing that filter, the unfiltered objects return to their original color intensity. Additional filters and groupings can then be specified.

Figure 17 shows the plot after specifying two additional filters, one on HbA1c values at or below 5.6 (normal) and the other on values at or above 6.5 (diabetes). All filters have been removed in this scatterplot.

After grouping by HbA1c ranges, it is easier to see the ages associated with each group. In addition, it appears that the areas of the rectangular objects, indicating BMI, are typically larger as the level of HbA1c increases in this random dataset. However, several of the rectangles are overlapping, so this cannot be determined with any certainty. It is also not possible to determine which group contains the most patients and which the least.

In Fig. 18, the non-overlap constraint has been strongly enforced in each group In addition, horizontal alignment constraints of a more moderate strength have been applied to the set of all males and the set of all females in both the top and middle groups (the middle group is shown in this figure as being currently selected). It is now possible to see that there are more females in the diabetes group (top) and the normal group (bottom), while more males fall into the middle category (normal). For females, it appears that the largest rectangles, indicating higher BMI values, are in the diabetes group.

To determine if this is indeed the case, a filter is added on BMI values in the obese category (30 and above for this age group). Figure 19 shows obese patients for each

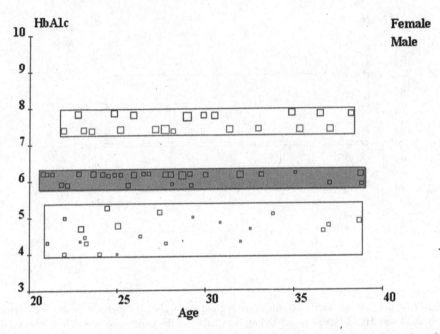

Fig. 18. After strongly enforcing non-overlap constraints on all groups and moderately enforcing horizontal alignment constraints on all blue objects and on all red objects in the top and middle groups. (Color figure online)

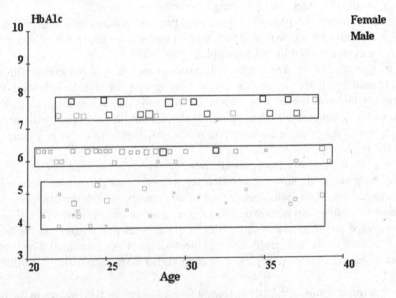

Fig. 19. After applying a filter on the area of the rectangle. Visible rectangles represent patients who fall into the obese category, defined here as a BMI of 30 and above.

strata. It is now evident that all females in the obese category are in the top group. Males in the obese category are primarily in the top group, with two in the middle group.

The application of non-overlap and horizontal alignment constraints has moved the graphic objects from their actual data value positions in Figs. 18 and 19. While their current positions are still somewhat indicative of their HbA1c and Age values, the associations are no longer accurately portrayed. The options available to the user for revealing the actual data values of these attributes are to right-click on an individual object to view all data properties; apply filters to identify objects by HbA1c and/or Age values; or restore the original placement of objects within each groups by setting the associated near constraint to its maximum value and all other constraints to zero.

5   Conclusions

In this paper, we have presented a constraint-based approach to visualizing and exploring multivariate datasets, with layouts not limited to node-link diagrams. In particular, we have demonstrated the usefulness of this approach in revealing graphic objects that are hidden by other objects and in physically separating and stratifying objects based on the attribute values of the data they represent. These capabilities are supported by a filtering mechanism for selecting and automatically grouping graphic objects based on their attribute values. Different constraint strengths can then be specified for groups of objects versus those specified for the layout overall. Filters can also be added after groups have been formed to highlight commonalities in the data amongst both grouped and ungrouped objects. The functionality described here supports data exploration activities while providing the user with greater control over object positioning.

This work adds to the repertoire of approaches available to users for exploring and presenting multivariate data. We plan on evaluating our prototype implementation with users and will apply their feedback to further development of this interactive, constraint-based approach to visualization.

References

1. Lucas, W., Gordon, T.: User control of force-directed layouts. In: 11th International Joint Conference on Software Technologies, vol. 1, pp. 91–99 (2016)
2. Kleinberg, J.M.: Authoritative sources in a hyperlinked environment. J. ACM **46**(5), 604–632 (1999)
3. Srivastava, J., Cooley, R., Deshpande, M., Tan, P.-N.: Web usage mining: discovery and applications of usage patterns from web data. ACM SIGKDD Explor. Newsl. **1**(2), 12–23 (2000)
4. Heer, J., Bostock, M., Ogievetsky, V.: A tour through the visualization zoo. Commun. ACM **53**(6), 59–67 (2010)

5. Pantazos, P., Lauesen, S.: Constructing visualizations with InfoVis tools – an evaluation from a user perspective. In: International Conference on Information Visualization Theory and Applications, pp. 731–736 (2012)

6. Shneiderman, B.: Creativity support tools: accelerating discovery and innovation. Commun. ACM **50**(12), 20–32 (2007)

7. Lucas, W., Shieber, S.M.: A simple language for novel visualizations of information. In: Filipe, J., Shishkov, B., Helfert, M., Maciaszek, L.A. (eds.) ENASE/ICSOFT 2007. CCIS, vol. 22, pp. 33–45. Springer, Heidelberg (2008). doi:10.1007/978-3-540-88655-6_3

8. Lucas, W.: An interactive approach to constraint-based visualizations. In: Yamamoto, S. (ed.) HCI 2014. LNCS, vol. 8521, pp. 54–63. Springer, Cham (2014). doi:10.1007/978-3-319-07731-4_6

9. Ryall, K., Marks, J., Shieber, S.M.: An interactive constraint-based system for drawing graphs. In: 10th Annual Symposium on User Interface Software and Technology, pp. 97–104. ACM Press (1997)

10. Dwyer, T., Marriott, K., Schreiber, F., Stuckey, P., Woodward, M., Wybrow, M.: Exploration of networks using overview+detail with constraint-based cooperative layout. IEEE Trans. Visual. Comput. Graph. **14**(6), 1293–1300 (2008)

11. Dwyer, T., Marriott, K., Wybrow, M.: Dunnart: a constraint-based network diagram authoring tool. In: Tollis, I.G., Patrignani, M. (eds.) GD 2008. LNCS, vol. 5417, pp. 420–431. Springer, Heidelberg (2009). doi:10.1007/978-3-642-00219-9_41

12. Yi, J.S., Kang, Y.A., Stasko, J.: Jacko. J.: Toward a deeper understanding of the role of interaction in information visualization. IEEE Trans. Visual. Comput. Graph. **13**(6), 1224–1231 (2007)

13. Shneiderman, B.: Dynamic queries for visual information seeking. IEEE Softw. **11**, 70–77 (1994)

14. Heer, J., Shneiderman, B.: Interactive dynamics for visual analysis. Commun. ACM **55**(4), 45–54 (2012)

15. Shneiderman, B.: The eyes have it: a task by data type taxonomy for information visualizations. In: IEEE Symposium on Visual Languages, pp. 336. IEEE Computer Society (1996)

16. Ahlberg, C.: Spotfire: an information exploration environment. SIGMOD Rec. **25**(4), 25–29 (1996)

17. Yi, J.S., Melton, R., Stasko, J.T., Jacko, J.A.: Dust & magnet: multivariate information visualization using a magnet metaphor. Inf. Visual. **4**, 239–256 (2005)

18. Anscombe, F.J.: Graphs in statistical analysis. Am. Stat. **27**(1), 17–21 (1973)

I-Codesign: A Codesign Methodology for Reconfigurable Embedded Systems

Ines Ghribi[1,2]([✉]), Riadh Ben Abdallah[1], Mohamed Khalgui[1,3], and Marco Platzner[4]

[1] LISI Lab, University of Carthage, Carthage, Tunisia
ines.ghrr@gmail.com, riadh.benabdallah@gmail.com,
khalgui.mohamed@gmail.com
[2] Faculty of Science of Tunis, University of Tunis el Manar, Tunis, Tunisia
[3] Systems Control Lab, Xidian University, Xi'an, China
[4] University of Paderborn, Paderborn, Germany
platzner@upb.de

Abstract. Hardware/software codesign involves various design problems including system specification, design space exploration and hardware/software partitioning. An effective codesign process requires accurately predicting the performance, cost and power consequence of any design trade-off in algorithms or hardware characterization. In order to satisfy these design constraints we developed a new codesign methodology: I-codesign. It starts with describing the system specification with probabilistic estimations of the execution scenarios along with real-time and inclusion/exclusion parameters. Then, a three phase partitioning approach is applied to the specification where each phase deals with a specific set of constraints. An embedded controller code is generated at the end of the methodology that acts at run-time on the reconfiguration requests.

Keywords: Codesign · Real-time · Reconfiguration · Partitioning · Probabilistic software

1 Introduction

Hardware/software co-design has been a recognized research field for about a decade. Within that time, it has moved from an emerging discipline to a mainstream technology. Researchers developed some basic approaches to the design of embedded software running on CPUs, and their work formed the roots of a hardware/software codesign methodology. In fact, the complexity of designing embedded systems is constantly increasing which motivates the need for using more efficient tools and design methodologies. Designing at a higher level of abstraction reduces the number of components with which the designer has to deal, and thus increasing design productivity. This paradigm shift in design requires methodologies and automated tools to support design at higher levels abstractions [1]. Hardware/software co-design is the technique of designing

© Springer International Publishing AG 2017
E. Cabello et al. (Eds.): ICSOFT 2016, CCIS 743, pp. 153–174, 2017.
DOI: 10.1007/978-3-319-62569-0_8

concurrent hardware and software components of an embedded system [2,3]. Generally, hardware/software co-design starts with specification then modeling the system behavior at the system level [4]. The hardware/software partitioning step follows. This step is a combinational optimization problem that assigns the system functions to the target architecture on the software and hardware domain under the condition of meeting the design constraints [5]. This is a key task in the system level design, because the decisions made during this step directly impact the performance and cost of the final implementation. One of the main performance issues in embedded systems design is to guarantee the results within a given time [6,7]. Such systems, which have to fulfill posed constraints, are called real-time systems [8,9]. In these systems, time at which results of a computation are available is crucial. Another challenge in designing embedded systems is dealing with reconfigurablility, since they have the capability to modify their functionalities, to add or to remove components and to modify interconnections among them. The basic idea behind these systems is to have a system that autonomously modifies its functionalities according to the changing application inputs [10].

In [11], we present a new technique for modeling and partitioning of reconfigurable embedded systems. The software model is composed of probabilistic tasks where each task executes a set of elementary functions. A directed acyclic graph (DAG) models each task where the vertices are functions connected with edges. The edges are valued with both probability values and communication costs. The probability on the edges gives an estimation of the execution progress of the tasks. Hence, the most probabilistic execution scenarios are placed together on the same processing unit (PE) during the partitioning. Hence, the traffic circulation on the interconnection network is minimized. The functions could be related with inclusion/exclusion constraints. A three phases partitioning approach for the proposed probabilistic software model is also proposed. A functional partitioning step deals with hard constraints and aims to optimize the number of processors by evaluating inclusion/exclusion constraints. The second step generates initial partitions or clusters by evaluating the most probabilistic executions of the software model. Finally, generated partitions are optimized with iterative techniques by evaluating the combination of their communication costs and their probability values. A reduction of the communication costs and the traffic circulation on the network was proved.

In the present work, we introduce a new co-design methodology using the described modeling and partitioning techniques called "I-Codesign". It is divided into four major tasks: (1) writing the system specification according to the new probabilistic specification model; (2) partitioning the task functions into clusters under several execution constraints; (3) Checking real-time, memory and energy constraints at each partitioning phase; (4) Generation of a controller matrix that supervises, synchronizes and handles the reconfiguration of the software and hardware components at run-time. A reconfiguration is assumed to be any addition/removal of a task set, or the modification of the execution path at the task level. We developed a framework tool to walk through our methodology steps. The input of the tool is a software specification according to I-codesign plus a hardware description of a set of processors equipped with a quantified amount of memory and battery energy. While applying the partitioning approach, the memory and energy constraints are verified firstly at each iteration followed by the real-time constraints according to the earliest deadline first algorithm. The output of this tool is a generated matrix used by the controller in order to associate each task to a PE according to I-codesign for each implementation. A new design strategy is defined where each implementation scenario is treated separately and placed into the controller matrix.

The current paper is organized as follows: the next Section describes useful background. Section 3 presents the system model and the used notations in this paper. In Sect. 4 a new co-design methodology is introduced. Section 5 exposes a case study to evaluate our methodology. Simulations and results are given in Sect. 6 and finally we conclude in Sect. 7.

2   State of the Art

Software design and hardware design are required to be integrated closely and coordinated with each other. This leads to the development of a new design theory: hardware and software co-design. After a decade of research, hardware/software codesign has a rich literature that is impossible to survey exhaustively in one article. Thus, this short recap merely introduces some of the decade's major research themes [12].

One of the earliest codesign efforts was the SOS system from Prakash and Parker of the University of Southern California, which could synthesize an arbitrary multiprocessor topology and schedule and allocate processes onto the multiprocessor. The system formulated the synthesis problem as a mixed integer-linear program, so it was slow and could not handle large problems, but it was important foundational work.

About a year later, the CODES workshop in Colorado and the CASHE workshop in Austria introduced several pieces of significant research that had evolved in parallel. From these, hardware/software partitioning emerged as an important first step in creating models and algorithms. Two early systems, Vulcan from Stanford and Cosyma from the Technical University of Braunschweig, took complementary approaches to this basic problem [13]. Its partition method is mainly for software to optimize the calculation through co-processors. The input to both Vulcan and Cosyma was a C like program. Based on an analysis of the performance and cost of various implementations of the program, some of the program's functions were put in the ASIC while other parts were implemented in software running on the CPU [14–16].

Traditionally, HW/SW partitioning is carried out manually based on system designer's experience. Many approaches have been proposed recently to fulfill and optimize multiple objectives and costs. Although there exist a wide variety of problem formulation and cost definition, these are highly dependent on targeted system architectures. The most common problem described in literature is the optimization of execution time, hardware area and communication cost, targeted for simple single-software single-hardware system. The most common problem described in literature is the optimization of execution time, hardware area and communication cost, targeted for simple single-software single-hardware system. Other works have also incorporated different cost metrics and objectives in HW/SW partitioning, including power consumption, and software memory usage. Many researchers have applied general-purpose heuristics to hardware/software partitioning. In particular, genetic algorithms have been extensively used as well as simulated annealing [17,18]. Other less popular heuristics in this group are tabu search and greedy algorithms [19]. These methods tend to be used with data oriented applications. In more recent work, Banerjee et al. in [20] have presented a placement-aware method for simultaneous partitioning and scheduling of task graph. They also have considered some characteristics such as configuration prefetching and placement constraints. In the current paper, we used a combination of well-known heuristics that are usually applied to partitioning problems. First, the hierarchical clustering, a constructive heuristic that builds a partitioning in bottom-up fashion by grouping nodes using closeness-functions to estimate the costs, is used. Also, Kernighan-lin heuristic, an iterative heuristic that was substantially improved by Fiduccia and Mattheyses and later by many others, is applied [21]. It starts from an arbitrary partition and swaps pairs of nodes in order to improve the cost of the partition. Gain calculation of moving a node x from a cluster to another using a metric is calculated according to the following formula: $G_x = E_x - I_x$ where: E_x is the cost of edges connecting a node x with other clusters and I_x is the cost of edges connecting a node x within its own cluster. In the current work the cost of the edges is Probability × communication cost. The advantage of this heuristics is its rapidity and its capability of processing large amount of data.

Contribution

In the present work, we introduce a new co-design methodology based on constructive and iterative partitioning phases. The originality of this work compared with the previously proposed approaches in the literature resides in multiple aspects including:

- A probabilistic estimation of the software models aiming to predict the execution flow which leads to an improvement in the codesign results and a noticeable enhancement in the performance of the system,
- An original codesign methodology based on multiple constraints and feasibility analysis that show good performance enhancements especially in terms of execution time and communication cost,
- A novel reconfiguration approach at two levels: (i) the modeling level which considers multiple execution scenarios (configurations) and estimates the probability of each configuration, (ii) the partitioning level that considers the possible automatic reconfigurations by generating a controller matrix which is responsible of executing the proper modifications at run-time.

3   Formalization

We present in this section the formal definitions and notations of the system.

3.1   System Model

The system model is based on processing units PEs linked by interconnects. We assume that all the processors are identical in term of processing power, memory size and energy consumption relationship aspects. Each processor PE_i is characterized by its operating voltage/frequency ranges, its battery load and its internal memory.

Definition 1 (processing unit PE)
A processing unit PE is formalized by quintuplet (PID, f, V, $Weight_{max}$, BL) where: (i) PID: Processor identifier (ii) f: The range of frequency points, (iii) V: The range of voltage points, (iv) $Weight_{max}$: The maximum load in term of memory space that P could support, (v) BL: The available battery charge.

The energy consumption of the PE if executed at frequency f is calculated as: $E_{PE} = P_f. PE_{time}$ where:

– P_f: is the power consumption at frequency f.

Definition 2 (interconnect)
An interconnect L is a communication link between two PEs. It is characterized with the pair (LID, Th) where: (i) LID: The link identifier, (ii) Th: The bandwidth of L.

The hardware architectures are mainly homogeneous cores and some ASIC or FPGA built on an Mp Soc. It consists in a master processor and a several slave processors. Each tile in the architecture has a CPU, a local memory used for communications on the same processor and a communication interface. The tiles communicate with the shared memory via a multiple buses. The software tasks are affected to CPU while hardware tasks are placed either on the FPGA or the ASIC. The FPGA is placed on the master processor along with an Input/output interface for communications with the physical world. The controller code and its mapping table are stored on the master tile also for communication and reconfiguration reasons. Fig. 1 presents an example of the adapted hardware model.

In [11], we define a function F as the basic entity in the software model to execute elementary operations.

Definition 3 (Function)
A function F is a quadruplet (ci, pi, di, Si) where: (i) ci: The worst case execution time of F, (ii) pi: The period of F, (iii) di: The relative deadline of F, (iv) Si: Describes the memory size occupied by F.

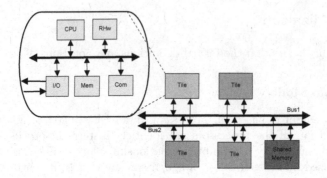

Fig. 1. Hardware model.

Each function F in the specification can be related to its predecessor F_p with an inclusion or exclusion constraint. The exclusion means that F has not to be executed on the same processor with F_p while the inclusion means that F and F_p have to be placed on the same PE. This constraint is modeled in the task representation by marking the mathematical symbol $\subset$ on F in case of inclusion and $\not\subset$ in case of exclusion. We formalize the exclusion/inclusion constraints as follows.

- **Exclu(F)** groups the set of functions that have not to be executed on the same processor and at the same time with the function F. This constraint is modeled in the task representation by marking the mathematical symbol '$\subset$' on the function F,
- **Inclu(F)** groups the set of functions that have to be executed on the same processor and at the same time with F. This constraint is modeled by marking the mathematical symbol '$\not\subset$' on F.

The processor and links affectation with functions are expressed as follows.

- **Assign-P(P_i)** groups the set of functions affected to the processor P_i,
- **Assign-L(L)** groups the set of communications affected to the link L.

A configuration is a path of k function that executes successively. These functions are related with precedence constraints. The configuration is defined as follows.

Definition 4 (Configuration)
A Configuration Conf is a set of functions. It is formalized by the triplet (CID, Cc_i, Dc_i) where: (i) CID: The configuration identifier, (ii) Cc_i: The worst case execution time of Conf, $Cc_i = \sum_1^k ci$ where k is the number of functions on the path, (iii) Dc_i: The relative deadline of Conf, which is the deadline of the leaf node function.

A task $T_i \in$, $i \in [1..m]$ is represented by a directed acyclic graph $T_i = (V_i, E_i)$, where (i) V_i is a set of nodes that correspond to behaviors or functions, and (ii) E_i is a set of arcs which describe connection between functions/behaviors. A task is defined as follows.

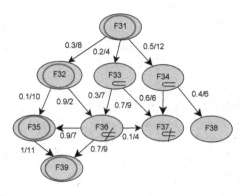

Fig. 2. Software task with a specified configuration path.

Definition 5 (Task)

A task T_i is a set of configurations. It is a doublet (TID, DAG) where: (i) TID: the task identifier, (ii) DAG: is the Directed Acyclic Graph that models the task.

All tasks are assumed to be independent. Figure 2 shows an example of a task T with inclusion/exclusion, probability and communication costs parameters [22]. It represents an example of a configuration and its path in the DAG of T. The software specification describes different implementation scenarios. At each iteration an implementation is designed to run on PEs. Each implementation includes a certain number of software tasks and it is defined as follows.

Definition 6 (Implementation)

An Implementation I is a set of tasks. It is formalized by the simplet IID where: (i) IID: is the identifier of the Implementation.

Hence, we can define the system to be a set of implementations, PEs and interconnects as follows.

Definition 7 (System)

A System Sys = {Implementation, PE, Interconnect}.

A reconfiguration scenario can be related to the current implementation of the system or to a configuration path in one of the implementation tasks. Hence, during execution another implementation could be loaded or another configuration path could be initiated. We define a reconfiguration scenario R as follows.

Definition 8 (reconfiguration R)

A reconfiguration R is a triplet (RID, event, target) where: (i) RID: The identifier of the reconfiguration R, (ii) event: The event that induces R, (iii) target: Specifies which implementation/configuration is concerned with the reconfiguration.

3.2   Problem Statement

We consider the partitioning of a task set composed of n tasks $\{T_1, \ldots, T_n\}$ on a set of m PEs $\{PE_1, \ldots, PE_m\}$. The aim of our methodology is the following:

(1) Respect the inclusion/exclusion constraints
   - $\forall F_k, F_h \in$ Assign-P(P_i), $F_k \notin$ Exclu (F_h).
   - $\forall F_k, F_h/F_k \in$ Inclu(F_h) then F_k and $F_h \in$ Assign-P(P_i).
(2) Respect the energy and the memory constraints
   - $\forall$ Fi $\in$ Assign-P(PE_i), $\sum_{Fi \in Assign-P(PE_i)}$ Si $\leq Weight_{max}$.
   - $\forall$ Fi $\in$ Assign-P(PE_i), $E_{PE_i} \leq$ BL.
(3) Respect real-time constraints:
   - The utilization of a function Fi is ui $=$ ci/pi. U_{tot}^i is the total utilization of the k function on a processor PEi, that is, $U_{tot}^i = \sum_1^k$ ci/pi ≤ 1.
   - The communication delays resulting of a function F_k on PE_i communicating with a function F_h placed on PE_j must not result in functions missing their deadlines.
(4) Evaluate the impact of the design constraints on the communication costs, the energy consumption and the number of preemption.

4   I-Codesign Methodology

The main purpose of I-codesign is to achieve a concurrent design between the probabilistic task model and the hardware architecture previously described in a manner that fulfills all the system requirements and respects the design constraints. I-codesign deals with a set of models and transformations. All the models are written in a system-level design language. Figure 3 shows the flow diagram of I-Codesign methodology extracted from an early work where I-codesign was first introduced [22]. In the proposed co-design methodology, the design flows begins with specification of the system behavior with formal models. The software part is composed of several implementation scenarios where each implementation scenarios executes a set of tasks. At each iteration an implementation scenario is specified for executing its tasks. Each task is modeled with a directed acyclic graph represented by a graph G = (V, E, W), V is a set of nodes where each node implements an elementary software function, E is a set of edges connecting the nodes and W records a set of weight for each node in V and edge in E. The weight of each edge in W represents data transfer between the nodes and it is weighted with two parameters: the communication costs of data transfer and a probabilistic estimation of the execution progress of the tasks. The next step is to map the system behavior to the hardware architecture. In this step, we perform HW/W partitioning and component selection at the same time. We developed a new partitioning method in (Ghribi et al. 2016). It starts with a functional partitioning step that evaluates the inclusion/exclusion constraints between task functions and creates clusters depending on this constraint. Couples that are concerned with inclusion or exclusion constraints are placed in

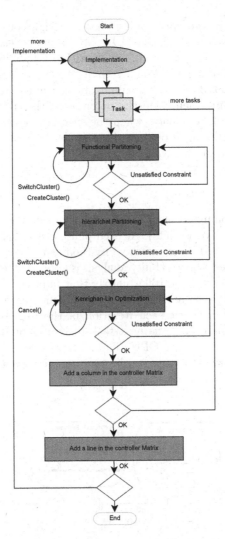

Fig. 3. I-Codesign flow diagram.

either the same or different processors. Each function F in the specification can be related to its predecessor F_p with an inclusion or exclusion constraint. The exclusion means that F has not to be executed on the same processor with F_p while the inclusion means that F and F_p have to be placed on the same PE. The hierarchical partitioning step follows. The remaining functions are evaluated by their connecting edge's probabilities and high probability values are treated first. This step aims to gather the most probabilistic executions on the same processor. Hence, the communications costs can be reduced. Finally, an optimization is performed using kernighan-Lin algorithm that evaluates both probability and communication cost on the edges connecting functions by gain calculation. At each of the partitioning phases, design constraints are verified. First, available energy and memory space are verified. Second, real-time constraints are evaluated using a scheduling algorithm feasibility test. A controller module is developed to supervise and reconfigure the system behavior. It constructs a mapping matrix for task assignments at the design phase. The matrix associates for each implementation the mapping of the corresponding tasks to the hardware architecture. Hence, when the system is executing the controller detects internal or external reconfiguration signals, refers to its matrix and perform a task migration mechanism.

4.1 HW/SW Partitioning

We define the partitioning problem in a manner that satisfies software constraints (spatial and temporal constraints). At each phase of the partitioning, we apply the appropriate rules first. Second, we verify the memory and energy constraints jointly. When validated, the feasibility analysis is applied. The partitioning phase is responsible of creating a controller matrix that indicates the proper mapping of the tasks for each software implementation. Since each implementation is composed of several tasks, at each iteration of the task partitioning module an entry is created indicating the next task to be executed, its corresponding implementation and the target CPU. The matrix is consulted at run-time at each reconfiguration request triggered by an internal/external signal/interrupt. Figure 4 depicts the partitioning module.

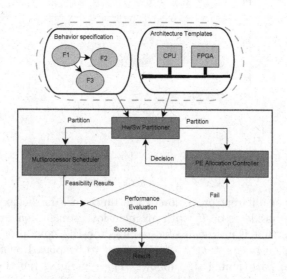

Fig. 4. Partitioning module diagram.

Real-Time Functional Partitioning. Evaluates the inclusion/exclusion constraints between task functions and creates clusters depending on this constraint. Couples that are concerned with inclusion or exclusion constraints are placed in either the same or different clusters. Once all the inclusions and exclusions are evaluated, a feasibility analysis is performed. If all clustered functions sets on the created clusters are schedulable on one of the available processors then the schedulability test is validated. Otherwise, the functional partitioning is applied again to create new clusters with schedulable function sets. Since any inclusion/exclusion constraint is hard, the clustered tasks are locked and cannot be moved any more. The pseudo-code below describes this partitioning phase.

```
program Functional Partitioning (Functional Graph)


    For each function F in T
    Extract Inclusion/Exclusion(F)
    If (inclusion){
    Cluster(F,F',C1)
    }
    else if (exclusion){
    Cluster(F,C1);
    Cluster (F',C2);
    }
    End If
    Lock(F);
    Lock(F');
    End For;
    GenerateFunctionalGraph();
    end.
```

Real-Time Hierarchical Partitioning. Clusters the remaining functions that have no inclusion/exclusion constraints. The functions are evaluated by their connecting edge's probabilities and high probability values are treated first. The available memory space is evaluated at each iteration. Once all the remaining functions are placed into clusters a feasibility analysis is performed. If all the functions sets on the created clusters are schedulable on one of the available processors then the schedulability test is validated. Otherwise, the hierarchical clustering is applied again to generate clusters with schedulable function sets. The pseudo-code below describes this partitioning phase.

```
program Hierarchical-partitioning ()

    For each Function F not clustered
    {
    ExtractHighestEdgeProbability(F);
    Cluster(F,F',C);
    End For;
    GenerateInitialClusters();
    end.
```

Real-Time Kernighan-Lin. Optimizes the generated clusters. This phase evaluates both probability and communication cost on the edges connecting functions by gain calculation. If the gain is positive, then the function is moved to another cluster if its energy consumption on the other cluster is less or equal to its energy consumption on the original cluster. Otherwise it is left on the original cluster. The pseudo code of the kernighan-lin optimization is described below.

```
program Kernighan-Lin()

For each Function F unlocked
{
G := GainCalculation(C1,C2);
If (G < 0)
Move(F,C2);
end if;
GenerateOptimizedClusters();
end.
```

Feasibility Analysis. The feasibility test at each partitioning phase verifies feasibility on the processors and on communication links: (i) it verifies first whether the created clusters are schedulable. Since we are using EDF algorithm the feasibility test verifies on each PE $\in \{PE_1, \ldots, PE_m\}$ the following inequation: $U = \sum_1^{N_i} c_i/p_i \leq 1$ where c_i is the execution time, p_i is the period and N is the number of functions placed on PE_i. (ii) The second test on the communication links verifies whether or not the communications delays between related functions affected to different PEs results in functions missing their deadlines.

4.2   Multiprocessor Scheduling with Precedence Constraint

The software specification is a set of independent tasks modeled with a directed acyclic graph where edges are functions and vertices are data dependencies. Hence, a function is ready to execute when all its predecessors are complete. We consider the scheduling of a set of functions with simultaneous release times, constrained deadlines and simple precedence. The policy proposed below is derived from [23]. A set of simple precedence is formalized by a relation $\rightarrow$. $F_i \rightarrow F_j$ states that F_i must execute before F_j. For a precise explanation of the precedence problem the following assumptions are considered:

- $\text{Pred}(F_i) = \{F_j \mid (F_j \rightarrow F_i)\}$
- $\text{succ}(F_i) = \{F_j \mid (F_i, F_j) \in \rightarrow\}$

The precedence constraint of the set of functions can be encoded as follows where d_i^* is the adjusted deadline of a function F_i:

$$d_i^* = min(d_i, min_{F_j \in succ(F_i)}(d_j^* - c_j)) \tag{1}$$

Theorem 1 (). *let $\wp = \{F_i\}$ a set of independent functions and $\rightarrow \subseteq \wp \times \wp$. Let $\wp^* = \{F_i^*\}$ be a set of independent functions such that d_i^* is given by the formula* (1). *We have $\wp$ feasible if only $\wp^*$ is feasible.*

The scheduling algorithm uses the adjusted parameters to perform the assignment of system applications to the software or hardware domain. Hence, the scheduling policy resides in adjusting the function deadlines according to the Eq. (1).

4.3 Controller Generation

A reconfiguration can be specified for a software implementation/configuration. We propose a controller that involves: (i) observation mechanisms of the system characteristics (energy, quality of service ...) (ii) reconfiguration mechanisms that acts on software tasks. The controller acts following internal or external events that induces configurations. A reconfiguration can add/remove implementation or change the configuration path of a task that belongs to the current implementation. Figure 5 extracted from [22] shows the class diagram of the controller. The controller class supervises the system environment. It receives internal or external events like user requests or peripheral entries and initiates necessary reconfiguration. The software specification is divided into configurations/implementation. Each configuration has a set of tasks to be executed when initiated. Initially, a boot configuration is loaded. However, a reconfiguration can occur at run-time which requires to reconfigure (replace, re-parameter, change the functionality, etc.) of the system tasks. Therefore, a pre-calculated mapping of all the possible configuration scenarios is necessary and will lead to better performance. Thus, we propose to build a controller module that manages the reconfiguration. It acts following internal or external events that induces reconfigurations. When executing the I-codesign process, a matrix is constructed based on the output of each partitioned configuration (task set). In fact, the task mapping to the execution platform is stored in the controller matrix along with its corresponding execution scenario. Figure 6 shows an example of the structure of the controller matrix.

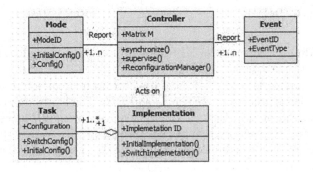

Fig. 5. Class diagram of the controller.

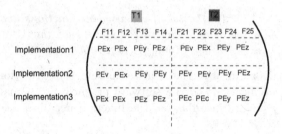

Fig. 6. An example of the controller matrix.

5   Case Study

We propose in this section to apply the I-codesign methodology to a software specification composed of three implementations: $S_1 = \{T1, T3\}$, $S_2 = \{T1, T3, T4\}$, $S_3 = \{T2, T3, T4\}$.

Motivational Example: We propose to apply the I-codesign techniques to S_1. It is composed of two independent tasks $T_1 = \{F_{11}, F_{12}, F_{13}, F_{14}, F_{15}, F_{16}\}$ and $T_3 = \{F_{31}, F_{32}, F_{33}, F_{34}, F_{35}, F_{36}, F_{37}, F_{38}\}$. T_1 and T_3 are represented respectively in Figs. 7 and 8 [22].

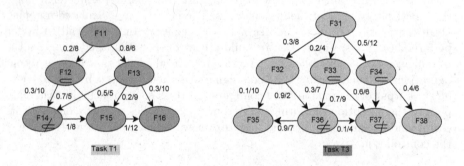

Fig. 7. Task T_1.   **Fig. 8.** Task T_3.

The scheduling properties of the tasks T_1 and T_3 are listed respectively in Tables 1 and 2.

This software model will be affected to a hardware architecture composed of three homogeneous processors PE_1, PE_2 and PE_3. The hardware units have the characteristics shown in Table 3. Each PE is running with its highest frequency f, voltage V and its memory size Si. We present in this section the results of I-codesign on S_1. The scheduling algorithm is EDF (Earliest Deadline First).

Table 1. Scheduling parameters of T_1.

Function	Execution time	Deadline	Period	Si
F_{11}	5	120	150	5
F_{12}	3	120	200	7
F_{13}	2	90	210	2
F_{14}	6	110	180	6
F_{15}	2	120	190	3
F_{16}	2	200	250	5

Table 2. Scheduling parameters of T_3.

Function	Execution time	Deadline	Period	Si
F_{31}	3	60	150	4
F_{32}	3	80	200	2
F_{33}	5	90	210	5
F_{34}	5	110	180	6
F_{35}	5	120	190	3
F_{36}	4	160	210	1
F_{37}	1	180	220	5
F_{38}	4	190	260	4

Table 3. Processor characteristics.

PE	f (MHz)	V (V)	$Weight_{max}$ (byte)	Battery (watt)
PE_1	250/150	1.2/0.95	40	10
PE_2	300/200	1.3/1.08	40	10
PE_3	400/120	1.7/0.85	40	10

5.1 Functional Partitioning

The first step is to evaluate the inclusion/exclusion constraints and generate initial clusters with locked functions. These clusters will hold the functions which respect the inclusion/exclusion constraints. The functional partitioning creates two clusters. On the first cluster C1, F_{11} and F_{12} of T1 are affected with F_{36} and F_{37} of T3. F_{14}, F_{31}, F_{33} and F_{34} are affected to the second cluster C2. The functional graph is constructed for each task. Figure 9 represents the functional graphs of T1 and T3 respectively [22]. We affect C1 to PE_1's parameters value and C2 to PE_2's parameters value. Then, we verify the energy and memory constrains first then we check the real-time constraints. The consumed energy on PE_1 is E = 1.44 ≤ 10 and the consumed memory space is Mem = 27 ≤ 40 on PE_1. On PE2, E = 4 ≤ 10 and Mem = 12 ≤ 40. The feasibility analysis is verified easily using the CHEDDAR tool [24] for instance. In order to verify that the communication delays do not result in functions missing their deadlines we create message dependencies between functions and we affect each message with the communication cost between the corresponding functions using CHEDDAR tool. The Utilization Factor is U = 0.12 on PE1 and U = 0.2 on PE2. Hence, the feasibility test is valid.

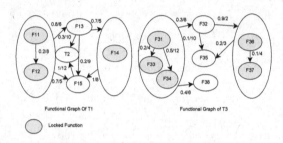

Fig. 9. Functional graph respectively of T_1 and T_3.

5.2   Hierarchical Partitioning

The hierarchical clustering aims to generate initial clusters by evaluating the probability as a metric. We dispose of a functional graph generated by the functional partitioning phase. We extract the highest edge's probability for each non clustered function F_j and cluster it with its related clustered functions. Hence, the link L_{ij} between F_i and F_j communicates only the less probabilistic traffic. The generated clusters are shown in Fig. 10 [22].

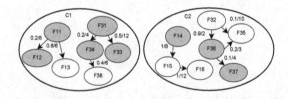

Fig. 10. Resulted clusters respectively of T_1 and T_3.

Then, energy and memory constraints are checked. The used memory size Mem = 35 ≤ 40 and E = 3.2 ≤ 10 on PE_1. On PE_2, Mem = 23 and E = 8.4 ≤ 10. The real-time constraints are verified. The Utilization Factor is U = 0.18 on PE1 and U = 0.29 on PE2. Hence, the feasibility test is valid.

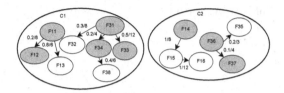

Fig. 11. Resulted clusters respectively of T1 and T3.

5.3 Kernighan-Lin Optimization

Kernighan-Lin optimizes the partitions based on some metrics. In our partitioning process we use the combination of two metrics: the probability on the connecting edges and the communication cost. The resulted clusters after applying the Kernighan-Lin optimization are represented in Fig. 11 [22]. After applying the Kernighan-Lin algorithm, we notice that F_{32} has been moved from the cluster C2 to C1. The available memory on PE_1 is 5 and the memory space of F_{32} is 2, the new energy consumption on PE_1 is E = 4.1. The utilization is measured with cheddar tool minding the communication delays on the links: U = 0.22. All the I-codesign constraints are valid. Figure 8 shows the final clusters C1 and C2 where C1 will be placed on PE_1 and C2 on PE_2 [22].

5.4 Scheduling Simulation Results

The scheduler receives the partitioning results as well as the real-time characteristics of each function. Its job is to determine which function executes on a processor at a given time. We start with adjusting the deadlines of the set of functions composing T1 and T3. Tables 4 and 5 present the adjusted values after applying the precedence constraint formula (1).

5.5 Controller Generation

The application controller use a matrix where each line contains the functions of tasks and the columns are the different system implementations. In this case,

Table 4. Adjusted scheduling parameters of T_1.

Function	Execution time	Deadline d_i	Period	d_i^*
F_{11}	5	120	150	88
F_{12}	3	120	200	104
F_{13}	2	90	210	90
F_{14}	6	110	180	110
F_{15}	2	120	190	120
F_{16}	2	190	250	190

Table 5. Adjusted scheduling parameters of T_3.

Function	Execution time	Deadline d_i	Period	d_i^*
F_{31}	3	60	150	60
F_{32}	3	80	200	80
F_{33}	5	90	210	90
F_{34}	5	110	180	110
F_{35}	5	120	190	120
F_{36}	4	160	210	115
F_{37}	1	180	220	180
F_{38}	4	190	260	190

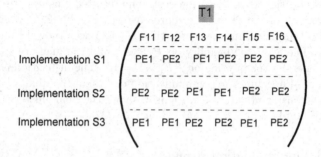

Fig. 12. Generated controller matrix.

Table 6. Comparison of the scheduling parameters with and without probabilistic estimations.

Parameter	Method	
	Using probability and CC	Using CC
Utilization factor U	0.22	0.3
Number of preemption	0	1

we have three implementations S_1, S_2 and S_3. Figure 12 shows the affectation of the task T1 in the controller matrix for each implementation scenario [22].

5.6   Evaluation

In this section, we evaluate the impact of the probabilistic aspect of the software tasks on the schedulability factors. We eliminate the probability on the edges and apply the partitioning based only on the communication costs. We schedule then the generated clusters. The tests are performed using CHEDDAR environment. Table 6 presents a comparison of some schedulability parameters between the partitioning results using the probability and the communication costs (CC) in one hand and the communication costs only on the other hand. It is clear that the probability enhances the schedulability quality along with the optimization of the traffic circulation.

6   Simulations

We have developed a tool environment to evaluate the potential communication costs, energy savings and execution costs for our methodology. The following subsections describe our tool and the assumptions made in its design. We show later some simulations results.

6.1   Simulation Methodology

We develop a co-design execution environment. It provides a toolbox in order to create a hw/sw system description according to the proposed design models and implements the co-design algorithms. It proposes a flexible task set generator for different scenarios and purposes. The tool places the software specification following several design constraints as inclusion/exclusion parameters, probabilistic execution of the software tasks, available memory and energy on the hardware units and real-time parameters. At each iteration, it constructs the controller table that stores all the possible execution scenarios. For simulation purposes the tool loads a specification file, reads the software and hardware characteristics, applies the co-design algorithms and generates the controller table along with memory and energy estimation.

6.2   Simulation Results

For performance simulation, we use ARTS framework which is a simulation tool for user-driven abstract MPSoC design explorations [25]. The framework features flexible configuration with respect to selection of task partitioning/mapping, ROTS protocols, communication topology.... The application model is based on static task graphs, where the exact functionality of a task is abstracted away and expressed using a set of timing constrains (execution time, deadline and offset). The PE models the behavior of an PI core, for example a CPU. It is characterized by supporting change of RTOS policies as well as task mapping during run-time. Based on which events are enabled for recording multiple files are generated that provide an overview of the architecture-under-test, and the profile of the application, the PE utilization, the memory or the communication. Hence, The framework allows to: (i) model processing elements (PE), memory units and interconnect, (ii) investigate PE utilization, memory usage, communication issues, and energy/power consumption, and (iii) analyze the causality between MPSoC components i.e. resource constrains and inter-dependencies. We have performed several simulations of the I-codesign methodology to determine the system parameters that affect the communication costs, the energy consumption and the number of preemption. In the following simulations, we compare

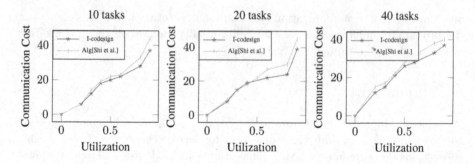

Fig. 13. Communication costs with 10, 20, and 40 tasks.

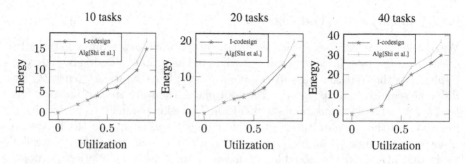

Fig. 14. Energy consumption with 10, 20, and 40 tasks.

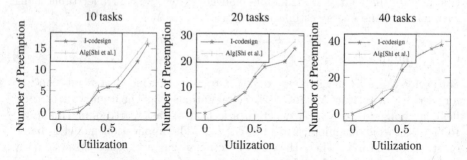

Fig. 15. Number of preemption with 10, 20, and 40 tasks.

the proposed work with the partitioning and scheduling algorithms Al [16]. We determine the effects of varying the number of tasks on the communication costs of the communicating functions placed on different PEs. Figure 13 shows the communication costs for task sets with 10, 20 and 40 tasks while Fig. 14 shows the energy consumption on the same task set [22]. Figure 15 presents the number of preemption with both algorithms using the same task set [22]. We notice that the I-codesign shows a good results for communications costs, energy savings and preemption values especially with high-range processor utilization values.

7   Conclusion

The task mapping onto tiles of the target architecture is an NP-complete design activity, and when performed at run-time may not get good results. This is due to the exiguous time and to the large number of solutions to be explored. In order to deal with these design problems, we introduce a new co-design methodology called I-codesign. The first original point in this methodology is the modeling techniques that relies on probabilistic estimations as well as modeling other constraints on the graphs such as the inclusion/exclusion constraint. Furthermore, the new partitioning combination of iterative, constructive and functional techniques allows the efficient and optimized placements of the software hardware specification while respecting the limited resources presented by the memory, the energy and real-time constraints. The second original contribution is the proposed controller module that stores all the possible reconfiguration scenarios and acts at run-time whenever a reconfiguration event occurs. The improvement of the proposed techniques is highlighted in terms of both communication costs (the number of exchanged messages), the consumed energy and consequently the required CPU time.

References

1. Shaout, A., El-mousa, H., Mattar, B.: Specification and modeling of HW/SW CO-design for heterogeneous embedded systems. In: Proceedings of World Congress on Engineering, Hong Kong, pp. 273–278 (2009)
2. Teich, J.: Hardware software codesign: the past, the present, and predicting the future. Proc. IEEE **100**, 1411–1430 (2012)
3. Cheng, O., Abdulla, W., Salcic, Z.: Hardware software codesign of automatic speech recognition system for embedded real-time applications. IEEE Trans. Industr. Electron. **58**, 850–859 (2011)
4. Wainer, G.: Applying modelling and simulation for development embedded systems. In: Proceedings of 2nd Mediterranean Conference on Embedded Computing (MECO) (2013)
5. Tang, J.W., Hau, Y.W., Marsono, M.: Hardware software partitioning of embedded system-on-chip applications. In: 2015 Proceedings of IFIP/IEEE International Conference on Very Large Scale Integration, pp. 331–336 (2015)
6. Banerjee, A., Mondal, A., Sarkar, A., Biswas, S.: Real-time embedded systems analysis; from theory to practice. In: Proceedings of 19th International Symposium on VLSI Design and Test (VDAT), Ahmedabad, pp. 1–2 (2015)
7. Joshi, P.V., Gurumurthy, K.S.: Analysing and improving the performance of software code for real time embedded systems. In: Proceedings of 2nd International Conference on Devices, Circuits and Systems (ICDCS), pp. 1–5 (2014)
8. Pillai, P., Shin, K.G.: Real-time dynamic voltage scaling for low-power embedded operating systems. In: Proceedings of 18th ACM Symposium on Operating Systems Principles, vol. 35, pp. 89–102 (2001)
9. Nikolic, B., Awan, M.A., Petters, S.M.: SPARTS: simulator for power aware and real-time systems. In: Proceedings of IEEE 10th International Conference on Trust, Security and Privacy in Computing and communications, pp. 999–1004 (2011)
10. Wang, X.W., Chen, W.N., Wang, Y., Peng, C.L.: A co-design flow for reconfigurable embedded computing system with RTOS support. In: Proceedings of ICESS 2009, International Conference on Embedded Software and Systems, pp. 467–474 (2009)

11. Ghribi, I., Abdallah, R., Khalgui, M., Platzner, M.: New Codesign solutions for modeling and partitioning probabilistic reconfigurable embedded software. In: Proceedings of 29th conference on European Simulation and Modeling Conference (EUROSIS) (2015)

12. Vahid, F., Gajski, D.D.: Incremental hardware estimation during hardware/software functional partitioning. In: Proceedings of IEEE Transactions on Very Large Scale Integration Systems, pp. 516–521 (2002)

13. Ernst, R., Henkel, J., Benner, T., Holtmann, U.: The COSYMA environment for hardware/software cosynthesis of small embedded systems. In: Proceedings of Microprocessors and Microsystems (1996)

14. Camposano, R., Wilberg, J.: Embedded system design. In: Proceedings of Design Automation for Embedded Systems (2001)

15. Shi, R., Yin, S., Yin, C., Liu, L., Wei, S.: Energy-aware task partitioning and scheduling algorithm for reconfigurable processor. In: Proceedings of IEEE 11th International Conference on Solid-State and Integrated Circuit Technology), pp. 1–3 (2012)

16. Rui, S., Yin, S., Chongyong, Y.: Energy-aware task partitioning and scheduling algorithm for reconfigurable processo. In: Proceedings of IEEE 11th International Conference on Solid-State and Integrated Circuit Technology), Xi'an, pp. 1–3 (2012)

17. Janakiraman, N., Kumar, P.N.: Multi-objective module partitioning design for dynamic and partial reconfigurable system-on-chip using genetic algorithm. J. Syst. Archit. 60, 119–139 (2014)

18. Poornima, B., Kumar, V.: A multilevel partitioning approach for efficient tasks allocation in heterogeneous distributed systems. J. Syst. Archit. 54, 530–548 (2008)

19. Liu, P., Wu, J., Wang, Y.: Integrated heuristic for hardware/software co-design on reconfigurable devices. In: Proceedings of 13th International Conference on Parallel and Distributed Computing, Applications and Technologies, pp. 370–375 (2012)

20. Banerjee, S., Bozorgzadeh, E., Dutt, N.: Physically-aware HW-SW partitioning for reconfigurable architectures with partial dynamic reconfiguration. In: Proceedings of 42nd Design Automation Conference, pp. 335–340 (2005)

21. Fiduccia, C.M., Mattheyes, R.M.: A linear time heuristic for improving network partitions. In: Proceedings of 9th Conference on Design Automation, pp. 175–181 (1982)

22. Ghribi, I., Abdallah, R., Khalgui, M., Platzner, M.: New co-design methodology for real-time embedded systems. In: Proceedings of 11th International Joint Conference on Software Technologies, Lisbon (2016)

23. Forget, J., Boniol, F., Grolleau, E., Lesens, D., Pagetti, C.: Scheduling dependent periodic tasks without synchronization mechanisms. In: Proceedings of 16th IEEE on Real-Time and Embedded Technology and Applications Symposium (RTAS), pp. 301–310 (2010)

24. Singhoff, F., Legrand, J., Nana, L., Marce, L.: Cheddar: a flexible real time scheduling framework. In: Proceedings of 2004 Annual ACM SIGAda International Conference on Ada: The Engineering of Correct and Reliable Software for Real-Time Distributed Systems Using Ada and Related Technologies, pp. 1–8 (2004)

25. Mahadevan, S., Storgaard, M., Madsen, J., Virk, K.: ARTS: a system-level framework for modeling MPSoC components and analysis of their causality. In: Proceedings of 13th IEEE International Symposium on Modeling, Analysis, and Simulation of Computer and Telecommunication Systems, pp. 480–483 (2005)

$CRMPSoC$: New Solution for Feasible Reconfigurable MPSoC

Imen Khemaissia[1](✉), Olfa Mosbahi[1], Mohamed Khalgui[2], and Zhiwu Li[3,4]

[1] Faculty of Sciences, Tunis El-Manar University, 2092 Tunis, Tunisia
khemaissia-imen@hotmail.com, olfamosbahi@gmail.com
[2] Cynapsys Company, Tunisia-France-Germany, LISI Lab, INSAT Institute,
University of Carthage, Tunis, Tunisia
khalguimohamed@gmail.com
[3] Institute of Systems Engineering, Macau University of Science and Technology,
Taipa, Macau, China
[4] School of Electro-Mechanical Engineering, Xidian University,
Xi'an 710071, China
zhwli@xidian.edu.cn

Abstract. This paper is dealing with the reconfiguration of a flexible real-time Network-on-Chip (NoC) in Multiprocessors System-on-Chip MPSoC architectures. We assume that each NoC's node is composed of a processor and a router. A processor is assumed to be composed of dependent periodic and aperiodic operating system tasks. The paper addresses low-power adaptations of MPSoC when dynamic reconfigurations of the periodic and aperiodic tasks (sharing resources) are applied at run-time to save or improve the performance. The reconfiguration is defined as any operation allowing the addition-removal-update of periodic dependent OS (Operating System) tasks that share resources. For two added dependent tasks assigned to different processors, a message is added automatically on the NoC. After a such scenario, several real-time constraints may be violated and the power consumption increased. In order to resolve this problem, a new approach $CRMPSoC$ (Abbrev. Cynapsys-Reconfigurable MPSoC) that is composed of two steps is proposed: (1) Applying a reconfiguration: Selection of reconfiguration scenarios, and (2) System Feasibility: A multi-agent architecture based

This research work is carried out within a MOBIDOC PhD thesis of the PASRI program, EU-funded and administered by ANPR (Tunisia). This national project is a collaboration between LISI Lab at University of Carthage, Cynapsys (French-German company installed in Tunisia), Systems Control Lab at Xidian University in China and Macau University of Science and Technology in Macau. We thank all directors of Cynapsys for their technical and financial stable supports. Special thank to all Master and Graduate Students who partially supported this project. This work is partially supported by Science and Technology Development Fund, MSAR, under Grant No. 066/2013/A2.

M. Khalgui is also with ITIA Institute, National Council of Research, Rome 00161, Italy.

Z.W. Li is also with the Faculty of Engineering, King Abdulaziz University, Jeddah 21589, Saudi Arabia.

© Springer International Publishing AG 2017
E. Cabello et al. (Eds.): ICSOFT 2016, CCIS 743, pp. 175–198, 2017.
DOI: 10.1007/978-3-319-62569-0_9

on a master/slave model is defined where a slave agent is assigned to each
node to verify the system/bus feasibility, and a master is proposed for
the whole architecture if any perturbation occurs at run-time by proposing software or hardware solutions. Since the kernel is not reconfigurable,
we develop a new middleware that will support the different steps of our
approach. The latter is applied to a real case study for the evaluation of
the paper's contribution.

Keywords: Embedded system · Reconfigurable MPSoC · Multi-agent ·
Real-time and low-power scheduling · Middleware

1 Introduction

The new generation of embedded systems is based on the MPSoC oriented technologies since they are widely used today to run various applications in industry
[51]. We assume that the MPSoC is composed of n nodes where each one contains:
(i) a processor and (ii) a router. Due to possible external or also internal distur-
bances, the system can be automatically adapted by adding/removing/updating
OS periodic tasks to/from/in the processors. Nevertheless, some realtime constraints may be violated and the system becomes unfeasible. The reconfiguration
can be also hardware by activating/deactivating a processor of the architecture
[1]. Many projects and researches are dealing today with the reconfiguration of
real-time embedded systems under real-time and energy constraints [2,8,11,34],
more specifically the reconfiguration of MPSoC architectures [29–32]. Also, we
found multiple research works on low-power execution of MPSoC architectures
in [9,17,29,32,52]. A fair amount of algorithms are proposed to schedule the OS
tasks of embedded systems [7,18,19,25,27,28]. Although all of them are interesting, no one in the related works deals with the reconfiguration of a real-time
MPSoC architecture with low-power. We note that no one in all our previous
conference works can resolve the global problem that we are dealing with in the
current paper. The contribution of the current paper is original and resolves a
global problem dealing with low-power-reconfiguration of MPSoC oriented applications implemented by periodic/aperiodic OS tasks/messages under precedence
constraints and with shared resources.

We assume in the current work that n processors are linked via the NoC. Each
processor is implemented by periodic/aperiodic OS tasks which can exchange
messages on the NoC. They are assumed to be under precedence constraints
and with shared resources. The well-known scheduling policies earliest deadline
first (EDF) and First In First Out are used to schedule the periodic and aperiodic tasks, respectively. The immediate priority ceiling protocol IPCP [27] is
used to manage the precedence constraints of dependent tasks. Before any reconfiguration scenario, the system is assumed to be feasible, i.e., the utilization of
each processor is equal or less than 1. Since a reconfiguration is assumed to be
a run-time software operation allowing the addition-removal-update of software
tasks and messages, this scenario can push the execution of new-old tasks to

violate real-time deadlines or to possibly increase the energy consumption or a message can take a long time to arrive to its destination. In order to guarantee the respect of the real-time and precedence constraints, a new complete approach is developed at Cynapsys [57] which is a professional company in the embedded technologies. This approach is achieved on two steps: (1) Application of reconfiguration scenarios by adding, removing or updating tasks or messages, and (2) Feasibility analysis of each processor and also the NoC after any reconfiguration scenario. We propose a multi-agent architecture based on the master/slave model to handle feasible reconfigurations of *RMPSoC*. Two types of agents are defined: (i) A master agent: Controls the evolution of the whole system's environment before applying software-hardware reconfigurations and checks the feasibility of the OS/NoC, (ii) A slave agent: Checks the power consumption and the respect of real-time constraints of each processor. The contribution of this paper is applied to FPGA Stratix III and a middleware is developed to handle run-time reconfiguration scenarios with Nios II and to arrange the new lists of tasks and messages to be executed after each scenario [4]. The middleware based on agents and deployed on each processor listens to input reconfigurations, arranges the parameters of tasks and controls also the traffic on the NoC. The rest of the paper is organized as follows: Sect. 2 reviews the related works. Section 3 formalizes the reconfigurable MPSoC architectures followed by a case study. Section 4 represents a methodology for a reconfigurable feasible real-time application. The architecture is implemented, simulated, and analyzed in Sect. 5. Finally, Sect. 6 concludes this work.

2   Background

We expose and analyze several research works which are related to the contribution. Since this paper addresses the reconfigurable feasible NoC in adaptive MPSoC architectures, we start first by presenting the characteristics of MPSoC and NoC. Then we review some interesting related papers dealing with the real-time scheduling of OS tasks.

2.1   MPSoC and NoC Characteristics

The MultiProcessors System-on-Chip (MPSoC) uses multiple processors usually targeted for embedded applications. It is used by platforms that contain multiple usually heterogeneous processing elements with specific functionalities reflecting the need of the expected application domain [33]. All these components are linked to each other by an on-chip interconnect. These architectures meet the performance requirements of multimedia applications, telecommunication architectures, network security and other application domains while limiting the power consumption through the use of specialized processing elements and architectures. Because of their comparatively high performance, flexibility, and power efficiency, the MPSoC is based on NoC solutions [46–50]. Network on chip (NoC) is a new paradigm assigned for the interconnections inside a system on chip (SoC) that presents a viable communication infrastructure [42]. Although all of them are interesting, there is no related work that deals with the real-time reconfigurable NoC in MPSoC architectures under low-power constraints.

2.2   Reconfigurable MPSoC

There are many related works dealing with the reconfigurable MPSoC in the recent years. The work in [45] proposes a configuration exploration tree for MPSoC architectures with configurable processors and bus interface. The authors in [30] present a method for mapping streaming applications, with real-time requirements, onto a reconfigurable MPSoC. In this method, the network performance interface and the NoC is integrated in the performance models of the applications. A solution is developed in [31] that consists in synthesizing a custom bus architecture for reconfigurable computing architectures. In this research, we develop at Cynapsys Corporation a new approach that deals with the reconfigurations of real-time MPSoC under low-power and precedence constraints and shared resources.

2.3   Low-Power Solutions on MPSoC

The authors in [9] propose a novel dynamic power management scheme for adaptive pipelined MPSoCs, suitable for multimedia applications. The paper [17] presents a global framework for power/energy estimation and optimization of heterogeneous Within this framework, a power modeling methodology is defined, and an open platform is developed. This methodology takes into account all the aspects of embedded systems; the software, the hardware, and the operating system. The authors in [29,32] describe a NoC architecture for reconfigurable multiprocessor system-on-chip in.

2.4   Real-Time Scheduling

Several successful studies in the literature deal with the real-time scheduling of OS tasks. The work in [25] proposes the Earliest Deadline First EDF and the Rate Monotonic RM to schedule periodic tasks. The work in [27] presents the original priority ceiling protocol OPCP and immediate priority ceiling protocol IPCP in order to solve the scheduling problem of the tasks that share resources. The research work in [28] proposes the stack resource policy SRP that allows processes with different priorities to share a single run-time stack. In this paper, we use the EDF for the scheduling of periodic tasks since it is optimal under some assumptions.

In summary, a lot of successful investigations have been done in the domain of reconfigurable MPSoC-based embedded technologies. None of the previous works takes into account the feasibility at run-time of NoC in an MPSoC architecture under real-time and energy constraints.

3 Reconfigurable MPSoC *RMPSoC*

In this section, we start by formalizing the reconfigurable MPSoC *RMPSoC* before exposing a case study that explains the problem under consideration.

3.1 Formalization of *RMPSoC*

We assume that *RMPSoC* consists of the matrix N_{i*j} of nodes, i.e., $RMPSoC = \{N_{1,1}, N_{1,2}, \ldots, N_{2,1}, N_{2,2}, N_{i,j}, \ldots, N_{l,c}\}$ ($i \in [1...l]$ and $j \in [1...c]$) where l and c are respectively the numbers of the rows and columns of the network on chip NoC which is used to link all the nodes of *RMPSoC* [32]. *RMPSoC* is assumed to be reconfigurable and adapted to its environment or to add-relax new and old services by adding/updating/removing OS tasks to/from the processors. We assume that each node $N_{i,j}$ is composed of: (a) Processor $Pr_{i,j}$: Executes periodic/aperiodic OS tasks $\tau_{i,j,k}$ ($i \in [1...l]$, $j \in [1...c]$ and $k \in [1...n_{i,j}]$) that share resources and under precedence constraints, (b) Router $R_{i,j}$: Is responsible of the message's forwarding in the NoC. The latter has a buffer that contains the list of messages to be added from a source node to a destination one. The NoC architecture is illustrated in Fig. 1. We note that the different processors of *RMPSoC* share data in a global memory M_G. According to Liu and Layland in [25], each

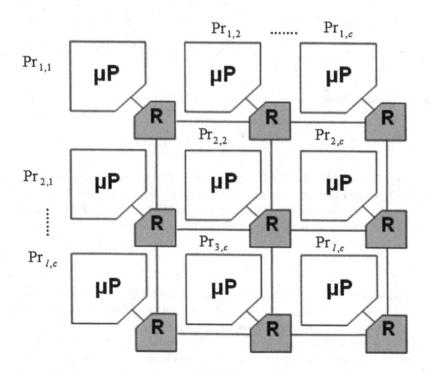

Fig. 1. NoC architecture.

periodic task $\tau_{i,j,k}$ ($i \in [1...l]$, $j \in [1...c]$ and $k \in [1..n_{i,j}]$) may produce many jobs. It is described by:

- Release time $R_{i,j,k}$: The time when a job becomes available for execution. Since the tasks are synchronous, $R_{i,j,k} = 0$,
- Period $T_{i,j,k}$: Is the regular inter-arrival time,
- Deadline $D_{i,j,k}$: The absolute deadline is equal to the release time plus the relative deadline,
- WCET $C_{i,j,k}$: the time needed to compute a job, and
- static priority $S_{i,j,k}$: The highest static priority is equal to 1, i.e., $S_k = 1$ represents $\tau_{i,j,k}$ with the highest static priority.

For the aperiodic tasks, they are characterized by a deadline d_k, a release time r_k, and a WCET c_k. We assume that any aperiodic task arrives according to the poisson process based on a poisson distribution with a rate λ_r^k and its WCET is exponentially distributed with the same mean $\frac{1}{\lambda_C^k}$. Also, we consider that the aperiodic tasks can be with hard or soft deadlines.

We assume that the tasks of $RMPSoC$ share software resources with precedence constraints. We assume that $T_{i,j,k} = D_{i,j,k}$. Each task in $RMPSoC$ is characterized by inclusion and exclusion sets according to user requirements respectively where:

- $Inclusion_{set}(\tau_{i,j,k})$: the set of processors that can handle the execution of $\tau_{i,j,k}$.
- $Exlusion_{set}(\tau_{i,j,k})$: the set of processors that cannot handle the execution of $\tau_{i,j,k}$.

For the periodic tasks that share resources, their processor utilization is given by [5, 18]:

$$U_{per}(Pr_{i,j}) = (\sum_{k=1}^{n_{i,j}} \frac{C_{i,j,k}}{T_{i,j,k}} + \frac{B_{i,j,k}}{T_{i,j,k}}), \forall k \in [1...n_{i,j}] \tag{1}$$

where $B_{i,j,k}$ is the blocking factor that is defined as the time to spend by a task with a higher priority when blocked. It waits the termination of a task with a lower priority. In this work, we assume that the blocking factor $B_{i,j,k}$ is equal to 0 or 1 [18]. The utilization of the aperiodic tasks is as follows:

$$U_{pro} = \frac{\lambda_r^k}{\lambda_C^k} \tag{2}$$

The independent tasks are scheduled by using the EDF algorithm for the periodic tasks and the FIFO for the aperiodic ones. The immediate priority ceiling protocol IPCP is used to schedule the tasks that share resources. To manage the dependent tasks, we can use the technique proposed in [5, 19]. For example, let us define two dependant tasks $\tau_{i,j,e}$ and $\tau_{i,j,f}$ such that $\tau_{i,j,e}$ precedes $\tau_{i,j,f}$. The deadlines of the tasks are assigned as follows:

if $\tau_{i,j,e}$ precedes $\tau_{i,j,f}$ **then** $S_{i,j,e} < S_{i,j,f}$. The deadline $D_{i,j,e}$ is equal to:

$$D_{i,j,e} = min(D_{i,j,e}, (D_{i,j,f} - C_{i,j,e})) \tag{3}$$

By Eq. (3), we guarantee that the precedence constraint will be satisfied. We note that the initial utilization of each processor U_{bef} is equal to:

$$U_{bef}(Pr_{i,j}) = U_{per}(Pr_{i,j}) + U_{pro}(Pr_{i,j}) \tag{4}$$

According to [3,4], the energy to be consumed by a processor is proportional to the processor utilization. It is given by:

$$P_{i,j} \propto U_{bef}(Pr_{i,j})^2 \tag{5}$$

Let we assume a reconfiguration scenario at a particular time t. We can apply a software reconfiguration to add or remove OS software tasks and U_{bef} increases to be U_{aft}.

We assume that the source task $\tau_{i,j,h}$ exchanges a message $m_p(\tau_{i,j,h}; \tau_{a,b,k})$ with a target task destination $\tau_{a,b,k}$. A periodic message $m_p(\tau_{i,j,h}; \tau_{a,b,k})$ in [5] is characterized by:

- A size $S_{mp}(\tau_{i,j,h}; \tau_{a,b,k})$,
- A transmission period $T_{mp}(\tau_{i,j,h}; \tau_{a,b,k})$,
- A deadline $D_{mp}(\tau_{i,j,h}; \tau_{a,b,k})$,
- A Worst Case Transmission Time $WCTT_p$ $C_{mp}(\tau_{i,j,h}; \tau_{a,b,k})$, where:

$$WCTT = S_{mp}(\tau_{i,j,h}; \tau_{a,b,k})/debit_{NoC} \tag{6}$$

and
- A static priority $SP_{mp}(\tau_{i,j,h}; \tau_{a,b,k})$

We assume that an aperiodic message $m_{ap}(\tau_{i,j,h}; \tau_{a,b,k})$ is characterized by:

- A size $S_{map}(\tau_{i,j,h}; \tau_{a,b,k})$,
- A random transmission period $T_{map}(\tau_{i,j,h}; \tau_{a,b,k})$,
- A deadline $D_{map}(\tau_{i,j,h}; \tau_{a,b,k})$,
- A Worst Case Transmission Time $WCTT_{ap}$ $C_{map}(\tau_{i,j,h}; \tau_{a,b,k})$, where:

$$WCTT = S_{map}(\tau_{i,j,h}; \tau_{a,b,k})/debit_{NoC} \tag{7}$$

and
- A static priority $SP_{mp}(\tau_{i,j,h}; \tau_{a,b,k})$

In this work, we assume that after each addition of a pair of tasks a new message is added automatically. The purpose of this research is to seek the optimal path between the source task and the destination task under real-time constraints. According to [40], the bus utilization is calculated as follows:

$$U_{bus}(m_p(\tau_{i,j,h}; \tau_{a,b,k})) = \sum_{p=1}^{m} \frac{C_{mp}(\tau_{i,j,h}; \tau_{a,b,k})}{T_{mp}(\tau_{i,j,h}; \tau_{a,b,k})} \tag{8}$$

where m is the number of messages.

Fig. 2. Stratix III FPGA development board.

3.2   Case Study: Stratix III FPGA

The proposed approach in the current paper is applied to an FPGA Stratix III[1]. We use an FPGA-optimized network-on-chip architecture [53] (Fig. 2).

In order to develop new module on FPGA, we have used Quartus II [54]. Moreover, we have used SOPC Builder [55] which is made by Altera to automate the connection of soft-hardware components to create a complete computer system that runs on any of its various FPGA chips. The integrated development environment Nios II IDE [56] is used to create Nios II processors. It is a software development tool for graphical Nios II family of embedded processors. The Nios II IDE provides a platform for a coherent development that works for all Nios II processor systems. Thus, we illustrate $RMPSoC$ through a running example in order to explain the proposed methodology by using theoretical tasks. Suppose that a stratix FPGA contains four Nios II processors $Pr_{1,1}$, $Pr_{1,2}$, $Pr_{2,1}$ and $Pr_{2,2}$. We define the NoC as the communication architecture between the components of the MPSoC. Initially, $RMPSoC$ is assumed to be feasible, i.e., it meets its real-time constraints with low-power properties. Table 1 lists the parameters of the different processors. We assume that its initial utilization of periodic tasks is equal to 0.5 and all the tasks are released at the time $R_i = 0$ with $T_i = D_i$. We assume that the aperiodic tasks/messages arrive with $\lambda_C = 0.5$ and $\lambda_r = 0.1$. Then their utilizations is equal to 0.2. Thus, the initial utilization of each processor is equal to 0.7 and the energy consumption is 0.49. We assume also that the NoC can initially support all the added messages since its utilization is equal to 0.95.

---

[1] We are very grateful for the company Cynapsys which provides us this FPGA. It is characterized by: (a) High-performance Stratix III EP3SL150F1152 FPGA, (b) DDR2 SDRAM and QDR II SRAM, (c) PSRAM and flash memory, (d) USB 2.0 MAC/PHY, (e) Graphics and character LCD displays, and (f) On-board embedded USB-BlasterTM download cable.

Table 1. The characteristics of the initial periodic tasks.

$Pr_{1,1}$			$Pr_{1,2}$			$Pr_{2,1}$			$Pr_{2,2}$		
tau_i	C_i	T_i/D_i	tau_i	C_i	T_i/D_i	tau_i	C_i	T_i/D_i	tau_i	C_i	T_i/D_i
τ_1	1	20	τ_6	1	10	τ_{11}	2	10	τ_{16}	2	40
τ_2	1	10	τ_7	2	40	τ_{12}	4	20	τ_{17}	2	20
τ_3	2	10	τ_8	4	40	τ_{13}	1	20	τ_{18}	1	10
τ_4	2	40	τ_9	1	20	τ_{14}	1	40	τ_{19}	1	20
τ_5	1	10	τ_{10}	2	10	τ_{15}	1	40	τ_{20}	2	10
τ_{h1}	2	10	τ_{s1}	1	20	τ_{h1}	2	10	τ_{s1}	1	20

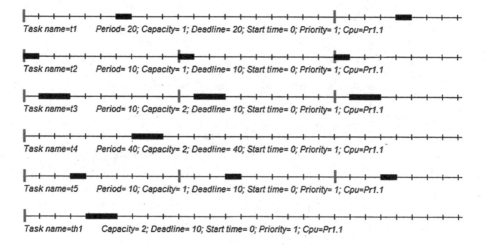

Task name=t1   Period= 20; Capacity= 1; Deadline= 20; Start time= 0; Priority= 1; Cpu=Pr1.1

Task name=t2   Period= 10; Capacity= 1; Deadline= 10; Start time= 0; Priority= 1; Cpu=Pr1.1

Task name=t3   Period= 10; Capacity= 2; Deadline= 10; Start time= 0; Priority= 1; Cpu=Pr1.1

Task name=t4   Period= 40; Capacity= 2; Deadline= 40; Start time= 0; Priority= 1; Cpu=Pr1.1

Task name=t5   Period= 10; Capacity= 1; Deadline= 10; Start time= 0; Priority= 1; Cpu=Pr1.1

Task name=th1   Capacity= 2; Deadline= 10; Start time= 0; Priority= 1; Cpu=Pr1.1

Fig. 3. Initial scheduling of $Pr_{1,1}$.

Table 3 indicates the periodic/aperiodic tasks that are dynamically added to the different processors. We assume that the aperiodic utilization of the added tasks/messages is equal to 0.1. The processor utilization after the reconfiguration $U_{aft}(Pr_{1,1})$, $U_{aft}(Pr_{1,2})$, $U_{aft}(Pr_{2,1})$ and $U_{aft}(Pr_{2,2})$ will be respectively 1.96, 1.8225, 1.8225 and 1.69. Since the processor utilization of all the processors is greater than 1, the system is infeasible. Also the energy consumption increases to be 1.1, 1.1 and 1.21, respectively.

After the addition of several messages, the bus utilization becomes equal to 1.2 and several messages cannot be supported by the NoC. Moreover, the messages take a long time to be routed. For that new software solutions are proposed for the NoC feasibility.

In the next sections, new technical software solutions are proposed in order to satisfy the real-time constraints and to reduce the power consumption (Fig. 3 and Table 2).

Table 2. The characteristics of the initial messages.

Message	$CM_i(\tau_k, \tau_l)$	$DM_i(\tau_k, \tau_l)/TM_i(\tau_k, \tau_l)$	taille
$m(\tau_2, \tau_4)$	1	10	12
$m(\tau_5, \tau_7)$	1	20	14
$m(\tau_2, \tau_3)$	2	20	13
$m(\tau_5, \tau_{13})$	1	10	25
$m(\tau_{12}, \tau_6)$	5	50	16
$m(\tau_8, \tau_2)$	2	20	14
$m(\tau_8, \tau_9)$	1	10	20
$m(\tau_{13}, \tau_{10})$	2	40	10
$m(\tau_8, \tau_2)$	2	20	14
$m(\tau_8, \tau_9)$	1	10	20
$m(\tau_{13}, \tau_{10})$	2	40	10

Table 3. The characteristics of the added periodic tasks.

$Pr_{1,1}$			$Pr_{1,2}$			$Pr_{2,1}$			$Pr_{2,2}$		
tau_i	C_i	T_i/D_i	tau_i	C_i	T_i/D_i	tau_i	C	T	tau_i	C	T
τ_{b1}	6	30	τ_{c1}	2	40	τ_{d1}	2	40	τ_{e1}	3	30
τ_{b2}	4	20	τ_{c2}	3	30	τ_{d2}	7	35	τ_{e2}	2	10
τ_{b3}	3	30	τ_{c3}	7	35	τ_{d3}	2	10	τ_{e3}	2	20
τ_{b4}	1	10	τ_{c4}	2	10	τ_{d4}	3	30	τ_{e4}	3	30
τ_{bs1}	2	10	τ_{ch1}	1	20	τ_{dh1}	2	10	τ_{es1}	1	20

4   New Middleware for the Feasible Reconfigurable MPSoC

We propose in the current paper a new middleware that deals with the feasible real-time reconfigurable MPSoC architectures as an extension to the contributions in [1] since in the latter, we do not propose which layer will manage the addition/removal/ update of OS tasks/messages. The different services offered by this layer are stated as follows: (i) Application of reconfiguration scenarios in different processors, (ii) Verification of each processor's feasibility and (iii) Verification of the NoC feasibility. For the two last steps, a multi agent architecture following the Master-Slave model is defined: (i) Master Agent Ag_M: responsible of the whole system feasibility and the NoC feasibility, (ii) Slave Agent $Ag_{i,j}$: defined for each node $N_{i,j}$. It informs Ag_M if the energy increases or if the local real-time constraints are not satisfied. Figure 5 summarizes the whole contribution of this current research. It shows the different states of the system and the proposed strategy to resolve any destabilization that can occur before and after applying any reconfiguration scenario (Fig. 4 and Table 4).

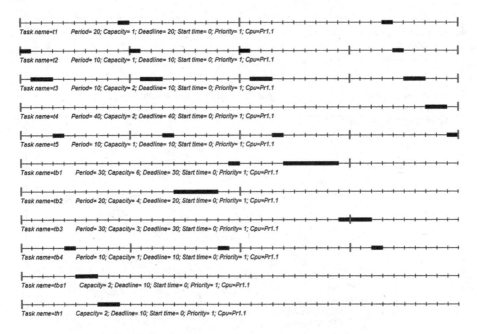

Fig. 4. Scheduling of $Pr_{1,1}$ after a reconfiguration scenario.

Table 4. The characteristics of the added messages.

Message	$CM_{ep}(\tau_k, \tau_l)$	$DM_{ep}(\tau_k, \tau_l)/TM_{ep}(\tau_k, \tau_l)$	*taille*
$m(\tau_{b2}, \tau_{b4})$	1	10	15
$m(\tau_{b3}, \tau_{c1})$	1	20	10
$m(\tau_{d4}, \tau_{b1})$	2	20	10
$m(\tau_{c1}, \tau_{c3})$	1	10	12
$m(\tau_{c2}, \tau_{b2})$	5	50	12
$m(\tau_{e1}, \tau_{b1})$	2	20	10
$m(\tau_{e2}, \tau_{b3})$	1	10	10
$m(\tau_{d3}, \tau_{b1})$	2	40	10
$m(\tau_{b2}, \tau_{d4})$	2	20	20
$m(\tau_{d1}, \tau_{c3})$	1	10	10
$m(\tau_{bs1}, \tau_{es1})$	2	40	20

4.1 OS Feasibility

Many solutions are proposed to re-obtain the system feasibility in all the processors/NoC of *RMPSoC* after applying any reconfiguration scenario that violates real-time or energy constraints.

- Periods and λ_C modification, or
- WCETs and λ_C modification, or

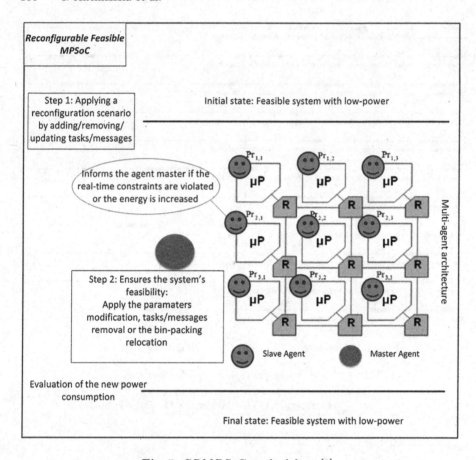

Fig. 5. $CRMPSoC$ methodology [1].

- Removal of unimportant tasks.
- Relocation of Tasks according to the Bin-packing.

Solution 1: Modification of Parameters. The utilization must be changed in order to guarantee a stable energy consumption. A technical solution to be proposed by Ag_M allows to modify the parameters of all the old and new tasks after any reconfiguration scenario. In this work, we suggest the modification of periods as a solution 1.1 or WCETs as a solution 1.2 to meet all the assumed constraints after such a scenario. We consider that the new utilization after the reconfiguration is less than/equal to the utilization before the reconfiguration and then we try to substitute the new utilization by the new parameters until we obtain the new formulas to calculate the periods/WCETs in function of $U_{per}(Pr_{i,j})$. According to [1], the new periods become:

$$T_{i,j,k}^{(r)} = \left\lceil (\sum_{k=1}^{n} (\frac{C_{i,j,k} + B_{i,j,k}}{U_{per}(Pr_{i,j})}) \right\rceil \qquad (9)$$

After the modification of the periods, the new processor utilization of periodic tasks $U_{perT}^{(r)}$ is given by:

$$U_{perT}^{(r)}(Pr_{i,j}) = \sum_{k=1}^{n} \frac{C_{i,j,k}}{T_{i,j,k}^{(r)}} + \frac{B_{i,j,k}}{T_{i,j,k}^{(r)}} \tag{10}$$

where n is the number of periodic tasks and r is the reconfiguration number. Then, we can formulate the new power consumption of the periodic tasks as follows:

$$P_{perT}^{(r)}(Pr_{i,j}) \propto (U_{perT}^{(r)}(Pr_{i,j})^2) \tag{11}$$

According to Eq. (9), the new period of old and new tasks to be executed by $Pr_{1,1}$ becomes equal to 42 Time Units. It is equal to 76 for the tasks of $Pr_{1,2}$. The period of tasks in $Pr_{2,1}$ and $Pr_{2,1}$ is equal to 63 and 68, respectively. Thus the new processor utilizations of $Pr_{1,1}$, $Pr_{1,2}$, $Pr_{2,1}$ and $Pr_{2,2}$ are equal to 0.5. Solution 1.1 can stabilize the utilization of all the processors of $RMPSoC$ and can consequently maintain the power consumption.

If we modify the WCET of tasks, then the new $C_k^{(r)}$ are given by:

$$C_{i,j,k}^{(r)} = \begin{cases} \left\lfloor \dfrac{U_{per}(Pr_{i,j}) - \sum_{k=1}^{n} \frac{B_{i,j,k}}{T_{i,j,k}}}{\sum_{k=1}^{n} \frac{1}{T_{i,j,k}}} \right\rfloor \\[2em] 1, if \dfrac{U_{per}(Pr_{i,j}) - \sum_{k=1}^{n} \frac{B_{i,j,k}}{T_{i,j,k}}}{\sum_{k=1}^{n} \frac{1}{T_{i,j,k}}} \leq 0 \end{cases} \tag{12}$$

After the modification of the WCETs, the new processor utilization of the periodic tasks $U_{perC}^{(r)}$ is given by:

$$U_{perC}^{(r)}(Pr_{i,j}) = (\sum_{k=1}^{n} \frac{C_{i,j,k}^{(r)}}{T_{i,j,k}} + \frac{B_{i,j,k}}{T_{i,j,k}}) \tag{13}$$

The new power consumption is as follows:

$$P_{perC}^{(r)}(Pr_{i,j}) \propto (U_{perC}^{(r)}(Pr_{i,j})^2) \tag{14}$$

According to Eq. (12), the new constant WCET of tasks (old and new) to be executed by $Pr_{1,1}$ is equal to 1 Time Units. The constant WCET of tasks to be executed by $Pr_{1,2}$, $Pr_{2,1}$ and $Pr_{2,2}$ becomes 2 Time Units. Thus, the new utilizations of $Pr_{1,1}$, $Pr_{1,2}$ and $Pr_{2,1}$ are equal to 0.55, 0.51 and 0.45, respectively. Solution 1.2 can minimize the processor utilization of all the processors of $RMPSoC$ and the power consumption is reduced too. Also, we need to modify $lamda_C^k$ of the aperiodic tasks to maintain their utilizations. It is given by:

$$\lambda_{Ck}^{(i)} = \lambda_{Ck} \times \frac{U^{(aft)}(mic_i)}{U_{bef}(mic_i)}, \ \forall j \in [0, i] \tag{15}$$

Solution 2: Tasks Removal. As a second solution, Ag_M proposes the removal of some tasks/messages according to their priorities. Before the removal of a dependent task, we should verify if the tasks which are dependent has a lower priority or not. In this case, we remove them too. Otherwise, the task cannot be removed. If we consider the removal of the following tasks: A_1 and A_4 from $Pr_{1,1}$, then its processor utilization becomes 1. If we remove the unimportant tasks (with the lowest priority) from all the processors, then we can minimize the processor utilization. This solution can provide a feasible system after any reconfiguration scenario but the results of the processor/NoC utilization depends on the number of the added and removed tasks. Solutions 1 and 2 are proposed to maintain or reduce the power consumption.

Solution 3: Relocation of Tasks According to the Bin-Packing. The bin-packing algorithm can be used in this work by the relocation of tasks according to different conditions that will be mentioned below. Based on it, Ag_M can reconfigure the system on two levels in order to be temporally feasible with a low-power consumption. We propose to locate all the added periodic tasks in one processor. Since we can calculate the processor utilization for each task, two steps must be done: (a) **Step 1:** We relocate the tasks by using one of the proposed algorithms of the bin-packing, and (b) **Step 2:** We modify their parameters by following Solution 1 if the current utilization of a processor exceeds 1. To apply the bin-packing, we should order the tasks in an increasing order and the processors in a decreasing order according to their utilization. In order to relocate a task $\tau_{i,j,k}$ to $Pr_{i,j}$, two conditions should be satisfied: (i) **Condition 1:** the processor $Pr_{i,j} \in Inclusion_{set}(\tau_{i,j,k})$, and (ii) **Condition 2:** $U_{bef}(Pr_{i,j}) \leq 1$. The bin-packing is characterized by five heuristics:

- Best Fit Decreasing BFD: For each task, the agent assigns it to a random processor that satisfies the three conditions and $U_{l,c}$ is maximal,
- Worst Fit Decreasing WFD: For each task, the agent assigns it to a random processor that satisfies the three conditions and $U_{l,c}$ is minimal,
- Next Fit Decreasing NFD: If the three conditions are not satisfied, the processor is considered as deactivated,
- First Fit Decreasing FFD: The agent assigns an added task to the first activated processor that can satisfy condition1, condition 2 and condition 3, and
- Random Fit Decreasing RFD: For each task, the agent assigns it to a random processor that satisfies the three conditions.

Algorithm 1, that is proposed in [1], describes the different followed steps in order to relocate the tasks according to the next fit decreasing NFD.

We choose to apply the FFD policy on the running example and we assume that $Pr_{1,1}$ can support the added tasks to $Pr_{1,2}$ and vice versa. For the tasks of $Pr_{1,2}$ can be added to $Pr_{2,2}$ and vice versa. We start by ordering the tasks in a decreasing order and the processors utilization in an increasing order. We have $U_{bef}(Pr_{1,1}) = U_{bef}(Pr_{1,2}) = U_{bef}(Pr_{2,1}) = U_{bef}(Pr_{2,2})$. If we re-order the periodic tasks, we get $\tau_{b1}, \tau_{b2}, \tau_{c3}, \tau_{c4}, \tau_{d2}, \tau_{d3}, \tau_{e2}, \tau_{b3}, \tau_{b4}, \tau_{c2}, \tau_{d4}, \tau_{e1}, \tau_{e3},$

Algorithm 1. Relocation of new tasks according to NFD.

Order the processors in an increasing order;
Order the tasks in a decreasing order;
for (each processor $Pr_{i,j}$) **do**
    for (each task $\tau_{i,j,k}$) **do**
        if ($Pr_{i,j}$ **is active**) and ($\tau_{i,j,k} \in Inclusion_{set}(\tau_{i,j,k})$) **then**
            Calculate the current processor utilization $U_{bef}(Pr_{i,j})$ after the addition of
            $\tau_{i,j,k}$;
        else
            if (($U_{bef}(Pr_{i,j}) \geq 1$) **then**
                Assign $\tau_{i,j,k}$ to $Pr_{i,j}$ that satisfies the conditions (conditions 1, 2 and 3);
                Re-Ccompute $U_{bef}(Pr_{i,j})$ after the addition of $\tau_{i,j,k}$ to $Pr_{i,j}$;
                break;
            else
                Close the current processor and open the next one;
                Re-Calculate the utilization of the newest opened processor;
            end if
        end if
    end for
end for

τ_{e4}, τ_{c1} and τ_{d1}, respectively. Every time we add a task, we should verify if the processor can include it. The algorithm of the FFD is applied as follows: τ_{b1} and τ_{b2} are packed into $Pr_{1,1}$ and $Pr_{1,2}$. τ_{c3} and τ_{c4} are added into $Pr_{1,1}$ and $Pr_{1,2}$ too, respectively. Since $Pr_{1,1} \notin SetInc(\tau_{d2})$, the current added task is put into $Pr_{2,1}$. We apply the bin-packing algorithm until we pack all the added tasks into the different processors. Once we finish the addition of tasks, Ag_M applies the parameters modification. The relocation of the periodic tasks according to the FFD is illustrated by Fig. 6.

4.2 NoC Feasibility

According to [1,5], if the bus cannot support the added messages, then we can modify the parameters of the messages or remove the unimportant ones. The new periods or the WCTT of each message is calculated according to [5] as follows:

$$T_{mp} = \left\lceil \frac{\sum\limits_{i=1}^{m} C_{mp}}{U_{NoC}(periodicmessages)} \right\rceil \tag{16}$$

or

$$C_{mp} = \begin{cases} 1, 0 < \frac{U_{NoC}(periodicmessages)}{\sum\limits_{i=1}^{m} \frac{1}{T_{mp}}} \leq 1 \\ \left\lfloor \frac{U_{NoC}(periodicmessages)}{\sum\limits_{i=1}^{m} \frac{1}{T_{mp}}} \right\rfloor, \frac{U_{NoC}(periodicmessages)}{\sum\limits_{i=1}^{m} \frac{1}{T_{mp}}} > 1 \end{cases} \tag{17}$$

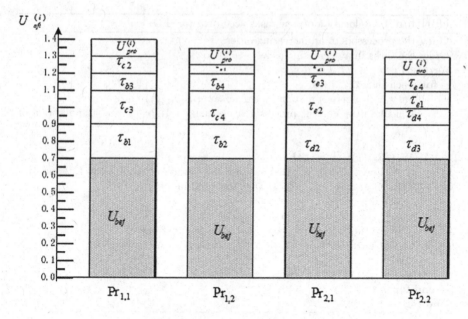

Fig. 6. Relocate new tasks in FFD.

where m denotes the number of messages.

After applying Eq. (16), the new utilization of NoC becomes equal to 0.8. Then the NoC is considered feasible. It is similar for the messages, i.e., if we remove the messages with the lowest priority the utilization of NoC will be reduced.

5   Experimentation

This section presents an experimentation that applies low-power reconfigurations of MPSoC-based architectures. We present first of all the localization of the middleware that will handle any reconfiguration scenario. Then, we present the implementation of the agent-based architecture. After that, we show theoretical simulations and analysis which are used to underline the benefits of this contribution. We propose to apply this contribution to Stratix III development board.

5.1   Localization of the Middleware

In order to handle run-time reconfiguration scenarios with Nios II, a middleware is developed to arrange the new lists of tasks and messages to be executed after each scenario Fig. 7. The middleware based on agents and deployed on each processor listens to input reconfigurations and arranges the parameters of tasks/messages. All the assumed tasks are defined statically and the middleware

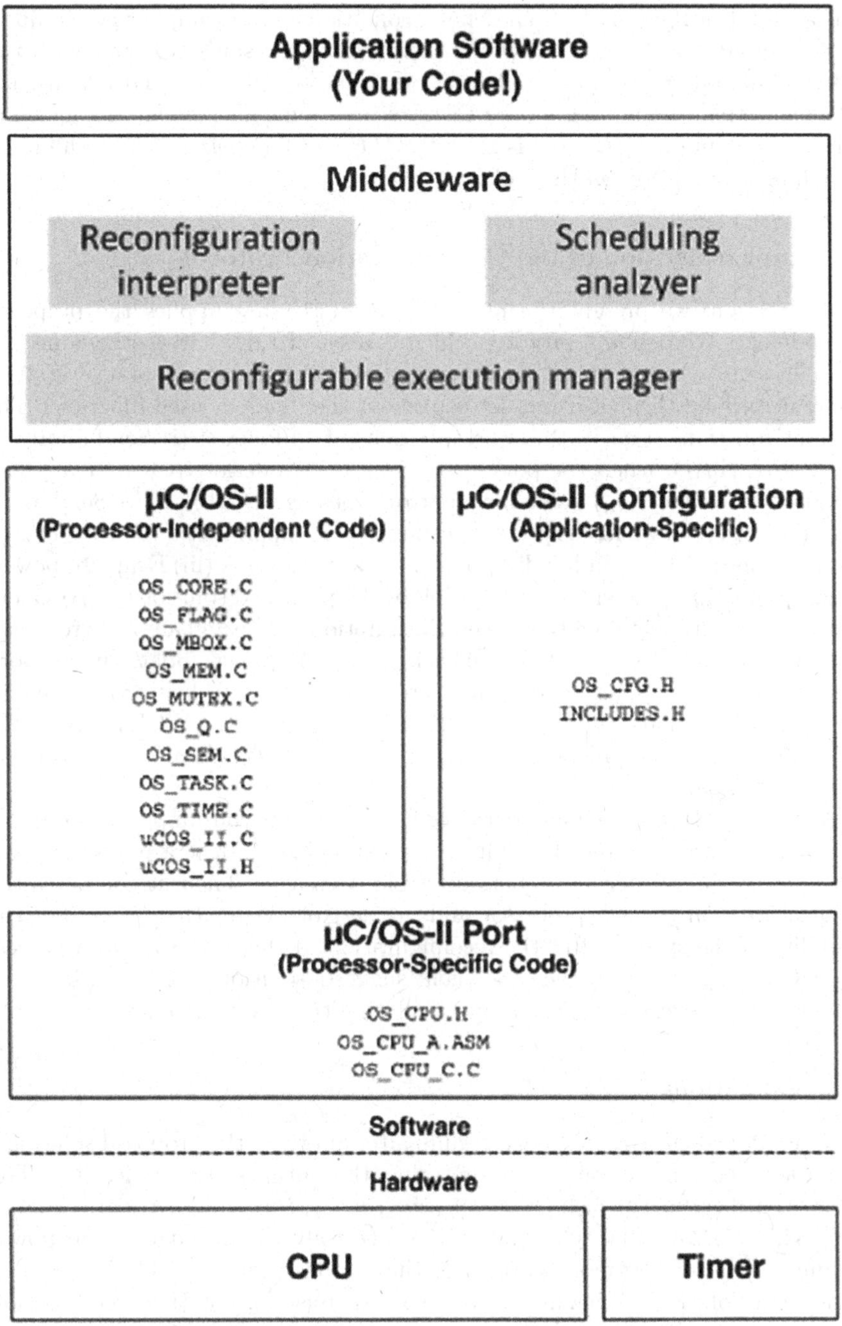

**Application Software
(Your Code!)**

Middleware

| Reconfiguration interpreter | Scheduling analzyer |

Reconfigurable execution manager

| **µC/OS-II** (Processor-Independent Code) | **µC/OS-II Configuration** (Application-Specific) |

```
OS_CORE.C
OS_FLAG.C
OS_MBOX.C
OS_MEM.C
OS_MUTEX.C
OS_Q.C
OS_SEM.C
OS_TASK.C
OS_TIME.C
uCOS_II.C
uCOS_II.H
```

```
OS_CFG.H
INCLUDES.H
```

µC/OS-II Port
(Processor-Specific Code)

```
OS_CPU.H
OS_CPU_A.ASM
OS_CPU_C.C
```

Software

Hardware

CPU   **Timer**

Fig. 7. Localization of the middleware.

runs a subset of them under well-defined conditions. For example, the modification of period is implemented by two instances of the same task but with two values of period. Since all reconfiguration scenarios are predicted off-line, the implementation of the middleware takes into account all possible implementations and executions. The goal is to test $RMPSoC$ for their feasibility and also the required feasibility on the NoC.

5.2   Implementation of the Communication Protocol

In this section, we present the main algorithm [1] that applies the proposed methodology. We define a protocol which is a set of rules and methods needed to facilitate the communication between the different agents of the system. Before describing the algorithm, let us present the different used functions. The different functions used in this work are defined as follows: (i) Send-approval-power($Ag_{i,j}$,Ag_M): when the power consumption is inferior to 1 after a reconfiguration scenario, $Ag_{i,j}$ sends an approval message to Ag_M, (ii) Send-alert-power($Ag_{i,j}$,Ag_M): when the power consumption is superior to 1 after a reconfiguration scenario, $Ag_{i,j}$ sends a disapproval message to Ag_M, (iii) Evaluate-power-consumption(Ag_M): after the application of the proposed solutions, Ag_M calculates the difference between the power consumption before and after the reconfiguration, (iv) Manage-removal($Ag_{i,j}$): each agent $Ag_{i,j}$ must update the memory after the removal of some tasks from a processor $Pr_{i,j}$, (v) App-sol1.1(): modification of the periods, (vi) App-sol1.2(): modification of the WCETs/WCTTS, (vii) App-sol2(): tasks/messages removal, and (viii) App-sol3(): relocation by using the bin-packing.

Algorithm 2 is proposed in order to control the power consumption by proposing some software solutions. It is with complexity $O(n^2)$. First, it reads the parameters of the initial periodic/aperiodic tasks/messages. Then, it computes the initial utilization of each processor and in the NoC. After that, it verifies the feasibility of the system after the reconfiguration. If the utilization of a processor/NoC is bigger than 1, then the agent suggests solution 1, 2 or 3. Finally, it evaluates the power consumption by calculating the power decrease.

5.3   Simulations

This section presents the obtained results after applying the proposed solutions. Before any reconfiguration, we assume that the initial system is feasible. The processor utilizations of each processor $Pr_{1,1}$, $Pr_{1,2}$, $Pr_{2,1}$ and $Pr_{2,2}$ are equal to 0.696532, 0.751534 and 0.803858, 0.7415 respectively. Figure 8 depicts the power consumption after the modifications of the periods and the WCETs. We can deduct that Solution 1.1 can maintain the power consumption. However, Solution 1.2 can minimize the power consumption since the curves show many variations. We can deduct that this theoretical simulation result by Solution 1.2 provides more benefits than Solution 1.1. Figure 10 visualizes the simulation result after

Algorithm 2. Allocations of added OS Tasks/messages to Reconfigurable MPSoCs.

for each processor reconfiguration scenario **do**
    Calculate the utilization U_{aft} and the NoC utilization;
    if $U_{aft} \leq 1$ or $U_{NoC} \leq 1$ **then**
        Send-approval-power($Ag_{i,j}, Ag_M$);
    else
        Send-alert-power($Ag_{i,j}, Ag_M$);
        Call(App-sol1.1()) or Call(App-sol1.2()) or Call(App-sol2())or Call(App-sol3());
    end if
end for
for each processor **do**
    Calculate the new utilization after the reconfiguration;
    Calculate the power consumption after the reconfiguration;
    Evaluate-power-consumption(Ag_M);
    Calculate the difference between values of the power consumption after and before
    a reconfiguration scenario.
end for

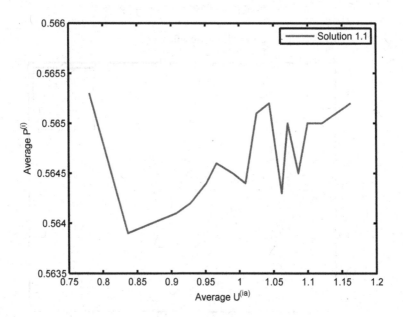

Fig. 8. Periods modification [1].

applying the bin-packing algorithm. The power consumption is between 0.5635 and 0.5655. In thus case, the variations can be ignored. This solution also is beneficial (Fig. 9).

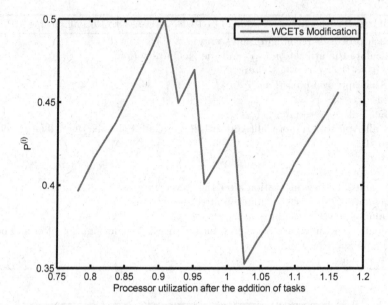

Fig. 9. WCETs modification [1].

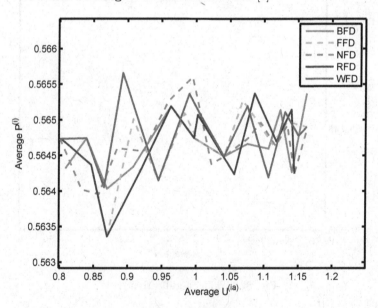

Fig. 10. Bin-paking1 [1].

6 Conclusion

We propose in this paper a run-time automatic global approach called $CRMPSoC$ for low-power reconfigurable MPSoC-based architectures. Before any reconfiguration scenario, the system is assumed to be feasible with low-power. However, after applying a reconfiguration scenarios, the power consumption can sometimes increase and some real-time constraints may be violated. To guarantee a feasible real-time system under low-power after a such scenario, a multi-agent architecture based on the master-slave model is proposed, where software/hardware technical solutions are applied: (1) Modification of the parameters, (2) Remove unimportant tasks/messages and (3) Relocation according the bin-packing algorithm. This new methodology is applied to confidential projects at Cynapsys. To our best knowledge, no work dealing with reconfigurable MPSoC under real-time and low-power constraints was proposed before. The paper's contribution is applied to the FPGA Stratix III in order to verify the effectiveness of our approach As a future work, we will be interested in aperiodic/sporadic tasks. Also, we will be interested in the reconfigurable routing of periodic/sporadic messages under low-power and low-memory constraints. Also, it sounds interesting to deal with quality of service of these systems for more performance and flexibility.

References

1. Khemaissia, I., Mosbahi, O., Khalgui, M., Li, Z.W.: New methodology for feasible reconfigurable real-time networked-on-chip NoC. In: Proceedings of the 11th International Joint Conference on Software Technologies (ICSOFT), Lisbon, Portugal, pp. 249–257 (2016)
2. Wang, X., Khalgui, M., Li, Z.W.: Dynamic low power reconfigurations of real-time embedded systems. In: Proceedings of 1st Pervasive Embedded Computing and Communication Systems, Algarve, Portugal, pp. 415–420, March 2011
3. Wang, X., Khemaissia, I., Khalgui, M., Li, Z.W., Mosbahi, O., Zhou, M.C.: Dynamic low-power reconfiguration of real-time systems with periodic and probabilistic tasks. IEEE Trans. Autom. Sci. Eng. **12**(1), 1–14 (2015)
4. Khemaissia, I., Mosbahi, O., Khalgui, M., Bouzayen, W.: New reconfigurable middleware for feasible adaptive RT-Linux. In: Proceedings of the 4th Pervasive Embedded Computing and Communication Systems, Lisbon, Portugal, pp. 158–167, January 2014
5. Khemaissia, I., Mosbahi, O., Khalgui, M.: Reconfigurable CAN in real-time embedded platforms. In: Proceedings of the 11th International Conference on Informatics in Control, Automation and Robotics (ICINCO), Austria, vol. 01, pp. 3355–3362 (2014)
6. Khemaissia, I., Mosbahi, O., Khalgui, M.: New automatic agent-based solutions for feasible reconfigurable MP-SoC architectures. In: Proceedings of the 14th International Conference on Application of Concurrency to System Design, Tunis, pp. 152–158 (2014)
7. Wu, N.Q., Zhou, M.C., Li, Z.W.: Short-term scheduling of crude-oil operations: petri net-based control-theoretic approach. IEEE Robot. Autom. Mag. **22**(2), 64–76 (2015)
8. Zhang, J.F., Khalgui, M., Li, Z.W., Frey, G., Mosbahi, O., Salah, H.B.: Reconfigurable coordination of distributed discrete event control systems. IEEE Trans. Control Syst. Technol. **23**(1), 323–330 (2015)

9. Javaid, H., Shafique, M., Henkel, J., Parameswaran, S.: System-level application-aware dynamic power management in adaptive pipelined MPSoCs for multimedia. In: Computer-Aided Design, San Jose, CA, pp. 616–623 (2011)
10. Gharsellaoui, H., Khalgui, M., Ben Ahmed, S.: New optimal preemptively scheduling for real-time reconfigurable sporadic tasks based on earliest deadline first algorithm. Int. J. Adv. Pervasive Ubiquit. Comput. IJAPUC **4**(2), 65–81 (2012)
11. George, L., Courbin, P.: Reconfiguration of uniprocessor sporadic real-time systems: the sensitivity approach. In: IGI-Global Knowledge on Reconfigurable Embedded Control Systems, pp. 167–189 (2011)
12. Khalgui, M., Mosbahi, O., Li, Z.W., Hanisch, H.-M.: Reconfiguration of distributed embedded-control systems. IEEE/ASME Trans. Mechatron. **16**(4), 684–694 (2011)
13. Khalgui, M., Mosbahi, O., Li, Z.W., Hanisch, H.-M.: Reconfigurable multi-agent embedded control systems: from modeling to implementation. IEEE Trans. Comput. **60**(4), 538–551 (2011)
14. Khalgui, M., Gharbi, A.: New solutions for feasible and coherent reconfigurations of multi-agent embedded software architectures. J. Ubiquit. Comput. Pervasive Netw. JUSPN **1**(1), 19–28 (2010)
15. Khalgui, M., Mosbahi, O., Li, Z.W.: Runtime reconfigurations of embedded controllers. ACM Trans. Embedded Comput. Syst. **12**(14) (2013)
16. Khalgui, M., Hanisch, H.M.: Reconfiguration protocol for multi-agent control software architectures. IEEE Trans. Syst. Man Cybern. Part C **41**(1), 70–80 (2011)
17. Ben Atitallah, R., Senn, E., Chillet, D., Lanoe, M., Blouin, D.: An efficient framework for power-aware design of heterogeneous MPSoC. IEEE Trans. Industr. Inform. **9**(1), 487–501 (2013)
18. Baker, T.: Stack-based scheduling of real-time processes. J. Real-Time Syst. **3**(1), 67–99 (1991)
19. Chetto, H., Chetto, M.: Some results of the earliest deadline scheduling algorithm. IEEE Trans. Softw. Eng. **15**(10), 1261–1269 (1989)
20. Coffman, E.G., Csirik, J., Galambos, M., Martello, S., Vigo, D.: Bin packing approximation algorithms: survey and classification, pp. 46–93. Springer, New York (2013). ISBN: 978-1-4419-7996-4. Edited by Hochbaum, D.S
21. Decreasing   Algorithms.   http://www.developerfusion.com/article/5540/bin-packing/6/
22. Albers, S., Mitzenmacher, M.: Average-case analyses of first fit and random fit bin packing. In: Proceedings of the Ninth Annual ACM-SIAM Symposium on Discrete algorithms, pp. 290–299 (1998)
23. Davis, T.: Bin packing, 29 November 2006. http://www.geometer.org/mathcircles
24. Ndoye, F., Sorel, Y.: Preemptive multiprocessor real-time scheduling with exact preemption cost. In: 5th Junior Researcher Workshop on Real-Time Computing, France (2011)
25. Liu, C.L., Layland, J.W.: Scheduling algorithms for multiprogramming in a hard real time environment. J. Assoc. Comput. Mach. **20**(1), 46–61 (1973)
26. Singhoff, F., Legrand, J., Nana, L., Marce, L.: Cheddar: a flexible real time scheduling framework. In: Association for Computing Machinery, pp. 1–8 (2004)
27. Chattopadhyay, S.: Embedded System Design. PHI Learning Pvt. Ltd., Delhi (2013). ISBN-8120347307
28. Burns, A., Gutierrez, M., Rivas, M.A., Harbour, M.G.: A deadline-floor inheritance protocol for EDF scheduled embedded real-time systems with resource sharing. IEEE Trans. Comput. **64**(5), 1241–1253 (2015)
29. Ahmad, B., Arslan, T.: Dynamically reconfigurable NoC for reconfigurable MPSoC. In: Custom Integrated Circuits Conference, San Jose, CA, pp. 277–280 (2005)

30. Holzenspies, P.K.F., Smit, G.J.M., Kuper, J.: Mapping streaming applications on a reconfigurable MPSoC platform at run-time. In: International Symposium System-on-Chip, Tampere, pp. 1–4 (2007)

31. Samahi, A., Bourennane, E.: Automated integration and communication synthesis of reconfigurable MPSoC platform. In: Second NASA/ESA Conference on Adaptive Hardware and Systems, Edinburgh, pp. 379–385 (2007)

32. Ahmad, B., Erdogan, A.T., Khawam, S.: Architecture of a dynamically reconfigurable NoC for adaptive reconfigurable MPSoC. In: First NASA/ESA Conference on Adaptive Hardware and Systems, Istanbul, pp. 405–411 (2006)

33. Sepulveda, J., Pires, R., Gogniat, G., Jiang Chau, W., Strum1, M.: QoSS hierarchical NoC-based architecture for MPSoC dynamic protection. Int. J. Reconfigurable Comput. **2012**(3) (2012)

34. Thramboulidis, K., Doukas, G., Frantzis, A.: Towards an implementation model for FB-based reconfigurable distributed control applications. In: Proceedings of the Seventh International Symposium on Object-Oriented Real-Time Distributed Computing, Vienna, pp. 193–200 (2004)

35. Lipari, G., Buttazzo, G.: Schedulability analysis of periodic and aperiodic tasks with resource constraints. J. Syst. Archit. **46**(4), 327–338 (2000)

36. Quan, G., Hu, X.S.: Minimal energy fixed-priority scheduling for variable voltage processors. IEEE Trans. Comput.-Aided. Des. Integr. Circuits Syst. **22**(8), 1062–1071 (2003)

37. Buttazzo, G.C., Bertogna, M., Yao, G.: Limited preemptive scheduling for real-time systems. a survey. IEEE Trans. Industr. Inform. **9**(1), 3–15 (2013)

38. Spuri, M., Buttazzo, G.: Efficient aperiodic service under the earliest deadline scheduling. In: Proceedings of IEEE Real-Time Systems Symposium, pp. 2–11, December 1994

39. Spuri, M., Buttazzo, G.: Scheduling aperiodic tasks in dynamic priority systems. Real-Time Syst. **10**, 179–210 (1996)

40. Bui, B.D., Pellizzoni, R., Caccamo, M.: Real-time scheduling of concurrent transactions in multi-domain ring buses. IEEE Trans. Comput. **61**(9), 1311–1324 (2012)

41. Santos, P.C., Nazar, G.L., Anjam, F., Wong, S., Matos, D., Carro, L.: Fully dynamic reconfigurable NoC-based MPSoC: the advantages of total reconfiguration. In: 7th HiPEAC Workshop on Reconfigurable Computing, Berlin, Germany (2013)

42. Bobda, C., Ahmadinia, A.: Dynamic interconnection of reconfigurable modules on reconfigurable devices. Des. Test Comput. **22**(5), 443–451 (2005)

43. Ishihara, T.: A multi-performance processor for reducing the energy consumption of real-time embedded systems. IEICE Trans. Fundam. Electron. Commun. Comput. Sci. **93**, 2533–2541 (2010)

44. Ghazalie, T.M., Baker, T.P.: Aperiodic servers in a deadline scheduling environment. Real-Time Systems, Department of Computer Science, Florida State University, Tallahassee, vol. 9, pp. 31–67 (1995)

45. Mishra, D., Samei, Y., Dang, N., Dömer, R., Bozorgzadeh, E.: Multi-layer configuration exploration of MPSoCs for streaming applications. In: Electronic System Level Synthesis Conference (ESLsyn) (2012)

46. Hansson, A., Goossens, K.: Trade-offs in the configuration of a network on chip for multiple use-cases. In: Proceedings of International Symposium on Networks on Chip (NOCS), Princeton, NJ, pp. 233–242 (2007)

47. Ching, D., Schaumont, P., Verbauwhede, I.: Integrated modelling and generation of a reconfigurable network-on-chip. Int. J. Embedded Syst. **1**(3/4), 218–227 (2005)

48. Stensgaard, M.B., Sparso, J.: Renoc: a network-on-chip architecture with reconfigurable topology. In: Second ACM/IEEE International Symposium on Networks-on-Chip, pp. 55–64, April 2008
49. Vallina, F.M., Jachimiec, N., Saniie, J.: Nova interconnect for dynamically reconfigurable NoC systems. In: IEEE Electro/Information Technology, pp. 9546–9550, May 2007
50. Bobda, C., Ahmadinia, A., Majer, M., Teich, J., Fekete, S., van der Veen, J.: Dynoc : a dynamic infrastructure for communication in dynamically reconfugurable devices. In: Field Programmable Logic and Applications, pp. 153–158, August 2005
51. Hajduk, Z., Trybus, B., Sadolewski, J.: Architecture of FPGA embedded multiprocessor programmable controller. IEEE Trans. Industr. Electron. **62**(5), 2952–2961 (2015)
52. Salehi, M., Ejlali, A.: A Hardware platform for evaluating low-energy multiprocessor embedded systems based on COTS devices. IEEE Trans. Industr. Electron. **62**(2), 1262–1269 (2015)
53. Obaid, Z.-A., Sulaiman, A., Hamidon, M.: FPGA-based implementation of digital logic design using altera DE2 board. Int. J. Comput. Sci. Netw. Secur. **9**(8), 186–194 (2009)
54. Altera, Getting started with Quartus II Simulation Using the ModelSim-Altera Software. https://www.altera.com/content/dam/altera-www/global/en_US/pdfs/literature/ug/ug_gs_msa_qii.pdf
55. Altera, Sopc Builder User Guide. https://www.altera.com/content/dam/altera-www/global/en_US/pdfs/literature/ug/ug_sopc_builder.pdf
56. Altera, Nios II Processor. https://www.altera.com/products/processors/overview.html
57. http://www.cynapsys.de/

Software Paradigm Trends

Bidirectional Model Transformations Using a Handcrafted Triple Graph Transformation System

Thomas Buchmann and Sandra Greiner[✉]

Applied Computer Science I, University of Bayreuth, 95440 Bayreuth, Germany
{thomas.buchmann,sandra1.greiner}@uni-bayreuth.de

Abstract. Model transformations are the core essence of model-driven software development. Over the years, languages and techniques for unidirectional batch transformations have become mature and are used frequently. However, some transformation problems rather demand for bidirectional and incremental transformations. Unfortunately, available model transformation languages support this kind of transformations only to a limited extent. In this paper, we present a solution for bidirectional and incremental model transformations using a handcrafted triple graph transformation system. As a real world use case, we show the feasibility of our approach in the context of model and code synchronization.

1 Introduction

Model-driven software development (MDSD) has become more and more popular during the last decade. The main goal of this development paradigm is to raise the level of abstraction from source code to higher level models. Starting from an initial model capturing the requirements, a series of models is derived over multiple levels of abstraction until the system is eventually implemented.

Usually, *modeling languages* are defined with the help of *metamodels* in the context of object-oriented modeling. The Object Management Group (OMG) provides a standard for describing metamodels, the *Meta Object Facility (MOF)* standard [1]. Over the years, the *Unified Modeling Language (UML)* [2] has been established as the standard modeling language for model-driven development. In its current version, UML comprises seven kinds of diagrams dedicated to structural modeling and seven kinds of diagrams which address behavioral aspects of a software system.

Model-driven Architecture (MDA) [3] has been proposed by the Object Management Group (OMG) as a result of a standardization process for core concepts in model-driven software development, which put strong emphasis on interoperability and portability. Ideally, the process starts with an initial model capturing the requirements of the system to be developed. In MDA, UML serves as the standardized modeling language. In order to achieve portability and interoperability, MDA makes use of so called platform independent (PIM) and platform specific models (PSM) and it uses UML to describe both of them.

In the academic world, the *Eclipse Modeling Framework (EMF)* [4] is the de-facto standard for research dedicated to model-driven engineering. EMF strictly focusses on principles from object-oriented modeling and only provides core concepts for defining

© Springer International Publishing AG 2017
E. Cabello et al. (Eds.): ICSOFT 2016, CCIS 743, pp. 201–220, 2017.
DOI: 10.1007/978-3-319-62569-0_10

classes, attributes and relationships between classes, formalized in its metamodel *Ecore*, which is based on a subset of MOF – *Essential MOF (EMOF)*.

Model transformations are the driving force behind model-driven software development. They describe how a source model is converted to a target model. Depending on the representation of the (target) models, we typically distinguish between *model-to-text (M2T)* and *model-to-model (M2M)* transformations.

Currently, the technology for defining and executing *unidirectional batch transformations* seems to be fairly well developed. Unfortunately, many transformation scenarios call for different kinds of transformations: After transforming a source model into a target model it may be necessary to modify and extend the target model. Consequently, subsequent changes to the source model need to be propagated in a way which allows to retain the modifications of the target model. These change propagations require *incremental* rather than batch transformations. In addition, changes to the target model may have to be propagated back to the source model. In these cases, transformations need to be *bidirectional*. Bidirectionality and incrementality result in a *round-trip engineering process* in which source and target models may be edited independently and changes need to be propagated back and forth.

The work presented in this paper was carried out in the context of the *Valkyrie* [5] project. Valkyrie is dedicated to the development of an UML-based environment for model-driven software engineering, mainly focusing on the provision of model transformation tools, e.g., for generating code from class diagrams and statecharts or for transforming PIM to PSM models. Please note that Valkyrie is built not only for, but also with model-driven engineering. To this end, and to reduce implementation effort, we reuse existing technology whenever possible.

A real-world application scenario of bidirectional model transformations is model and code synchronization in CASE tools: Code generated from structural models (e.g., class diagrams) needs to be refined with behavior, which is usually supplied by handwritten method bodies. Updates need to be propagated back and forth in a round-trip engineering process. Unfortunately, tool support for transformations of this kind is rather poor, which was unveiled by addressing this use case with Triple Graph Grammars [6] and QVT-R [7]. Therefore, we handcrafted a triple graph transformation system in the programming language Xtend[1], which allows to concisely specify rules for each transformation direction. The execution of the transformation rules is done in an incremental way. This paper is an extended version of our conference paper [8].

The paper is structured as follows: In Sect. 2, we briefly classify different model transformation approaches. While Sect. 3 introduces our application scenario, Sect. 4 describes conceptual and technical aspects of our approach. A critical discussion follows in Sect. 5 whereas related work is presented in Sect. 6. Section 7 concludes the paper.

2   Background

2.1   Model Transformations

Model transformations constitute the core essence of model-driven software development. Given a source model s and a target model t, both conforming to their respective

---

[1] http://www.eclipse.org/xtend.

metamodels, a model transformation describes how *s* is converted to *t*. Depending on the respresentation of the models *s* and *t*, we distinguish between *model-to-model (M2M)*, *model-to-text (M2T)*, *text-to-model (T2M)*, and *text-to-text (T2T)* transformations.

Throughout the years, a wide range of languages and tools for *model transformations* has been developed [9]. These approaches differ from each other in several aspects:

Computational Paradigms: Computational paradigms of model transformation languages comprise procedural, functional, object-oriented, or rule-based languages.

Transformation Direction: While some languages only provide support for unidirectional (i.e., from the source to the target model), other languages allow to formalize and execute bidirectional transformations (i.e., from source to target models and vice versa).

Execution Modes: While *batch* transformations create the complete target model in each transformation run from scratch, *incremental* transformations may be used to retain changes made to the target model.

Source/Target Model Relationships: If source and target model refer to the same model instance, the transformation is called *in-place* transformation. *Out-place* transformations operate on different instances of source and target models.

Source/Target Language Relationships: If both source and target model are instances of the same metamodel, the transformation is called *endogeneous*. In an *exogeneous* transformation, the metamodels or source and target models are different.

Different model transformation languages exist, ranging from general ones, like ATL [10] or QVT [11], graph based languages (e.g., Henshin [12] or eMoflon [13]) to domain-specific transformation languages such as the Epsilon family of transformation languages [14] or EMG [15].

2.2   Graph Transformations

Model instances may be interpreted as graphs, as a model typically constitutes a spanning containment-tree whose elements are interconnected with cross-tree edges. As a consequence, a model transformation is regarded as a problem in the domain of *graph transformations* [16]. In general, graph-based systems may be classified into two different categories: *Graph-rewrite systems* and *graph grammars*. For the application scenario of bidirectional model-to-model transformations, a special kind of graph grammars – triple graph grammars [17] – are used typically. *Graph rewriting* implies that the graphs are transformed by applying rewrite rules, which specify the replacement of a graph pattern (left-hand side) by a subgraph to be embedded into the overall host graph. *Triple Graph Grammars (TGG)* [17] interpret both source and target models as graphs and additionally a correspondence graph whose nodes reference corresponding elements from both source and target graphs, respectively, is used. TGGs allow to describe model transformations in a highly declarative way by means of production rules, which are used to describe the simultaneous extension of the involved graphs.

2.3   Triple Graph Transformation System

As stated earlier, graphs may be used to represent models in a natural way and graph transformations declaratively describe modifications of graph structures. In order to maintain consistency between interdependent and evolving models, a *graph transformation system* is necessary dealing with at least two graphs: a *source graph s*, and a *target graph t*. When incremental change propagation is required, an additional *correspondence graph c* is placed in between *s* and *t*, in order to maintain traceability links. Altogether, this results in a *triple graph transformation system (TGTS)* comprising rules for defining source-to-target and target-to-source transformations and actions for checking consistency and repairing inconsistencies. TGGs are able to automatically derive a corresponding TGTS from a TGG specification but, as described in [18] and [6], the TGG approach suffers from certain limitations which have been unveiled in our case study. As a consequence, we decided to provide an alternative implementation by handcrafting the TGTS which deals with the models involved in this use case. Please note that we intentionally decided to implement the TGTS manually rather than using graph transformation tools, like Henshin [12], to specify the corresponding forward and backward rules since we wanted to compare the bidirectional approaches with manual implementations of model transformations in a current programming language.

3   Round-Trip Engineering of UML Class Models and Java Source Code

3.1   Approach

For the use case of round-trip engineering between UML models and Java source code, we have to implement a *bidirectional incremental model-to-text transformation*: The UML model is represented as instance of its metamodel; Java source code is maintained as a set of text files. Since there is no language or tool available which supports the definition and execution of transformations of this kind, we have to combine multiple transformation languages and tools to solve the overall transformation problem.

Since the tools used in our alternative implementations of this use case [6,7] assume that source and target model are represented as EMF models, an EMF representation of Java source code is required. The abstract syntax tree (AST) which is maintained by the Eclipse Java editor cannot be used for this purpose because it is not based on EMF. Instead, we rely on the *MoDisco* framework [19] which provides an EMF based representation of Java source code. In addition, MoDisco's Java models are located on a higher level of abstraction than ASTs, which facilitates the development of model-to-model transformations. Furthermore, MoDisco offers a discoverer which transforms Java source code to a Java model (text-to-model), and a formatter (implemented with Acceleo[2]) operating in the opposite direction (model-to-text).

The specific advantage of our architecture, which is presented below, is the fact, that for the backward direction (i.e., from Java source code to the UML model), the user only needs to specify fields and not the accessor methods. After backward transforming the

---

[2] http://www.eclipse.org/acceleo.

changes to the UML model and subsequently invoking the M2T transformation, the missing accessor methods will be generated automatically.

It is important to note, that our approach is flexible enough to allow the round-trip engineering to start at either end. However, the forward and the backward transformations operate in considerably different ways, which will be explained below.

The forward direction (UML model to Java source code, as depicted in Fig. 1) consists of two steps, which could be carried out concurrently.

1. The model-to-text transformation is used to update Java source code such that it is consistent with the UML model. This transformation includes all required details, including accessor methods for properties and their bodies. Thus, it comprises both a structural and a behavioral transformation. For user-defined operations, methods with protected bodies are generated.
2. In parallel, the Java model is updated by executing the forward transformation rules specified in the TGTS. Please notice that these rules cover only structural transformations but ignore accessor methods.

After an update to the source code, a *backward transformation* is performed in two sequential steps:

1. The incremental discoverer is used to update the Java model. In particular, this propagation step includes annotations (if present); however, the round-trip may be initiated with Java source code without any annotations. After the synchronization, the Java source code and the Java model are equivalent.
2. Subsequently, updates to the Java model are propagated to the UML model by executing the backward transformation rules specified in the TGTS. All structural elements (classes, class hierarchies, and field declarations) are transformed into corresponding UML elements; if possible, opposite fields are grouped into associations. Accessor methods—annotated with @accessor—are ignored altogether. The signatures of ordinary methods are inserted into the UML model, too.

The *reference architecture* which is shown in Fig. 1 is used in our round-trip engineering scenario. It was also used in the alternative implementations using TGGs [6] and QVT-R [7]. Let us start by explaining the components of this architecture:

– A *model-to-text transformation* was implemented with the help of *Acceleo*, which directly generates Java source code from UML models. Acceleo is based on the template-based transformation language Mof2Text defined by the OMG [20]. The M2T transformation is unidirectional and complete inasmuch as it generates behavior (accessor methods) in addition to structure. Furthermore, the transformation operates incrementally. Manually supplied code fragments in the Java source code may be retained in subsequent generation steps by means of Java annotations (@generated tag) and protected blocks. In order to prevent the backward propagation of accessor methods into the UML model (see below), the transformation marks accessor methods with a non-standard Javadoc tag (@accessor).

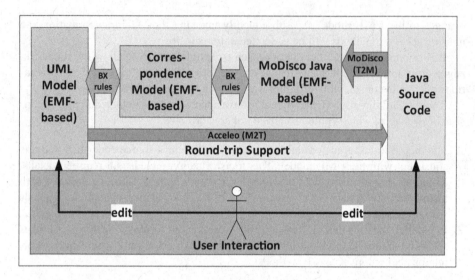

Fig. 1. Round-trip support in Valkyrie: Revised architecture (Source: [8].)

– The *text-to-model transformation* does not invert the model-to-text transformation; rather, it takes Java source code and transforms it into an equivalent Java model. To this end, we reuse the Java metamodel provided by the MoDisco framework. Since the discoverer provided by MoDisco operates in batch mode only, we implemented an *incremental discoverer* which listens to changes to the AST maintained by the Eclipse Java editor and translates them into updates of the Java model. Furthermore, the Java model was extended with universally unique identifiers (UUIDs), which are required by the respective transformation engines in order to reference elements of the source and the target model in the correspondence model. Please notice that propagation includes all elements of the AST, in particular accessor methods.
– The *Xtend rules*, which form the Triple Graph Transformation System (TGTS) operate on a UML model, a MoDisco Java model, and a correspondence model which stores a trace connecting elements of UML and Java models, respectively. In contrast to the transformation from UML to Java source code, the Xtend rules merely specify structural transformations—including methods with empty bodies for user-defined operations in the UML model—and ignore accessor methods. The TGTS may be executed in both directions. After changes have been performed on a source model, the target model is updated, based on the information stored in the source model, the correspondence model, and the target model and vice versa. The transformation of insertions has to be specified in the rules; changes and deletions are handled in a generic way by an abstract base rule. Altogether, the transformation developer specifies a set of Xtend rules describing forward and backward direction explicitly and obtains an incremental bidirectional transformation.

3.2 The Xtend Programming Language

As stated earlier, we implemented the same use case with the help of state-of-the-art technology for bidirectional and incremental model transformations [6,7]. The results obtained from these alternative implementations motivated us to try a hand-crafted TGTS, as some major drawbacks, like combinatorial explosion in the number of rules, a high cognitive complexity imposed to the transformation developer and the lack of reuse of transformation patterns, has been revealed. Consequently, we decided to manually implement a TGTS using a modern procedural and object-oriented programming language. The Xtend (See footnote 1) programming language, has its syntactical and semantical roots in the Java programming language. However, it focuses on a less verbose syntax and extra functionality such as type inference, extension methods and operator overloading. While being primarily an object-oriented language, Xtend also provides declarative features known from functional programming, e.g., lambda expressions. The Xtend language is statically typed and uses the type system of Java without modifications. Consequently, Xtend code is compiled into fully executable Java code, which allows for a seamless integration with existing Java libraries.

4 The TGTS for Bidirectional Incremental Transformations

Developing a TGTS by hand seems to be a tedious and laborious task: First, besides the generation of graphs, modifications and deletions have to be addressed. Second, each direction of the transformation has to be specified and considered explicitly. Additionally, it needs rules for checking consistency and establishing correspondences. In the following we describe how our TGTS is realized. First, we present the involved metamodels followed by giving one concrete scenario of our round-trip use case. Finally, the key concepts of the TGTS realization are provided. Detailed descriptions concerning the implementation of rules can be found in our previous article on this topic [8].

4.1 Metamodels

Eclipse UML2. Eclipse UML2 is part of the *Eclipse Modeling Project*[3]. It provides an Ecore-based implementation of the OMG UML2 specification [2]. Eclipse UML2 only constitutes the abstract syntax of UML2. Figure 2 depicts a simplified overview on relevant metaclasses involved in the transformation.

The Model, which is a specialization of a Package, forms the root of the containment hierarchy. A package contains PackageableElements which summarize, besides others, packages and all kinds of classifiers. A Class may store primitive Properties and, like Interfaces, Operations with different parameters. In contrast, an Association establishes a relationship between two or more classifiers. Its ends are contained as properties in either the association or the opposite classifiers. When both ends are navigable the association is said to be *bidirectional* otherwise *unidirectional*.

---

[3] http://www.eclipse.org/modeling/.

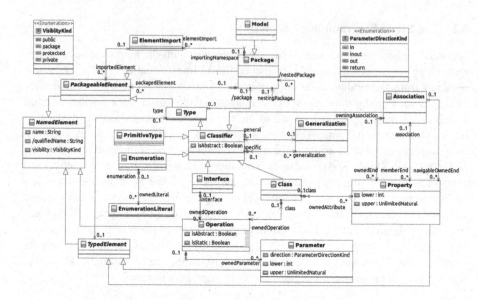

Fig. 2. Overview on relevant UML metaclasses (Source: [8]).

Java (MoDisco). Since a bidirectional and incremental M2T engine does not exist, it is necessary to represent Java source code as a model. Thus, we rely on the tool MoDisco [10], which allows to parse legacy Java code into an Ecore-compliant model instance. Relevant cutouts of the MoDisco Java metamodel are shown in Fig. 3.

In contrast to the UML metamodel, in this metamodel the Model forming the root of the containment hierarchy is no specialization of a Package but contains packages that are also structured hierarchically. They may contain classes, interfaces or enumerations which are summarized as AbstractTypeDeclarations. These type declarations reference an arbitrary number of bodyDeclarations which include methods or fields. A Modifier encapsulates the visibility and other properties of a method or field, like being static. The concept of an association is not present.

Besides the available types, in the Model a CompilationUnit is introduced for every handwritten classifier which serves as anchor points for the code generator.

Model Differences. While both metamodels share many similarities, major and minor differences challenge the bidirectional transformation. In particular, the UML2 metamodel resides on a higher level of abstraction by incorporating concepts, like associations or multiplicities for typed elements. These concepts have to be mapped to different Java concepts where multiplicities are expressed with arrays or collections. For associations a separate class is introduced that is annotated with a JavaDoc comment to distinguish it from regular classes. The association class is used to implement the association semantics controlling the access on the association ends.

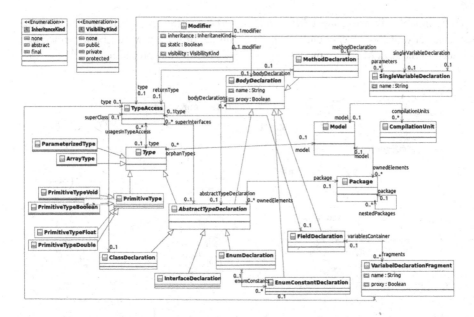

Fig. 3. Overview on relevant metaclasses of the Java MoDisco metamodel (Source: [8]).

4.2 Round-Trip Example

This section provides a brief example to illustrate a simple round-trip scenario in our use case. Figure 4 depicts single transformation steps as they occur in the transformation process explained in detail in Sect. 3. The figure provides cutouts of the UML model in concrete syntax as well as of the resulting Java model in the Ecore tree representation and in source code.

The transformation starts with a given UML model and an empty Java model. Subsequent changes are performed incrementally. In the initial (UML) model many persons may live at one Address where the ends of the association lives at are contained in the respective opposite class. This indicates a bidirectional association which is navigable in both directions. Moreover, a person might have a name and the Address stores the street name.

In the first step Java source code is generated from the UML model with the Acceleo M2T transformation. Figure 4 shows the class LivesAt, generated for the association, as well as the class Person and Address. The code generator adds accessor methods for every field. In parallel, our TGTS transforms the UML model into the equivalent Java MoDisco model by neglecting accessor methods. They are integrated into the Java model by the text-to-model transformation of the MoDisco Java discoverer (Step2).

In a subsequent step (Step 3) a new method, printAddress, is added to the class Address in the Java source code whereas the rest remains unchanged. Then, the modification is incrementally propagated back to the UML model by our TGTS (Step 4). As explained before, accessor methods are ignored by the Xtend transformation whereas the signatures of ordinary methods, like the added method printAddress, are integrated into the

UML model. Likewise, the UML model could be further modified by changing the multiplicity of the address end to infinity. This modification would be incrementally added to the Java MoDisco model as it was explained in our preceding article.

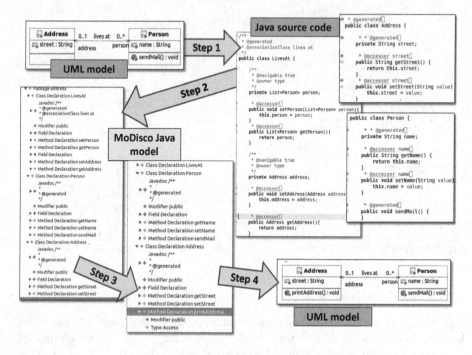

Fig. 4. Example round-trip scenario.

4.3 The Transformation System

This section provides insights in the realization of the TGTS. In the beginning the section presents the core of the TGTS, the correspondence model. Afterwards, an overview on the base concepts of the realization and on how to implement concrete rules is given.

Correspondence Model. In order to implement a TGTS, besides source and target graph, a correspondence graph is needed. For our use case the simple correspondence model, depicted in Fig. 5, serves this purpose.

A Transformation contains an arbitrary number of correspondence elements (Corr). In order to establish traceability links, such elements always refer to at least one EObject from the source model and one EObject from the target model. In general, the easiest kind of mapping are 1:1 mappings. Thus, for the abstract class at maximum one source and one target element are allowed. The String desc describes the element. The

EClass Corr is abstract to allow different and complex specializations. In our use case, however, it was sufficient to introduce one concrete class, BasicElem, without any further features. In case of 1:n mappings, which are also possible, no additional elements are created in the correspondence model nor is the upper bound for source or target elements extended. Rather the additional elements (2-n) are maintained manually in the rule that covers the basic (1:1) mapping.

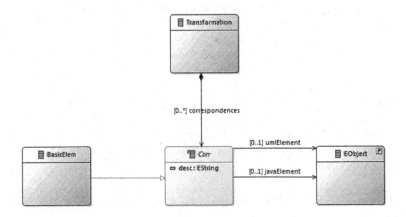

Fig. 5. Correspondence model (Source: [8]).

Rule Construction. When specifying a model transformation, the software engineer needs to decide whether the model elements should be transformed bottom-up, i.e., starting with the leaf nodes of the spanning containment tree, or top-down, starting at the root node. As declarative approaches perform a topological sort of model elements, software developers have very limited influence on the transformation order. Accordingly, when declaring the rules, the developer must typically assume the resulting ordering of the rules and, thus, the execution semantics. Contrastingly, when hand-crafting a TGTS, the transformation order is fully under the control of the user. In our round-trip scenario we chose to strictly follow a top-down approach on the highest level (i.e., on the element level). As a consequence, when transforming child elements, e.g., attributes or methods of classes, we can always be sure that the respective containers and the referred types already exist. Therefore, in our round-trip scenario the transformation starts at the respective root elements (i.e., the Model in both cases) and the primitive types. Next, the Package hierarchy is established. Once this is finished, type declarations (classes, interfaces, enumeration) and associations are transformed followed by the respective inheritance relationships. We further tackle properties and methods afterwards.

As we are hand-crafting our TGTS (unlike in previous approaches [6,7], where bidirectional model transformation formalisms were used), we need to explicitly specify both transformation directions. Furthermore, we need to address creation, deletion or update of existing elements. To reduce the specification effort, we made use of the fact that Xtend builds on the Java VM and it provides mechanisms for inheritance and method overloading.

The base class Elem2Elem (a cutout is depicted in Listing 1) serves as base for all transformation rules. For every element being transformed, it is necessary to specify the forward and the backward direction. Therefore, the two operations sourceToTarget and targetToSource are integrated in the abstract class. These two general methods implement basic behavior that is necessary in every transformation. First, the methods remove all unreferenced elements inside the target model of the respective direction, i.e., in our scenario the Java model in the forward and the UML2 model in the backward direction by invoking the methods seen in line 4 and 9 respectively. Such dangling references may occur in incremental transformations whenever an element of the source of the transformation direction was deleted. In this case, the target element is deleted as well as its correspondence element in the correspondence graph. The String parameter could be used to define specific deletion behavior depending on the name of the given description of an element. For instance, if a Java class is deleted, all additional manually created elements for this object type, e.g., the corresponding CompilationUnit, can be removed from the Java model as well.

Listing 1. Excerpts of abstract base class for transformation rules.

```
1  abstract class Elem2Elem {
2      ...
3      def void sourceToTarget(String s) {
4          deleteUnreferencedTargetElements(s)
5          corrModel.save(null)
6          targetModel.save(null)
7      }
8      def void targetToSource(String s) {
9          deleteUnreferencedSourceElements(s)
10         corrModel.save(null)
11         sourceModel.save(null)
12     }
13     def Corr getCorrModelElem(EObject ob) {
14         corrModel.contents.get(0).correspondences.
15         findFirst[ c |     c.umlElement == ob || c.
               javaElement == ob]
16     }
17     def getOrCreateCorrModelElem(EObject ob, String
           description) {
18         var Corr c = ob.getCorrModelElem
19         if (c == null) {
20             c = corrFactory.createBasicElem => [
21                 if (ob.eClass.EPackage instanceof
                       UMLPackage)
22                     umlElement = ob
23                 if (ob.eClass.EPackage instanceof
                       JavaPackage)
24                     javaElement = ob
```

```
25              desc = description
26          ]
27          corrModel.contents.get(0).correspondences += c
28          }
29       return c
30    } }
31    def getOrCreateSourceElem(Corr corr, EClass clazz) {
32       if (corr.umlElement == null)
33          corr.umlElement = createUMLElement(clazz)
34       return corr.umlElement
35    }
36    def getOrCreateTargetElem(Corr corr, EClass clazz) {
37       ...
38    }
39    ...
40 }
```

The methods getOrCreatCorrModelElem (Listing 1, lines 17–30) and getCorrModelElem (Listing 1, lines 13–16) are both used to retrieve the correspondence element for a given EObject. Due to their generic implementation they can be used in either direction. During the transformation, however, it might not be obvious if a correspondence element is already present which occurs when a new element has been created. Then, the getOrCreateModelElement method is invoked. When there is no correspondence element present yet, this method adds a new one to the correspondence graph linking the given object as either source or target element of the correspondence element. Thus, it updates the correspondence graph which is mandatory in the transformation rules. Contrastingly, whenever the programmer knows the correspondence element for a given EObject exists, the method getCorrModelElem searches the respective element in the correspondence graph.

Furthermore, with getOrCreateSourceElem (Listing 1, lines 31–35) the source element of the provided correspondence element is retrieved or a new object of the provided type is created and linked in the correspondence element. Consequently, this method comes into play when transforming in the backward direction – only then a source element (here, in the UML model) may be still missing when a new element was added in the target model (here, the Java Model). This method can be used to find or link the object as source element during the transformation. The method getOrCreateTargetElem (Listing 1, lines 36ff) behaves in exactly the same way except it covers the new creation of a target element (in the Java model).

In order to specify the transformation, concrete classes that inherit from the abstract Elem2Elem class are introduced for every 1:1 mapping of elements that can be identified. All of them cover the forward and backward direction, hence, they (re)implement the methods sourceToTarget and targetToSource. These redefinitions, however, always adhere to same basic pattern: In the forward direction, at first, all source elements of this rule are collected from the source model. Then, for every source object the correspondence model is examined whether it already contains an element referencing this source object. Such element is either retrieved or created by using the aforementioned method (getOrCreateCorrModelElement). With the correspondence element the reference to its target element could be used to get or (if not present yet) to create the respective target element (getOrCreateTargetElem). The maintenance of the structural features of the target object is addressed afterwards. Further elements that must be additionally created or maintained can be regarded upon the rule execution. At last, unreferenced elements, introduced through deletions in the source model, are deleted and the modified models are saved by calling the base implementation of the super method. The implementations for the backward direction behave exactly in the same way by interchanging source and target.

Listing 2. Excerpts of a concrete transformation rule for properties.

```
1  class Property2Attribute extends Elem2Elem {
2      ...
3      override def sourceToTarget(String s) {
4          sourceModel.allContents.filter(typeof(Property))
5          .forEach [ p |
6              val corr = p.getOrCreateCorrModelElement(s)
7              val fd = corr.getOrCreateTargetElem(JavaPackage
                   ::eINSTANCE.fieldDeclaration)
8
9              setOwnerJava(p, fd)
10             fd.originalCompilationUnit = fd.
                   abstractTypeDeclaration.
                   originalCompilationUnit
11
12             setNameJava(p,fd)
13             setTypeJava(p, fd)
14             setVisibilityJava(p, fd)
15         ]
16         super.sourceToTarget(s)
17     }
18
19     override targetToSource(String s) {
20         var allProperties = targetModel.allContents.filter(
                   typeof(FieldDeclaration))
21         .forEach [ fd |
22             val corr = fd.getOrCreateCorrModelElement(s)
23             val p = corr.getOrCreateSourceElem(UMLPackage::
                   Literals::PROPERTY)
24
25             p.name = fd.fragments.get(0).name
26             setTypeUML(fd, p)    // set type and
                   multiplicity
27             setOwnerUML(fd, p)   // set owner of the
                   property
28
29             p.visibility = javaToUMLVisibility(fd.modifier.
                   visibility)
30         ]
```

```
31          super.targetToSource(s)
32  }     }
```

Listing 2 provides an example for a concrete specialization of the Elem2Elem rule regarding the transformation of properties. It shows how the forward (lines 3–17) and backward (lines 19–31) transformation are implemented.

In the forward direction in a first step all source objects, the properties, are retrieved from the source model (Listing 2, line 4). Then, in the correspondence model for each source object a correspondence element referencing the source object is searched which would be retrieved or created if none is present yet (line 5). Next, the target element, the FieldDeclaration, can either be retrieved via the existing correspondence element or it is created and assigned to the target reference (line 7, getOrCreateTargetElem). In the following (lines 9–14), all structural features are maintained. For a field it is necessary to set the proper type and name and to establish the corresponding ownership. These assignments, which involve complex logic to treat every kind of property, are implemented in different operations as seen, e.g., in lines 12–14. In this way, it is possible to keep the basic transformation rule quite simple and understandable. Note, by outsourcing specific logic to methods, these methods might be reused in other rules, like when determining and setting the type of the parameters of an operation.

The backward direction behaves in exactly the same way except that source and target objects are interchanged. In contrast to the forward direction, the visibility could be assigned by only looking at the modifier visibility of the Java field.

Moreover, we like to point out that the implementation shown in Listing 2 handles all kinds of properties, i.e., those of primitive type and of non-primitive type. The latter are more complex to handle as they resemble association ends. If a property is of non-primitive type, it will be added to an association class that handles the access on the fields. The navigability and the owner of the association end are encoded in a JavaDoc comment for the Java field. This comment is used in the backward transformation to assign the end either to the opposite class or the association and to determine whether it is navigable. Note that the introduction of a separate class for the association further provides the benefit to be expandable to more complex UML association concepts, like n-ary relationships.

5   Lessons Learned

5.1   Implementation Effort

The obvious question is, why take the effort of implementing a TGTS by hand, when there are model transformation languages and tools, which provide native support for bidirectional and incremental model-to-model transformations. Our experiences with solving the transformation problem presented in this paper with TGGs [6] and QVT-R [7] have shown that a significant effort was required to specify bidirectional rules, even though the transformation developer does not need to take care of the different execution directions and the incremental mode of operation. In terms of LOC metrics, the QVT-R solution required **1905** lines of code. On the other hand, the Xtend solution presented in this paper only required **1032** lines of code, although both transformation directions had to be specified explicitly and code for handling the trace model and performing updates and deletions on the respective models were required (the latter ones come for free by the execution engines of both TGGs and QVT-R). If we only consider the forward and backward rules transforming the UML model into the Java model and vice versa, the Xtend solution only requires **738** lines of code. The tool for specifying the TGG rules, that was used in [6], only supports a graphical notation. Consequently it was not possible to apply a LOC metrics; however, the redundancy problem (see below) was shared with the QVT-R implementation.

5.2 Redundancy of the Rule Set

The structure of the metamodels involved in the transformation is similar in a number of places. This circumstance calls for a formalism which provides means to avoid redundancies by fostering reuse of already existing rule patterns. Both, the TGG approach and the QVT-R approach are highly declarative. Nevertheless, they miss language features, like inheritance, genericity or control structures, which are available in the Xtend language and extensively exploited in our hand-crafted TGTS. The lack of these features leads to a combinatorial explosion of the number of rules, both in the QVT-R [7] and the TGG approach [6], whereas we were able to reduce the number of rules in the TGTS significantly: Only one rule per model element was required. In addition, reuse and modularization is aided by object-oriented paradigms, as complex and recurring assignments may be easily extracted to operations, which may be called whenever appropriate.

5.3 Cognitive Complexity

The cognitive complexity imposed to the rule developer is another important factor. Both TGG and QVT-R are highly declarative approaches and they impose a higher cognitive complexity to the developer than the approach presented in this paper. Since only one single rule set is specified, which is executed in both directions, the developer needs to make sure that the rules are actually executable in both directions, which is not always easy. Furthermore, especially in the case of QVT-R, the execution semantics is confusing as it is not clear in which order statements specified in *when* and *where* clauses are actually executed.

In the Xtend approach presented in this paper, the cognitive complexity for the developer is reduced, as there are separate rules for each transformation direction. On the other hand, the developer needs to make sure that both transformation directions actually match.

5.4 Level of Abstraction

Highly declarative approaches, like TGG or QVT-R, reside on a high level ob abstraction. Their main benefit is the fact that only a single rule set is required for transformations in both directions and the respective execution engines take care of reaction to changes in the participating models (this reaction does not need to be specified by the transformation engineer).

The hand-crafted TGTS resides on the lowest level of abstraction, as the Xtend language primarily is a procedural object-oriented language which is augmented with some declarative language constructs like lambda expressions. However, in our use case this fact did not cause negative effects on the required implementation effort or on the complexity of the resulting forward and backward rules.

6 Related Work

Common approaches that are used to transform text (e.g., source code) to models are based on parsers for the specific text languages. Usually, these approaches work on the resulting parse trees and map the tree items to corresponding model elements. Typical limitations are maintenance problems when the underlying M2T templates are changed.

Hettel et al. [21] propose an approach towards model round-trip engineering based on abductive logic programming. In particular, this approach does not place restrictions such as injective behavior on the underlying transformations. A reference implementation is given which can be used to reverse unidirectional transformations based on the Tefkat language. It is a general approach, which could also be applied to other model transformation languages, like QVT. However, since the source transformation does not necessarily need to be injective, ambiguities have to be solved when reversing the transformation. At the end, the "best" solution has to be picked by the user or it has to be determined using some kind of heuristics.

Angyal et al. present in [22] an approach for model and code round-trip engineering based on differencing and merging of abstract syntax trees (AST). In this approach, the AST is regarded to be the platform-specific model (PSM) according to the taxonomy of models in MDA [3]. Nevertheless, in this approach the AST model has a very low level of abstraction because it exactly represents the code. Contrastingly, the discovered Java model which is used in our approach is on a higher level of abstraction. The round-trip engineering approach comprises two different round-trip tasks: one between PIM and PSM and one between PSM and code. The approach tries to prevent information loss during round-trip engineering by using a so called trace model which is used to synchronize the PIM and the PSM (the AST). Furthermore, the AST and the source code are updated using a fine grained bidirectional incremental merge based on three-way differencing. In our approach, information loss is prevented by using Javadoc tags as annotations. In case model and code are changed simultaneously and the changes are contradicting, one transformation direction has to be chosen, which causes that some changes might get lost.

In [23], Bork et al. describe an approach towards model and source code round-trip engineering, which is based on reverse engineering of M2T transformation templates. The idea of this approach is to use (customizable) code generation templates as a grammar to parse the generated (and later modified) code. The benefit of this approach compared to other approaches using plain Java parsers and the resulting parse tree as a source for the code to model transformation is that changes to the templates are automatically taken into account during reverse engineering. While the approach described in [23] requires considerable implementation effort since a template parser, reasoner and token creator have to be implemented, our approach just required the specification of respective Xtend rules that relate two elements of the respective metamodels.

Since MoDisco is able to parse source code which even contains syntax or compile errors into a corresponding Java model, our approach is also independent of the style of the generated code and it also does not depend on a (usually) fine grained parse tree. Furthermore, Javadoc tags can be used to add additional meta-information to the code. While the approach presented in [23] is able to round-trip engineer only code that has been generated with the corresponding templates, our approach is able to handle any code which complies to Java language specification version 5. In addition, the approach by Bork et al. requires bijective reversible templates. E.g., the approach will fail if an attribute name in a class contains the class name.

There are also approaches that are dedicated to model-to-model round-trip engineering. This task involves synchronizing models and keeping them consistent. Antkiewicz and Czarnecki propose an approach towards round-trip engineering for *framework-specific modeling languages* (FSML) [24]. FSMLs are a special category of DSLs which are defined on top of object-oriented application frameworks. In contrast to general round-trip engineering approaches, the approach presented in [24] does not have to deal with non-isomorphic mappings between the artifacts, as the problem domain is much smaller and only code for a specific framework is generated by the code generators of the FSML. The synchronization of the involved implementation model is based on a comparison inspired by CVS and reconciliation. In a last step, conflict resolution has to be carried out interactively by the user.

7   Conclusion and Future Work

In this paper, which is an extended version of our conference paper [8], we presented our approach of realizing bidirectional and incremental model transformations with the help of a hand-crafted Triple Graph Transformation System (TGTS). We applied the approach to the common use case of model and code synchronization, which is a standard example for round-trip engineering in CASE tools.

In our previous work [6, 7], we used state-of-the-art technology for bidirectional and incremental model transformations on this use case. The results revealed major drawbacks, like combinatorial explosion in the number of rules, a high cognitive complexity imposed to the transformation developer and the lack of reuse of transformation patterns. As a consequence, we decided to manually implement a TGTS using the Xtend language, a modern object-oriented programming language, which provides some high-level concepts, like lambda expressions. We had to explicitly specify forward and backward rules and to maintain trace information and the creation, update and deletion of model elements. Nevertheless, the overall effort in terms of LOC metrics was significantly lower than compared to our QVT-R implementation, as inheritance and reuse of transformation patterns was exploited to a large extent.

Current work addresses the application of our TGTS approach to other examples for bidirectional model transformations, as listed in [25]. Furthermore, we currently apply the approach to the synchronization of UML and Alf [26] models.

Future work comprises a quantitative and qualitative evaluation of our three implemented solutions for incremental round-trip engineering.

References

1. Object Management Group: Meta Object Facility (MOF) Version 2.5. OMG, Needham, MA. formal/2015-06-05 edn. (2015)
2. Object Management Group: Unified Modeling Language (UML). Object Management Group, Needham, MA. formal/15-03-01 edn. (2015)
3. Mellor, S.J., Kendall, S., Uhl, A., Weise, D.: MDA Distilled. Addison Wesley Longman Publishing Co. Inc, Redwood City (2004)
4. Steinberg, D., Budinsky, F., Paternostro, M., Merks, E.: EMF Eclipse Modeling Framework. The Eclipse Series, 2nd edn. Addison-Wesley, Boston (2009)
5. Buchmann, T.: Valkyrie: a UML-based model-driven environment for model-driven software engineering. In: Hammoudi, S., van Sinderen, M., Cordeiro, J. (eds.) Proceedings of the 7th International Conference on Software Paradigm Trends, ICSOFT 2012, Rome, Italy, 24–27 July 2012, pp. 147–157. SciTePress (2012)
6. Buchmann, T., Westfechtel, B.: Using triple graph grammars to realize incremental round-trip engineering. IET Softw. (2016). http://digital-library.theiet.org/content/journals/10.1049/iet-sen.2015.0125
7. Greiner, S., Buchmann, T., Westfechtel, B.: Bidirectional transformations with QVT-R: a case study in round-trip engineering UML class models and Java source code. In: Hammoudi, S., Pires, L.F., Selic, B., Desfray, P. (eds.) Proceedings of the 4rd International Conference on Model-Driven Engineering and Software Development, MODELSWARD 2016, Rome, Italy, 19–21 February 2016, pp. 15–27. SciTePress (2016)
8. Buchmann, T., Greiner, S.: Handcrafting a triple graph transformation system to realize round-trip engineering between UML class models and java source code. In: Maciaszek, L.A., Cardoso, J.S., Ludwig, A., van Sinderen, M., Cabello, E. (eds.) Proceedings of the 11th International Joint Conference on Software Technologies (ICSOFT 2016), ICSOFT-PT, Lisbon, Portugal, 24–26 July 2016, vol. 2, pp. 27–38. SciTePress (2016)
9. Czarnecki, K., Helsen, S.: Feature-based survey of model transformation approaches. IBM Syst. J. **45**, 621–645 (2006)
10. Jouault, F., Allilaire, F., Bézivin, J., Kurtev, I.: ATL: a model transformation tool. Sci. Comput. Program. **72**, 31–39 (2008). Special Issue on Second issue of experimental software and toolkits (EST)
11. Object Management Group: Meta Object Facility (MOF) 2.0 Query/View/Transformation Specification, Needham, MA. formal/2015-02-01 edn. (2015)
12. Arendt, T., Biermann, E., Jurack, S., Krause, C., Taentzer, G.: Henshin: advanced concepts and tools for in-place EMF model transformations. In: Petriu, D.C., Rouquette, N., Haugen, Ø. (eds.) MODELS 2010. LNCS, vol. 6394, pp. 121–135. Springer, Heidelberg (2010). doi:10.1007/978-3-642-16145-2_9
13. Anjorin, A., Lauder, M., Schürr, A.: eMoflon: a metamodelling and model transformation tool. In: Störrle, H., Botterweck, G., Bourdellès, M., Kolovos, D., Paige, R., Roubtsova, E., Rubin, J., Tolvanen, J. (eds.) Joint Proceedings of the Co-located Events at the 8th European Conference on Modelling Foundations and Applications (ECMFA 2012), Copenhagen, Denmark, Technical University of Denmark (DTU), p. 348 (2012). ISBN: 978-87-643-1014-6
14. Rose, L.M., Kolovos, D.S., Paige, R.F., Polack, F.A.C., Poulding, S.M.: Epsilon flock: a model migration language. Softw. Syst. Model. **13**, 735–755 (2014)
15. Popoola, S., Kolovos, D.S., Rodriguez, H.H.: EMG: a domain-specific transformation language for synthetic model generation. In: Van Gorp, P., Engels, G. (eds.) ICMT 2016. LNCS, vol. 9765, pp. 36–51. Springer, Cham (2016). doi:10.1007/978-3-319-42064-6_3

16. Ehrig, K., et al.: Model transformation by graph transformation: a comparative. In: Bruel, J.-M. (ed.) MODELS 2005. LNCS, vol. 3844, pp. 71–80. Springer, Heidelberg (2006). doi:10.1007/11663430

17. Schürr, A.: Specification of graph translators with triple graph grammars. In: Mayr, E.W., Schmidt, G., Tinhofer, G. (eds.) WG 1994. LNCS, vol. 903, pp. 151–163. Springer, Heidelberg (1995). doi:10.1007/3-540-59071-4_45

18. Buchmann, T., Dotor, A., Westfechtel, B.: Triple graph grammars or triple graph transformation systems? In: Chaudron, M.R.V. (ed.) MODELS 2008. LNCS, vol. 5421, pp. 138–150. Springer, Heidelberg (2009). doi:10.1007/978-3-642-01648-6_15

19. Brunelière, H., Cabot, J., Dupé, G., Madiot, F.: MoDisco: a model driven reverse engineering framework. Inf. Softw. Technol. **56**, 1012–1032 (2014)

20. Object Management Group: MOF Model to Text Transformation Language, Version 1.0. Object Management Group, Needham, MA. formal/2008-01 edn. (2008)

21. Hettel, T., Lawley, M., Raymond, K.: Towards model round-trip engineering: an abductive approach. In: Paige, R.F. (ed.) ICMT 2009. LNCS, vol. 5563, pp. 100–115. Springer, Heidelberg (2009). doi:10.1007/978-3-642-02408-5_8

22. Angyal, L., Lengyel, L., Charaf, H.: A synchronizing technique for syntactic model-code round-trip engineering. In: 15th Annual IEEE International Conference and Workshop on Engineering of Computer Based Systems (ECBS 2008), 31 March–4 April 2008, Belfast, Northern Ireland, pp. 463–472 (2008)

23. Bork, M., Geiger, L., Schneider, C., Zündorf, A.: Towards roundtrip engineering - a template-based reverse engineering approach. In: Schieferdecker, I., Hartman, A. (eds.) ECMDA-FA 2008. LNCS, vol. 5095, pp. 33–47. Springer, Heidelberg (2008). doi:10.1007/978-3-540-69100-6_3

24. Antkiewicz, M., Czarnecki, K.: Framework-specific modeling languages with round-trip engineering. In: Nierstrasz, O., Whittle, J., Harel, D., Reggio, G. (eds.) MODELS 2006. LNCS, vol. 4199, pp. 692–706. Springer, Heidelberg (2006). doi:10.1007/11880240_48

25. Westfechtel, B.: Case-based exploration of bidirectional transformations in QVT relations. Softw. Syst. Model. (2016). doi:10.1007/s10270-016-0527-z

26. OMG: Action Language for Foundational UML (ALF). Object Management Group, Needham, MA. formal/2013-09-01 edn. (2013)

Domain-Specific Modelling Using Mobile Devices

Diego Vaquero-Melchor, Antonio Garmendia, Esther Guerra[✉],
and Juan de Lara

Modelling and Software Engineering Group, Computer Science Department,
Universidad Autónoma de Madrid, Madrid, Spain
{diego.vaquero,antonio.garmendia,esther.guerra,juan.delara}@uam.es
http://miso.es

Abstract. Domain-Specific Languages (DSLs) are languages tailored for a specific application area, like logistics, networking or mobile app design. They capture the main primitives and abstractions within a domain, which permits modelling systems and problems within that domain in a succinct and natural way. DSLs are heavily used in software development paradigms like Model-Driven Engineering, and they are also a means to enable end-users to perform simple programming tasks in particular domains.

Traditionally, modelling using DSLs has been supported by desktop computers in static settings that neglect the surrounding contextual information. Instead, we claim that DSLs can also be very useful in a dynamic setting where they can profit from mobility and context. Therefore, in this paper, we identify several scenarios where modelling using mobile devices – like smartphones or tablets – is useful. We also propose an architecture and a tool, called *DSL-comet*, which enables mobile modelling using graphical DSLs, and supports seamless integration of desktop and mobile graphical modelling environments.

Keywords: Model-Driven Engineering · Domain-Specific Languages · Graphical modelling languages · Context · Mobile devices · DSL-comet

1 Introduction

Domain-Specific Languages (DSLs) [1,2] are "small" languages tailored to a particular domain. In contrast to general-purpose languages (GPLs) – like Java for programming or UML for modelling – DSLs target specific application areas, like networking, user interface design or logical circuits [1]. This way, DSLs provide useful primitives of the domain, which can be used to create simpler, more intentional system descriptions than those that would result from the use of GPLs. DSLs can be either graphical [1] or textual [3], though in this paper we will focus on graphical ones.

DSLs are heavily used in Model-Driven Engineering (MDE) [4], a software engineering paradigm that promotes an active utilization of models in all phases

© Springer International Publishing AG 2017
E. Cabello et al. (Eds.): ICSOFT 2016, CCIS 743, pp. 221–238, 2017.
DOI: 10.1007/978-3-319-62569-0_11

of software development. In MDE, models are used to specify, analyse, simulate, test, execute and generate code for the final applications, among other activities. While it is possible to define these models using GPLs like the UML, their construction using DSLs tailored to particular domains is very frequent in practice [1,5]. DSLs are also enablers for end-user development [6], as they permit users with no or little computer science background to perform concrete, simple programming tasks in particular contexts.

A primary goal of models in MDE is to serve as an automation mechanism for development tasks like code generation. Thus, although initial phases of modelling may take place in informal settings like whiteboards or using pen and paper, models need to become precisely defined to be machine processable. Traditionally, the modelling task takes place in desktop computers (or laptops) assisted by modelling tools, like those based in Eclipse/EMF [7]. While this is useful for late phases of model development, it introduces rigidity and prevents using models in flexible scenarios that imply mobility and collaboration or need to react to contextual information. Unfortunately, most tools for the creation of DSLs are targeted to desktop environments [1,3].

We claim that modelling using DSLs can benefit from mobility, collaboration and context in several situations. In this paper, we identify scenarios where mobile modelling is useful, and present an architecture and prototype tool for the discussed scenarios. Our approach permits the automatic generation of both desktop and mobile graphical modelling environments from a single description, as well as the seamless editing of models in both kinds of environments. Our desktop modelling environment is an Eclipse plugin based on the Sirius [8] graphical modelling platform. The mobile modelling environment is based on iOS, and permits model sharing and local collaborative model editing via local ad-hoc WiFi networks. Communication between the desktop and mobile environments is achieved through a dedicated server. Our tool is called *DSL-comet* (Domain Specific Language COllaborative Modelling EnvironmenT) and is freely available at the Apple's app store, and at http://miso.es/tools/DSL-comet.html. To illustrate its functionality, we will introduce a DSL for designing factory plants as a running example.

This is an extended version of our previous paper [9] presented at the 10th International Joint Conference on Software Technologies (ICSOFT). In this paper, we enhance the presentation of the motivating scenarios for mobile modelling, we present a more comprehensive description of the technical aspects of our tool and architecture using a different case study, and we expand the analysis of related works.

The rest of this paper is organized as follows. First, Sect. 2 motivates the need for mobile modelling using DSLs, describes several scenarios of interest, and elicits some technical requirements for tools aimed at supporting mobile modelling. Next, Sect. 3 describes the architecture we propose to support these scenarios. Section 4 introduces *DSL-comet*, the prototype tool that realizes this vision. Then, Sect. 5 presents a comparison with related research. Finally, Sect. 6 ends with the conclusions and open lines of future work.

2   Scenarios for Mobile Modelling

In this section, we discuss several scenarios where modelling can profit from mobility, context and collaboration. We will use these scenarios to elicit requirements for tools aimed at supporting domain-specific modelling in mobile devices.

2.1   Multi-device Modelling

Mobile modelling tools should keep models compatible with other devices. Therefore, in the first scenario, we deem necessary being able to use seamlessly models both in mobile and desktop environments. This means that models can be created in a desktop environment and then be used in a mobile device, or vice-versa. Figure 1 shows a schema of this scenario. A server is in charge of storing the models, which can be downloaded for their editing in mobile and desktop environments indistinctly, and then be uploaded to the server again.

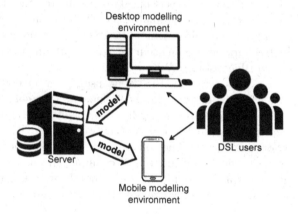

Fig. 1. Combined desktop and mobile modelling.

Applications of this scenario include modelling in remote locations (e.g., a wind turbine) through mobile devices. As an example, an operator of a factory may need to inspect a model of the factory plant on-site, change its parameters according to the current working location, or even create a model of the plant while visiting the factory. In this case, the operator would find preferable performing these modelling actions using a mobile device while staying on the plant. On the other hand, the same models may need to be analysed by other engineers at desktops in the company offices, or be used for simulation or run-time monitoring.

The seamless integration of desktop and mobile modelling also enables informal, agile meetings between engineers, who may use a combination of tablets and desktop monitors for model visualization.

Finally, this scenario is also applicable to the educational domain. In this setting, professors can create models and modelling exercises in their desktop computers, and students may access these exercises or modelling lessons for learning in mobility. Then, students may upload the solution to the exercises to the server, and be graded by the professors in their desktops.

From the analysis of this scenario, we derive as a technical requirement the need of a common format to represent models in desktop and mobile environments. This is more easily achievable if both environments are generated from a single definition of the DSL being used to build the models.

2.2 Mobile Collaborative Modelling

When modelling in mobility in remote locations (e.g., a farm or a building in the country side) one cannot assume the availability of a WiFi Internet connection or even mobile coverage. In this scenario, users can benefit from the short-range communication capabilities of mobile devices to enable *local* collaboration, e.g., for joint model construction or inspection. This eliminates the need to use a remote server to orchestrate and coordinate the collaboration, which may incur in long delays or can be impossible in remote locations where no data connection is available. Instead, collaboration can occur by using short-range communication of mobile devices like Bluetooth or WiFi.

Figure 2 illustrates this scenario. First, one user (user 1) downloads from the server a palette with the different kinds of elements that can appear in the model. Alternatively, the user may already have the palette stored locally in the mobile device. Then, this user sets a local WiFi network and invites other nearby users to the collaborative session. The collaboration rules may be customizable depending on the particular application. For example, it can be token-based, with either implicit or explicit assignment of the modification token. The figure shows a token-based collaboration, where only the user holding the modification

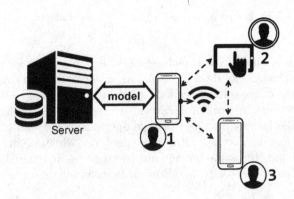

Fig. 2. Local collaborative modelling. User 1 starts the session, and user 2 has the modification token. All users' devices display an updated view of the model as it is being modified.

token (user 2) can change the model. In the meantime, the devices of all users participating in the session will display an updated view of the model as it is being modified. When the session finishes, the model can be stored either in the server or locally.

Applications of this scenario include those presented in Sect. 2.1, but enhanced with local collaboration facilities. In particular, local collaboration enables joint model creation, model revision and discussion, or the collaborative solution of modelling exercises in an educational setting.

2.3   Context-Based Modelling

Mobile devices can access contextual information, which can be useful in some modelling scenarios [10]. For example, a mobile modelling environment may present different parts of a model, or allow different editing actions, depending on the context. This context may include information about the device state – like battery, size of screen, orientation, or availability of a WiFi connection – and external information – like position, time or weather conditions –. Figure 3 illustrates the adaptation of a mobile modelling environment depending on the context.

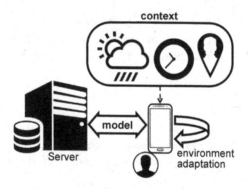

Fig. 3. Mobile contextual modelling.

For instance, in the factory example introduced in Sect. 2.1, the mobile app may present a model of the plant where the engineer is located, updating this view when the engineer moves to a different location. This way, it becomes easier for the engineer to monitor or modify the operating conditions of the machines nearby the current location.

Domotics is another domain where this scenario applies. Similarly to the factory example, a mobile app could present a model of the devices (TVs, blinds, lights, heating, etc.) inside the room where the house owner is currently located. This view would get updated when the owner moves to a different room. By manipulating the model, the owner may interact with the home devices.

2.4 Requirements for Mobile Domain-Specific Modelling

From an analysis of the presented scenarios, we identify the following requirements for a mobile modelling platform:

Rq1. Models should be compatible in mobile and desktop applications. The environment should enable the seamless use of models in desktop and mobile devices.

Rq2. In order to allow multi-device modelling (scenario 1), the generation of both desktop and mobile environments should be easy. Moreover, the effort needed to generate one desktop and one mobile environment should be the same as the effort needed to generate only one of them.

Rq3. Model visualization in the mobile environment should be adapted to the reduced screen size.

Rq4. Model editing in the mobile environment should be adapted to support typical mobile interaction gestures (e.g., swipe, tap and pinch).

Rq5. In order to allow mobile collaborative modelling (scenario 2), the platform should support local collaboration in the mobile environment.

Rq6. In order to allow context-based modelling (scenario 3), the platform should enable context adaptation in the mobile environment, and incorporation of context information and the corresponding adaptation rules in the DSL definition.

The next section describes an architecture that addresses scenarios 1 and 2 and requirements Rq1 to Rq5. Scenario 3 and requirement Rq6 are left for future work.

3 Architecture

Figure 4 shows the scheme of our proposed architecture, which provides support for scenarios 1 and 2. It considers two main phases: DSL definition (label 1) and DSL use (label 2).

In the first phase, the DSL developer defines the DSL. This includes the definition of the DSL abstract syntax (the concepts of interest, together with their properties and relations), concrete syntax (their visualization), and semantics (what the models mean, typically enacted by model simulators or code generators). In this work, we focus on the abstract and concrete syntax, and leave the semantics for future work.

In MDE, the abstract syntax of a DSL is described through a meta-model. Implementation-wise, we use standard tools based on the Eclipse Modelling Framework (EMF) [7] to create the meta-models. Therefore, meta-models are built using Eclipse in a desktop environment, and then they are uploaded to the server once their definition is complete.

The graphical concrete syntax (which we call palette) can be defined either from the mobile environment or from Eclipse in the desktop [11]. In both cases, it is defined using a wizard that allows assigning icons and shapes to the different

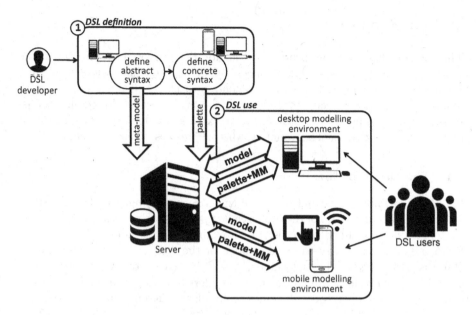

Fig. 4. Our proposed architecture.

meta-model elements. This palette is stored as a model in the server. For this purpose, we have created a meta-model to describe graphical concrete syntaxes in a platform-independent way.

To enable combined modelling, we use the same definition (abstract syntax meta-model and concrete syntax description) to synthesize both a desktop and a mobile modelling environment, thus covering requirements Rq1 and Rq2. The desktop environment is realised as a Sirius editor, while we have built our own tool called *DSL-comet* to allow the editing of models in mobile devices. *DSL-comet* supports typical visualization and interaction styles for mobile devices, thus covering requirements Rq3 and Rq4.

The DSL users can build models using any of the two generated environments, and store the models either locally or in the server. This permits the seamless editing of models both in the mobile device and the desktop environment. In case of mobility, it is also possible to set up a collaborative modelling session between several nearby users by temporarily designating one of their mobile devices as a local server. This enables collaboration without requiring an internet connection, as demanded by requirement Rq5.

Currently, we use a MongoDB NoSQL database to store the models, meta-models and palettes. Technically, all these artefacts are stored in JSON format, and they are converted into XMI to ensure compatibility with the desktop environment.

Once we have seen the main parts of the architecture we propose, in the next section we detail its main features. As a running example, we will use a DSL for factory plants.

4   Tool Support

This section describes our prototype tool for the proposed architecture. The tool, named *DSL-comet* (Domain Specific Language COllaborative Modelling EnvironmenT) is made of three components: a desktop client, a server, and a mobile app. The desktop client is based on Eclipse, the server is based on Node.js, and the client is a native iOS app. Next, we explain the three components. More information about the tool is available at http://miso.es/tools/DSL-comet.html.

4.1   The Desktop Client

In order to define the abstract syntax of the DSL, we use our tool DSL-tao [12]. The distinguishing feature of the tool is that it permits constructing meta-models by composing predefined patterns. As an example, the window at the back of Fig. 5 shows an excerpt of the meta-model for the factory DSL, specified using DSL-tao. According to the meta-model, a factory may contain different types of machines (generators, terminators and assemblers) connected through conveyors and controlled by operators. Machines manipulate different types of parts, like handles, knobs and hammers. Moreover, two attributes in class Machine permit configuring whether a machine is busy or broken.

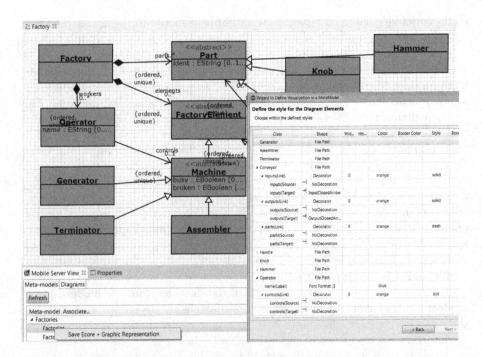

Fig. 5. Meta-model of a DSL for factory plants (back). Wizard to define the concrete syntax of the DSL (front).

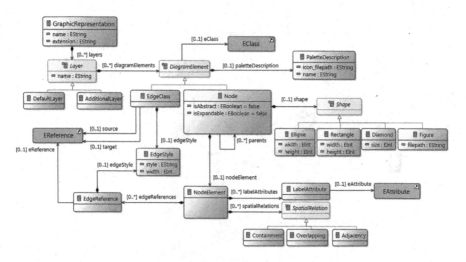

Fig. 6. Excerpt of *GraphicRepresentation* meta-model.

Once the meta-model of the DSL is complete, we need to define its concrete syntax. This is performed using a dedicated wizard, which is shown at the front of Fig. 5. The specified concrete syntax is internally described through a platform-independent meta-model called *GraphicRepresentation* that records the selected appearance for the classes and relations in the DSL meta-model (shape, colour, etc.) as well as the palette that the generated modelling environments will provide to create instances of the different classes. An excerpt of the meta-model is shown in Fig. 6. The diagram elements are organized into layers. This is useful to occlude elements or show more details. However while the generated desktop graphical editor supports layers, currently the mobile editor does not.

Layers contain graphical elements (class DiagramElement), which point to the meta-model classes they represent. Objects can be represented as nodes (class Node) or edges (class EdgeClass). Class EdgeClass provides attributes for setting the references acting as the source or target of the edge, from the available references of the class. Moreover, the EdgeStyle contain the information about the graphical style of the edge (e.g., dash, dot or solid). With respect to the Nodes, there are different styles of representation, either defining a predefined figure (e.g., Ellipse, Rectangle or Diamond) or an external one (e.g., SVG). Some of its attributes can be selected as the label of the node (class LabelAttribute), and spatial relations between nodes (adjacency, overlapping, containment) can be defined. However currently, the mobile editor does not support spatial relations, but the desktop editor does. Common graphical descriptions among different objects can be reused using abstract nodes (attribute isAbstract in class Node) and inheritance relations (references Node.parents). As we will see in Sect. 4.3, "expandable" nodes (Nodes with isExpandable true) can include non-graphical objects, especially useful in mobile devices because of their reduced screen size (Rq3 in Sect. 2.4).

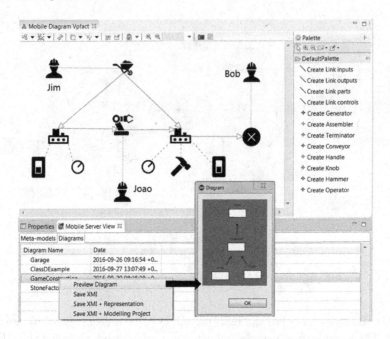

Fig. 7. Screenshot of the Sirius desktop client.

From the DSL meta-model and the concrete syntax description, we generate a desktop graphical modelling environment based on Sirius. Although we currently target Sirius, other technologies like Graphiti [13] or EuGENia [14] could be targeted as well. Figure 7 shows a screenshot of the resulting desktop editor. Since it is a Sirius-based editor, its generation accounts to producing an *odesign* model that describes the modelling workbench.

The desktop client provides a dedicated view called *Mobile Server View* to interact with the remote server. This view has two tabs. The first one, named *Meta-models*, lists all meta-models stored in the server and its corresponding graphic representation. The window in the back of Fig. 5 shows this tab. By right clicking on one of the listed meta-models it is possible to download it, together with its concrete syntax. Additionally, the client has also functionalities to upload the meta-model and the concrete syntax in the server. We allow a single meta-model to have several concrete syntax representations.

Figure 7 shows the second tab of the view, called *Diagrams*. It displays the list of diagrams (i.e., models) stored in the server. By right clicking on a model, a contextual menu with several options appears. From the options in this menu, it is possible to obtain a pre-visualization of the selected model (as shown in the figure), download the model in XMI format (standard format to persist EMF models), and download the graphical information of the model (e.g., position of nodes). As an example, Fig. 7 shows a model previously created in a mobile device, which has been downloaded (both its XMI and graphical information) to the desktop environment from the server. Sirius stores the graphical information attached to models in *aird* files.

4.2 The Server

We have developed a remote server to store models, meta-models and palettes (called artefacts henceforth). The server is deployed on the Heroku [15] platform and uses "Node.js" [16] technology. The server can be accessed from http://miso.es/tools/DSL-comet.html.

There are two ways to manage artefacts in the server: either using REST services or through the web-based application. In order to enhance scalability, we store artefacts in a MongoDB [17] database using JSON format. The advantage this format brings is that other external tools can use our artefacts directly.

On the other hand, the desktop clients use EMF technology, which is not directly accessible on mobile platforms. To solve this problem, we have developed some services to convert back and forth between JSON and XMI. This technique has the advantage of providing a lighter, portable format for using models in mobile apps. Other mobile platforms may use these services to work with meta-models.

4.3 The iOS Client

The mobile client has been developed for iOS devices (i.e., iPhone and iPad). It has been designed to use the minimum internet traffic, and therefore, it does not require data connectivity most of the time. An internet connection is only necessary to download palettes and meta-models from the server though. Once those files are downloaded, the user may create and edit diagrams with no need for connectivity.

Figure 8 shows the main screen of the mobile app, where the same model shown in Fig. 7 is being edited. The image is decorated with labels depicting its main functionalities.

Label 1 corresponds to the canvas where the model is drawn. We have specially kept in mind the reduced screen size of mobile devices when creating the app (from 4.0 in. in an iPhone 5s, to 12.9 in. in an iPad Air). The user may drag classes from the bottom palette (label 2) to the canvas, in order to create instances of them. This palette can be collapsed to save space.

The user can add annotations (such as notes, hand-made drawings and temporal alerts) to the diagram, using the button with label 4. A new model can be created (label 5) and saved locally or in the server (label 6).

Label 7 points to the search tool, which is useful to find elements on the canvas using filters. Users may initiate a collaboration session with nearby users (label 8), select a new palette (label 9) and share the model via Airdrop[1]. Finally, it is possible to take a screenshot of the current model (label 11) and save it on the camera roll or send it via Twitter or e-mail.

Tool Workflow. The app user can either use a palette from the server or use a local one (see Fig. 9). Taking into account that this tool may be used without internet connection, the app can download a palette and store it locally on the mobile device.

---

[1] Airdrop is a file sharing technology of iOS similar to Bluetooth.

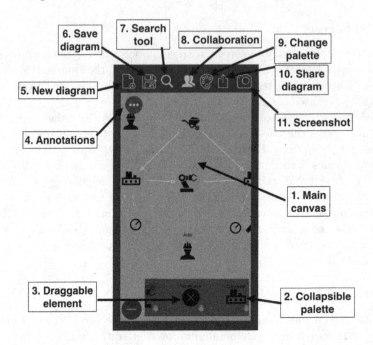

Fig. 8. Screenshot of the editor on an iPhone SE.

Model editing is done by gestures in the mobile touch screen. Draggable elements are created by dragging from the palette. As the palette may be too long, we support scrolling to show more elements. The canvas itself supports zoom-in (open pinch) and zoom-out (close pinch).

Connecting elements is done by a long press from the source node to the target one. The tool is able to resolve the admissible relationships that may exist between those two elements. If several relationships are possible, the user can select the desired one.

If an object is selected in the canvas, the application displays a detailed view with its attributes and output connections (see Fig. 10). The user can update its attributes and the visual representation gets updated accordingly. Given that models can become large, the application includes a search tool where the user can ask for any object using filters, as shown in Fig. 11. The filters allow searching for nodes having a certain value in some selected attributes, as shown in Fig. 12.

When defining a DSL (see Sect. 4.1), the DSL developer can declare some references as "Expandable". Figure 13 shows an instance of the Conveyor class with the default behavior, which is representing the links between the conveyor and the three parts it contains (a hammer, a handle and a knob) as edges. By setting the part reference of the Conveyor class as "Expandable", those parts would not be shown in the canvas. Instead, the details view of the conveyor would include an option to create instances of Part, as Fig. 14 shows. If we select the *Create Link Parts* option, the new view in Fig. 15 will be shown. From this view, we can create instances associated to the conveyor that will not appear

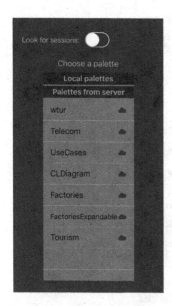

Fig. 9. Selecting a palette.

Fig. 10. Example of a node details.

Fig. 11. Filtering by class type.

Fig. 12. Filtering by attributes.

on the canvas. This is especially useful in a mobile app to save space, given the reduced size of the screen of mobile devices.

Once the user has created the model, it can be saved either on the server or locally. The model can also be shared via Airdrop or via some external apps

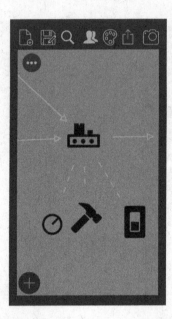

Fig. 13. Example of a conveyor without expandable items.

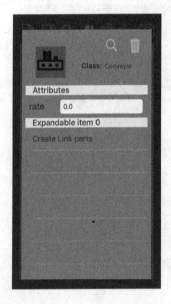

Fig. 14. A conveyor with an expandable reference.

Fig. 15. Creating a part linked to the conveyor.

like Google Drive or Dropbox (Fig. 16). The model is serialized as a ".demiso" file with XML schema. This file extension is detected by the operative system, whereby it will show the user the option to open those files with the *DSL-comet* app.

Fig. 16. Some sharing options.

Collaboration Support. The mobile app allows a group of nearby users to work together on a diagram without an internet connection. For this purpose, first, one of the users needs to offer a diagram in collaboration. The user's device will become the *local server* of the session. Then, one or more users can connect to this local server. The role of this server is to store the diagram information and send the model changes to the clients periodically, so that every connected device has a synchronized model status.

We use a token-based collaboration approach, where only the user holding the token (initially the server) can modify the model. Any model change is sent to the server device, and from there, it is propagated to all connected clients, so that they see the synchronized model on their screens. Clients may ask for the token at any point, and the collaboration server has to agree (or deny) to grant the token.

5 Related Work

Many tools have been proposed along the years to create graphical DSLs, like AToM^3 [18], EuGENia [14], GMF [19], Graphiti [13], MetaEdit+ [1] or Sirius [8]. However, most of them target the generation of graphical editors for the desktop, but not for mobile devices.

Some recent works allow creating graphical DSL environments for modelling in the web, like AToMPM [20], EuGENia Live [21] or WebGME [22]. However, although these environments can be utilized within a mobile device using a web browser, this poses several drawbacks. First, the web environments are not tailored to the particularities of mobile devices, whereas a mobile app is optimized for its execution in the mobile, and enables forms of visualization and interaction gestures especially designed for the reduced space of a mobile device. Second, web applications require connectivity, which might not be available when modelling in remote locations. Finally, relying on a web application for collaborative modelling might involve greater delays than the local short-range form of collaboration we support.

On the other hand, although MDE has been used to produce mobile applications [23], few works report on mobile domain-specific modelling environments. Some of them are described next.

CEL [24] is a mobile iOS application to create UML class diagrams, with no support for collaboration or model sharing. FlexiSketch [25] is a sketching mobile modelling tool especially tailored for software requirements modelling, and it supports collaboration. However, none of these two tools support combined modelling in desktop and mobile.

The flexibility that touch screens provide for modelling has also been explored. For instance, Calico [26] is a sketching tool, where the sketched elements can be scrapped and reused in other parts of the diagrams. It works on a digital whiteboard, not on mobiles, but relies on touch-based interaction.

Some works allow programming in mobile devices using graphical languages [27]. However, such languages are fixed, and the environment is created ad-hoc for them. Instead, we enable the creation of arbitrary graphical DSLs, where their environment is configured with the DSL descriptions. We believe that our tool could greatly simplify the construction of these kinds of applications.

Altogether, we can conclude that our approach is novel as it permits creating both a desktop and a mobile DSL modelling environment, multi-device modelling in the mobile and the desktop, and collaboration using mobile devices.

6   Conclusions

In this paper, we have presented our proposal for enabling mobile domain-specific modelling, showing some scenarios of interest and a working prototype tool called *DSL-comet*. We claim that enabling modelling on mobile devices present interesting opportunities for MDE, including more flexibility and the use of contextual information.

We are currently improving our prototype tool to support more advanced collaborative model editing. In the short term, we will also address scenario 3 and requirement Rq6 related to contextual modelling, which implies specifying the contextual information of interest and adaptation rules in the DSL definition. We would like to combine the tool with Wodel [28], a system to generate modelling exercises, so that students can make those exercises in mobile devices. Finally, we plan to conduct empirical user studies to evaluate our proposal for different domains.

Acknowledgements. This work was supported by the Spanish Ministry of Economy and Competitivity (TIN2014-52129-R), and the R&D programme of the Madrid Region (S2013/ICE-3006).

References

1. Kelly, S., Tolvanen, J.: Domain-Specific Modeling - Enabling Full Code Generation. Wiley, Hoboken (2008)
2. Mernik, M., Heering, J., Sloane, A.M.: When and how to develop domain-specific languages. ACM Comput. Surv. **37**, 316–344 (2005)
3. Voelter, M.: DSL Engineering - Designing, Implementing and Using Domain-Specific Languages (2013). dslbook.org
4. Brambilla, M., Cabot, J., Wimmer, M.: Model-Driven Software Engineering in Practice. Morgan & Claypool, San Rafael (2012)
5. Whittle, J., Hutchinson, J.E., Rouncefield, M.: The state of practice in model-driven engineering. IEEE Softw. **31**, 79–85 (2014)
6. Ko, A.J., Abraham, R., Beckwith, L., Blackwell, A.F., Burnett, M.M., Erwig, M., Scaffidi, C., Lawrance, J., Lieberman, H., Myers, B.A., Rosson, M.B., Rothermel, G., Shaw, M., Wiedenbeck, S.: The state of the art in end-user software engineering. ACM Comput. Surv. **43**, 21 (2011)
7. Steinberg, D., Budinsky, F., Paternostro, M., Merks, E.: EMF: Eclipse Modeling Framework, 2nd edn. Addison-Wesley Professional, Boston (2008)
8. Sirius (2016). https://eclipse.org/sirius/
9. Vaquero-Melchor, D., Garmendia, A., Guerra, E., de Lara, J.: Towards enabling mobile domain-specific modelling. In: ICSOFT 2016, vol. 2, pp. 117–122. ICSOFT-PT, SciTePress (2016)
10. Bettini, C., Brdiczka, O., Henricksen, K., Indulska, J., Nicklas, D., Ranganathan, A., Riboni, D.: A survey of context modelling and reasoning techniques. Pervasive Mob. Comput. **6**, 161–180 (2010)
11. Garmendia, A., Pescador, A., Guerra, E., de Lara, J.: Towards the generation of graphical modelling environments aided by patterns. In: Sierra-Rodríguez, J.-L., Leal, J.P., Simões, A. (eds.) SLATE 2015. CCIS, vol. 563, pp. 160–168. Springer, Cham (2015). doi:10.1007/978-3-319-27653-3_16
12. Pescador, A., Garmendia, A., Guerra, E., Cuadrado, J.S., de Lara, J.: Pattern-based development of domain-specific modelling languages. In: MODELS, pp. 166–175. IEEE (2015)
13. Graphiti. https://eclipse.org/graphiti/
14. Kolovos, D.S., Rose, L.M., Abid, S.B., Paige, R.F., Polack, F.A.C., Botterweck, G.: Taming EMF and GMF using model transformation. In: Petriu, D.C., Rouquette, N., Haugen, Ø. (eds.) MODELS 2010. LNCS, vol. 6394, pp. 211–225. Springer, Heidelberg (2010). doi:10.1007/978-3-642-16145-2_15
15. Heroku (2016). https://www.heroku.com/
16. Node.js (2016). https://nodejs.org/
17. MongoDB (2016). https://www.mongodb.org/

18. de Lara, J., Vangheluwe, H.: AToM^3: a tool for multi-formalism and meta-modelling. In: Kutsche, R.D., Weber, H. (eds.) FASE 2002. LNCS, vol. 2306, pp. 174–188. Springer, Heidelberg (2002). doi:10.1007/3-540-45923-5_12

19. GMF. http://www.eclipse.org/modeling/gmp/

20. Syriani, E., Vangheluwe, H., Mannadiar, R., Hansen, C., Mierlo, S.V., Ergin, H.: AToMPM: a web-based modeling environment. In: Joint Proceedings of MODELS Invited Talks, Demonstration Session, Poster Session, and ACM SRC, Proceedings of CEUR Workshop, vol. 1115, pp. 21–25 (2013). CEUR-WS.org

21. Rose, L.M., Kolovos, D.S., Paige, R.F.: Eugenia live: a flexible graphical modelling tool. In: XM @ MoDELS, pp. 15–20. ACM (2012)

22. Maróti, M., Kecskés, T., Kereskényi, R., Broll, B., Völgyesi, P., Jurácz, L., Levendovszky, T., Lédeczi, Á.: Next generation (meta)modeling: web- and cloud-based collaborative tool infrastructure. In: MPM @ MoDELS, Proceedings of CEUR Workshop, vol. 1237, pp. 41–60 (2014). CEUR-WS.org

23. Vaupel, S., Taentzer, G., Harries, J.P., Stroh, R., Gerlach, R., Guckert, M.: Model-driven development of mobile applications allowing role-driven variants. In: Dingel, J., Schulte, W., Ramos, I., Abrahão, S., Insfran, E. (eds.) MODELS 2014. LNCS, vol. 8767, pp. 1–17. Springer, Cham (2014). doi:10.1007/978-3-319-11653-2_1

24. Lemma, R., Lanza, M., Olivero, F.: CEL: modeling everywhere. In: ICSE, pp. 1323–1326. IEEE/ACM (2013)

25. Wüest, D.: FlexiSketch: a mobile sketching tool for software modeling. In: Uhler, D., Mehta, K., Wong, J.L. (eds.) MobiCASE 2012. LNICST, vol. 110, pp. 225–244. Springer, Heidelberg (2013). doi:10.1007/978-3-642-36632-1_13

26. Mangano, N., LaToza, T.D., Petre, M., van der Hoek, A.: Supporting informal design with interactive whiteboards. In: CHI, pp. 331–340. ACM (2014)

27. Danado, J., Paternò, F.: Puzzle: a mobile application development environment using a jigsaw metaphor. J. Vis. Lang. Comput. **25**, 297–315 (2014)

28. Gómez-Abajo, P., Guerra, E., de Lara, J.: Wodel: a domain-specific language for model mutation. In: SAC, pp. 1968–1973 (2016)

Applying MDA to Rule and Data Generation for Compliance Checking

Deepali Kholkar$^{(\boxtimes)}$, Sagar Sunkle, and Vinay Kulkarni

Tata Consultancy Services, Pune, India
{deepali.kholkar,sagar.sunkle,vinay.vkulkarni}@tcs.com

Abstract. Compliance to regulations is a critical problem for enterprises. Increasing regulation and need for reduced time-to-market has led enterprises to look to technology to scale and automate their compliance efforts. Automated compliance checking approaches proposed in research need human experts to formally encode rules, as well as to extract the relevant data from enterprise data stores. We present a model-driven architecture (MDA) and method to semi-automate generation of formal rules and extraction of relevant data for compliance checking, based on OMG's MDA methodology. We demonstrate how building a fact-oriented model of the regulation is central to both relating it to the enterprise as well as deriving formal specification of rules. We illustrate our approach using a real-life case study of the MiFID-2 financial regulation.

Keywords: Model-driven engineering · Model-Driven Architecture (MDA) · Regulatory compliance · Rule base · Rule languages · Production rule systems · Formal logic · SBVR · CIM · PIM · PSM · Data integration

1 Introduction

Modern enterprises operate in an unprecedented regulatory environment [1]. Increasing regulation and heavy penalties on non-compliance have placed regulatory compliance among the topmost concerns of enterprises worldwide[1]. Enterprises are increasingly looking to technology to aid their overall compliance process and efforts.

Industry uses GRC frameworks[2] for compliance management and tracking. These are document-oriented systems that help human experts maintain traceability between various artefacts in the compliance life-cycle. Documents such as legal text of regulations, compliance process descriptions, audit reports, etc. can be linked using tagging mechanisms[3]. Actual implementation of compliance to regulations happens through organizational processes and IT systems.

---

[1] Top Ten Problems Faced by Business, http://www.bmgi.com/resources/articles/top-ten-problems-faced-business.

[2] MetricStream, http://www.metricstream.com/.

[3] OpenCalais, http://www.opencalais.com/.

© Springer International Publishing AG 2017
E. Cabello et al. (Eds.): ICSOFT 2016, CCIS 743, pp. 239–263, 2017.
DOI: 10.1007/978-3-319-62569-0_12

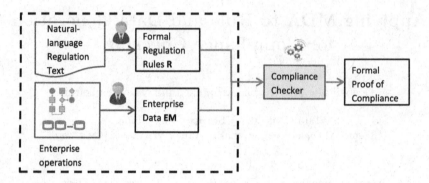

Fig. 1. Formal approach to compliance checking [9].

Compliance checking, i.e. validating whether the enterprise adheres to applicable regulations, can be done at two levels - *design-time*, i.e. checking the organization's business process definitions, and *run-time* compliance, i.e. checking enterprise data resulting from process execution.

Several approaches for automated compliance checking have been proposed in literature [2–8]. All of these use formalisms to encode rules, and a reasoning engine to check compliance of operational details of the enterprise, as illustrated in Fig. 1. Operational details could be enterprise business processes or data, depending on whether design-time or run-time compliance is to be checked, and are encoded in the same formalism as the rules. The rule engine produces as output a trace or formal proof of compliance, as shown in Fig. 1 [9].

Most approaches in literature focus on design-time checking [2–4] of business processes. Of the run-time approaches, some use execution paths generated from business process models for compliance checking. Others use production rule systems (PRS) to check data from enterprise application databases [4]. These systems, also known as business rule management systems (BRMS), are widely employed in practice. BRMS allow rules to be declaratively specified and evaluated on enterprise data, outside of core application code. This approach offers several advantages, viz. visibility, centralized definition, and easier maintenance of rules.

Business rules are the most critical component of any application and drive all the business processes in the organization. It is therefore imperative that domain experts are able to directly specify, maintain, and control business rule repositories [40]. However, rule languages have program-like syntax, requiring programmers to encode rules. This leads to two separate teams to maintain rule bases - domain experts to specify rules and programmers to encode them, leaving room for gaps in understanding. In addition, manual coding of rules is effort- and cost-intensive, also, vulnerable to error.

The entire process of interpreting natural-language (NL) regulations, relating them to enterprise information, specifying rules in BRMS, extraction of relevant data for compliance checking, and deciphering the results, all constitute a huge workload on human experts, accounting for the high effort and cost of compliance in practice [10]. Automation in the end-to-end process to the extent possible is highly desirable to bring down effort and cost.

Research approaches as well as BRMS, automate only the compliance checking step, relying on human experts to create both rule and data specifications. The problem of *relating* the regulation to the enterprise, i.e. identification of relevant enterprise data is simplified in current approaches by assuming correspondence between terminology used on both sides. In reality, there are several issues involved. One, the relation is not a direct mapping. The regulation uses a conceptual information model at a different level of abstraction from that used by the enterprise in its systems. The corresponding model of enterprise information may span several enterprise systems and databases. Moreover, there is typically an overlap between data in various systems. Finally, there is no mapping or common enterprise-wide view of the data [9]. Currently, these issues are surmounted by teams of business, legal, and operations experts working together.

We focus on these two specific problems in the automated compliance checking context, viz.

1. Creation of formal specification of regulation rules from natural-language regulation text and
2. Identification and extraction of enterprise data relevant to a regulation from application databases

Both these tasks cannot be completely automated, and require expert intervention. We therefore present a semi-automated solution to aid human experts. In order to relate the regulation to the enterprise, we need to map their conceptual models. We therefore proposed creation of models as abstractions of the regulation and enterprise. Models are suitable for mapping as opposed to NL text, since they are a precise, structured representation adhering to a specific meta-model. Model-driven engineering (MDE) [11,12] advocates creation of machine-manipulable models from which code can be generated in an automated manner. We apply the MDE process defined by the Object Management Group (OMG) in their model-driven architecture (MDA) standard, to our two problems in the compliance context, listed above.

In this paper, we present a model-driven architecture that uses separation of concerns to create models at a suitable level of abstraction for each step of the compliance process. We show how meta-model mapping between the model layers enables automated generation of downstream models. Specifically, we demonstrate how building a model of regulation rules helps automate generation of the rule base in a rule language, as well as map to relevant data within the enterprise. In the next few sections, we describe our approach and illustrate it using a real-life case study of the MiFID-2 financial regulation.

2 Our Solution Approach

We first give a more precise definition of our problem. Taking a model-theoretic view[4], the regulatory compliance checking problem can be formally defined as

$$EM \models R \tag{1}$$

where EM denotes the model of an enterprise that needs to satisfy the formally specified set of regulation rules R. EM signifies the relevant enterprise details to be checked for compliance to R, as depicted in Fig. 1. If EM satisfies R, EM is a *model* of R, by model theory.

Existing compliance checking approaches automate the checking of EM against R, given EM and R [9]. Our earlier-stated two problems of the compliance process can now be defined as

1. Creation of the formal specification **R** of regulation rules
2. Obtaining the relevant enterprise data **EM** for checking compliance to R

We have elected to use a model-based approach for derivation of EM and R and for relating them. The key issues are creation of these models from natural-language information sources, and choice of modeling languages. In the next few subsections, we describe the technologies used in our solution approach and the rationale behind each choice.

Regulation text is unstructured information available as NL text. We choose to take the knowledge representation (KR) [13] approach as a means to arrive at a structured abstraction of the regulation and then its conceptual model, from unstructured NL information. A brief overview of KR follows in the next subsection.

2.1 Knowledge Representation

Knowledge representation [13] is the construction of systems that contain symbolic representations of information in a problem space, such that the representations have the following properties

- they express *propositions* about the problem space
- they capture the *intentional stance* or *goals* of the problem space, and cause the system to *behave* in accordance with these goals.

This definition is as per the Knowledge Representation Hypothesis [14].

Such systems are *knowledge-based systems* (KBS) and the representations constitute a *knowledge base* (KB) [13]. E.g. a KBS representing the game of chess captures propositions about playing pieces and moves, as also the rules and goals of the game.

---

[4] Stanford Encyclopedia of Philosophy: Model theory, http://plato.stanford.edu/entri es/model-theory/.

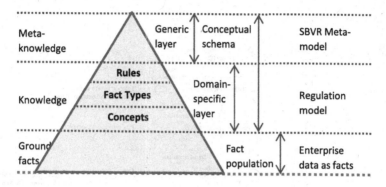

Fig. 2. Layers of a fact-oriented model [9].

We proceed to build a knowledge base of regulation rules, referred henceforth as regulation KB. The representations in the regulation KB express propositions about the problem domain of the regulation. The goals of building our regulation KB are, to

1. Establish compliance to regulation rules
2. Identify the data EM_{data} needed for checking compliance to the rules [9].

We choose the fact-oriented modeling (FOM) formalism [15, 16] to represent the regulation KB. The next sub-section gives an overview of FOM.

2.2 Fact-Oriented Modeling

The fact-oriented formalism captures knowledge about the universe of discourse in the form of *facts*, also called fact types. Fact types are *propositions* about things in the universe of discourse e.g. *Customer holds account, account has balance.* Customer, account and balance are *concepts*, or *things* in the universe of discourse. *Rules* are built by imposing modalities such as *obligation* and *necessity* onto compositions of fact types. e.g. *It is obligatory that* account *has* balance *if* customer *holds* account.

The fact-oriented model thus represents knowledge in three layers: concepts, fact types based upon concepts, and rules based upon fact types, as shown in Fig. 2. FOM supports reasoning with data provided as a population of *ground facts*, shown by the *fact population* layer in Fig. 2. E.g. for the fact type *customer holds account*, a population of ground facts would give data of accounts held by specific customers e.g. <u>Cust001</u> *holds* <u>AC10076</u>, <u>Cust002</u> *holds* <u>AC30012</u>.

FOM is thus suitable for modeling the regulation knowledge base for the following reasons

– Sentences from NL text of regulations can be expressed as propositions or *fact types* in FOM.
– Regulation *rules* can be modeled as compositions of these fact types.

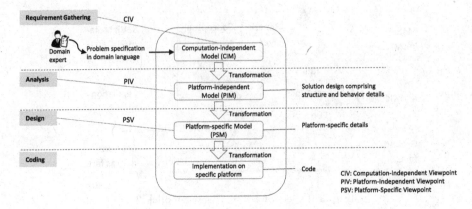

Fig. 3. Layers in MDA.

- Representation of rules in terms of fact types and concepts identifies the concept model on which a rule depends, fulfilling the second goal of our regulation KB.
- FOM maps to first-order logic, and is thus useful for translating rules from the regulation KB into logical form R.
- Given a fact population for EM_{data}, a reasoning engine can reason about the truth of the set of rules R, as given by Eq. 1.

In the next subsection we give a brief overview of OMG's MDA standard, on which our compliance architecture is based.

2.3 MDA

MDA advocates creation of abstract, machine-readable models of the problem and solution space, stored in standardized repositories [11]. Models can be repeatedly accessed to generate implementation artefacts such as schemas, code, test harnesses, deployment scripts [11,12]. Models give a higher-level abstraction over code that is easier to understand and maintain.

Principles of MDA. MDA emphasizes separation of concerns, where domain, structural, and platform details are encapsulated in separate layers of abstraction [12]. The three layers of MDA are illustrated in Fig. 3. A description of the problem space in purely domain-specific terms is captured in the computation-independent model (CIM)[5]. The next layer is the platform-independent model (PIM) that captures design details of the solution in terms of structure and behavior, however, devoid of technology platform details. Finally, the platform-specific model (PSM) is the realization of the PIM on a specific technology platform.

---

[5] Model Driven Architecture - A Technical Perspective, http://www.omg.org/cgi-bin/doc?ormsc/2001-07-01.

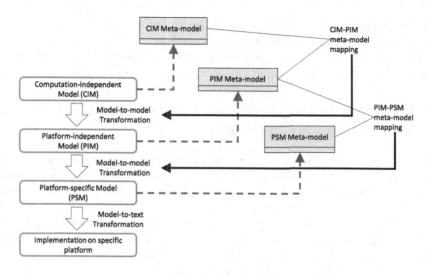

Fig. 4. Model mapping and transformations in MDA.

The three layers of MDA correspond to phases of the software development lifecycle (SDLC), as shown in Fig. 3. CIM is the specification of a system created in the Requirements Gathering phase, PIM corresponds to the Analysis, and PSM to the Design phase [17].

Model Mapping and Automated Transformation. Models being machine-operable, successive model layers and finally implementation code can be derived from previous layers by meta-model mapping and automated transformation. In addition to productivity and cost benefits over manual development, this enables traceability all the way from the CIM to the code, making it easier to track impact of change. Moving to new technology platforms or a different design choice requires only the relevant model layer and mapping to be changed, and downstream model layers can be generated afresh to reflect the change. E.g. to derive the PSM for a different technology platform, the PIM needs only to be mapped to the meta-model for the new platform, and its PSM generated.

The mapping and transformations between the three layers are illustrated in Fig. 4. A mapping is a set of rules for deriving one model layer from another, and is based on the meta-models of the two layers. PIM-PSM mapping can be used to generate a realization of the logical PIM on physical execution infrastructure[6]. If both PIM and PSM are MOF-compliant models, model-to-model transformation techniques and tools such as QVT[7] can be used to generate the PSM.

---

[6] Model Driven Architecture - A Technical Perspective, http://www.omg.org/cgi-bin/doc?ormsc/2001-07-01.

[7] Meta Object Facility (MOF) 2.0 Query/View/Transformation Specification, http://www.omg.org/spec/QVT/1.2/.

Implementation code on the chosen technology platform can then be generated from the PSM using model-to-text transformation.

In the next section, we describe our application of MDA for automated derivation of rules and data for compliance checking.

3   MDA Applied to Rule and Data Generation for Compliance Checking

Our model-driven architecture for compliance checking comprises two parts, to address the two problems defined earlier, viz. (a) MDA for creation of rule base R and (b) MDA for extraction of enterprise data EM, where R and EM are as shown in Fig. 1.

In arriving at an MDA for rule base creation, we focus on the specific requirements of rule engines, and select modeling languages accordingly, as described in the next subsection. We use the rule model obtained in this process as basis for the architecture for enterprise data extraction.

3.1   MDA for Rule Base Generation

All rule engines work on the basic premise that there is information available as *facts*, based on which, truth status of *rules* is to be determined.

Rule engines can be classified into the following three principal kinds[8] based on the reasoning algorithm used

1. Pure inferencing engines such as Prolog, DR-Prolog. These either use forward chaining i.e. data-driven inferencing about rules beginning with available data or information, or backward chaining, i.e. goal-driven inferencing beginning with a *goal* or query given by the user, and testing for the truth value of its contained goals one by one, on available data.
2. Production Rule Systems (PRS) such as JBoss Drools that combine inferencing using forward or backward chaining or both, called hybrid reasoning, with actions based on the conclusions drawn.
3. Reactive rule engines that do complex event processing, i.e. detect events from available information, and react to them.

Applying MDA principles to our context of modeling rules, domain experts can provide the specification of regulation rules in domain language, as the CIM. The common conceptual model used by all rule engines comprising *rules* dependent on *facts*, forms the PIM. Individual rule languages form the PSM, that can be generated from the PIM, by mapping PIM and PSM meta-models. The textual rules in the syntax of the rule language can be generated by model-to-text transformation from the PSM.

MDA thus provides an alternative to encoding rules by hand and offers the possibility of switching to or maintaining multiple implementations of a rule base on various platforms by mapping their PSMs to a common PIM.

---

[8] Production Rule Representation, http://www.omg.org/spec/PRR/.

In the next few subsections, we discuss the choice of modeling languages for each layer of our MDA.

Choice of CIM and PIM. We need a language for domain experts to specify rules using domain terminology, as the CIM. SBVR was devised by OMG as a standard for capturing the vocabulary used by a business domain, definitions and relations between terms, and business rules governing the domain. SBVR is a fact-oriented modeling language [15,16], that captures rules as compositions of facts. This is the same conceptual model as that used by all rule engines, making SBVR the natural choice of model. Figure 2 shows the layers of a fact-oriented model, where the SBVR meta-model makes up the *meta-knowledge* layer. An SBVR model of regulation rules created by instantiating this meta-model constitutes the *knowledge* layer, while enterprise data forms the *ground facts*.

OMG provides a MOF-compliant meta-model for SBVR, and also a controlled natural language notation for specifying the model, called SBVR Structured English (SE)[9]. SBVR SE is a restricted subset of natural language, with a well defined set of keywords that connect phrases denoting concepts and their relations. We use SBVR SE for the CIM, since it is a structured, yet near-natural language notation in which the vocabulary and rules for any domain can be specified, fulfilling the criteria for a CIM.

Since SE is intended as a means to populate the SBVR model, its elements have a direct correspondence with the SBVR meta-model. A translation scheme from SE to an SBVR model can thus be worked out. It therefore follows that we use SBVR as the PIM. SBVR SE and SBVR model have often been clubbed in literature and classified as a CIM [39]. We choose to treat SE as a CIM notation for the aforementioned reasons, and the SBVR model as a PIM since it captures structure and behaviour of domain entities using a specific meta-model. A concept model captures the structure, while rules using logical formulations built upon the concept model encode the behaviour. The SBVR meta-model subset we use is described in detail in the next section.

SBVR Meta-Model. We use a subset of the OMG SBVR meta-model[10], shown in Fig. 5, for capturing regulation rules. The meta-model comprises three sections, as shown in the figure.

1. **Meaning Vocabulary:** This is the meta-model for capturing structure or the body of *concepts*. *Noun concepts* denote entities, while *verb concepts*, also called *fact types*, signify relations. Fact types take the form *role verb role*, where *role* denotes a noun concept. *General concepts* and *concept types* specialize concepts and help create concept hierarchies. Attributes of a concept are captured as *characteristics*.

---

[9] Semantics of Business Vocabulary and Business Rules: Annex A: SBVR Structured English, http://www.omg.org/spec/SBVR/1.2/.

[10] Semantics of Business Vocabulary and Business Rules, http://www.omg.org/spec/SBVR/1.2/.

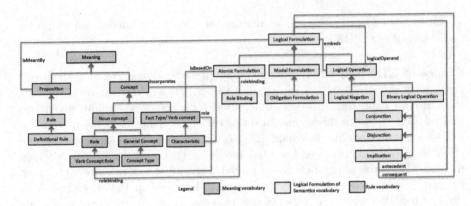

Fig. 5. SBVR meta-model [9].

2. **Logical Formulation of Semantics Vocabulary:** This section comprises *logical formulations* of fact types. Compound logical formulations e.g. *conjunctions, implications, negations* are composed of *atomic formulations*. Each atomic formulation is based on a fact type from the body of concepts.

3. **Rule Vocabulary:** This section specifies rules, based on logical formulations. We use *definitional rules* to denote necessity formulations, and *operative rules* to denote obligations. A rule inherits from *Proposition*, that is *meant by* a logical formulation that is a formal expression of the rule in terms of fact types.

SBVR thus provides a comprehensive meta-model for capturing the *semantics* of rules as logical formulations over fact types and concepts. The next subsection takes stock of other existing general-purpose rule languages.

Why SBVR? There are several general-purpose rule languages and notations in addition to SBVR, such as Production Rule Representation (PRR), RuleML, SWRL, W3C RIF. SWRL, RuleML and W3C RIF are especially designed for capturing ontologies for the semantic web. SWRL combines the capabilities of RuleML and OWL. PRR has been explicitly devised to create a generic representation of rules that addresses all types of production rule systems.

We choose SBVR as PIM because of (a) its semantic fact-oriented model that captures the dependence hierarchy of rules on fact types and concepts, crucial for inferencing, and (b) its multi-layer modeling capability, supported by its MOF-compliant meta-model, that allows multiple layers of instantiation. We choose SBVR over other languages for its inherent mapping to SE. Any other rule language as PIM would require designing the CIM-PIM mapping from SE.

The expressiveness of SBVR is sufficient to capture a generic platform-independent representation of rules. The SBVR meta-model, being a FOM, maps directly to the common conceptual model of rule languages such as DR-Prolog and PRS such as Drools, although they have different platform-specific models.

SBVR captures both structure and behavior in a single notation, whereas when PRR is used to capture rules, structure needs to be defined using UML class models. The next subsection describes platform-specific models for rules.

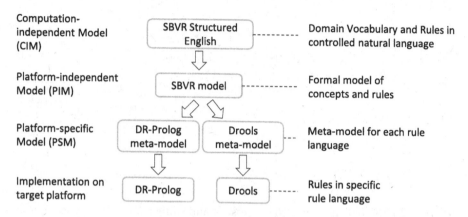

Fig. 6. Model-driven architecture for rule base generation.

Choice of PSM. As mentioned earlier, DR-Prolog and Drools are rule definition languages representative of two different classes of rule systems, viz. backward chaining rule engine and production rule system respectively. We select DR-Prolog as the rule language for our architecture. Its language meta-model therefore forms our PSM.

The rule definition meta-model of DR-Prolog maps directly to the SBVR meta-model, since both are fact-oriented models. We create the PIM-PSM map between SBVR and DR-Prolog meta-models and use it for transformation of the PIM instance to PSM instance. We then translate the PSM instance to rules in DR-Prolog syntax.

The resultant architecture for rule base generation is depicted in Fig. 6. MDA also allows multiple PIM-PSM layers to be used, with each PSM becoming the PIM for the next layer. E.g. if we choose a PRS as our rule platform, it was possible to use SBVR as PIM and PRR as a PSM, since PRR captures the model for the PRS class of systems. The PRR model then becomes the PIM for a Drools PSM.

In the next section we describe our architecture for extraction of enterprise data, followed by the detailed method for using the architecture.

3.2   MDA for Enterprise Data Extraction

The SBVR PIM of regulation rules created in the rule generation architecture described above is used as the basis for data extraction. The SBVR model is a fact-oriented KB that captures rules and their dependence on fact types.

The fact types on which rules are based denote the propositions whose truth value must be determined in order to evaluate whether the rule holds. This set of

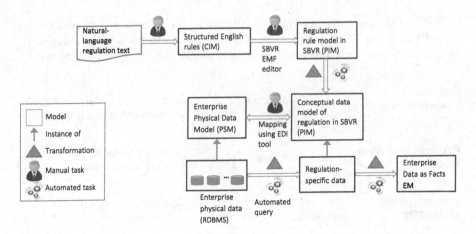

Fig. 7. Model-driven architecture for enterprise data extraction.

fact types therefore constitutes the necessary and sufficient *model* of information needed from the enterprise, for determining compliance. This is actually the *conceptual data model* of the regulation, as we illustrate in the case study section. Building a fact-oriented KB of the regulation thus addresses the second goal of the regulation KB. Building an FOM is in fact, a way to get the conceptual model for any problem space, from unstructured information.

The enterprise provides data as *ground facts* corresponding to this *conceptual model*. These are checked for compliance to the rules by a reasoning engine, addressing the first goal of the regulation KB. For instance, in the simplistic rule about customer account, the fact types *customer holds account*, and *account has balance* denote the *model* of information needed to check compliance to the rule. The enterprise has to provide ground facts for these fact types, such as *Cust001 holds Acct101, Cust002 holds Acct102, Acct101 has Rs 2000*, as data.

Our model-driven architecture for data extraction comprises several layers of models and model transformations to arrive from regulation NL text to the enterprise data, depicted in Fig. 7. The first two model layers are the SE CIM and SBVR PIM described earlier. The model layers in this architecture are listed below.

1. Regulation rules expressed in SE (CIM)
2. Rule model in SBVR (PIM)
3. Conceptual data model of regulation, extracted from the SBVR rule model (PIM)
4. Enterprise physical data model (PSM).

Our overall architecture, a union of the individual architectures for rule base creation and data extraction, is shown in Fig. 8. The SBVR PIM of rules is central to generation of both rules and data, and therefore forms the pivotal model of the overall architecture. Transformations from one model layer to the next are described in the next section, as part of our method for using this architecture for automated generation of rules and data.

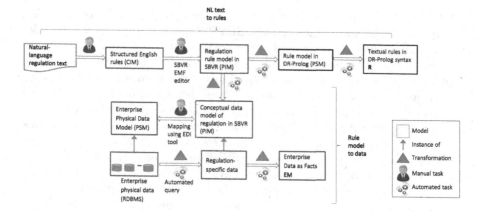

Fig. 8. Overall model-driven architecture for rule and data generation.

4 Method for Using the MDA for Rule and Data Generation

4.1 Rule Base Generation Using SBVR

We create our regulation rule base in the DR-Prolog language, in an automated manner from the SBVR model of rules. We first create the CIM and PIM of regulation rules using SBVR. The constructs of the SBVR PIM are then mapped to constructs of DR-Prolog, which is the PSM. This PIM-PSM mapping is used for transformation from SBVR to DR-Prolog.

Creation of CIM and PIM of Regulation Rules in SBVR. We use the Eclipse Modeling Framework (EMF)[11] model-to-model and model-to text conversion tools to import the MOF-compliant SBVR meta-model supplied on the OMG SBVR website to EMF Ecore format and to generate code for an SBVR editor.

We build the SBVR model of regulation rules in the following steps

1. Domain experts mark in the NL regulation text, the statements representing rules to be checked, definitions of terms used in the rules, and data descriptions relevant to the rules.
2. Domain experts then write each NL rule statement in the controlled natural language SBVR SE. This is the CIM of the regulation. SBVR SE is written using a restricted English vocabulary, defined in the OMG SBVR specification[12] and specific font styles, viz. the term font for designating noun concepts, general concepts, concept types and roles; Name font for individual concepts

---

[11] IBM Eclipse Modeling Framework, http://www.eclipse.org/modeling/emf/.
[12] Semantics of Business Vocabulary and Business Rules: Annex A: SBVR Structured English, http://www.omg.org/spec/SBVR/1.2/.

or names; *verb* font for designations of fact types; and keyword font for other words in definitions and statements. SBVR SE rule statements for the rules in our case study are illustrated in the next section.

3. Rules in regulation text are expressed in terms of concepts at a high level of abstraction. High-level concepts and fact types from regulation rules are explicated using propositions obtained from definitions or data descriptions within the regulation text, or knowledge from domain experts, in terms of more basic concepts and fact types. This process is iteratively followed until no further explication of concepts is possible [9].

4. We mapped the SE meta-model to the SBVR meta-model. However, we create the SBVR PIM corresponding to the captured SE statements manually using the SBVR editor, since automation of the CIM-PIM translation from SE to SBVR model is ongoing work, its detailed description is therefore not included in this paper.

The next section deals with transformation of rules from the SBVR PIM to the target rule language DR-Prolog.

Translation from PIM to PSM: SBVR to DR-Prolog. The SBVR meta-model has almost a one-to-one correspondence with the conceptual model of DR-Prolog. We create the PIM-PSM map between SBVR and DR-Prolog meta-models, by mapping their elements. E.g. A rule is defined as *element of guidance* in SBVR, and maps to *defeasible rule* in DR-Prolog, *implication* maps to *implication rule*, *atomic formulation* maps to *predicate*. The entire PIM-PSM map for DR-Prolog has not been included here for want of space.

A custom program generates the DR-Prolog PSM from the SBVR PIM in accordance with this PIM-PSM map. From the DR-Prolog PSM, another program generates rules in textual format in the corresponding DR-Prolog syntax.

In the next few sections, we describe the method for extraction of enterprise data relevant to the modeled rules.

4.2   Extraction of Enterprise Data

The first step is extraction of the conceptual data model from the SBVR model of regulation rules.

Extraction of Conceptual Data Model of Regulation. The leaf-level fact types and concepts from the SBVR rule model constitute the *conceptual* model of regulation data, as described earlier. The conceptual data model defines the data expected from the enterprise for checking compliance.

The meta-model for concepts and fact types in the SBVR model, is the section shown in blue in Fig. 5, except for the entity *Proposition*. Instances of this meta-model represent the concepts used in the regulation KB. Concepts at the leaf level represent the conceptual model of data expected from the enterprise [9]. We use this conceptual model to retrieve enterprise data as described in the next subsection.

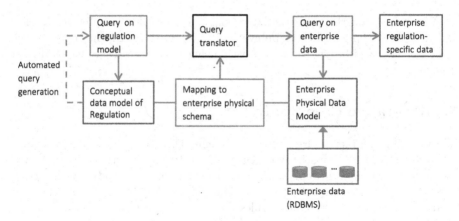

Fig. 9. Query translation in the EDI tool [9].

Retrieval of Enterprise Data. In industry practice of compliance, compliance experts, operations, and systems experts are required to analyze regulation text, interpret it in the context of enterprise processes, and identify the enterprise data mapping for a regulation. Data relevant to a regulation is typically distributed across several enterprise systems, with no enterprise-level view of data. Data integration is needed in order to create a common conceptual view of enterprise data. Extraction of data for compliance checking thus poses a schema integration problem, and we tackle it as such [9].

We use an in-house enterprise data integration (EDI) tool [18] for schema integration. It allows mapping of multiple physical database schemas to a single conceptual schema. It also facilitates queries to be written on the conceptual schema that are translated to queries on the enterprise physical database schemas using the mapping.

Using our approach, the conceptual data model of regulation obtained earlier becomes the conceptual schema that needs to be mapped to enterprise data. This conceptual schema is imported into the EDI tool. Domain experts then map it to the distributed physical database schemas (PSM) of the enterprise. This is a PIM-PSM mapping. Tables and columns of the PIM are mapped to tables and columns of the PSM.

We then generate queries on the conceptual data model, in an automated manner, for retrieval of requisite data corresponding to each *concept* and *fact type* in the conceptual model. These are translated by the EDI tool to queries on enterprise physical tables using the above PIM-PSM mapping, as depicted in Fig. 9.

As shown in Fig. 9, the translated queries on execution fetch the required data to be checked for compliance. We provide a one-time PSM-PSM map between enterprise physical data model i.e. tables, columns, and datatypes, and DR-Prolog fact meta-model, i.e. facts, attributes, and datatypes. A fact generator program transforms the fetched enterprise data into ground facts in DR-Prolog.

We thus obtain the requisite data EM_{data} to check for compliance to regulation rules R using model mappings and automated transformations. In the next section, we illustrate our approach using a case study of the MiFID-2 regulation[13].

5   Illustrative Case Study

The MiFID-2 (Markets in Financial Instruments Directive) regulation lays down obligations on financial institutions regarding the types of transactions that must be included/excluded in reporting trades to the regulatory body. We illustrate here the relevant excerpt from the original regulation text and the chain of models created for the regulation rules.

Regulation Text. The original regulation text containing inclusion and exclusion rules for transactions is shown below.

Meaning of transaction

1. *For the purposes of Article 26 of Regulation (EU) No. 600/2014, the conclusion of an acquisition or disposal of a financial instrument referred to in Article 26(2) of Regulation (EU) No. 600/2014 shall constitute a transaction.*
2. *An acquisition referred to in paragraph 1 shall include:*
   (a) a purchase of a financial instrument;
   (b) entering into a derivative contract in a financial instrument.
3. *A disposal referred to in paragraph 1 shall include:*
   (a) sale of a financial instrument;
   (b) closing out of a derivative contract in a financial instrument.
   ..
4. *A transaction for the purposes of Article 26 of Regulation (EU) No. 600/2014 shall not include:*
   (a) a securities financing transaction as defined in Regulation [Securities Financing Transactions]
   (b) a contract arising exclusively for clearing or settlement purposes;
   (c) an acquisition or disposal that is solely a result of custodial activity;

The next sub-section illustrates the CIM created by writing the above natural-language regulation rules in Structured English.

CIM of Regulation Rules in SE. The inclusion and exclusion rules from the regulation text are encoded in SBVR SE as below.

Rule_Inclusion: It is obligatory that <u>transaction</u> *is included in MiFID reporting* if the <u>transaction</u> *is an* <u>acquisition</u> or a <u>disposal</u>.

---

[13] MiFID-2: http://ec.europa.eu/finance/securities/isd/mifid2/index_en.htm.

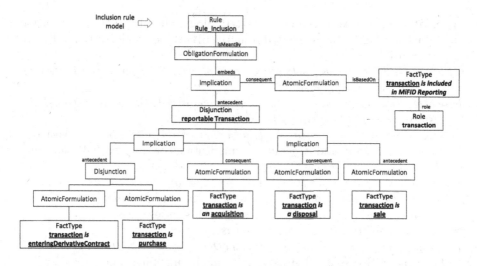

Fig. 10. SBVR model of MiFID-2 rules.

Rule_Exclusion: It is obligatory that transaction *is excluded from MiFID reporting* if the transaction *is a* securities financing transaction or clearing or settlement contract or an acquisition or disposal *arising from* custodial activity.

The keywords *It is obligatory that* denote the obligation modality of the rule. Rule_Inclusion is built upon fact types *transaction is included in MiFID reporting*, *transaction is an acquisition*, and *transaction is a disposal*. Transaction, acquisition, and disposal are concepts; *is included in MiFID reporting* is a characteristic of a transaction.

Acquisition and disposal are high-level concepts defined in terms of other concepts, e.g. purchase and sale. These definitions are captured as definitional rules as follows

Acquisition *is a* purchase or entering a derivative contract.

Disposal *is a* sale or closing a derivative contract.

Purchase is further explicated by domain experts in terms of propositions on elements such as *buyer* and *seller* defined in the data description section in the regulation, as well as concepts such as *trade type* from their own knowledge of the domain.

Purchase *is a* transaction with trade type equal to Buy and transaction *has* buyer and transaction *trades* instrument and instrument is equities or bonds.

The next section shows the SBVR model constructed from these SE rules.

PIM of Rules in SBVR. The SBVR model corresponding to the above SE rules is created using the SBVR editor, and shown in Fig. 10. This PIM of rules is programmatically translated to a DR-Prolog model of MiFID-2 rules using the SBVR-DR-Prolog PIM-PSM mapping. From the DR-Prolog model, MiFID-2 rules in DR-Prolog syntax are generated, illustrated in the next sub-section.

Translated Regulation Rules in DR-Prolog. The inclusion and exclusion rules in DR-Prolog syntax generated from the SBVR model illustrated in Fig. 10 are shown below.

defeasible (rule_inclusion, obligation, includeInMiFIDReporting (TransRef), [reportableTransaction(TransRef)]).

defeasible (rule_exclusion, obligation, excludeInMiFIDReporting(TransRef), [exclusionTransaction(TransRef)]).

Since the antecedent *reportableTransaction* of the inclusion rule is a disjunction of *acquisition* and *disposal*, the implications or simple DR-Prolog rules specifying this relation follow.

fact (reportableTransaction(TransRef)):- fact (acquisition(TransRef)).

fact (reportableTransaction(TransRef)):- fact (disposal(TransRef)).

Definitional rules get translated as simple DR-Prolog rules, as

fact (acquisition(TransRef)):- fact (purchase(TransRef)).

fact (acquisition(TransRef)):- fact (enteringDerivativeContractInFI(TransRef)).

The generic SBVR-to-DR-Prolog meta-model mapping and translator can thus be used to translate any SBVR model of rules to a rule base in DR-Prolog in an automated manner.

The SBVR model for the entire set of SBVR SE statements for the regulation constitutes the source from which the conceptual model of the regulation is extracted. The conceptual model of our MiFID-2 regulation case study is shown in the next subsection.

Extracted Conceptual Data Model. The conceptual data model of the MiFID-2 regulation comprises leaf-level concepts and fact types from all of the defined rules, such as the concepts transaction and trade type, and facts trade type equal to Buy, and transaction *has* buyer from the definition of purchase.

The conceptual model automatically extracted from the SBVR rule model is shown in the upper half of Fig. 11. The list of characteristics within each concept is an illustrative subset, the exhaustive list not shown due to space constraints. Mapping of this conceptual model to the bank's physical data model is illustrated in the subsection below.

Enterprise Data Extraction. The enterprise physical schema comprises several sub-schemas from component sub-systems, such as Deal and Securities sub-systems seen in Fig. 11. Domain experts perform the mapping of concepts from the MiFID-2 regulation conceptual schema to the bank's physical database schema.

The Transaction concept from the regulation schema maps to the Trans and Deal tables from the enterprise Deal sub-system database, while Instrument maps to the Security Master table from the Securities sub-system. Buyer, Seller and Executing Firm entities from the conceptual schema map to the Client Master table of the enterprise database. Individual characteristics of concepts

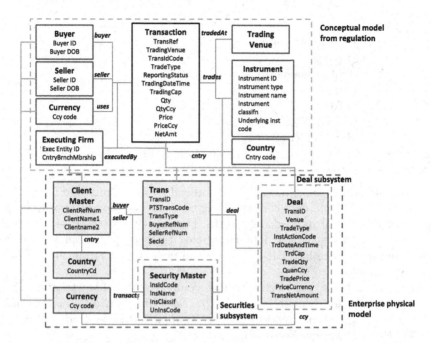

Fig. 11. Conceptual to physical data mapping in EDI [9].

such as <u>transaction</u> are mapped to columns of corresponding tables, in this case Trans and Deal.

Two of the sample queries we generate automatically, for retrieving data for Transaction and Instrument tables in the conceptual schema, are shown here. Queries for fact types that relate concepts mapping to different tables are translated as joins, such as query 2 below, corresponding to the fact type <u>transaction</u> *trades* <u>instrument</u>.

(1) **SELECT** * **FROM Transaction** ;
(2) **SELECT** * **FROM** Instrument i , **Transaction** t
    where i . InstrumentID = t . InstrumentID ;

These queries are translated by the EDI tool into queries on corresponding enterprise tables (1) Trans and Deal, and (2) Securities respectively. The translated query corresponding to query (1) is shown below

SELECT t1 . TransID ,
       t1 . TradeType ,
       t1 . InstActionCode ,
       t1 . TrdDateAndTime ,
       t1 . TrdCap ,
       t1 . TradeQty ,
       t1 . QuanCcy ,
       t1 . TradePrice ,

```
        t1 . PriceCurrency ,
        t1 . TransNetAmount ,
        t2 . transType ,
        t2 . PTSTransactionCode ,
        t1 . Venue ,
        t2 . SecId ,
        t2 . BuyerRefNum ,
        t2 . SellerRefNum
FROM DealSchema . Deal t1 , TradeSchema . Trans t2
WHERE t1 . TransID = t2 . TransID
```

The translated query, on execution, transforms data from Trans and Deal enterprise tables (PSM) into data corresponding to the transaction concept from the regulation conceptual data model (PIM). The retrieved data (PIM) is transformed by our fact generator into DR-Prolog transaction ground fact model (PSM) and from there into DR-Prolog ground facts in text format by PSM-to-text transformation.

The fact schema for each concept comprises its characteristics. E.g. the fact schema for transaction is *fact(transaction(TransRef, TradingVenue, TransIdCode, TradeType, ReportingStatus, TradingDateTime, TradingCap, Qty, QtyCcy, Price, PriceCcy, NetAmt))*.

The schema for each fact type, e.g. transaction *trades* instrument comprises the fact type, with concept names replaced by their unique key fields, viz. TransRef for transaction and InstrumentID for instrument, i.e. *trades(TransRef, InstrumentID)*.

The listing of two sample sets of ground facts, for a purchase and a closing a derivative contract transaction is shown below.

```
/* Set 1: Purchase transaction*/
fact ( transaction ( '1010000023TATA' , '' , 'Buy' , 'NEWT' , '
    2015−11−06T09 : 16 : 36 : 143232 ' , 'MTCH' , 2500 ,_ , 150 , 'INR' ,
    375000 ) ) .
fact ( instrument ( 'INE467B01029' , 'ESXXXX' ) ) .
fact ( currency ( 'INR' ,_ , 'Active' ) ) .
fact ( tradedAt ( '1010000023TATA' , 'XXXX' ) ) .
fact ( trades ( '1010000023TATA' , 'INE467B01029' ) ) .


/* Set 2: Closing out of Derivative Contract */
fact ( transaction ( '000CMEC000' , 'AB4' , 'Sell' , 'NEWT' , '
    2015−11−06T09 : 11 : 36 : 143232 ' , 'DEAL' , 5 , _ , 75.43 , 'GBP' ,
    377150 ) ) .
fact ( hasSeller ( '000CMEC000' , 'AFXS5XCH7N0Y05NIXW17' ) ) .
fact ( hasUnderlyingInstrument ( '000CMEC000' , 'GB0008706128' ) ) .
fact ( instrument ( 'GB0008706128' , 'FFICNX' ) ) .
fact ( currency ( 'GBP' ,_ , 'Inactive' ) ) .
```

We thus complete the process of (a) conversion of rules from MiFID-2 regulation NL text into rules in DR-Prolog language, and (b) discovering the conceptual model of the MiFID-2 regulation from regulation text, and mapping it to the physical data model of the bank, as well as automated extraction of relevant data from the bank's databases in the form of facts, for checking compliance to the regulation.

The next section discusses related work.

6 Related Work

Compliance checking approaches in literature [2–8] use formal representations of regulation rules. In all of these, experts need to directly code rules in the rule language. Most formal compliance checking approaches check business process models for compliance against regulations [2,3,5,6]. Various approaches have been developed for relating regulations to enterprise business processes such as constructing an execution trace as in [19], finding paths in process structure tree as in [20], or labels placed manually on a business property specification language diagram as in [21]. Labels from business processes are presumed to map to labels used in the formal models of rules.

A system for defeasible logic representation of regulations and compliance checking is presented in [8] that we use as the compliance engine in our work. In our earlier works, vocabulary mapping has been proposed to address the problem of semantic disparity between regulations and enterprise [22,23]. Generation of NL proof explanations of (non-) compliance, and handling regulatory change have been described in [24] and [25] respectively, while an initial framework for compliance has been introduced in [26].

Other work that makes use of models in the compliance context are a model that enables traceability of delegation of obligations from regulations and their refinement into software requirements given by [27], and a language for modeling norms and their inter-relations and analysis of various compliance alternatives in [28,29] using goal-oriented analysis. Ontologies are suggested in [30] to tackle semantic disparity. A conceptual model of the regulatory compliance management process and activities involved is used as basis to survey and rank business process compliance management frameworks in [31]. We address some of the recommendations from this work such as making compliance requirement specification possible for business users and extending use of logic to the business context, through the use of CNL and SBVR for capturing rules.

Another classification of compliance checking approaches based on the granularity of checks, i.e., whether business processes, tasks, attributes or pure data is checked, and finally whether checking takes place by making use of an inference engine and/or queries to models of enterprise information is presented in [4]. Existing business process compliance management approaches are surveyed for generalizability and applicability in [32], reporting that available frameworks support only a single model specification, do not check entire regulations but only excerpts, and lack evaluation. Although we have described mapping to enterprise physical databases for run-time compliance in this paper, our approach can be applied to a data model sourced from the enterprise's business processes, tool repositories, or indeed any other source.

Several approaches propose SBVR for encoding rules, such as semi-automated approaches to generate SBVR from natural language descriptions [33–35], expression of anti-money laundering rules in SBVR [36], and capture of legal rules in [37], for precise capture and revealing inconsistencies. Requirements for translation from SBVR to Formal Contract Logic (FCL), a proprietary defeasible logic language are defined in [38]. The source SBVR and desired target FCL specification are given, however, the mapping or transformation between the two specifications is not given.

A model-driven rule generation approach has been proposed in [39], that suggests using a combination of MDA and Ontology Definition Metamodel (ODM) for generating rules. Use of SBVR as CIM and the authors' own proprietary general purpose rule language as PIM is proposed, but the language or its mapping to SBVR or PSMs has not been worked out.

7   Conclusion and Future Work

MDA has typically been applied for code generation in technical problem spaces. We explored its application to a business problem space, viz. regulatory compliance.

We demonstrated that use of fact-oriented modeling enables (a) building a regulation model from unstructured, natural language text, by stating available information as facts, (b) identifying the conceptual model of the regulation, and (c) mapping conceptual models at different levels of abstraction on the regulation and enterprise side in order to arrive at relevant enterprise data, through our worked-out approach and the illustrative case study.

Use of MDA provides another great benefit of traceability from computation-independent regulation rules to their formal specification and related enterprise data, through each intermediate model layer.

Separation of concerns helped break the model-building task into distinct parts, automatically defining a process for creating the model, involving the appropriate stakeholder at each level. Domain experts were able to give the requirement i.e. rules in a Structured English CIM. Modelers were able to further specify structure of rules in terms of hierarchies of logical formulations in an SBVR PIM. A one-time mapping to platform-specific constructs, in our case, DR-Prolog rule language, was provided by IT experts. The rule base code was then automatically generated using the generic mappings.

Use of MDA thus meant the rule base no longer needed to be manually encoded by IT teams, but could be specified by domain experts in controlled natural language. MDA made the task of model-building manageable, and also scales to large code bases by automated code generation from model mappings.

The SBVR model serves as a general-purpose PIM for rules, that can be used to map to and generate rule implementations on multiple PSMs for rule languages such as DR-Prolog and Drools. Creating the meta-model map for Drools and automated generation of the rule base using this mapping is part of ongoing work, as is automated translation of the SBVR SE CIM to SBVR PIM.

Our model-based generators described in this work were custom-written programs. We plan to implement specification-based translation using model-to-model and model-to-text transformation tools in order to gain further productivity and maintainability benefits of MDA.

The success of model-based techniques depends upon the quality of models built. We are working on automated population and correctness checking of models at build-time using natural-language processing and machine learning techniques.

References

1. Thomson Reuters: State of regulatory reform 2016 - a special report (2016)
2. Governatori, G., Rotolo, A.: A conceptually rich model of business process compliance. In: APCCM 2010, pp. 3–12 (2010)
3. Awad, A., Weidlich, M., Weske, M.: Consistency checking of compliance rules. In: Abramowicz, W., Tolksdorf, R. (eds.) BIS 2010. LNBIP, vol. 47, pp. 106–118. Springer, Heidelberg (2010). doi:10.1007/978-3-642-12814-1_10
4. El Kharbili, M., de Medeiros, A.K.A., Stein, S., van der Aalst, W.M.P.: Business process compliance checking: current state and future challenges. In: Loos, P., Nuttgens, M., Turowski, K., Werth, D. (eds.) MobIS. LNI, vol. 141, pp. 107–113 (2008)
5. Governatori, G., Hoffmann, J., Sadiq, S., Weber, I.: Detecting regulatory compliance for business process models through semantic annotations. In: Ardagna, D., Mecella, M., Yang, J. (eds.) BPM 2008. LNBIP, vol. 17, pp. 5–17. Springer, Heidelberg (2009). doi:10.1007/978-3-642-00328-8_2
6. Governatori, G.: Representing business contracts in RuleML. Int. J. Cooper. Inf. Syst. **14**(2–3), 181–216 (2005)
7. Governatori, G., Rotolo, A.: A conceptually rich model of business process compliance. In: APCCM 2010, pp. 3–12 (2013)
8. Dimaresis, N.: A system for modal and deontic defeasible reasoning. Int. J. Cooper. Inf. Syst. **14**(2–3), 181–216 (2007)
9. Kholkar, D., Sunkle, S., Kulkarni, V.: From natural-language regulations to enterprise data using knowledge representation and model transformations. In: Proceedings of the 11th International Joint Conference on Software Technologies (ICSOFT 2016), vol. 2: ICSOFT-PT, Lisbon, Portugal, 24–26 July, pp. 60–71 (2016)
10. English, S., Hammond, S.: Cost of Compliance 2014. Thomson Reuters Accelus, London (2014)
11. Kleppe, A., Warmer, J., Bast, W.: MDA Explained - The Model Driven Architecture: Practice and Promise. Addison Wesley Object Technology Series. Addison-Wesley, Boston (2003)
12. Kulkarni, V., Reddy, S.: Separation of concerns in model-driven development. IEEE Softw. **20**(5), 64–69 (2003)
13. Brachman, R.J., Levesque, H.J.: Knowledge Representation and Reasoning. Elsevier, Amsterdam (2004)
14. Smith, B.C.: Reflection and Semantics in a Procedural Language. Massachusetts Institute of Technology, Cambridge (1982)
15. Nijssen, G.: SBVR: semantics for business. Bus. Rules J. **8**(10) (2007). http://www.brcommunity.com/a2007/b367.html

16. Halpin, T.: Fact oriented modeling - past, present and future. In: Krogstie, J., Opdahl, A.L., Brinkkemper, S. (eds.) Conceptual Modelling in Information Systems Engineering, pp. 19–38. Springer, Heidelberg (2007). doi:10.1007/978-3-540-72677-7_2

17. Alhir, S.S.: Understanding the model driven architecture. Methods and tools (2003). http://www.methodsandtools.com/archive/archive.php?id=5

18. Reddy, S.: A model driven approach to enterprise data integration. In: COMAD 2010, p. 202 (2010)

19. Sadiq, S., Governatori, G., Namiri, K.: Modeling control objectives for business process compliance. In: Alonso, G., Dadam, P., Rosemann, M. (eds.) BPM 2007. LNCS, vol. 4714, pp. 149–164. Springer, Heidelberg (2007). doi:10.1007/978-3-540-75183-0_12

20. Awad, A., Smirnov, S., Weske, M.: Resolution of compliance violation in business process models: a planning-based approach. In: Meersman, R., Dillon, T., Herrero, P. (eds.) OTM 2009. LNCS, vol. 5870, pp. 6–23. Springer, Heidelberg (2009). doi:10.1007/978-3-642-05148-7_4

21. Liu, Y., Müller, S., Xu, K.: A static compliance-checking framework for business process models. IBM Syst. J. 46(2), 335–362 (2007)

22. Sunkle, S., Kholkar, D., Kulkarni, V.: Solving semantic disparity and explanation problems in regulatory compliance - a research-in-progress report with design science research perspective. In: Gaaloul, K., Schmidt, R., Nurcan, S., Guerreiro, S., Ma, Q. (eds.) CAISE 2015. LNBIP, vol. 214, pp. 326–341. Springer, Cham (2015). doi:10.1007/978-3-319-19237-6_21

23. Sunkle, S., Kholkar, D., Kulkarni, V.: Toward better mapping between regulations and operations of enterprises using vocabularies and semantic similarity. CSIMQ 5, 39–60 (2015)

24. Sunkle, S., Kholkar, D., Kulkarni, V.: Explanation of proofs of regulatory (non-)compliance using semantic vocabularies. In: Bassiliades, N., Gottlob, G., Sadri, F., Paschke, A., Roman, D. (eds.) RuleML 2015. LNCS, vol. 9202, pp. 388–403. Springer, Cham (2015). doi:10.1007/978-3-319-21542-6_25

25. Sunkle, S., Kholkar, D., Kulkarni, V.: Model-driven regulatory compliance: a case study of know your customer regulations. In: MoDELS 2015, pp. 436–445 (2015)

26. Sunkle, S., Kholkar, D., Kulkarni, V.: Toward (semi-)automated end-to-end model-driven compliance framework. In: ModSym+SAAAS@ISEC 2016, pp. 33–38 (2016)

27. Breaux, T.D., Anton, A.I., Spafford, E.H.: A distributed requirements management framework for legal compliance and accountability. Comput. Secur. 28(1–2), 8–17 (2009)

28. Ingolfo, S., Siena, A., Susi, A., Perini, A., Mylopoulos, J.: Modeling laws with Nomos 2. In: Sixth International Workshop on Requirements Engineering and Law (RELAW), pp. 69–71, 16 July 2013

29. Ingolfo, S., Jureta, I., Siena, A., Perini, A., Susi, A.: Nòmos 3: legal compliance of roles and requirements. In: Yu, E., Dobbie, G., Jarke, M., Purao, S. (eds.) ER 2014. LNCS, vol. 8824, pp. 275–288. Springer, Cham (2014). doi:10.1007/978-3-319-12206-9_22

30. El Kharbili, M., Stein, S., Markovic, I., Pulvermüller, E.: Towards a framework for semantic business process compliance management. The impact of governance, risk, and compliance on information systems (GRCIS). CEUR Workshop Proceedings, Montpellier, France, 17 June 2008, vol. 339, pp. 1–15 (2008)

31. El Kharbili, M.: Business process regulatory compliance management solution frameworks: a comparative evaluation. In: Ghose, A., Ferrarotti, F. (eds.) Asia-Pacific Conference on Conceptual Modelling (APCCM 2012), CRPIT, Melbourne, Australia, vol. 130, pp. 23–32. ACS (2012)

32. Becker, J., Delfmann, P., Eggert, M., Schwittay, S.: Generalizability and applicability of model-based business process compliance-checking approaches - a state-of-the-art analysis and research roadmap. BuR Bus. Res. J. 5(2), 221–247 (2012)

33. Bajwa, I.S., Lee, M.G., Bordbar, B.: SBVR business rules generation from natural language specification. In: AAAI Spring Symposium: AI for Business Agility, pp. 2–8. AIII (2011)

34. Lévy, F., Nazarenko, A.: Formalization of natural language regulations through SBVR structured English. In: Morgenstern, L., Stefaneas, P., Lévy, F., Wyner, A., Paschke, A. (eds.) RuleML 2013. LNCS, vol. 8035, pp. 19–33. Springer, Heidelberg (2013). doi:10.1007/978-3-642-39617-5_5

35. Njonko, P.B.F., El Abed, W.: From natural language business requirements to executable models via SBVR. In: 2012 International Conference on Systems and Informatics (ICSAI). IEEE (2012)

36. Abi-Lahoud, E., Butler, T., Chapin, D., Hall, J.: Interpreting regulations with SBVR. In: Fodor, P., Roman, D., Anicic, D., Wyner, A., Palmirani, M., Sottara, D., Lévy, F. (eds.) Joint Proceedings of the 7th International Rule Challenge, The Special Track on Human Language Technology and the 3rd RuleML Doctoral Consortium, Seattle, USA, 11–13 July 2013. CEUR Workshop Proceedings, vol. 1004 (2013). CEUR-WS.org

37. Johnsen, A.S., Berre, A.J.R.: A bridge between legislator and technologist - formalization in SBVR for improved quality and understanding of legal rules. In: International Workshop on Business Models, Business Rules and Ontologies, Bressanone, Brixen, Italy (2010)

38. Kamada, A., Governatori, G., Sadiq, S.: Transformation of SBVR compliant business rules to executable FCL rules. In: Dean, M., Hall, J., Rotolo, A., Tabet, S. (eds.) RuleML 2010. LNCS, vol. 6403, pp. 153–161. Springer, Heidelberg (2010). doi:10.1007/978-3-642-16289-3_14

39. Diouf, M., Maabout, S., Musumbu, K.: Merging model driven architecture and semantic web for business rules generation. In: Proceedings of the First International Conference on Web Reasoning and Rule Systems, Innsbruck, Austria, 7–8 June 2007, pp. 118–132 (2007)

40. Bauer, E.: The Business Rules Approach (2009). http://is.uni-paderborn.de/fileadmin/Informatik/AG-Engels/Lehre/WS0809/SE/Sonstiges/Seminar/Version1.0/Seminar.NAQ.Eduard.Bauer.v1.0.pdf

Software System Theory of the Forbidden Within Discrete Design

Iaakov Exman[(⊠)]

Software Engineering Department,
The Jerusalem College of Engineering – JCE - Azrieli, Jerusalem, Israel
iaakov@jce.ac.il

Abstract. Many "theoretical" frameworks have been proposed for software systems design with a plethora of techniques, scopes and degrees of sophistication. However, a clear delineation of the *forbidden* in software design terms is almost universally absent in all these frameworks. This absence is surprising, as other engineering disciplines obviously display forbidden regions. This paper claims that an acceptable software design theory should clearly demarcate the forbidden in contrast to the possible. Algebra is argued to be the mathematical field appropriate to determine boundaries of forbidden regions. To this end, a spectral approach is demonstrated, in which matrix eigenvectors play a central role. Such boundaries of forbidden regions are illustrated by a case study.

Keywords: Software theory · Forbidden regions · Forbidden domains · Boundary · Algebra · Eigenvectors · Models · Discrete software design · Hierarchical software systems

1 Introduction

Forbidden regions surrounding possible solutions to engineering problems are ubiquitous in mature engineering disciplines and their underlying basic sciences. A central claim of this work is that Software Engineering deserves such a theory implying a definition and delineation of forbidden regions or domains. This is true in particular for software embedded in larger systems, which without forbidden domain restrictions may cause critical failures and endanger human life.

An aeronautical engineering example is a case that really happened above the Atlantic Ocean, of an airplane flying at high altitude that inadvertently entered a weather storm area. The pilots should have tried to either totally avoid the well-known storm area, or once inside that area to escape the storm from below, gaining speed through the airplane descent. Instead the inexperienced pilots, tried to climb above the storm causing an increasing loss of speed. The final outcome was the free fall of the airplane in the middle of the ocean. This is just one example that there are clearly *forbidden maneuvers* for any given aircraft – dictated by aerodynamics theory – that may result in total loss of control with unfortunate consequences.

Another example, this one in civil engineering, is the famous Tower of Pisa. The tower was obviously planned to be vertical, with a nice view of the surrounding area. Along time, it gradually became inclined. Without reinforcements, it would continue to

© Springer International Publishing AG 2017
E. Cabello et al. (Eds.): ICSOFT 2016, CCIS 743, pp. 264–283, 2017.
DOI: 10.1007/978-3-319-62569-0_13

increase its angle relative to the vertical axis, and finally fall. The *statics* theory, an old branch of physics, states the laws of the relevant *forbidden region*. Roughly one says that, the tower cannot be more inclined than some angle, in which the projection of the tower center of mass passes a threshold distance of the building ground basis.

There are uncountable cases of forbidden regions in science and technology. We shall, later on, motivate forbidden regions in software, by two examples of physics.

1.1   Models of the Possible are *not* a Theory

We wish to emphasize, early in this paper, that models of the possible are not a theory; therefore they do not produce forbidden regions. The widely used UML (Unified Modeling Language) diagrams [25] are an example of software design models and not a theory. They can be indefinitely modified at will by software engineers while developing a software system. They impose no restrictions, and do not highlight design problems, since they do not imply any design quality criteria.

The same occurs with code in a programming language, say Java or Python. These languages are below a suitable level of abstraction to generate software design criteria. Thus, the currently used compilers help in eliminating language syntax bugs, but otherwise allow indefinite program variations.

1.2   Forbidden Domains are Essential for a Software Theory

The main thrust of this paper – which is an update and extension of the paper by Exman [11] – is the claim that forbidden regions or domains are essential for a Software Theory. This is based on the following assumptions:

- *Hierarchical software system composition problem* – a theory of software composition should solve the design problem of a hierarchical software system, through increasingly simpler subsystems, down to indivisible components;
- *Existence of forbidden region boundaries* – these boundaries should restrict composition variability, for pragmatic reasons, which limit the search effort in design space, and for more fundamental reasons, such as keeping conceptual integrity, facilitating system development, comprehension and maintenance.
- *Formal algebraic criteria* – representing software systems by matrices, enables the full power of linear algebra formalism, obtaining boundaries determined by quality of design criteria, viz. suitable eigenvectors of those matrices.

1.3   Related Work

This concise literature review focuses into two topics, forbidden regions and linear algebra. It omits non-software references, such as "forbidden transitions" in pure physical systems.

a- Forbidden Regions

The notions of forbidden regions or forbidden domains have appeared in several contexts in the scientific literature, with differing meanings. The common idea of all the contexts is the existence of a problem sub-space where a solution cannot be found. We provide here just a limited sample of papers specifically referring to algorithms in embedded and/or pure software systems.

Aneja and Parlar [2] describe transportation-related algorithms for optimal single facility location problems with forbidden regions. These regions are those were location is not permitted, but one can travel through them, such as a lake. Wu et al. [27] estimate answer sizes for XML queries by excluding forbidden regions and assuming some distribution over the remainder of a two-dimensional diagram.

A whole area of embedded systems referring to forbidden regions is that dealing with robots. Abbot et al. [1] discuss ways of preventing robot manipulators to enter forbidden regions of a workspace. Payandeh and Stanisic [17] state that in order to train a novice operator of a robotic manipulator, one may define "forbidden regions virtual fixtures" (FRVF); when an operator moves the manipulator in these regions, a graphical clue can be generated, a force feedback can be generated or an embedded command in the FRVF can maintain the robot at a safe configuration.

Devadas and Aydin [4] discuss real-time dynamic power management in which they explicitly enforce device sleep intervals, the so-called forbidden regions. The goal is to enhance energy savings. This is done by time-demand analysis, which determines duration and frequency of forbidden regions to preserve the temporal correctness of all the tasks. They show that the problem of generating feasible schedules for preemptive periodic real-time tasks in which all device sleep intervals are longer than the device break-even times, is NP-Hard in the strong sense.

b- Linear Algebra

Matrices of several types have been used to analyze software design, in which an essential feature is a spectral approach using matrix eigenvectors, delimiting "forbidden regions". For comparisons about the applicability of the referred matrices to software design, we refer the reader to e.g. Exman [8] and Exman and Sakhnini [9].

Besides the Modularity Matrix one finds the Laplacian matrix [26], see e.g. Exman and Sakhnini [9], the Design Structure Matrix (DSM), see e.g. Sullivan et al. [24], and the affinity matrix, see e.g. the work by Li and Guo [15].

1.4   Organization of the Paper

The remainder of the paper is organized as follows. Section 2 deals with forbidden domains in physical systems, to motivate the later sections which refer to software systems. Section 3 introduces the software algebraic theory that we use. Section 4 describes a generic design algorithm dealing with forbidden regions. In Sect. 5, we discuss a case study, focusing on a design pattern, to illustrate the theory and the idea of forbidden regions. A discussion in Sect. 6 ends the paper.

2   Sources of Forbidden Domains: Physical Metaphors

In this section we deal with sources of forbidden domains within two physical realms. These serve as metaphors motivating the software theory to be introduced in the next section. One metaphor refers to transverse standing waves generated with a Slinky toy. The other refers to wave-functions of the so-called "particle in a box".

2.1   The 1st Physical Metaphor: Standing Waves in a Slinky

Slinky is a toy made of a pre-compressed helical spring – cf. e.g. Slinky [20, 21]. It has been used for concrete and intuitive demonstrations of properties of physical waves. Here we focus on transverse waves.

Let us imagine the following experiment. A slinky is stretched horizontally on the floor – or on a table – by two persons, grasping its end-points. If both persons move their hands laterally, in parallel to the floor (see the arrows in Fig. 1), but perpendicularly to the slinky axis, each person generates *transverse waves* travelling towards the other person. In Fig. 1 a stretched slinky depicts an **S** due to the schematic grasping hands lateral motion.

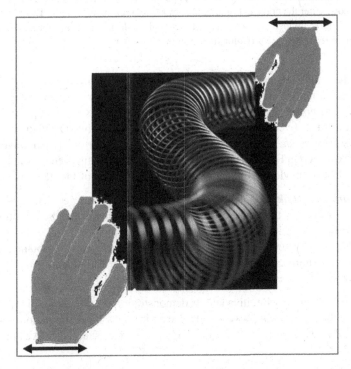

Fig. 1. Slinky transverse wave – two schematic hands move laterally a slinky, the helical spring. The motion, in the direction shown by the arrows, is perpendicular to the slinky axis. The hands' oscillation back and forth generates a transverse wave with an **S** form.

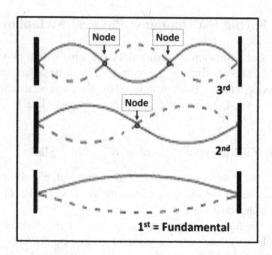

Fig. 2. Transverse standing waves in a slinky bounded by its end-points – the dashed lines show the amplitude of wave oscillation in each slinky point. Three permitted wave modes are shown: 1- The 1st fundamental (lowest) wave, the mode number is 1 and it has no nodes; 2- The 2nd wave mode number is 2, because it has two half-waves with a node in between; its continuous (blue) line is a full sinusoidal wave since it has zero vibration at the left-most point, goes up before the node, goes down after the node and returns to zero at the right-most point; 3- The 3rd wave mode number is 3 and is divided by two nodes. Fractional mode numbers are forbidden (see text). Figure adapted from Ref. [11]. (Color figure online)

Once the hands' motions of both persons are synchronized, *standing waves* are obtained. Standing waves divide the slinky in an integer number of equal parts, delimited by the *nodes* (see Fig. 2). These nodes are fixed in space and do not oscillate, despite the fact that overall, the slinky is oscillating as a whole. Oscillation modes are characterized by *mode numbers*, i.e. the number of sinusoidal half-waves of the vibration, explained in Fig. 2. Thus, we state the limitations imposed on slinky motions and the oscillation modes forbidden by the physical nature of the motions:

- **Boundaries** *on slinky behavior* – besides the material and geometry of the slinky itself, the nature of the *boundaries*, be they fixed walls or hands in motion, is the most significant limitation of behavior;
- **Forbidden** *slinky oscillation modes* – *Standing waves* can be obtained only for integer mode numbers; fractional mode numbers are forbidden by the destructive interference of waves travelling in opposite directions.

The slinky toy is very intuitive and its demonstration is easily reproduced. Dynamic views of oscillating standing waves can be seen in a graphical simulation – as shown by the standing wave in [22] – and in a video – see e.g. standing waves on a slinky in [23].

2.2 The 2nd Physical Metaphor: Wave-Functions of a Particle in a Box

Our 2nd metaphor, the particle in a box, is a gradual intermediate transition from the slinky physical metaphor (in the previous Subsect. 2.1), to the software theory to be described in the next Sect. 3. The two physical metaphors have in common the same "wave" solutions, as seen below. This 2nd metaphor and the software theory in Sect. 3 have in common that solutions are obtained by means of eigenvectors, either from an eigenvalue equation here, or from the eigenvectors of a matrix in the software theory.

This 2nd metaphor demands deeper physics knowledge to fully understand its details. But this should not discourage a reader which is not familiar with this specialized knowledge. The reader may skip the details; they are not essential to understand the overall meaning of this example. For a gradual elementary introduction to the subject, the reader may look at [18].

The "particle in a box" is a simple quantum mechanics' problem – see e.g. Messiah [16]. The particle has mass m. The so-to-speak box is one-dimensional!, has finite length ℓ, and zero potential. The particle is confined and cannot escape the two bounding walls with infinite potential.

The problem to be solved is an eigenvalue problem. In such a problem, when a matrix or operator H multiplies an eigenvector vk one obtains back the same eigenvector multiplied by a constant, the respective eigenvalue λk. This has the form:

$$H \cdot vk = \lambda k \cdot vk \tag{1}$$

Specifically this is the Schrödinger equation in which H is the Hamiltonian operator, and the kth eigenvector vk fits the eigenvalue λk, standing for an energy value. As the potential inside the box is null, the particle Hamiltonian reduces just to a Laplacian. Some solutions of this problem, the *wave functions*, are seen in Fig. 3.

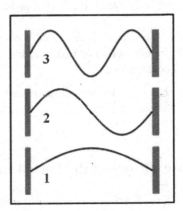

Fig. 3. Wave functions of the particle in a one-dimensional box – these waves are indexed by integers, seen in the above diagram. Just three of the possible solutions are shown in this figure. Intermediate energy values are forbidden. Note that their form is identical to the slinky waves of Fig. 2. Figure adapted from Ref. [11].

The meaning of the *wave functions* of the particle in a box problem is certainly different from the slinky transverse standing waves, but their form (seen in Fig. 3) is identical to the slinky waves (in Fig. 2) for similar reasons. Also here the wave functions vanish in the confining walls.

The conclusions from this 2nd metaphor are analogous to the slinky ones:

- **Boundaries** *of behavior of a Particle in a box* – besides the mass of the particle itself the *boundaries'* nature, i.e. the infinite potential in the fixed walls and the box length ℓ, is the most important behavior limitation;
- **Forbidden** *energy values* – Wave functions, the solutions to the eigenvalue problem, have discrete energy values, indexed by integers; other energy values are forbidden.

2.3   Common Features of Both Physical Metaphors

The two physical metaphors described in this section have very different underlying physical systems. A slinky is a real macroscopic toy made of metal or plastic materials, obeying classical mechanics, which can be hand held, stretched and oscillated. A particle in a box is a microscopic system obeying quantum mechanics, and rather serves as a thought experiment useful to demonstrate the simplest quantum system enclosed between walls.

Nonetheless, there are some striking similarities between these two kinds of systems. These common features are abstracted from the conclusions we extracted from each of them:

- **Boundaries** *on behavior* – the nature of the *boundaries* of these systems, either fixed walls or hands in motion, have a significant influence on the system behavior. For instance, a particle confined by finite (instead of an infinite) potential has a very different behavior.
- **Forbidden** *non-solutions* – The actual solution *waves* obtained are discrete and can only be indexed by integer numbers. For instance, fractional number indices are forbidden by the system constraints.

We shall compare these characteristics with those of software systems design in the next sections. It turns out that software systems also have clear similarities to these physical systems.

3   A General Software Theory of the Forbidden

A general Software Theory of the Forbidden is presented in this section in two parts: a set of basic axioms and mechanisms to delimit forbidden domains from algebraic structures which describe design sub-spaces for the desired software system.

3.1   Basic Axioms

The starting point of our software theory is a couple of basic axioms formulated in the two next text-boxes and explained in the paragraphs following the axioms.

Axiom 1 – Bounded Design Space

The design space of any particular software system is composed of a discrete and finite number of components.

The *Design Space* of a software system, in terms of numbers of components, is larger than the actual final design of the desired software system. The former contains all the potential components for that system. On the other hand, the final output design of a certain software system is obtained by the search results within the Design Space limited by the boundaries of the forbidden domains. *Components* are used here in the generic sense of Sect. 1.2. They are either subsystems in a given hierarchical level or the smallest indivisible parts of the system.

Axiom 2 – Hierarchical Design Sub-spaces

The design space of any particular software system is hierarchical, with each design sub-space corresponding to an abstraction level of the hierarchy. Adjacent sub-spaces are related by collapsing/expanding operations.

Any particular software system is assumed to be composed as a hierarchy of abstraction levels. One goes up in the hierarchy by collapsing sub-systems into a higher system level. One goes down the hierarchy by expanding a higher system level into sub-systems in the lower level, recursively until one reaches the lowest indivisible components. Likewise, the Design Space of a software system is hierarchical, with sub-spaces corresponding to the abstraction levels.

These axioms are needed for two purposes:

a. *Design Space Bounded size* – to assure that the search process for the final Software System output design is efficient;
b. *Software System Comprehensibility* – comprehensibility is a far reaching demand from the Software System design. It concerns system development, maintenance, improvement and fundamental principles, as conceptual integrity – see Brooks [3], Jackson [14], and Exman [12].

The two axioms are needed for design efficiency, since just discreteness and finiteness of design space, in the 1st axiom, are not enough to guarantee a small enough space for efficiency. The 2nd axiom is necessary, as we still envision the design process as not fully automatic. Automated computation is alternated with human intervention, justifying the importance of comprehensibility.

3.2   Algebraic Structures and Forbidden Software Compositions

Design Sub-Spaces and the final Software System design at a certain hierarchical abstraction level are both represented by an algebraic structure. Typically such algebraic structure is a matrix – say the Modularity Matrix, see e.g. Exman [7] – or a Laplacian Matrix – see e.g. Exman and Sakhnini [9]. The algebraic structure may also be a graph obtained from a matrix, for instance the algebraic structure of a Modularity Lattice – see e.g. Exman and Speicher [10] – or a bipartite graph which originates and is intimately linked to the Laplacian Matrix. In this paper we focus on matrices.

The physical metaphors of Sect. 2 are clearly suggestive of our software theory of the forbidden. Its most important characteristics are as follows:

a. *Boundaries around a software system and its modules* – the Software System boundaries idea is ubiquitous in object oriented software, and known as *encapsulation*. An outer boundary separates the software system from its environment. The inner boundaries separate system modules from each other.

b. *Forbidden compositions are delimited by matrix Eigenvectors* – the above referred boundaries imply forbidden regions. Eigenvectors fitting certain eigenvalues of the chosen matrices delimit forbidden compositions. One still needs conjunction with a formal definition of cohesion – see e.g. Exman [8] and Exman and Sakhnini [9]. The final design discrete components are determined by suitable elements of the relevant eigenvectors.

c. *Outliers in forbidden regions eliminated by redesign* – outlier matrix elements in forbidden regions point out to undesirable couplings between modules. These should be eliminated by software system redesign, usually done by human intervention of software engineers.

These characteristics are put together in a software system design algorithm, capable to deal with forbidden regions. This algorithm is presented in the next section, in pseudo-code format.

4   Generic Design Algorithm with Forbidden Regions

In this section we present our algorithm with boundaries capable of excluding forbidden regions. This is a generic algorithm displayed in pseudo-code. In order to design an actual software system, one must first choose a specific matrix type, say Modularity Matrix or Laplacian matrix. Then, suitable specific procedures should be applied to select eigenvalues and get modules from their respective eigenvectors.

The generic algorithm consists of four phases:

a. *Initialize* a matrix and a cohesion threshold;

b. *Search Loop* calculating eigenvalues and corresponding eigenvectors, to obtain modules;

c. **Check modules' cohesion** whether they comply with the threshold;
d. **Redesign** if indicated by outliers.

The generic design algorithm is shown in the next text-box.

Generic Design Algorithm – with Forbidden Regions

<u>Init:</u>
Design Sub-Space = obtain suitable matrix;
Set lower cohesion threshold;

<u>Search Loop – obtain modules:</u>
    While (there are low cohesion modules)
        Do {
        Obtain matrix eigenvalues/eigenvectors;
        Select suitable eigenvalues;
        Pick corresponding eigenvectors;
        Get modules from eigenvector elements;
        Calculate modules' cohesion;
        <u>Forbidden boundary – cohesion check:</u>
        If (module cohesion < threshold)
            {split module;
                Repeat while loop}
        Else
            End While}

<u>Forbidden region redesign:</u>
If (outlier left)
    {Redesign matrix as needed;}

Cohesion is calculated by the inverse of the sparsity of a module (which is itself a sub-matrix). The sparsity is the ratio of zero-valued matrix elements to the total number of matrix elements in the matrix or sub-matrix. A typical sparsity threshold is 50%. Modules should have high-cohesion (low sparsity). The environment, i.e. matrix elements outside modules, should display low cohesion (high sparsity).

5 Case Study: Boundaries of the Forbidden

In this section we describe the well-known *Command* design pattern, given in the GoF (so-called "Gang of Four") book by Gamma et al. [13] as a case study. The main goal here is to illustrate the boundaries of the forbidden. The design pattern is first presented in terms of the UML class diagram. Next, we demonstrate the *Generic Design Algorithm* of Sect. 4, in a series of steps, starting with the chosen Modularity Matrix – see Exman [7]. We could as well choose a Laplacian Matrix – see Exman and Sakhnini [9]. The specific steps, following the algorithm are:

a. *Obtain a matrix* – we choose the Modularity Matrix to represent the design pattern; such a matrix is symmetrized and weighted by means of an affinity;

b. *Get eigenvalues/eigenvectors* – use the suitable approach for the chosen matrix; for a Modularity Matrix the eigenvectors are listed in decreasing order of their respective eigenvalues; then one takes the highest eigenvectors that completely span the matrix size;

c. *Obtain the module sizes* – from the respective eigenvector positive elements;

d. *Illustrate the case of an outlier* – by intentionally adding an arbitrary matrix element coupling two modules; this shows how one deals with elements in the forbidden region;

e. *Collapse sub-systems* – to illustrate the hierarchy of the Software System levels.

5.1   The Command Design Pattern – Its Class Diagram

The goal of the Command design pattern is to enable abstraction of commands, say in a text editor application. It decouples an object that invokes an action, by clicking a *Save* menu-item, from another object that actually performs the file saving action. Moreover, the Command pattern enables generic features such as Undo and Redo, independently of whether the specific action is a saving or printing a file.

Figure 4 shows a class diagram of the Command design pattern. It is similar to the Command class diagram of this pattern in the GoF book (see Gamma et al. [13], p. 233). The Command pattern in this class diagram has the following classes:

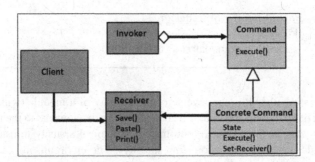

Fig. 4. Command Design pattern UML Class Diagram – the invoker, a menu-item or button, once clicked triggers commands execution. The Concrete-Command inherits the abstract Command class (both with a beige color) and actually executes an action on the Receiver (a document). Figure adapted from Ref. [11]. (Color figure online)

- An invoker, say a menu-item or button, to be clicked in order to activate execution of a command;
- An abstract Command which characterizes the pattern;
- A Concrete Command class inheriting the abstract Command to actually execute a specific command;
- A Receiver, which represents an abstraction of a document file.
- A client, which in fact does not belong specifically to this design pattern.

Design patterns, declared as reusable software architectural units, could be expected to have well-defined standard forms. But any such standard does not exist.

The Command section of the GoF book (Gamma et al. [13]) displays no less than four different class diagrams of this pattern, besides the pattern generic diagram similar to Fig. 4. The situation is even worse when considering the Internet literature on design patterns and their implementations in a variety of programming languages.

As was stated in Sect. 1.1, UML allows indefinite variability for any software system. It is a flexible design model, *not* a theory with forbidden regions. Therefore, the next logical step is to translate the Command class diagram into a Modularity Matrix, enabling a theory which limits forbidden regions.

5.2   Boundaries by the Modularity Matrix

A Modularity Matrix (see Exman [5–7]) was chosen for the Command pattern case study linking structors (generalizing classes) to provided functionals (generalizing methods). The standard Modularity Matrix, by the Linear Software Models is square and block-diagonal. The Command pattern Modularity Matrix displayed in Fig. 5 is indeed square and block-diagonal.

Structor →		Command	Concrete Command	Client	Invoker	History	Receiver
Functional		S1	S2	S3	S4	S5	S6
execute	F1	1	1				
Set-receiver	F2	0	1				
Create-objects	F3			1	0	0	
Bind-cmd	F4			1	1	0	
Undo	F5			0	1	1	
Receiver-action	F6						1

Fig. 5. Command Design pattern Modularity Matrix – it is square and block diagonal with 6 Structors (columns) and Functionals (rows). Diagonal blocks (blue background) are modules: Top-Left = essential Command pattern roles, with structors S1, S2 and functionals F1, F2 designations (again marked by beige color); Middle = generic classes; Bottom-Right = Receiver. Zero-valued elements outside the modules are omitted for simplicity. Figure adapted from Ref. [11]. (Color figure online)

A Modularity Matrix, containing only the system structors and functionals, establishes a boundary between the software system and its environment. The diagonal blocks also set well-defined boundaries among modules.

5.3   Eigenvectors Delimit the Forbidden Regions

A spectral approach applied to the Modularity Matrix has been developed [8] to find the software system module sizes and eventual outliers, based upon the matrix eigenvectors and eigenvalues. The approach is formally described by an eigenvalue equation, entirely analogous to Eq. (1) in Subsect. 2.2:

$$M \cdot vk = \lambda k \cdot vkZ \tag{2}$$

M is a symmetrized and weighted Modularity Matrix; vk stands for the kth eigenvector of M; the eigenvector vk fits to its eigenvalue λk. Symmetrizing and weighting details by an affinity expression are not essential to understand the arguments and conclusions of this paper. More details can be found in the paper by Exman [8].

The Command pattern Modularity Matrix eigenvectors and eigenvalues are shown in Fig. 6. The eigenvalues are sorted in decreasing order. One can easily verify that the positive eigenvector elements in the first three eigenvectors span the whole matrix. These eigenvector elements correspond to the module sizes shown in Fig. 5. The elements of these eigenvectors have only zero-valued or positive values, in contrast to the remaining eigenvectors.

		Modules				
Eigenvectors	1	2	3	4	5	6
	0	0.707	0	0	0.707	0
	0	0.707	0	0	-0.707	0
	0.5	0	0	-0.707	0	-0.5
	0.707	0	0	0	0	0.707
	0.5	0	0	0.707	0	-0.5
	0	0	1	0	0	0
Eigenvalues →	1.52	1.367	1	1	0.633	0.48

Fig. 6. Command pattern eigenvectors/eigenvalues – the three first eigenvectors fitting the first three eigenvalues – to the left of the red vertical separator – span the Modularity matrix *modules*. Positive eigenvector elements (blue background) obtain the matrix module sizes in Fig. 5. Here the module sizes fit the eigenvalues' order. Figure adapted from Ref. [11]. (Color figure online)

Had we chosen a Laplacian Matrix (see Exman and Sakhnini [9]) instead of the Modularity Matrix to solve our case study, the generic eigenvalue Eq. (2) would still be valid. On the other hand, the specific eigenvalues and eigenvectors would be different, as well as their meaning and the way to obtain the module sizes. These Matrix specifics are not essential for the understanding the results of this paper. The generic approach, viz. the fact that eigenvectors delimit the boundaries of the forbidden regions, is the important message.

5.4   Redesign to Eliminate Forbidden Outliers

The treatment of existing outliers can be illustrated by intentionally adding a 1-valued matrix element to the block diagonal matrix of the Command pattern in Fig. 5 as follows. The outcome matrix in Fig. 7 has an added element, in row F2 and column S3, which indeed is an outlier. The latter element couples the *upper-left* module (over-lapped by row F2) with the *middle* module (overlapped by column S3), while itself being outside the borders of both these modules.

The outlier in Fig. 7 is revealed by the *Forbidden boundary – cohesion check* within our Generic Design Algorithm (in Sect. 4) as follows:

1. *The eigenvector module size* – it fits a large module of size 5 * 5 which is the result of coupling of the *upper-left* module of size 2 * 2 with the *middle* module of size 3 * 3;
2. *The cohesion of the large module* – is too low, as it has a total of 16 zero-valued elements, 5 inside the coupled modules and 11 in the forbidden regions of the environment of these modules, viz. in rows F3 to F5 below the upper-left module and in columns S3 to S5 above the middle module. Its sparsity is then calculated as 16/25 = 0.64, which is higher than the threshold of 50%. Thus this larger coupled module must be split.

Structor →		Command	Concrete Command	Client	Invoker	History	Receiver
Functional ↓		S1	S2	S3	S4	S5	S6
execute	F1	1	1				
Set-receiver	F2	0	1	1			
Create-objects	F3			1	0	0	
Bind-cmd	F4			1	1	0	
Undo	F5			0	1	1	
Receiver-action	F6						1

Fig. 7. Command pattern Modularity Matrix with outlier – this is the matrix in Fig. 5, with an added outlier element in row F2 and column S3 (with dark blue hatched background). Zero-valued matrix elements outside the modules are omitted for clarity. Figure adapted from Ref. [11]. (Color figure online)

Our Generic Design Algorithm determines that outliers – 1-valued matrix elements in forbidden matrix regions – i.e. outside the diagonal modules, should be eliminated and the matrix redesigned.

5.5   Hierarchical Sub-spaces of the Command Design Pattern

We finally illustrate the meaning of the Hierarchical Design Sub-Spaces of Axiom 2 in Subsect. 3.1. The modules of the Modularity Matrix of the Command design pattern, in Fig. 5, have its structors and functionals explicitly shown. Each of these three modules may be collapsed into the next higher level of the hierarchy for this system, to obtain the Modularity Matrix in Fig. 8. This is a 3 * 3 matrix. Expanding this higher level matrix into the next lower level, obtains back the matrix in Fig. 5.

Structor →		Command roles	Generic Classes	Receiver
Functional ↓		S1	S2	S3
Execute command	F1	1		
Generic function	F2		1	
Receiver Action	F3			1

Fig. 8. Collapsed high-level Modularity Matrix of the Command Design pattern – modules of Fig. 5 were collapsed to single matrix elements: Top-Left = essential Command pattern roles; Middle = generic classes; Bottom-Right = Receiver of the action. Zero-valued matrix elements are omitted for clarity. Figure adapted from Ref. [11].

Performing one further collapsing operation into the highest level of the Command pattern hierarchy, one obtains the Modularity matrix in Fig. 9, which is a 1 * 1 matrix.

Structor →		Command Design pattern
Functional ↓		S1
Execute Command	F1	1

Fig. 9. Collapsed highest-level Modularity Matrix of the Command Design pattern – modules of Fig. 8 were collapsed into a single matrix element.

The whole hierarchy of the Command design pattern, viz. the upper-level system, the next level sub-systems and the lower-level sub-sub-systems, is shown in Fig. 10, to

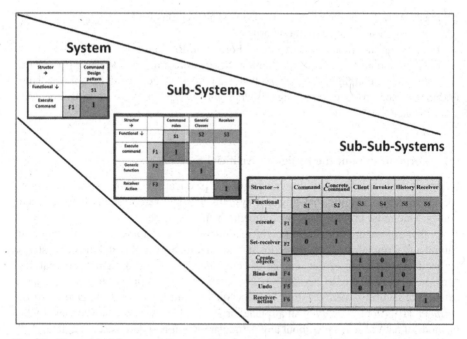

Fig. 10. Hierarchical System of Command Design pattern – the three Modularity Matrices in the Command design pattern hierarchy. Top-Left: fully collapsed system; Middle: collapsed sub-systems; Bottom-right: fully expanded sub-sub-systems to the resolution of Fig. 5.

illustrate the idea of a hierarchical software system. Note that this is the final designed system. The Hierarchical Design Sub-Spaces have the same pyramidal structure, in which each abstraction level corresponds to a sub-space, which in turn is represented by one Modularity Matrix.

6 Discussion

This paper has shown, motivated by physical systems' metaphors, that generic formal quality criteria for software system design are provided by Linear Algebra, within the theory of Linear Software Systems. Here we discuss the nature of such criteria and why they are essential.

6.1 The Theoretical Importance of Forbidden Regions

The idea of focusing on Forbidden Regions is somewhat surprising, since apparently one would most probably prefer an emphasis on positive rather than negative design criteria. But the purpose of real theories is to *simultaneously* provide positive and negative criteria. When one says that some decisions are desirable, one is concomitantly saying that other decisions are undesirable.

Positive criteria declare that some design space regions lead to desirable properties of a software system, such as modularity.

What is the theoretical importance of Forbidden Regions?

Their importance is to call the attention of software engineers to design problems, say undesirable coupling between software modules, which must be solved. Thus, Forbidden Regions are clear signals that the design process is still not fully accomplished.

6.2   Formalization of the Design of Artificial Systems

In principle one could refute the validity of the physical metaphors, since there is no special reason to assume that physical systems and software systems behave analogously. One must provide further arguments with this respect.

A first argument is the existence of a common body of knowledge covering both natural and artificial systems, which justifies similar treatment of both kinds of systems. An example, referring to the science of aerodynamics, is that designed artificial systems, be it an airplane or the software embedded in its computers, behave to a large extent like natural systems. Citing Herbert Simon from his book *The Sciences of the Artificial* [19] (in p. 7): "Given an airplane, or given a bird, we can analyze them by the methods of natural science without any particular attention to purpose or adaptation...".

A second argument is the hierarchical structure which is common to social systems, natural systems and software systems. Referring to software systems, we find it so important for this paper, that we explicitly stated hierarchy in Axiom 2, and in the explanations surrounding this axiom in Subsect. 3.1. Again citing Herbert Simon's book [19] (in p. 184): "...my central theme is that complexity frequently takes the form of hierarchy and that hierarchic systems have some common properties independent of their specific content." This is further and thoroughly discussed by Simon in Chap. 8 "The Architecture of Complexity: Hierarchic Systems" of the same book.

The issue of the validity of physical metaphors for software systems is much deeper, but space limitations of this paper prevent us to embark in the broader discussion that this issue deserves.

6.3   Why Eigenvectors?

Eigenvectors are important for dimensionality reduction. Specifically, in the context of software engineering, as shown in Sect. 5.3 of this paper, they enable modularity in a software system represented by a Modularity Matrix, or alternatively by a Laplacian matrix, in each of the abstraction levels of the hierarchical software structure.

Eigenvectors reduce and simplify the set of vectors describing a software system. Accordingly, the corresponding modules have the effect of reducing a large software system to a smaller set of sub-systems that are easier to comprehend.

Formally, software system modularity implies lack of dependence among different modules. In terms of Modularity matrices – e.g. the matrix in Fig. 5 – modules are mutually independent since each module is composed by a set of structors and functionals which is disjoint to the sets of structors and functionals of all other modules.

Modules exactly reflect the eigenvectors' mutual orthogonality. Eigenvectors – e.g. the first three in Fig. 6 in Subsect. 5.3 – have zero-valued pairwise scalar products. The same is true for any structor from a given module: it is orthogonal to structors belonging to any other modules of the same Modularity Matrix. Mutatis mutandis, any functional from a given module is mutually orthogonal to any functional belonging to other modules of the same Modularity matrix.

6.4   Search Efficiency Issues

The 1st axiom on the Software System Design Space in Subsect. 3.1 of this paper, tells that the Design Space is discrete and finite. It does not guarantee that the Design Space is small. Search in the Design Space could still take a long time.

The 2nd axiom in Subsect. 3.1 – demanding a hierarchical Design Space for a software system – is the basis of an intuitive argument for the claim that, while the overall Design Space for the whole system may not be small, the Design Sub-Space for each subsystem in any level in the Design Space hierarchy is expected to be of bounded size.

For instance, looking at each abstraction level of our case study – the Command Design pattern shown in Fig. 10 – one sees that the maximal size of each module is bounded by a 3 * 3 matrix. In general, one expects for a multi-level hierarchy of a large system, that in each abstraction level the subsystem matrix size is bounded by a small integer. In other words, design space search in each module is efficient for all hierarchy levels.

6.5   Main Contribution

This paper claims that real software system theories need to be of practical use for software design. Such theories should provide formal design quality criteria, supporting system modularity. Concomitantly these theories should point out to *forbidden system compositions*, signaling undesired modules' coupling in need of software system redesign.

References

1. Abbot, J.J., Marayong, P., Okamura, A.M.: Haptic virtual fixtures for robot-assisted manipulation. In: Thrun, S., Brooks, R., Durrant-Whyte, H. (eds.) Robotics Research. Springer Tracts in Advanced Robotics, vol. 28, pp. 49–64. Springer, Berlin (2007). doi:10. 1007/978-3-540-48113-3_5
2. Aneja, Y.P., Parlar, M.: Algorithms for weber facility location in the presence of forbidden regions and/or barriers to travel. Transp. Sci. **28**(1), 70–76 (1994). doi:10.1287/trsc.28.1.70

3. Brooks, F.P.: The Mythical Man-Month - Essays in Software Engineering – Anniversary. Addison-Wesley, Boston (1995)
4. Devadas, V., Aydin, H.: Real-time dynamic power management through device forbidden regions. In: Proceeding IEEE Real-Time and Embedded Technology and Applications Symposium, pp. 34–44 (2008). doi:10.1109/RTAS.2008.21
5. Exman, I.: Linear software models, extended abstract. In: Jacobson, I., Goedicke, M., Johnson, P. (eds.) Proceeding. GTSE 2012, SEMAT Workshop on a General Theory of Software Engineering, pp. 23–24. KTH Royal Institute of Technology, Stockholm (2012)
6. Exman, I.: Linear Software Models, GTSE 2012, SEMAT Workshop on a General Theory of Software Engineering. KTH Royal Institute of Technology, Stockholm (2012). Video presentation of Ref. [5]: http://www.youtube.com/watch?v=EJfzArH8-ls
7. Exman, I.: Linear software models: standard modularity highlights residual coupling. Int. J. Softw. Eng. Knowl. Eng. **24**(2), 183–210 (2014). doi:10.1142/S0218194014500089
8. Exman, I.: Linear software models: decoupled modules from modularity matrix eigenvectors. Int. J. Softw. Eng. Knowl. Eng. **25**(8), 1395–1426 (2015). doi:10.1142/S0218194015500308
9. Exman, I., Sakhnini, R.: Linear software models: modularity analysis by the Laplacian matrix. In: Proceeding 11th International Joint Conference on Software Technologies, ICSOFT-PT, vol. 2, pp. 100–108, Lisbon, Portugal (2016). doi:10.5220/0005985601000108
10. Exman, I., Speicher, D.: Linear software models: equivalence of modularity matrix to its modularity lattice. In: Proceeding 10th ICSOFT International Joint Conference on Software Technologies, Colmar, France, pp. 109–116 (2015). doi:10.5220/0005557701090116
11. Exman, I.: Software theory of the forbidden in a discrete design space. In: Proceeding 11th International Joint Conference on Software Technologies, ICSOFT-PT, vol. 2, pp. 131–137. Lisbon, Portugal, SciTePress (2016a). doi:10.5220/0006004601310137
12. Exman, I.: The modularity matrix as a source of software conceptual integrity. In: Proceeding SKY 2016 - 7th International Workshop on Software Knowledge, Porto, Portugal, pp. 27–35. SciTePress (2016b)
13. Gamma, E., Helm, R., Johnson, R., Vlissides, J.: Design Patterns. Addison-Wesley, Boston (1995)
14. Jackson, D.: Conceptual design of software: a research agenda. CSAIL Technical report, MIT-CSAIL-TR-2013-020 (2013). http://dspace.mit.edu/bitstream/handle/1721.1/79826/MIT-CSAIL-TR-2013-020.pdf?sequence=2
15. Li, X.-Y., Guo, L.: Constructing affinity matrix in spectral clustering based on neighbor propagation. Neurocomputing **97**, 125–130 (2012). doi:10.1016/j.neucom.2012.06.023
16. Messiah, A.: Quantum Mechanics, vol. I. North-Holland Publishing Co., Amsterdam (1961). Chap. III, Reprinted by Dover Publications (2014)
17. Payandeh, S., Stanisic, Z.: On application of virtual fixtures as an aid for telemanipulation and training. In: Proceeding HAPTICS 2002 10th Symposium on Haptic Interfaces for Virtual Environment and Teleoperator Systems, pp. 18–23 (2002), doi:10.1109/HAPTIC.2002.998936
18. Particle in a Box. https://en.wikipedia.org/wiki/Particle_in_a_box
19. Simon, H.A.: The Sciences of the Artificial, 3rd edn. MIT Press, Cambridge (1996)
20. Slinky (2016a). https://en.wikipedia.org/wiki/Slinky
21. Slinky, Wave Phase changes at fixed end (2016b). http://hyperphysics.phy-astr.gsu.edu/hbase/sound/slinkv.html#c1
22. Standing wave (2016a). https://upload.wikimedia.org/wikipedia/commons/7/7d/ Standing_wave_2.gif
23. Standing wave, Standing waves on a Slinky (2016b). http://hyperphysics.phy-astr.gsu.edu/hbase/sound/slnksw.html#c1

24. Sullivan, K.J., Griswold, W.G., Cai, Y., Hallen, B.: The structure and value of modularity in software design. In: Proceeding ESEC/FSE 8th European Software Engineering Conference and 9th SIGSOFT International Symposium Foundations Software Engineering, pp. 99–108. ACM (2001). doi:10.1145/503209.503224

25. UML, Specification, OMG (Object Management Group) (2015). http://www.omg.org/spec/UML/

26. Weisstein, E.W.: Laplacian Matrix, From Mathworld–A Wolfram Web Resource (2016). http://mathworld.wolfram.com/LaplacianMatrix.html

27. Wu, Y., Patel, J.M., Jagadish, H.V.: Estimating answer sizes for XML queries. In: Jensen, C.S. et al. (ed.) EDBT 2002. LNCS, vol. 2287, pp. 590–608. Springer, Heidelberg (2002). doi:10.1007/3-540-45876-X_37

Enabling Legacy Applications
for Multi-tenancy Without Reengineering

Uwe Hohenstein[✉] and Preeti Koka

Siemens AG, Corporate Technology, Otto-Hahn-Ring 6, 81730 Munich,
Germany
{Uwe.Hohenstein,Preeti.K}@siemens.com

Abstract. Multi-tenancy is an architectural style to share resources amongst
several tenants. It is an important facet of Cloud Computing and often considered
a key element to make Software-as-a-Service (SaaS) profitable. Indeed, SaaS
providers adopt multi-tenancy to optimize resource usage and to save operational
costs. While literature often discusses how to develop new, green-field software
with multi-tenancy, this paper focuses on adding multi-tenancy to existing,
brown-field software. This is particularly relevant in the context of Cloud
migration where legacy software should be moved into the Cloud. The major
contribution of this paper is to present an approach to leave the application's
source code untouched, i.e., to add some new components in order to enable the
application for multi-tenancy. To this end, we apply the aspect-oriented language
AspectJ in an industrial case study to evaluate what can be achieved with such an
approach as well as to enumerate the benefits and drawbacks in detail. In a
nutshell, the approach is appropriate to handle REST applications and/or backend
services. The following important facets of multi-tenancy can be achieved:
Tenant management; tenant-specific authentication and data isolation among
multiple tenants for various database servers and strategies; tenant-specific customization by modifying existing behavior, particularly, removing functionality
but also to introduce new functionality; and as a by-product, to monitor all
tenants' activities as a prerequisite for a tenant-specific billing.

Keywords: Multi-tenancy · Cloud migration · Aspect-orientation · AspectJ ·
Industrial application · Case study

1 Introduction

The NIST definition [21] defines Cloud computing as "a model for enabling ubiquitous, convenient, on-demand network access to a shared pool of configurable computing resources (e.g., networks, servers, storage, applications, and services) that can be
rapidly provisioned and released with minimal management effort or service provider
interaction". Software-as-a-Service (SaaS) is thereby one service model besides
Platform-as-a-Service (PaaS) and Infrastructure-as-a-Service (IaaS). SaaS is a delivery
model that enables customers, the so-called *tenants*, to lease and use services without
buying a software license and setting up a local installation [17]. Moreover, tenants pay
only for what they use to what extent according to the pay-as-you-go principle.

© Springer International Publishing AG 2017
E. Cabello et al. (Eds.): ICSOFT 2016, CCIS 743, pp. 284–308, 2017.
DOI: 10.1007/978-3-319-62569-0_14

The goal of SaaS providers is to save operational cost in order to be competitive by means of an efficient utilization of hardware and software resources and improved ease of maintenance [3]. This let SaaS providers usually adopt a multi-tenant architecture [5]. Multi-tenancy is a software architecture principle that lets several tenants share a common infrastructure. It is widely agreed that a well-economical SaaS application has to pursue a multi-tenant architecture.

Since software is more and more becoming an on-demand service drawn from the Cloud, industries are interested in offering SaaS to enter new businesses. Having a huge amount of legacy applications, there is a strong interest in moving these applications into the cloud first for entering SaaS business while preserving investments. As a side effect, applications can also benefit from features such as elasticity and pay-as-you-go. But industries have the challenge to convert legacy applications into multi-tenant SaaS without spending too much time and effort on refactoring [4].

Several papers such as [3, 29] discuss multi-tenant architectures with pros and cons according to what is shared by the tenants: the topmost web frontend, middle tier application servers, the underlying database. Others, e.g., [1], define further degrees of sharing and categorize migration types to cloud-enable applications.

Striving for multi-tenancy, the SaaS provider has to balance between easy implementation and saving operational costs by efficient resource utilization. The simplest approach to make an application multi-tenant with lowest development effort is a virtualization approach [14]. This approach let each tenant obtain a virtual machine (VM) containing an application server, the application and a DB server. The ease of this approach is paid by a higher consumption of resources and higher costs especially in public clouds where each VM (one for each tenant) has to be paid. Even on premises more equipment than necessary has to be provided. Moreover, each tenant requires a database server license or additional costs for using a database as a Cloud service.

At the other edge of the scale, fully efficient multi-tenancy [5] let all the tenants share all resources: one Tomcat, one application, and one database server amongst all tenants. However, a significant re-engineering of applications is required to set up a fully multi-tenant application, thus leading to high development costs [23].

Recent technologies facilitate further approaches. Particularly, container technologies enable another approach to make application deployments multi-tenant, lying in between the previous two extremes. This implementation involves deploying the application stack (application server, application and database server) on a separate container for each tenant. Containers such as Docker are more light-weight than virtual machines, but still produce more load and thus require more resources than fully efficient multi-tenancy. As an advantage, tenant-specific customizations become easier since each container can be equipped with a different software variant.

In fact, SaaS applications have to be customizable or configurable to fulfil the varying functional requirements of individual tenants [14]; customers want to add or modify specific features. From the SaaS provider's view, various degrees of feature sets could be offered with different prices, especially a "freemium" version with a reduced function set. Several papers such as [2, 9] recognize tenant customization as one important requirement and challenge, and [17] states that it is not trivial to adapt the business logic and data to the requirements of the different tenants. Most work on customization focuses on product-line approaches [26] to offer variability. Using aspect-oriented programming (AOP) is sometimes proposed to achieve configurability, e.g., by [29, 34].

In this paper, we also apply AOP, however, at a broader scope to migrate existing applications into fully multi-tenant SaaS applications. We investigate how to benefit from the aspect-oriented language AspectJ [16] in this context. We have a clear idea in mind: To add multi-tenancy to existing applications without any reengineering and without explicitly modifying the source code. To explore our idea, we use an existing industrial application that was originally not developed for a multi-tenant environment and serves users of exactly one tenant. More precise, each tenant obtains one dedicated application instance deployed on a Tomcat application server and using an Oracle database on premise so far. That is, the application is managed per tenant similar to traditional application service providers. We then elaborate upon the feasibility to realize the AOP idea thereby illustrating the major advantages of our migration approach. Hence, this paper takes a practical view on Cloud migration and presents a low-effort approach for offering legacy applications as multi-tenant SaaS in a Cloud.

In a nutshell, it is possible to achieve tenant isolation, to modify existing behavior in a tenant-specific manner, to introduce new services for specific tenants, and to monitor requests per tenant for billing purposes. Enabling such multi-tenancy facets is achieved without explicitly touching source code or building a new application; only a restart of Tomcat is required after having deployed some additional components. Hence, we obtain a simple and cheap mechanism by only adding components to existing applications – without any further reengineering and refactoring of source code.

The motivation for our work is manifold. The approach is a first step to let existing applications become Cloud-ready and to enable entering the SaaS business fast and easily. Such a first trial can explore SaaS business opportunities, maybe offering reduced functionality, and to expand business to a larger customer base with low expenses. Being easily applicable to other applications, our solution reduces time-to-market and saves development effort. And finally, free demo versions of existing applications can be made publicly available in a Cloud as a teaser. Since no profit can be directly made in that case, we benefit from small investments in development.

This paper is an extended version of [10] where we have already outlined the basic ideas for the previously mentioned software running in Tomcat and using an Oracle database. Here, we extend the mechanism to cover other database servers and further data isolation strategies according to [6].

The remainder of this paper is structured as follows. Section 2 presents related research and deduces the necessity for this work. Before discussing the migration approach in depth, we give in Sect. 3 a short introduction into the aspect-oriented AspectJ language, as far as it is necessary to understand how we applied AspectJ. Section 4 introduces the application, which we used in a concrete industrial study to prove effectiveness, in its original single-tenant form. We present our approach to migrate to a multi-tenant Cloud application with low programming effort in detail by discussing the components that implement important facets of multi-tenancy such as tenant isolation and customization. In Sect. 5, we elaborate upon the flexibility of the AspectJ approach to cover other database servers and further data isolation strategies in addition to our previous work [10]. Section 6 presents an evaluation of the AspectJ approach with regard to implementation effort, modularity, and adaptability. Moreover, the lessons learned are discussed. Finally, the conclusions summarize the discussion and presents future ideas.

2   Related Work

A lot of recent research focuses on migrating legacy applications into the cloud, e.g., suggesting checklists and methodologies to perform migrations. For example, ARTIST [24] provides methods, techniques, and tools to guide companies in moving applications into the cloud in three phases pre-migration, migration, and post-migration. The approach attempts to better support the complex, time-consuming, and expensive tasks during migration.

Decisions to migrate existing services to the cloud can be complicated as the benefits, risks, and costs of using the Cloud are complex. [11] states that a migration should also consider organizational and socio-technical factors. Their Cloud Adoption Toolkit offers a collection of tools for decision support and helps to identify relevant concerns and match them to appropriate technologies. A particular cost modeling tool can be used to compare the cost of different cloud providers and deployment options. A case study presents in detail this tool.

Binz et al. [4] discuss vendor lock-in as a major difficulty for migrating existing applications into and between different clouds. The CMotion framework models entities and their dependencies as a basis for supporting migration. Anyway, adapters have to be implemented manually.

This work in the area of cloud migration is quite general and does not address the integration of multi-tenancy into legacy applications. Indeed, our approach combines migrating applications to the Cloud with adding multi-tenancy to legacy applications.

In fact, the specific topic of multi-tenancy is often considered as a challenge in research. Several papers, for example [6] and [15], describe the possible variants of multi-tenancy. Momm and Krebs [23] consider approaches to reduce resource consumption and discuss some cost aspects of sharing. Wang et al. [33] make recommendations on the best multi-tenant variant to use based on the number of tenants, the number of users per tenant, and the amount of data per tenant. Guo et al. [9] discuss the implementation principles for application-level multi-tenancy and explore different approaches to improve isolation of security, performance, availability, and administration. Fehling et al. [8] come up with prospects for the optimization of multi-tenancy by distributing the tenants with respect to Quality of Service.

Bezemer et al. [2] present an architectural approach for reengineering applications to enable multi-tenancy in software services. The discussion especially considers a multi-tenancy reengineering of workflow and UI configuration. A specific multi-tenancy reengineering pattern takes into account a multi-tenant database, tenant-specific authentication, and configuration. This reengineering pattern is applied to an existing single-tenant application in a case study. However, the reengineering effort was relatively little due to a well-designed and layered architecture. In an additional work [3], they manually transform the ScrewTurn wiki case to a multi-tenant application and encounter security, data protection, data isolation, configurability, performance isolation of tenants, and scalability issues for tenants from different continents, as the core challenges. Unfortunately, the authors do not solve all the previously mentioned issues. Beside implementation effort, they consider the recurrence of maintenance tasks such as patches or software updates as another driver for operational cost.

In contrast to this general work on strategies and their impact on resource consumption, our approach tackles the problem of adding multi-tenancy by avoiding reengineering efforts.

Further research considers tenant-specific customizations as an important requirement for multi-tenancy, e.g., case studies such as [15, 18] which try to configure multi-tenant applications for tenants. The elements of an application that need to be customized are graphical user interface, business logic, service selection and configuration, and data [30]. Customization could be performed in two ways [29]: A source-code based approach allows customizing SaaS applications by integrating new tenant-specific source code. Such an approach has been pursued by [13, 35]. In spite of giving tenants more flexibility in the customization process, this approach has several disadvantages. At first, each tenant must know the implementation details of the SaaS application. Then, security regulations of the application might be violated if tenants are able to integrate source code. Since all the tenant-specific extensions have to be retained, software upgrades become more complicated for the SaaS provider. [32] considers source code based approaches as too complex.

An alternative composition-based approach let SaaS applications be customized by composing variants. An application template contains customization points [20], i.e., unspecified parts, which can be configured by selecting predefined components from a provided set [19, 22, 25].

Adopting work from the area of product-line engineering, Pohl et al. [26] point out four key concerns to be addressed for customization: modeling customization points and variations, describing relationships among variations, validating customzations performed by tenants, and dis-/associating variations from/to customization points during runtime.

Shahin et al. [29] tackle all these concerns and propose the Orthogonal Variability Modeling (OVM) to model customization points and variations and to describe the relationships among variations. Tenants' customizations are validated by a Metagraph-based algorithm. An aspect-oriented extension of the Business Process Execution Language (BPEL) is used to associate and disassociate variations to/from customization points at run-time. The approach is illustrated by a Travel Agency example.

Three of the above concerns are dealt with by [20]. They also use Metagraphs to model customization points, variants, and their relationships. Moreover, they propose an algorithm to validate customizations made by tenants. [30, 31] handle only the modeling of customization points and variants using an ontology-based customization framework with OVM. Tenants are guided through the customization process to avoid unpredictable customizations.

Walraven et al. [32] investigate middleware component models with respect to offering software variations to different tenants and come to the conclusion that support is too inflexible. Using Google AppEngine, they propose a multi-tenancy support layer that combines dependency injection with middleware support. They evaluate operational expenses and flexibility for an online booking scenario. The approach requires that dedicated customization points are inserted into the code for applying customization. Similarly, Wang and Zheng [34] apply aspect-orientation in a case study, but still rely on preparing the software architecture accordingly.

In spite of providing interesting insights in multi-tenancy and configurability, all this research starts from green-field or need to insert customization points in the existing application. In contrast, our approach leaves the original application unchanged. To our knowledge, there is also no work combining an approach to migrate applications to the Cloud with adding multi-tenancy for a legacy application by avoiding major code changes.

3   Aspect-Oriented Programming in AspectJ

Aspect-orientation (AO) is a paradigm that helps to develop software in a modular manner [12]. AO provides systematic means for effectively modularizing crosscutting concerns (CCCs). CCCs are those functionalities that are typically spread across several places in the source code and often lead to lower programming productivity, lower degree of code reuse, and poor traceability and quality [7]. Special aspect-oriented languages offer advanced concepts to modularize CCCs and to avoid the well-known symptoms of non-modularization such as code tangling and code scattering.

Our approach relies on the AspectJ language [16]. AspectJ is an extension of the Java language introducing a new concept of aspect to Java. An *aspect* changes the dynamic structure of a program by intercepting certain points of the program flow, the so-called *join points*. Join points can be method and constructor calls or executions, field accesses, and exceptions etc. *Pointcuts* syntactically specify those join points in the flow by means of a signature expression. The actions to be taken before and/or after the join points are defined by *advices*.

AspectJ, as presented in [16], is a language of its own, in fact, an extension of Java. Hence, it requires a dedicated AspectJ compiler. Usually, the AJDT plug-in will be installed in Eclipse. However, an AspectJ compiler requires changes in the build process, which is often not desired, so for us: We do not want to re-compile the existing application. Then, using Java annotations is an alternative. The following is an example for a simple aspect with annotations:

```
@Aspect class MyAspect {
  @Before("execution(* MyClass*.get*(..))")
  public void myAdvice() {
    do something in Java before specified join points
} }
```

An annotation @Aspect lets the Java class MyAspect become an aspect. The method myAdvice is a @Before advice that adds Java logic before those joinpoints that are captured by the pointcut. The pointcut is specified within @Before as a string: Any execution of any method starting with get, having any parameters and any return type, belonging to a class starting with MyClass. Wildcards can be used to determine several methods of several classes. A star "*" in names denotes any character sequence; "*" used as a type stands for any type. Parameter types can be fixed with data types or left open (. .). Similarly, @After and @Around advices can be used to execute an advice after or around join points, resp. An aspect can also declare attributes and methods; it can also extend another aspect.

This is only a very brief overview of AspectJ. Concrete examples will be discussed in the successive section. It is important to note that this is pure Java code that runs with any Java compiler. So-called load-time weaving (LTW) lets the advices be woven into the code whenever a class is loaded by the class loader.

4   Adding Multi-tenancy to Existing Applications

In this paper, we use an existing industrial Java application that provides customers a REST service in the travel management domain. The application runs in a Tomcat application server and uses an Oracle database (DB) for storing data at the backend. Currently, the application is shipped as a single-tenant application to individual customers and deployed at the customer site. Thus, each customer obtains a full application stack consisting of Tomcat, the application, and an Oracle database server.

The intention is to deploy this application in a public cloud thereby enabling it for multi-tenancy. This means that Tomcat, the application and the database have to be shared amongst several tenants. Further details about the application are subject to confidentiality and irrelevant for the message of this paper.

4.1   Tomcat and Oracle Basics

Tomcat and Oracle have some specific concepts the understanding of which is necessary for the remainder of this paper. Tomcat provides several forms of user authentication, a form-based for Web application, basic authentication for REST services etc. Having enabled authentication, Tomcat shields the application by asking for a user and a password. User, passwords, and user roles are stored for each application in a configurable "user/roles store" like an XML file, a relational DB, a JDNI store etc. When a user logs in to an application, the Tomcat container checks that store for valid credentials. The application can also restrict functionality to users with specific roles. The legacy application we use in our case study applies Tomcat's basic authentication. To this end, a dedicated schema Auth(entication) in Oracle contains the user/roles tables. The connect string with a specific user/password is part of the Tomcat configuration file.

In Oracle, each user requires a password to login; the user obtains an associated DB *schema* with the same name. Every user can create the same set of tables with the same statement – in his schema. Thus, an Oracle user/schema corresponds to a tenant "database". Schemas are isolated from each other. To access data in another schema (i.e., of another user), tables can be prefixed by a schema name. However, the owner of the foreign schema must explicitly grant access to the user. In the following, we use the notion schema.table to refer to a table in a specific schema.

A *database instance* is the Oracle notion of a database server. Such an instance has exactly one *database* being associated. A JDBC driver connects to that database.

4.2   Tenant and User Management

The major concern of this paper is to enable an existing Tomcat application for multi-tenancy, i.e., to share the Tomcat application server, the application, and the Oracle database instance amongst tenants. According to [2], one important prerequisite for multi-tenancy is an appropriate tenant/user management. In particular, the following workflow should be supported:

1. Tenants must be given a possibility to register for using the application.
2. A SaaS administrator should be able to approve or deny the tenant for using the application depending on whether a contract about payment details has been set up between the SaaS provider and the tenant.
3. If the SaaS provider has approved a tenant, the tenant obtains a dedicated database. Moreover, the tenant is allowed to register its users.
4. All the registered tenants' users should be able to use the application.

4.3   Initial DB Setup for Multi-tenancy

The original application keeps its data in a database schema. Indeed, there might be several, however, we collapse them to one referred to as Appl. We assume another schema, referred to as Auth, which contains the Tomcat authentication tables Users and User_Roles with Tomcat users with their roles. Tomcat accesses these tables to check the password for any login to the application during authentication. Only Tomcat users in the Users table can authenticate.

During an initial database setup, the Users table in the Auth schema is extended with a column tenant to keep the association between a user and the tenant s/he belongs to. Moreover, a new Oracle user/schema Admin is created that is exclusively used by the SaaS administrator to keep information about tenants. The setup also creates a new table Tenants in this schema to keep registered tenants with their administrators and a UserMonitoring table for monitoring purposes (cf. Sect. 4.7).

The newly introduced tenant administration service (cf. Sect. 4.4) requires a SaaS administrator to perform tenant management. To this end, a new Tomcat user SaaS with a new role SaaS is added to the Users and User_Roles tables.

Finally, an SQL script createApplicationTables.sql is required to create all the application's tables in any new tenant schema.

All these steps do not affect the existing application, but only require some SQL scripts to be executed.

4.4   Tenant Administration Service

New services are required for tenant administration purposes, especially for registering tenants and users, to support the workflow in Subsect. 4.2. The existing application source code is not affected. Hence, we implemented a new REST server to provide corresponding functionality:

1. POST TenantService allows a tenant to register for using the application. Everybody is allowed to invoke this service. The request payload has to specify a name TenantX for the tenant and an administrator by name and password. Name and password are required to let a tenant register users in Step 3. This information is stored in a table Admin.Tenants(name, admin, password, approved, ...).

2. PUT TenantService/Tenants/{TenantX} can be used by the SaaS administrator to enable or disable access for TenantX; the request body contains {"approve":Yes} or {"approve":No} accordingly. Only the SaaS administrator is allowed to invoke the service. To this end, we set up a new organizational Tomcat role SaaS which allows the administrator to manage tenants. If the SaaS administrator approves TenantA, then approved=1 is set for TenantA in the Admin.Tenants table; the record for TenantA's admin is copied from Admin. Tenants (cf. Step 1) to the Auth.Users table. Moreover, the tenant administrator obtains a new Tomcat role TAdmin in the Auth.User_Roles table. This role allows him to register tenant's users for the application. The approved tenant obtains an Oracle user and schema TenantA, i.e., a database to keep the tenant's application data isolated. Finally, all the application tables are created in the new schema by executing the SQL script createApplicationTables.sql in schema TenantA.

3. POST TenantService/Tenants/{TenantX} lets the tenant administrator for TenantX create a user to make a user known to the application. The invoker requires the TAdmin Tomcat role for Tomcat authentication. The request payload specifies the name of the user and a password, which both are inserted to the Auth. Users table. Furthermore, the user obtains one or more roles, which enables him to use the application with the above credentials. The association of a user to his tenant is stored in the tenant column of the Auth.Users table. Table 1 shows the contents of the Users and User_Roles tables after the administrator AdminA for TenantA has registered UserA1 and UserA2; an explanation describes when each record has been added.

4. The users UserA1 and UserA2 of TenantA are then able to login to the application and to use it.

Table 1. Database contents for authentication (adopted from [10]).

Users	user_name	user_pass	tenant	
	… existing users	…	NULL	
	SaaS	SaaS	NULL	in 4.3
	AdminA	PwA	TenantA	Step 2
	UserA1	PwA1	TenantA	Step 3
	UserA2	PwA2	TenantA	Step 3

User_Roles	user_name	role_name	
	… existing users	… existing roles	
	SaaS	SaaS	in 4.3
	AdminA	TAdmin	Step 2
	UserA1	User	Step 3
	UserA2	User	Step 3

These services can simply be deployed as a new application in Tomcat in order to become immediately effective. Services rely on the following Tomcat roles giving privileges to the various types of users:

- A new SaaS role for the administrator of the SaaS applications to perform administrative tasks such as tenant approval;
- a new TAdmin role for a tenant administrator to enable registering tenant's users;
- User for the users of the application: Indeed, there may be several with specific privileges. For the ease of discussion, we collapse them to one User schema.

4.5 Data Isolation

Tenants and their users are now known to Tomcat and allowed to access the application since Tomcat authenticates against the Auth.User/UserRoles tables. However, *all* these users access the same application and use the original tables in the Appl schema. Hence, there is no effective data isolation between different tenants as requested by [9]. To achieve data isolation, a user's data must be stored in the tenant's schema (i.e., database). This means that every database access of a logged-in user must be re-directed to the correct tenant schema. In fact, AspectJ comes here into play since it enables intercepting every user authentication without explicitly modifying, recompiling, or rebuilding the original application. Then, the user can be determined and the corresponding TenantX for the user derived. The following code sketches a corresponding AspectJ aspect:

```
@Aspect public class MTE {
  @Around(
      "execution(* com.siemens.app.ExistingAppl.svc*(..))
       && !within(com.siemens.aspects.MTE)")
  public Object interceptRequests
                  (ProceedingJoinPoint jp) {
    (1) determine user from HTTPRequest and
        derive role & tenant (from Users table);
    (2) store user/tenant/role for later usage;
    (3) switch acces to tenant database;
    return jp.proceed(jp.getArgs()); /* call original
                                logic of svc* method */
} }
```

We do not use the AspectJ language and its compiler because we do not want to change the build process. Instead, we rely on pure Java with AspectJ annotations and load-time weaving. The annotation @Aspect let the Java class MTE (MultitenancyEnabler) become an aspect. The method interceptRequests is annotated with @Around and defines an advice to be executed at join points. These join points are specified by a pointcut string within the @Around annotation. The advice intercepts any execution of methods starting with svc... belonging to the class

ExistingAppl (i.e., the basic REST service) with any parameters (..) and returning any type (*). We could also specify several method signatures individually and combine them with '||' (logical OR) without wildcards.

The @Around method interceptRequests implements the logic to be executed at each join point, i.e., any execution of a svc... method specified by the pointcut, and replaces the original behavior with its body. The parameter jp of type ProceedingJoinPoint is used to execute the original logic at the join points in the advice by means of jp.proceed(). Furthermore, jp also gives access to the context of invocation such as the parameter values (jp.getArgs()) and the signature of the concrete svc... method (jp.getSignature()). Since the method is implicitly invoked by jp.proceed() inside the aspect, an endless loop will occur. This is avoided by adding !within(MTE) in the pointcut to not intercept any invocation that occurs within the aspect itself.

Please note only the pointcut "execution(* com.siemens.app. ExistingAppl.svc*(..))" of advice interceptRequests depends on the application code. This pointcut specifies what methods or services are intercepted, here of class ExistingAppl that implements the REST service.

One open point now is how to get the user name from Tomcat authentication (cf. (1) in the code above). Unfortunately, there are several ways to pass the authentication context to the application, and it is unknown what mechanism has been used in the original application. For instance, the application can declare a HttpServletRequest req variable. Such a variable declaration can be annotated with @Context in a service class which let the value be injected by the Tomcat container. The HttpServletRequest can then be used to derive authentication information, e.g., by req.getUserPrincipal().getName(). Another way is to specify an additional @Context HttpServletRequest parameter in a service method. Besides not knowing the used mechanism, even a global variable req is usually private and not accessible from an external aspect.

Investigating the behavior of Tomcat, we noticed that Tomcat invokes for authentication in any case a _handleRequest method of a class WebApplicationImpl. Thus, a @Before advice in the MTE aspect can intercept the method execution in order to extract the HttpRequest and then the user name:

```
@Before("execution
          (* com.sun.jersey.server.impl.application
          .WebApplicationImpl._handleRequest(..))
          && this(w) && !within(com.siemens.aspects.MTE)")
public void getUserInfo(JoinPoint jp,
                        WebApplicationImpl w) {
  String user = w.getThreadLocalHttpContext()
             .getRequest().getUserPrincipal().getName();
  determine role and tenant for user;
}
```

Please note AspectJ is able to intercept JARs, even of 3rd party tools like Tomcat without having the source available!

The clause `this(w)` binds the variable w to the called object of type `WebApplicationImpl`. The method `getThreadLocalHttpContext()` is used to get the request-local `HttpContext`, which is then used to derive the `HttpRequestContext` and the `Principal` of the user who has logged in. The tenant to whom the user belongs can be determined by using the `Auth.Users` table.

The user and tenant information has to be passed to the `interceptRequests` advice. This is simply possible since information can be shared amongst several advices within the same aspect. Hence, the `getUserInfo` advice can store the user information in a variable within the `MTE` aspect, which is the used by the `interceptRequests` advice in the sense of Laddad's wormhole pattern [16].

Please note this advice is only specific to Tomcat but is independent of the application. Any other application server will require slight modifications of this advice.

Finally, we have to take care of tenant isolation. Using another advice within `MTE`, we intercept every access to a database `Connection` and re-direct access to the tenant schema. For JDBC accesses, the advice looks as follows:

```
@Around("call(java.sql.Connection
                java.sql.DriverManager.getConnection(..)
        && !within(com.siemens.aspects.MTE)")
public Object interceptGetConnection
                          (final ProceedingJoinPoint jp) {
    get the user and tenant (stored locally in MTE);
    Connection con = (Connection) jp.proceed(jp.getArgs());
                    // original logic gets connection
    Statement stmt = con.createStatement();
    // switch to tenant's database/schema:
    stmt.execute("SET SCHEMA '" + tenant + "'");
    return con;
}
```

Every successive database operation will use the tenant schema, i.e., database. Indeed, an `@After` advice would have been sufficient here. However, `@Around` is more flexible to handle other databases with different concepts such as an explicit database name in the URL. Section 5 will dive into the details and will also illustrate how to implement other strategies such as sharing the original tables between several tenants.

4.6   Customization

Several papers like [29] emphasize the importance of tenant-specific customizations of an application for business, thereby considering customization as a major challenge of multi-tenancy. Again, AspectJ can be used to give an application a tenant-specific behavior without explicitly touching the source code. To this end, each tenant-specific behavior requires one dedicated aspect, e.g., `TenantAModifier` for TenantA, which defines the specific tenant behavior. Since the logic of the aspect is technically applied to the overall application, the aspect must determine the expected tenant and only apply the logic to that tenant. That is why the aspect has to implement an interface `GenericModifier`, which demands for a method `getTenantName()`; it should return the tenant name of the modifier, i.e., "TenantA" for aspect `TenantAModifier`. Using `getTenantName()`, an advice can then compare the calling tenant with the expected one and modify the logic only for that tenant:

```
if (nameOfCallingTenant.equals(getTenantName()) {
  … modify logic …
} else { // don't modify behavior
    return jp.proceed(jp.getArgs()); // original logic
}
```

An `@Around` advice can define pointcuts where to modify logic. Inside the advice, the original call can be ignored by omitting `jp.proceed()`. Hence, functionality can be disabled, for example, by returning an empty result, a result masked out with stars '*', or an HTTP code 403 (FORBIDDEN) in case of REST services. Similarly, the original logic can be modified or extended. Especially information to be returned can be changed by using the original logic.

Adding new REST services offering additional functionality that is *not* part of the original application is more complicated since the logic will be implemented in a different class. We have to use static introduction to this end in the following manner:

```
@Aspect public class TenantAModifier
                                implements GenericModifier {
  @DeclareParents(
        defaultImpl=com.siemens.newfunc.NewFunction.class,
        value="com.siemens.app.ExistingAppl")
  public com.siemens.nf.NewFunctionIF mix;
}
```

Then, a new GET service `/newFunctionality`, can be implemented in the class `NewFunction`.

```
@Path("newFunctionality")
public class NewFunction implements NewFunctionIF {
  @GET public Response svcNewGetOperation(...) { ... }
}
```

The new logic implemented in `svcNewGetOperation` becomes available in class `ExistingAppl` (implementing the original REST service) because `ExistingAppl` inherits from the newly introduced superclass `NewFunction` – although its definition is done in another class. This happens because `@DeclareParents` places a new superclass `NewFunction` of interface `NewFunctionIF` on top of those classes that are specified by the `value` clause, here the single class `ExistingAppl`. The interface `NewFunctionIF` is only required for enabling a syntactic cast from `ExistingAppl` to `NewFunction`; the variable `mix` is of no further importance.

Thanks to AspectJ, the application itself does not have to be prepared or modified for allowing intercepted code at the right place. The powerfulness certainly depends on the power of the pointcut syntax and the context information available at the intercepted join points. The approach suffers only if certain points in the code cannot be addressed by pointcuts. Moreover, the application code has to be available to find appropriate join points; the weaving itself does not require the source code and is satisfied with byte code! This point is the major advantage of our approach: Other customization approaches require special, prepared customization points, where to plug in tenant logic. However, this would violate our goal not to touch the original application.

4.7 Monitoring

Every SaaS provider has to define a billing model for charging his tenants for using the application. In turn, a SaaS provider has expenses for running the application, especially in a public cloud. Then, he has to pay for the all used resources. In fact, the billing model must be appropriate to make profit. The investment covers both the operational costs in a Cloud as well as the costs for developing an application or SaaS-enabling it [23] and later maintenance [2].

Many proposed billing models for SaaS are post-paid. Tenants receive a bill and pays for usage periodically. Hence, the SaaS provider has to monitor and aggregate the consumption costs for each tenant [27] for billing purposes. If a SaaS provider charges his tenants by a fixed rate per month or based upon other factors such as the number of users (registered or in parallel), then it is important to throttle exhaustive usage by a single tenant because the SaaS providers' revenue will be reduced or even lost otherwise.

Consequently, it is necessary to monitor and log the activities of all tenants' users and the costs they produce. As [28] discusses, such a tracking is the task of the SaaS providers. The support given by underlying Cloud platforms is only rudimentary and not detailed enough to determine the costs for resources for each tenant individually.

To enable a tenant-specific monitoring, we have added the following table to the `Admin` schema in order to track tenants' user activities as shown in Table 2.

Table 2. Table UserMonitoring.

id	name	tenant	operation	timestamp	elapsed
1	UserA1	TenantA	Operation1	2016-11-10 17:00:01	12 ms
2	UserA2	TenantA	Operation2	2016-11-10 17:00:02	21 ms
3	UserB1	TenantB	Operation2	2016-11-10 17:00:03	10 ms

We again use AspectJ to intercept any user actions (maybe filtering out a few relevant ones by a pointcut). To this end, we extend the `interceptRequests` advice from Subsect. 4.5 to compute the elapsed time around `jp.proceed()`:

```
long start = System.nanoTime();
Object o = jp.proceed(args);
double elapsed = (double) (System.nanoTime() - start);
createLogEntry(user, tenant, elapsed,
                    jp.getSignature().toShortString());
```

createLogEntry logs the elapsed time together with the signature of the method, tenant, user etc. at a central place. Dedicated pointcuts can define what has to be tracked; this might depend on the application. The table now gives an overview over all user activities and forms the basis for several scenarios. Using the table, tenants can be charged back for their consumed resources. Moreover, it is possible to check profit-making, i.e., whether the chosen billing model for one/all tenant(s) is appropriate to make profit. Also the (elapsed) execution times or the number of service requests for each user or tenant can be accumulated; if thresholds are exceeded, further access is throttled or rejected. Hence, a SaaS provider is able to timely react on frequent and massively active tenants by throttling them before costs rise. Even further use cases can be supported. For example, if a Service Level Agreement (SLA) specifies a maximum number of concurrent users, a @Before advice is able to check the current number of concurrent users for a tenant in the UserMonitoring table before executing a service request. Similarly, if an SLA states a threshold for the number of registered users, the Users table can be used to supervise the limit in the user registration process. Finally, all the monitoring information might be used to implement auto-scaling features that enable Cloud elasticity.

4.8   Configuration

AspectJ load-time weaving requires an additional configuration file aop.xml that specifies what aspects (<aspects>) are active and what packages (<include ...>) should be intercepted by the aspect logic. The following content is an example:

```
<aspectj>
  <aspects>
    <aspect name="com.siemens.aspects.MTE"/>
    <aspect name="com.siemens.aspects.TenantAModifier"/>
    <aspect name="com.siemens.aspects.TenantBModifier"/>
  </aspects>
  <weaver> <include within="com.siemens.app.*"/>
  </weaver>
</aspectj>
```

5   Other Types of Database Servers and Isolation Strategies

We want to expand the scope of our investigation and discuss what has to be done to apply the principle to other database servers beside Oracle and to other data isolation strategies following Chong et al. [6]. This paper was one of the first to investigate multi-tenant data architectures and distinguishes between "separate databases", "shared database, separate schemas", and "shared database, shared schema" for an SQL Server. This section follows this structure and also investigates PostgreSQL and SQL Server databases as further candidates.

5.1   Separate Databases

Storing the tenant's data in a separate database offers the highest degree of data isolation. In principle, using a separate database server for each tenant is an even higher isolation. For a strong isolation it is important to authenticate units for each tenant individually. Hence, there is essentially no difference between using a separate database server (i.e., an instance, containing several databases) and a database (within such a database server) as far as individual privileges can be defined for the units.

Oracle has a notion of a "database", but this is closely related to a database server, named instance: Each instance can only be associated with one database. Hence, we have to set up an instance for each tenant. An Oracle JDBC URL thus refers to the instance as `jdbc:oracle:thin:@<Host>:1521:<Instance>`. This means for multi-tenancy that we have to replace `<Instance>` in the URL with the respective tenant's instance name in order to switch from the existing instance to the tenant one. To this end, the pointcut for the `interceptGetConnection` advice from Subsect. 4.5 can still be used with minor changes of the advice:

```
@Around("call(java.sql.Connection java.sql.DriverManager
          .getConnection(String, String, String))
  && args(url,usr,pw) && !within(com.siemens.aspects.MTE)")
public Object interceptGetConnection(ProceedingJoinPoint
                   jp, String url, String usr, String pw) {
  get the user and tenant (stored in MTE);
  url = exchange instance name with tenant name in URL;
  usr = tenant;    // provide credentials
  pw  = password;  // for database connect
  return jp.proceed(url,usr,pw);
}
```

PostgreSQL has both options, one DB server or one database for each tenant; the URL `jdbc:postgresql://<Host>:<Port>/<Database>` specifies the host, the database, and optionally the port number (if several PostgreSQL instances run on the same host):. The tenant-specific substitutions can be done analogous to Oracle in the `interceptGetConnection` advice using the same pointcut:

url = replace host or database with tenant name in URL;

The URL of the SQL Server resembles the PostgreSQL URL: `jdbc:sqlserver://<Host>\<ServerName>;databaseName=<Db>`, i.e., server name and database name can be specified in addition to the host name. Hence, it is possible to change the DB server and/or database for corresponding tenants by a URL modification. Again, the same pointcut can be used with slight modifications of the related advice.

To sum up, only the advice has to be adapted to handle the different formats of URLs while keeping the original pointcut.

Furthermore, the Tenant Administration Service must create a tenant-specific database or server when a tenant has been approved. Here, the implementation depends on DB-specific concepts and dialects. Moreover, a user for the tenant with a password is required to provide database access in the MTE aspect. However, it is quite easy to organize the syntactic variants in Java. For example, users are created in Oracle with

```
CREATE USER TenantA IDENTIFIED BY <Pw>;
```

while PostgreSQL requires

```
CREATE ROLE TenantA WITH LOGIN ENCRYPTED PASSWORD '<Pw>',
                 TEMPLATE applicationTables;
CREATE DATABASE TenantA WITH OWNER=TenantA;
```

and SQLServer a statement like

```
CREATE USER TenantA IDENTIFIED BY <Pw>;
```

In general, the database set up of the original application has to be understood, i.e., what databases and schemas are available, which tables are tenant-specific etc. According to that, the creation of tables can be done during setup (cf. Subsect. 4.3) by executing `createApplicationTables.sql` in the tenant instance. PostgreSQL has a so-called template mechanism for handling the pre-creation of tables, views, stored procedures etc. during database creation (see the statement above).

5.2 Separate Schemas

A schema is basically a special concept of some database servers. The idea of a schema is to have a dedicated and isolated space within a database, e.g., one for each tenant. In such a schema, the same set of tables etc. can be created. Sometimes, even individual users and privileges can be specified for a schema.

In order to take care of data isolation, we can use the same pointcut `interceptGetConnection` as before in Subsect. 5.1 to intercept the request of a database connection for all types of database systems. The corresponding advice does not need to change the URL, but simply switches the schema by a statement that uses a database-specific syntactic variant. That is, all tenants connect to the same database setting the schema afterwards. How to use the Oracle schema for multi-tenancy has already been demonstrated in the `interceptGetConnection` advice in Sect. 4.5:

```
SET SCHEMA TenantA;
```

Furthermore, the Tenant Administration Service (cf. Sect. 4.4) has to create a schema for each tenant:

```
CREATE USER TenantA IDENTIFIED BY <Pw>;
```

As already mentioned in Subsect. 4.1, each Oracle user possesses a schema with the same name. Hence, there is no explicit schema definition.

PostgreSQL uses a different advice for the same pointcut due to a different syntax:

```
SET SEARCH_PATH TO "TenantA";
```

Again, the Tenant Administration Service has to create a tenant-specific schema, when a tenant has been approved:

```
CREATE ROLE TenantA WITH LOGIN ENCRYPTED PASSWORD '<Pw>'
CREATE SCHEMA "TenantAschema" AUTHORIZATION TenantA
```

SQL Server has a different syntax to switch the schema, too:

```
ALTER USER TenantA WITH DEFAULT_SCHEMA = TenantAschema;
```

User and schema have to be created in the Tenant Administration Service:

```
CREATE USER TenantA ...;
CREATE SCHEMA TenantAschema AUTHORIZATION TenantA;
```

The creation of tables can be done during setup by executing `createApplicationTables.sql` in the particular tenant schema.

Please note there is a strong danger of SQL injection in any case if a user can issue SQL arbitrary statements: a user can switch to another tenant's schema! Special prevention is required to prevent SQL injection.

If a database server does not support a dedicated schema concept, all the tenant-specific tables can be replicated in the same database by adding a tenant suffix: `<Table>_TenantA`. However, more effort is required because all SQL statements are affected due to changing table names in all queries. Furhermore, authentication with user/password is lost compared to an explicit schema concept. The principles of the next subsection can be applied to provide a smarter solution.

5.3 Shared Schemas

A third approach uses the same database and the same set of tables for all the customers. Thus, each table contains the data of several tenants. This certainly requires a discriminator column in each tenant-specific table, the `TenantId`. As an immediate consequence, every INSERT on such a table has to provide this `TenantId`, while queries (including delete and updates) must filter for the tenant's id by `TenantId=<id>`.

Indeed, this is the lowest level of data isolation, which requires the highest effort for application development. Anyway, AspectJ is able to handle the new arising challenges in a modular manner with general principles.

As a presumption, all tenant-specific tables must be known and handled. However, the `createApplicationTables.sql` script can be maintained, since `ALTER TABLE` statements can add the new `TenantId` column afterwards.

In contrast to the previous strategies, the Tenant Administration Service is not affected by this isolation strategy as no tenant-specific database or schema is required. In general, there is no dependency on the type of database server.

As already mentioned, all queries issued by the application have to be changed at runtime to add a filter `TenantId=<id>`. The interception is not an issue and can be done by pointcuts, e.g., for SQL queries executed by `executeQuery` in JDBC:

```
@Around("call(java.sql.ResultSet
                  java.sql.Statement.executeQuery(String))
     && !within(com.siemens.aspects.MultitenancyEnabler)")
public Object interceptExecute(ProceedingJoinPoint jp) {
  String theQuery = (String)jp.getArgs()[0];
  theQuery = "modified query";
  return jp.proceed(jp.getArgs());
}
```

The pointcut `interceptGetConnection` used in Subsects. 5.1 and 5.2 is no longer necessary. The principle is easy, but disguises a lot of technical issues. For example, let us assume the following original SQL query with two tenant-specific tables `Tab1` and `Tab2`:

```
SELECT *
FROM Tab1 t1 LEFT OUTER JOIN Tab2 t2 ON t1.id=t2.fk
WHERE t1.col1=10 OR t2.col2=20
```

Simply adding "AND `TenantId = <id>`" does not work since `TenantId` is ambiguous due to the two tables with a `TenantId` column. Even an addition "AND `t1.TenantId=<id>`AND `t2.TenantId=<id>`" is incorrect because of `OR` in the `WHERE` clause, which changes the original semantics drastically. Obviously, brackets are required around the `OR` condition. Next, `LEFT OUTER JOIN`s must be treated carefully. A condition "(t1.col1=10 OR t2.col2=20) AND t1.TenantId=<id>AND t2.TenantId=<id>" returns wrong results in many database servers as such a condition in the `WHERE` clause diminishes the outer join by implicitly forcing a join. Finally, `SELECT *` has additional `TenantId` columns for which an existing cursor is not prepared. In sum, the correct form is:

```
SELECT concrete columns without TenantId
FROM Tab1 t1 LEFT OUTER JOIN Tab2 t2 ON t1.id=t2.fk
   AND t1.TenantId=<id>AND t2.TenantId=<id>
WHERE (t1.col1=10 OR t2.col2=20)
AND t1.TenantId=<id>
```

This simple example already shows some important pitfalls. Further points to be handled appropriately are inner queries with IN and EXISTS. Hence a lot query string parsing and manipulation is required for queries, making the logic in the advice quite complex. This has to be done for DELETE and UPDATE statements in the same manner. Furthermore, INSERT statements have to be modified, too, because of the new TenantId column. Here, the TenantId value has to be added to the VALUES clause.

One nasty challenge are stored procedures. Again, it is easy to intercept the invocation of stored procedures in JDBC. But the source code of those procedures is not directly accessible because of being stored in the database. The solution we suggested is as follows:

- Modify the code of all the stored procedures manually, i.e., modifying the SQL statements according to the previous discussion (this does not require a re-compilation of the application code);
- add a new parameter TenantId to each procedure in order to transport the tenant information to the procedure;
- modify the procedure call by passing the TenantId as a parameter to the procedure call during interception.

So far, the use of JDBC for database accesses has been discussed. Hence, the question arises what happens if an object/relational (O/R) framework such as Hibernate or EclipseLink is used. There are two general options:

- To intercept JDBC at a deeper level, i.e., inside the O/R framework or within a connection pool. Please remember that AspectJ is able to intercept even 3rd party libraries without having source code available. The pointcuts do not need to be changed, however, the packages to be intercepted are specific to a particular framework and must be listed in the aop.xml configuration file (cf. Subsect. 4.8).
- As an alternative, the higher O/R requests can be intercepted by pointcuts. Different String modifications then become necessary for query languages such as JPQL of the JPA standard. This is more complex since the new TenantId properties must be added to the persistent Java classes to match the changed table structures with the TenanId column. This might have an impact on the build process and/or Java code.

6   Evaluation

6.1   Modularity and Adaptability

Separation of concerns is one of the driving forces of aspect oriented programming. Bringing in the notion of reuse without compromising the advantages of separation of concerns is an important consideration for application development. The positive impact of code reuse during application development and maintenance should not be under-weighed.

The strategies to enable multi-tenancy follow the best practices of using AspectJ and the individual concepts can be reused across other similar applications. All the multi-tenancy logic is concentrated in classes to be added to the application's WAR file thereby adjusting the aop.xml configuration file accordingly. Moreover, tenant specific logic is also clearly separated in particular classes. Only a restart of Tomcat is required for the multi-tenancy configuration to take effect.

All the multi-tenancy components rely on simple mechanisms that can easily be applied to other legacy Java applications to make them multi-tenant. Thus, development cost can be reduced for other applications. Indeed, REST services are easier to handle than applications with a graphical user interface since there are pure Java methods annotated with @GET, @PUT etc., which are the entry points for functionality. Anyway, background logic of other applications can be handled the same way.

The MTE aspect that takes care of tenant isolation mainly depends on tools, i.e., the application server and the database server, especially the isolation strategy to apply. This aspect has to be adapted if MTE should be applied to applications using JBoss and/or MySQL, for instance. Sticking to the same technologies allows for an immediate reuse of the MTE aspect. The pointcuts to intercept DB accesses rely on JDBC or an object/relational framework and are not DB-specific. Hence, only switching the persistence technology requires a modification of pointcuts.

However, the pointcut interceptRequests in MTE depends on the application methods to be intercepted just as customization does; other applications require different pointcuts and/or advices.

Anyway, any adaption and modification is made in central components – outside the original application. Reusability can be further enhanced. An abstract aspect can implement an advice but leaves out the pointcut, while application-specific sub-aspects reuse the general logic and only specify the concrete pointcuts.

6.2   Implementation Effort

Taking a look at the lines of code, the simplicity of the approach becomes obvious:

- The new Tenant Administration Service has about 400 lines of Java code;
- The aspect MTE consists of ca. 150 lines all together for the Oracle schema approach, however, a shared-schema approach requires about 500 lines of code due to a more complex logic;
- The effort for a customizing TenantXModifier aspect depends on what should be modified. To give an impression, disabling functionality in a REST service requires 10 lines, a simple modification of service behavior 23 lines, and introducing a new REST service about 60 lines.

6.3   Lessons Learned

The lack of comprehension and maintainability of aspect-orientation is often criticized. Since we only have a small number of dedicated aspects serving a very special purpose such as tenant isolation, customization, and monitoring, we did not detect any problems in this respect. Indeed, the impact of multi-tenant aspects to behavior is clearly arranged.

As explained throughout the paper, we could benefit a lot from aspect-orientation to achieve our goal to leave code untouched. Especially, the possibility to intercept 3-rd-party tools such as Tomcat and to exchange information between advices according to the "Wormhole Pattern" [16] helped a lot.

However, we also recognized some limitations. The first idea was to have a `Users` table in each tenant schema instead of global table. As a consequence, Tomcat authentication has to use the corresponding tenant database. However, we failed to intercept the start-up of Tomcat to bring in the logic. That is the reason why the approach relies on the single `Users` table of the existing application.

6.4   Advantages

We achieve with our AspectJ approach the general advantages of full multi-tenancy such as cost saving by sharing resources (hardware, application server, database etc.) amongst tenants and reducing operational expenses (OPEX). But the major additional advantage of our approach lies in the fact that the source code of the existing application does not need to be touched explicitly.

In fact, Tenant Administration Service (cf. Sect. 4.4) is just a new service to be deployed in the Tomcat application server as a WAR file. Tenant isolation is achieved by adding a new `MTE.class` to the deployed application WAR. Additional files `TenantXModifier.class` in the WAR provide a tenant-specific behavior for each Tenant*X*. Only a restart of Tomcat is required to apply the `MTE` aspect thanks to AspectJ load-time weaving. Adding a new tenant class can even be done at runtime without a restart by just deploying the `TenantXModifier` class and adjusting the aop. xml file.

Hence, the approach offers a cost-efficient way to speed up time-to-market by migrating existing applications quickly into SaaS-offerings. The approach also allows for a flexible configuration, e.g., for various tenant isolation strategies (one DB for each tenant, one schema for each tenant, or one single-table for all tenants).

7   Conclusions

While research has investigated many facets of multi-tenancy for designing and implementing new applications, this paper focuses on migrating legacy single-tenant to fully multi-tenant applications. This is an important and necessary step to offer an existing application as Software-as-a-Service (SaaS).

There are a couple of approaches and methodologies that demonstrate how to convert legacy applications into multi-tenant software. However, they require to re-engineer the legacy source code to a large extent. In contrast, our approach consists of simply adding components to the legacy application – *without* explicitly touching the application's source code.

We propose several components, being implemented as aspects in AspectJ, which have to be added to an application's WAR file. The major component for tenant isolation depends only on technological choices such as application server, database server, and the chosen data isolation strategy. Furthermore, tenant customization depends on the application; pointcuts specify what to intercept in the application and advices implement the customization.

In order to validate the approach, we used an existing industrial REST application that runs in Tomcat and uses an Oracle database. In particular, we discuss how to achieve three main concerns in detail:

- tenant isolation [5] for different strategies and database servers;
- tenant-specific customization of behavior;
- monitoring tenants' user activities for billing purposes.

We elaborated upon how to benefit from the aspect-oriented language AspectJ in order to achieve these points. We presented the AspectJ approach in detail and evaluated the approach with regard to modularity, adaptability, and implementation effort. The effort to be spent for the overall principle requires only a few 100 lines of aspect code. We also concluded with some lessons learnt. The approach can directly be adapted to other Java applications, especially REST services.

In general, REST services are easier to handle than applications with a graphical user interface since there is pure Java code without any parts in HTML or Javascript. In order to evaluate the limits, our future work will consider applications with a graphical user interface. First experiences show that the MTE (Multi-Tenancy Enabler) aspect works well for achieving data isolation. Moreover, logic can be customized on a per-tenant basis as far as no GUI is concerned. Further investigations are required to evaluate customizing the UI.

Currently, applying the presented aspects to other applications requires some copy&paste of code and an adjustment of pointcuts and advice logic. This is also true for the MTE aspect which depends on technologies. Feature modelling tools might be useful to generate the aspect code according to a domain-specific language that describes the database server, data isolation strategy, and application server. Alternatively or in addition, we think of providing a reusable aspect framework. The idea is to have an aspect hierarchy that reflects technological choices. If for example an application uses JBoss and SQLServer with a shared schema isolation approach, then an application-specific sub-aspect has to derive from an Oracle_JBoss_SharedSchema aspect. The sub-aspect itself only contains those parts that are specific to the application, e.g., the database URL and pointcuts.

In case of too much load, several Tomcat instances have to be started with a load balancer in front. Hence, migrating an application into the cloud is much more than just adding multi-tenancy. Taking care of scalability issues and replacing software components with Cloud services is also subject to future work.

References

1. Andrikopoulos, V., Binz, T., Leymann, F., Strauch, S.: How to adapt applications for the Cloud environment - Challenges and solutions in migrating applications to the cloud. Computing 95(6), 493–535 (2013)

2. Bezemer, C., Zaidman, A. Platzbeecke, B. Hurkmans, T., Hart, A.: Enabling multitenancy: an industrial experience report. In: Technical Report of Delft University of Technology, TUD-SERG-2010-030 (2010)
3. Bezemer, C., Zaidman, A.: Challenges of reengineering into multitenant SaaS applications. In: Technical Report of Delft University of Technology, TUD-SERG-2010-012 (2010)
4. Binz, T., Leymann, F., Schumm, D.: CMotion: a framework for migration of applications into and between clouds. In: SOCA 2011, pp. 1–4 (2011)
5. Chong, F., Carraro, G.: Architecture strategies for catching the long tail (2006). https://msdn.microsoft.com/en-us/library/aa479069.aspx. Accessed Nov 2016
6. Chong, F., Carraro, G., Wolter, R.: Multi-tenant data architecture (2006). http://msdn.microsoft.com/en-us/library/aa479086.aspx. Accessed Nov 2016
7. Elrad, T., Filman, R., Bader, A. (eds.): Theme section on aspect-oriented programming. CACM **44**(10) (2001)
8. Fehling, C., Leymann, F., Mietzner, R.: A framework for optimized distribution of tenants in cloud applications. In: IEEE 3rd International Conference on Cloud Computing (CLOUD), pp. 252–259 (2010)
9. Guo, C., Sun, W., Huang, Y., Wang, Z., Gao, B.: A framework for native multi-tenancy application development and management. In: CEC/EEE 2007: International Conference on Enterprise Computing, E-Commerce Technology and International Conference on Enterprise Computing, E-Commerce and E-Services, pp. 551–558 (2007)
10. Hohenstein, U., Koka, P.: An approach to add multi-tenancy to existing applications. In: ICSOFT 2016, pp. 39–49 (2016)
11. Khajeh-Hosseini, A., Greenwood, D., Smith, J., Sommerville, I.: The cloud adoption toolkit: supporting cloud adoption decisions in the enterprise. Softw. Pract. Exp. **42**(4), 447–465 (2012)
12. Kiczales, G., et al.: Aspect-oriented programming. In: Proceedings of the European Conference on Object-Oriented Programming (ECOOP), Finland, pp. 230–242 (2007)
13. Kong, L., Li, Q., Zheng, X.: A novel model supporting customization sharing in SaaS applications. In: International Conference on Multimedia Information Networking and Security (MINES), pp. 225–229 (2010)
14. Krebs, R., Momm, C., Kounev, S.: Architectural concerns in multi-tenant SaaS applications. In: CLOSER 2012, pp. 426–431 (2012)
15. Kwok, T., Nguyen, T., Lam, L.: A software as a service with multi-tenancy support for an electronic contract management application. In: International Conference on Services Computing (SCC), pp. 179–186 (2008)
16. Laddad, R.: AspectJ in Action: Practical Aspect-Oriented Programming, 2nd edn. Manning, Greenwich (2009)
17. Lee, W., Choi, M.: A multi-tenant web application framework for SaaS. In: 2012 IEEE 5th International Conference on Cloud Computing (CLOUD), pp. 970–971 (2012)
18. Lee, J., Kang, S., Hur, S.: Web-based development framework for customizing java-based business logic of SaaS application. In: 14th International Conference on Advanced Communication Technology (ICACT), pp. 1310–1313 (2012)
19. Li, Q., Liu, S., Pan, Y.: A cooperative construction approach for SaaS applications. In: 2012 IEEE 16th International Conference on Computer Supported Cooperative Work in Design (CSCWD), pp. 398–403 (2012)
20. Lizhen, C., Haiyang, W., Lin, J., Pu, H.: Customization modeling based on metagraph for multi-tenant applications. In: 5th International Conference on Pervasive Computing and Applications (ICPCA), pp. 255–260 (2010)

21. Mell, P., Grance, T.: The NIST definition of cloud computing. National Institute of Standards and Technology, September 2011. http://csrc.nist.gov/publications/nistpubs/800-145/SP800-145.pdf. Accessed Nov 2016

22. Moens, H., Truyen, E., Walraven, S., Joosen, W., Dhoedt, B., De Turck, F.: Developing and managing customizable software as a service using feature model conversion. In: IEEE Network Operations and Management Symposium (NOMS), pp. 1295–1302 (2012)

23. Momm, C., Krebs, R.: A qualitative discussion of different approaches for implementing multi-tenant SaaS offerings. In: Proceeding Software Engineering 2011, pp. 139–150 (2011)

24. Orue-Echevarria, L., et al.: Cloudifying applications with ARTIST: a global modernization approach to move applications onto the cloud. In: CLOSER 2014, pp. 737–745 (2014)

25. Park, J., Moon, M., Yeom, K.: Variability modeling to develop flexible service-oriented applications. J. Syst. Sci. Syst. Eng. **20**(2), 193–216 (2011)

26. Pohl, K., Böckle, G., van der Linden, F.: Software Product Line Engineering: Foundations, Principles and Techniques. Springer, New York (2005)

27. Ruiz-Agundez, I., Penya, Y., Bringas, P.: A flexible accounting model for cloud computing. In: SRII 2011, pp. 277–284 (2011)

28. Schwanengel, A., Hohenstein, U.: Challenges with tenant-specific cost determination in multi-tenant applications. In: 4th International Conference on Cloud Computing, Grids and Virtualization 2013, pp. 36–42 (2013)

29. Shahin, A., Samir, A., Khamis, A.: An aspect-oriented approach for SaaS application customization. In: 48th Conference on Statistics, Computer Science and Operations Research 2013, Cairo University, Egypt, pp. 1–15 (2013)

30. Tsai, W., Shao, Q., Li, W.: OIC: ontology-based intelligent customization framework for SaaS. In: IEEE International Conference on Service-Oriented Computing and Applications (SOCA), pp. 1–8 (2010)

31. Tsai, W., Sun, X.: SaaS multi-tenant application customization. In: IEEE 7th International Symposium on Service Oriented System Engineering (SOSE), pp. 1–12 (2013)

32. Walraven, S., Truyen, E., Joosen, W.: A middleware layer for flexible and cost-efficient multi-tenant applications. In: Kon, F., Kermarrec, A.-M. (eds.) Middleware 2011. LNCS, vol. 7049, pp. 370–389. Springer, Heidelberg (2011). doi:10.1007/978-3-642-25821-3_19

33. Wang Z. et al.: A study and performance evaluation of the multi-tenant data tier design pattern for service oriented computing. In: IEEE International Conference on eBusiness Engineering, (ICEBE), pp. 94–101 (2008)

34. Wang, H., Zheng, Z.: Software architecture driven configurability of multi-tenant SaaS application. In: Wang, F.L., Gong, Z., Luo, X., Lei, J. (eds.) WISM 2010. LNCS, vol. 6318, pp. 418–424. Springer, Heidelberg (2010). doi:10.1007/978-3-642-16515-3_52

35. Zhou, X., Yi, L., Liu, Y.: A collaborative requirement elicitation technique for SaaS applications. In: 2011 IEEE International Conference on Service Operations, Logistics, and Informatics (SOLI), pp. 83–88 (2011)

An Incremental Approach to Testing AOP

André Restivo[1]([⊠]), Ademar Aguiar[1], and Ana Moreira[2]

[1] Faculdade de Engenharia da Universidade do Porto, Porto, Portugal
{arestivo,agguiar}@fe.up.pt
[2] Faculdade de Ciências e Tecnologia, Universidade Nova de Lisboa,
Lisbon, Portugal
amm@fct.unl.pt

Abstract. Breaking down applications into smaller modules is a common way for software developers to cope with the increasing complexity of their projects. A common barrier to this endeavor is the presence of crosscutting concerns that prevent reusability and reduce comprehensibility. The promise of AOP (Aspect-Oriented Programming) is that, by using it, developers will be able to organize these crosscutting concerns into their own units of modularity. However, AOP does not tackle the problem of having tangled automatic tests. This paper presents a technique using incremental testing and invasive aspects to modify and adapt tests, enabling the development of unit tests that are free of crosscutting concerns and thus easier to reuse. Using a medium scale project, we will show that without using this technique, due to the presence of invasive aspects, some unit tests would have to be discarded or modified to accommodate the changes made by them.

1 Introduction

Humans often struggle when asked to cope with complex problems; and developers are only human. So its natural that when working on large software projects, developers need to simplify the problem by decomposing the larger problem into several smaller and more manageable ones. We usually call these smaller pieces of software *modules*.

In order to obtain as many benefits as possible from this kind of decomposition, there are several characteristics that developers should aim to achieve. Elements in the same module should be as related to each other as possible, normally referred to as having high cohesion, and they should know as little as possible about other modules, also known as having low coupling. This kind of decomposition leads to modules that can be easily described, reused, replaced, and tested in isolation.

Many of the characteristics of classical paradigms, like Object Oriented Programming (OOP) with encapsulation and information hiding, are aimed at providing the framework for developers to achieve high quality decompositions. However, these decompositions suffer from the *tyranny of the dominant decomposition* [14] that states that when programs are modularized following any given

© Springer International Publishing AG 2017
E. Cabello et al. (Eds.): ICSOFT 2016, CCIS 743, pp. 309–331, 2017.
DOI: 10.1007/978-3-319-62569-0_15

decomposition criteria, all the concerns that do not align with that criteria end up tangled and scattered throughout several modules of the system. Aspect-Oriented Programming (AOP) aims at encapsulating these crosscutting concerns into separate units of modularity [8].

The way in which most AOP languages provide a way to isolate crosscutting into their own separate modules is by allowing developers to specify set of points in the execution flow (*joinpoints*), using a specific pointcut designator language, that when reached cause the execution of other pieces of code (*advices*) that still maintain access to the original execution context. These new modules are normally called *aspects* and are the counterpart to *classes* in OOP. This technique effectively allows modules to change the behavior of other modules.

AOP is just one facet of something larger called Aspect-oriented software development (AOSD). The objective of AOSD is that all stakeholders of a software project should benefit from this higher concern isolation. Not only at the code level, but also in the requirements [15] and design [3] phases.

By using aspects, developers are able to separate each concern into its own unit of modularity. Having concerns untangled improves reusability as the code of each module pertains only to a single concern. However, the actual code is not the only artifact that can be reused between projects. Other artifacts, like tests, suffer from the same entanglement problems. Not being able to reuse tests is a major difficulty in the implementation of AOSD. In this paper, we argue that due to the nature of aspects, some unit tests cannot be reused in different contexts thus impeding module reusability. We also argue that testing modules in isolation becomes harder when using AOP.

The technique [16] that we will present in the following sections, uses automatic dependency detection and incremental compilation, together with some *Java* annotations, allowing the coexistence of classical testing methodologies together with AOP code while still keeping the code reusable. A support tool to help developers implement this technique will also be described.

In Sect. 2, the problem we propose to tackle will be identified. Section 3 describes a technique, based on incremental testing, that aims at solving the proposed problem. In Sect. 4 we discuss the advantages of trying different compilation orders to extract more information from the testing process. Section 5 presents a *Eclipse* [5] based implementation of the technique. Our efforts to validate the solution are presented in Sect. 6. Finally, Sects. 7 and 8 describe related work and our conclusions.

2   The Problem

To better illustrate the problem we will start by presenting a very simple *AspectJ* example.

Imagine we have a base class called *Question* that represents a multiple choice question in an exam (see Listing 1.1 for a simplified sample of the class). Each question is composed of several choices that can be added and retrieved from the class.

Listing 1.1. Question Class.

```
1  package question;
2  public class Question {
3    public void addChoice (String choice) {
4      choiceList.add(choice);
5    }
6    public String getChoice(int number) {
7      return choiceList.get(number);
8    }
9    public boolean contains(String choice) {
10     return choiceList.contains(choice);
11   }
12   /* ... */
13 }
```

This class is part of a larger module *question* that contains several tests. One of these tests adds some choices to the question and verifies if they are present and in the correct order (see Listing 1.2 for a simplified version of the test).

Listing 1.2. Question Test.

```
1  package question;
2  public void testChoices () {
3    Question q = new Question("Choose_a_color?");
4    q.addChoice("blue");
5    q.addChoice("red");
6    q.addChoice("green");
7
8    assertEquals("blue", q.getChoice(0));
9    assertEquals("red", q.getChoice(1));
10   assertEquals("green", q.getChoice(2));
11 }
```

In order for the entire module to be considered as as single reusable artifact, when the *question* module is reused in another project, it should also be possible to reuse the test in that project without any modifications.

As our code does not contain any AOP code, and as long as the project we are moving is also aspect free, moving it should not be a problem as in OOP classes do not interfere with the inner working of other classes. This class and its test would always work in the same way regardless of any other artifacts present in the system. This would not be the case if aspects were present in one of the two projects as we will show next.

Imagine that we add an aspect called *RandomizeChoices*, in a separate *randomize* package, that changes the positions of the choices at random as they are added (see Listing 1.3 for a small excerpt of this aspect). In this example, the *addChoice* pointcut captures all calls to the *addChoice* method in the *Question* class, not made inside this aspect, and the advice replaces that call with some code that randomizes the position in which the choice is placed.

Listing 1.3. RandomizeChoices Aspect.

```
1   package randomize;
2   public aspect RandomChoices {
3     pointcut addChoice(List list , String choice) :
4       cflow( call( void Question.addChoice(..) )) &&
5       !within(Randomize) &&
6       target(list) && args(choice) &&
7       call(boolean List.add(..) );
8
9     boolean around(List list , String choice) :
10    addChoice(list , choice) {
11      int position = random.nextInt(list.size() + 1);
12      list.add(position , choice);
13      return true;
14    }
15  }
```

Having this aspect in the system will make the *testChoices* test fail five times out of six. This happens even without any changes to the code of the *Question* class, the test or any code this class depends on.

In OOP, the problem of having code from outside a module influencing the outcome of a test is solved by using *mocks* and *stubs* [6]. The difference is that, when dealing with objects, only the code the module depends on can alter its behavior. As we just saw, that is not the case when using aspects. In the next paragraphs we will describe some naive solutions for this problem.

Moving the Test. One possible solution would be to move and change the offending test from the *question* module to the *randomize* module. The test would have to be changed so that it tests for the existence of the choice not by looking for it in the expected position but by using the *contains* method (see Listing 1.4). This would make the test run successfully when both modules are present in the system but the test would not run in the absence of the *randomize* module. Besides that, the original behavior of the *question* module, where choices are kept in the same order in which they are introduced, would not be tested at all in both scenarios.

Changing the Test. A similar alternative would be to change the test without moving it to the *randomize* module. This way the test would be executed whether the *randomize* module is present in the system or not. In this particular case, as the changes introduced by the aspect are not very significant, the original module could be tested with or without the aspect module present. In more extreme cases that might not be possible. Besides that, the original behavior would also never be tested. This alternative would also entangle two different concerns as the test for one behavior is now part of a different module.

Listing 1.4. Modified Question Test.

```
1   package randomize;
2   public void testChoices() {
3       Question q = new Question("Choose_a_color?");
4       q.addChoice("blue");
5       q.addChoice("red");
6       q.addChoice("green");
7
8       assertTrue(q.contains("blue"));
9       assertTrue(q.contains("red"));
10      assertTrue(q.contains("green"));
11  }
```

Using Aspects to Change the Test. A more interesting approach would be to use aspects to affect the behavior of the test. By adding a new aspect to the *randomize* module, that changes the behavior of the original test, and implements a new test for the modified behavior, we would have the best of both worlds. With this approach both tests would be able to coexist, however when both modules are present, the original test would never be executed. Although having some advantages, the problem with this approach is the same as in the previous one. The difference is that the entangling now happens in the *Random-Choices* module and the original test is never executed.

Using Aspects to Exclude the Test. A very similar alternative, with very similar problems, would be to add an aspect in the aspect module, that would remove the original test altogether and add a new test for the modified behavior. This way the *Question* tests would work as planned when the module is used in isolation and the *randomize* module would have a different test for its own behavior. This might be the best of these naive approaches. It almost reaches the desired result and it is easy to implement. The only major problem is that the original test is not executed in a system where both modules are present.

None of these solutions gives us a scenario where modularity is preserved in its entirety. However, we could summarize the principles of what would be a good solution:

1. **Obliviousness.** Tests should only test the behavior of their own modules.
2. **Completeness.** All concerns should have their own tests and all tests should run at least once in all contexts.
3. **Correctness.** When a module is reused in a different context, tests should still work correctly.

The naive approaches presented all fail in at least one of these principles as can be verified in Table 1. We can also verify that none of the approaches follows the *completeness* principle as the composed system does not allow for the original code to be tested in isolation.

In the next section, we will describe a technique based on incremental compilation that allows the usage of unit tests without breaking modularity. For the

Table 1. Analysis of naive approaches.

Approach	Obliviousness	Completeness	Correctness
Moving the test	✗	✗	✓
Changing the test	✗	✗	✗
Using aspects to change the test	✓	✗	✓
Using aspects to exclude the test	✓	✗	✓

sake of completeness, we will explore four different ideas that will converge into our final proposition and we will explain how these compare to one another in several different aspects.

3   Incremental Testing

The technique that we propose to solve the problems delineated in the previous section are based in an incremental testing solution. This solution is only applicable if the original software is designed so that low-level modules do not depend on higher level modules. Software systems should be built layer by layer, with each layer adding more functionalities. If this is accomplished, then the modules dependency graph is in fact a *directed acyclic graph* (DAG).

As all developers know, even in well-designed softwares, this is rarely the case. Most software systems have at least a few circular dependencies and although AOP can help in this matter, it is very difficult to remove all of these from large software systems. In graph theory, these collection of nodes that form circular dependencies are called *strongly connected components*, and although they cannot be easily removed, they can be merged. We do this by considering each *strongly connected component* in the graph as a super module (see Fig. 1). In this way, we can consider that all software systems can be thought of as being a DAG of module dependencies.

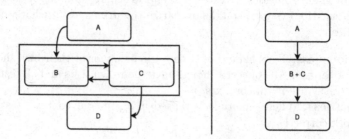

Fig. 1. Merging circular dependencies.

When the dependency graph of a project is derived, we can be sure that we will have at least one low-level module, lets call it module A, that does not depend upon any other module. As this module does not depend on any other module, we can separate it from the rest of the code, compile it and test it in isolation, shielding it from the potential influence of higher level aspects.

After testing this initial module (or even all modules that do not depend on other modules), we can take another module that only depends on this module, lets call it module B and test both of them together. Classic OOP unit testing techniques like *mocks* and *stubs* can be used to prevent errors in the source code of module A to influence the tests from module B. Integration tests can be used to assure that any eventual residual errors in module A do not propagate into the behavior of module B.

It is clear that the addition of this additional incremental compilation step would not change or improve the results in a pure OOP project. However, if module B contains AOP code, tests from module A can be influenced by aspects on module B making them fail. All tests from module A have already been run once in isolation, so all we need is to make sure that tests that fail under the influence of aspects from module B are not run again. This process can be repeated for every module in the system until all tests have run at least once.

The initial objective behind this approach [20], was to use tests in order to detect unexpected interferences caused by aspects. Interactions happen when a module containing invasive aspectual code changes the behavior of another module, these interactions are called unexpected interferences when this happens in unforeseen and undesirable ways.

When the source code is thoroughly tested, these interferences can be easily detected using the described approach. However, there will be no apparent difference between an unexpected interference and an expected interaction. The developer must be able to differentiate between the two of them and act accordingly. Interferences must be fixed and interactions must be dealt with; not because they are wrong but because they impede the testing process as they pollute the test results with false positives.

In order to remove these false positives and fix the testing process, the developer must be able to specify that changes introduced by expected interaction are desirable. If this is done, the testing process can ignore any tests that fail due to that interaction, but only after the test has been successfully executed without the offending aspect. Our first proposal used code annotations to enable the developer to specify these interactions but this initial idea slowly evolved into a simpler solution. In the following sections, we will describe that evolution and present the advantages and drawbacks of each new iteration.

3.1 Method-Test Approach

The first iteration in our approach was to consider tests as a certificate that a certain concern was implemented correctly. Methods are what end up implementing these concerns so there is a relation between methods and the tests for the concerns that they implement. For every concern in the system, the developer should be able to create a test for it and place annotations in each method that implements it with a reference to that test.

In this first iteration, the way in which the DAG of dependencies was extracted from the source code was also based on annotations. The developer had to declare for each method, the tests it depends on. Notice that developers do not specify which methods the method depends on, but the tests that were created to test that method. This means that every time an aspect is added to the system, in our incremental testing process, and a previously tested test fails, we can pinpoint which methods are affected by that interaction.

The final proposed annotation, allowed the developer to declare any expected interactions. This annotation had to be placed on any advices, referencing the tests they expected to break. Figure 2 contains a representation of the connections obtained by these annotations. Listing 1.5 represents a sample of the code needed to implement this approach for the example we have been using.

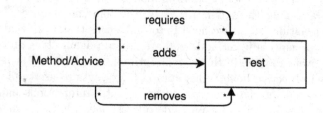

Fig. 2. Method-test approach [16].

Listing 1.5. Method-Test Approach.

```
1   package question;
2   public class Question {
3     @Adds("QuestionTest.testChoices")
4     public void addChoice (String choice) {
5       choiceList.add(choice);
6     }
7     @Adds("QuestionTest.testChoices")
8     public String getChoice(int number) {
9       return choiceList.get(number);
10    }
11  }
12
13  /* Inside Question Test Suite */
14  package question;
15  public void testChoices() {
16      ...
17  }
18
19  /* Inside Randomize Aspect */
20  package randomize;
21  public aspect RandomChoices {
22      ...
23
24      @Removes("QuestionTest.testChoices")
```

```
25    @Adds("RandomizeTest.testChoices")
26    boolean around(List list, String choice) :
27      addChoice(list, choice) {
28        ...
29      }
30  }
31
32  /* Inside Randomize Test Suite */
33  package randomize;
34  public void testChoices() {
35      ...
36  }
```

With these annotations in place, it would be possible to extract the DAG of dependencies, using the *requires* and *adds* annotations, and only run the tests not removed by subsequent advices by means of the *removes* annotation.

This initial approach had two major drawbacks, first the extensive use of annotations imposes a lot of extra work on the developer, and secondly the relation between methods/advices and tests is artificial, making the whole process awkward to use.

3.2 Concern-Test Approach

Our second iteration focused mainly on dealing with the artifial relation between tests and methods by adding a new annotation that would represent a *concern*. In this approach, each method has an annotation stating which concern it implements. These concerns can be derived from the requirements phase making faults easier to trace.

In this solution, methods and advices no longer add, remove or depend on tests but on concerns. To do this we just need to have an annotation applied to each test with a reference to the concern it tests. Figure 3 shows the relationships

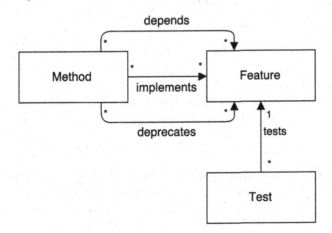

Fig. 3. Concern-test approach [16].

between the code artifacts derived from the annotations in the code. Listing 1.6 represents a sample of the code needed to implement this approach for the example we have been using.

Listing 1.6. Concern-Test Approach.

```
1
2   package question;
3   public class Question {
4     @Implements("questionHasChoices")
5     public void addChoice (String choice) {
6       choiceList.add(choice);
7     }
8     @Implements("questionHasChoices")
9     public String getChoice(int number) {
10      return choiceList.get(number);
11    }
12  }
13
14  /* Inside Question Test Suite */
15  package question;
16  @Tests("Question.questionHasChoices")
17  public void testChoices() {...};
18
19  /* Inside Randomize Aspect */
20  package randomize;
21  public aspect RandomChoices {
22    ...
23
24    @Requires("Question.questionHasChoices")
25    @Removes("Question.questionHasChoices")
26    @Implements("questionsAreRandom")
27    boolean around(List list, String choice) :
28      addChoice(list, choice) {
29        ...
30      }
31  }
32
33  /* Inside Randomize Test Suite */
34  package randomize;
35  @Tests("Randomize.questionsAreRandom")
36  public void testChoices() {
37    ...
38  }
```

To apply this second strategy, we start by selecting a module whose methods do not depend on any concern from another module. We then run all tests defined for concerns in that module. In each iteration we add a new module that only requires concerns added by modules that have already been tested. Anytests, from previously tested modules, that fail after a new module is added indicate that there is an interaction between some concern implemented in that module and the concern that the failing test is testing.

Having a richer set of metadata this approach allows us to better understand which concerns are interacting with each other. Developers can therefore reason more easily about the cause of the interaction and evaluate if it is expected or if it is an unexpected interference.

3.3 Module-Test Approach

To reduce the extra work imposed on the developer, in this next iteration we focused on removing most of the needed annotations.

As in other the previous iteration, we considered our modules as being defined in the way the used language, in this case *AspectJ*, defined its own units of modularity – *Java* packages. To prevent cases where the desired modules and the language defined modules do not coincide, we added an optional annotation so that each class/aspect could define to which module it belongs. This might seem a step in the wrong direction but it will allow us to remove most of the other annotations.

Tests defined inside a module are considered as being used to test some concern of the module. In this approach we do not care about the particular concern or method that is being tested. This removed the burden to add annotations for each test. Besides that, instead of using annotations, all information about the dependency between modules was now extracted directly from the source code using code inspection. .

The only mandatory annotations, are between tests and only when expected interaction are detected. The *replaces* annotations identify cases where a test represents a concern, developed as an invasive aspect, that changes the behavior of another concern that is tested by the other test. Figure 4 shows the relationships between the code artifacts derived from the annotations in the code. Listing 1.7 represents a sample of the code needed to implement this approach for the example described in the beginning of this paper.

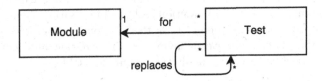

Fig. 4. Module-test approach [16].

Listing 1.7. Module-Test Approach.

```
1   package question;
2   public class Question {
3     public void addChoice (String choice) {
4       ...
5     }
6     public String getChoice(int number) {
7       ...
8     }
9   }
10
11  /* Inside Question Test Suite */
12  package question;
13  public void testChoices () {
14      ...
15  }
16
17  /* Inside Randomize Aspect */
18  package randomize;
19  public aspect RandomChoices {
20      ...
21    boolean around(List list , String choice) :
22      addChoice(list , choice) {
23          ...
24      }
25  }
26
27  /* Inside Randomize Test Suite */
28  package randomize;
29  @Replaces("question . QuestionTest . testChoices")
30  public void testRandomChoices() {
31      ...
32  };
```

However, as the extra work imposed on the developer is drastically reduced, so is the ammount of metadata about the relation between artifacts. When interactions are detected we can still get information about which test failed and which modules caused the interaction and this information should be enough for the developer to identify the origin of the problem and act accordingly. We believe that the trade-off between having less information and less repetitive work is a very positive one as it made the technique usable.

3.4   Advice-Test Approach

The last iteration was an easy evolution from the previous one where the only mandatory annotation was used to remove tests in the presence of expected interactions. We considered replacing that last annotation with advices that would disable the test. Listing 1.8 shows how that can be accomplished by simply adding an around advice that does not call the original captured joinpoint from the test.

Listing 1.8. Module-Test Approach.

```
1   public class Question {
2     public void addChoice (String choice) {...}
3     public String getChoice(int number) {...}
4   }
5
6   /* Inside Question Test Suite */
7   public void testChoices() {...};
8
9   /* Inside Randomize Aspect */
10  boolean around(List list, String choice) :
11    addChoice(list, choice) {
12    ...
13    }
14    void around() : testChoices() { /* do nothing */}
15
16  /* Inside Randomize Test Suite */
17  public void testRandomChoices() {...};
```

Although this approach does not use any annotations, besides the optional one that changes the way modules are defined as language constructs, the incremental compilation process is still needed to ensure that disabled tests are run at least once during testing.

3.5   The Process

The process used for all these approaches is, in its essence, the same:

1. Identify all modules, their tests and dependencies. This can be done using annotations or code inspection.
2. Execute a *strongly connected* analysis of the dependency graph, agglomerating modules involved in circular dependencies, thus transforming it into a DAG of modules.
3. Execute a *topological sort* to determine in which order the modules must be compiled.
4. For each module:
   (a) Compile it together with the previously tested modules.
   (b) Execute the tests defined for the features provided by this module.
   (c) Execute the tests defined by previous modules not removed by other modules.

When a test fails in step 4b, it means that the module being added to the system has an error. This error can either be caused by a test not working properly, an error in the code of this module, or even a problem related to errors in the previously compiled modules that was not detected by the implemented tests.

When a test fails in step 4c, it means we have encountered an interaction between the code of the module being tested and one of the modules previously compiled. Depending on the selected approach, the information given to the developer can be different. If using the *Concern-Test*, it should be possible to pinpoint the concern that is being interfered-with. The other approaches would only reveal the test being broken.

4   Compilation Order

Although AOP improves modularity, sometimes reasoning about interactions between modules is not as easy as in OOP. This happens as reasonings about the base code can become invalid once aspects from other modules are taken into account.

When unit tests uncover faults, it is also important to be able to pinpoint easily where the fault originated. In this section, we will explore how modular testing can be used to reason about unexpected interactions that are the source of faults.

By transforming our dependency graph into a directed acyclic graph and then incrementally compiling and testing its modules using a topological sort order, we might get not one compilation order but several ones as can be seen in Fig. 5.

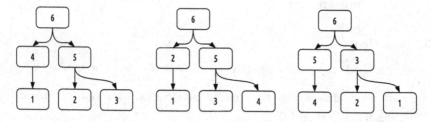

Fig. 5. Some possible compilation orders.

Using any one of those orders is enough to use our testing approach but we can take advantage of this fact to extract even more information from the tests.

For example, in Fig. 6, we can compile incrementally the four modules in three different ways: {C, B, A, D}, {C, B, D, A} or {C, D, B, A}. Let us imagine the following scenario:

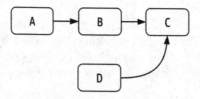

Fig. 6. Dependency example.

1. When testing using the order {C, B, A, D}, tests for module C, B and A pass and when module D is added a test from itself fails. The only information we can extract from this test is that something is wrong with the composition of module D with the remaining modules.
2. When testing using the order {C, D, B, A}, tests for modules C, D and B pass and when module A is added a test from module D fails. Using this order there is some more information we can extract from the test. Not only is there something wrong with module D but that something seems to be originating from module A. As module A does not depend or interact with module D directly, the developer could extrapolate that module A is changing something in module B that is changing something in module C which is breaking module D. The developer could then add some annotation to module A stating that it broke module D.
3. We could easily confirm this problem by running the tests using the order {C, B, D, A} and noticing that only when module A was added into the system did module D break.

In Figs. 7 and 8 we can observe how we can extract two different informations depending on the compilation order. In Fig. 7, when module D is added, we cannot pinpoint if there is an interaction with another module. In Fig. 8, when module A is added, module D fails its tests revealing an interaction between the two modules.

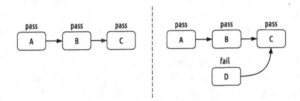

Fig. 7. Module D is added after module A.

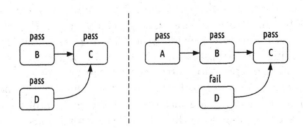

Fig. 8. Module A is added after module D.

To ensure the maximum amount of information is extracted from these tests, the module where the test failed should be added as soon as possible to the system. This allows us to deduce that if, at that time, a unit test fails, then the problem lies in the added module as the only other modules added all passed their tests.

On the other hand, if all tests still pass when the module is added, then the fault is in a higher level module. One that is changing the behavior of the module or the behavior of a module this module depends on.

Taking this into consideration, after discovering that module D, from the previous example, has a test that fails. We should compile the modules incrementally in the following order: C, D, B and A. The test that failed previously will either fail when module D is added, uncovering a fault in that same module, or when modules A and B are added, pointing to an interaction between one of those modules and module D.

This means that, to extract the maximum amount of information from a fault, the process should be prepared to re-execute the complete incremental compilation approach, introducing the module that caused the fault as early as possible.

The strategy that has been delineated throughout these last two sections can be summarized in four clear steps:

- **Develop Modules with Few or no Circular Dependencies.** The main objective of using AOP is to prevent crosscutting concerns from polluting the code. This will help make the code more modular which will improve several other aspects like reusability and maintainability. A code base where modules have circular dependencies removes a lot of these advantages so it should be already a top priority to have as few of these as possible. When using this strategy, it becomes even more important to observe this principle as circular dependencies prevent an incremental compilation strategy.
- **Use Classic Unit Testing Techniques.** Testing techniques for OOP code have already been thoroughly discussed in the literature. We argued that they are not enough for the AOP case, but they should be used as a starting point. By using stubs and mocks, the developer can isolate each module from the behavior of lower-level modules.
- **Use Incremental Testing.** In order to isolate tests from the behavior of possible higher level modules containing invasive aspects, we should use an incremental testing strategy. This strategy complements the use of classical unit testing techniques by providing protection from higher level modules without breaking the encapsulation within each module.
- **Try Different Composition Orders.** If a fault is detected, try different composition orders in order to better pinpoint the origin of the fault. This should be done only after a fault has been detected. The faulty module should be added as soon as possible so that all possible interactions can be analyzed.

5   Implementation

During the course of the work, two different plugins were developed: *DrUID* and *Aida*. Both are based on the usage of annotations throughout the code that contain information about which interferences are expected. These tools were implemented as *Eclipse* plugins.

AspectJ was chosen as the target language for several reasons. First, it is one of the most used aspect-oriented languages. Secondly, as it is Java based, it can be used with *Eclipse*, an IDE where plugin development is straightforward. With *Eclipse* we also get two other important benefits in the form of the tools JDT and AJD for Java and AspectJ languages respectively. They allow access to the source code abstract syntax tree. Although the implementation is *AspectJ* oriented, the technique we proposed is applicable to other aspect-oriented languages following the same principles.

5.1   DrUID

DrUID (UID as in Unexpected Interference Detection) [17,21] was the first attempt at creating a plugin to help developers follow the methodology being explored throughout this paper. In order to accomplish this, the plugin allows developers to define several characteristics about system artifacts using Java annotations.

Several aids have been implemented to guide the developer in this process in the form of Eclipse *quick fixes* and *quick assists*. Each time a file is saved in Eclipse, the annotations are inspected and any errors are reported. Besides that, a dependency graph is created and shown in a graphical form that allows the developer to navigate through the code following the dependencies between artifacts.

5.2   Aida

Aida [18] is an evolution of the DrUID tool, built from scratch, having the main objective of removing most of the burden put on the developer to annotate his code. It also has a bigger focus on the testing process. In this tool, we started by removing the notion of annotating features manually. We did this by considering each test as a feature. This means that the developer only needs to create test cases for each individual behavior. Obviously, this also removed the need to specify which test case tests what feature.

Using code inspection, we were also able to remove the need of specifying the dependencies between features. At the cost of losing some of the details of the dependency graph used in DrUID, with Aida we rely only on the dependencies between modules. In the end, we were down to only two types of annotations:

– **@TestFor.** Used to indicate which module each test is testing.
– **@ReplacesTest.** Used to indicate that a test replaces another test. It also indicates that if the module the test is related to is present in the system, then the replaced test does not have to be run.

Modules are defined as being contained inside Java packages by default. A third optional annotation (**@Unit**) can be used to alter this behavior. The dependencies between modules are automatically calculated by using the information provided by the JDT and AJDT Eclipse plugins.

With the dependency graph calculated, the test process is very similar to that of *DrUID*. We start by extracting the dependency graph from the source code, then we order the modules by sorting them topologically and test them adding each module incrementally to the system.

After running the complete set of tests, *Aida* is capable of reporting, both graphically and in text, on eventually detected errors and interferences. This allows the developer to add **@ReplaceTest** annotations, when an interaction is expected, or correct his code if the interaction was unexpected.

5.3   Current Issues

There are still some issues with the implementation of these tools. *Aida* has been a major step forward as it removes most of the burden of declaring the dependencies from the developer, but there are still a couple of issues.

The first problem is that not all dependencies can be detected. At the moment, Aida is able to detect dependencies caused by: import declarations, method and constructor calls, type declarations and advices. These encompass most of the cases, but soft dependencies, like the ones created using reflection are not detected.

The second problem is that every time the project is tested, all the tests have to be run again. This problem is augmented by the fact that most tests are being run several times. This problem could be mitigated by doing some code analysis to figure which tests might have their results altered by the introduction of a new module in the incremental compilation process.

6   Validation

To validate the approach we used it in several small sized projects and a medium sized one. The characteristics that we were looking for in a candidate project were that it had to be developed in *AspectJ*, it had to have few circular dependencies between modules and it had to have a test framework.

Unfortunately, all the existing open source projects we considered fail in one of these three aspects. For example, the two most used testbed projects for *AspectJ* are *AJHotDraw* [13] and *Health Watcher* [7]. The first of these has an architecture with a dependency graph so complicated that most of the code is part of a mass of 14 different packages that depend on each other forming a *strongly connected component*. The second one is a much cleaner project, but unfortunately, there are no tests developed for it.

Having failed to elect a good and popular testbed where to run our testing process, we ended up developing our own testbed. A simple school information system [19] was implemented featuring personal information for students, teacher and administrators, course information, class schedules, infrastructure information and grading. Figure 9 shows the dependencies between the implemented packages.

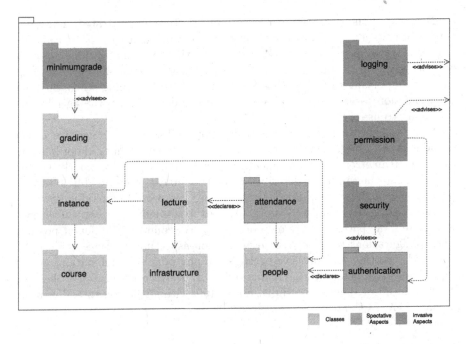

Fig. 9. School testbed packages.

After implementing the base packages, some packages containing aspects were added to the system:

Authentication. Spectative aspect that adds a login and password attributes to the Person class. Offers methods to login and logoff as well as a way to verify who is logged in.

Attendance. Adds a list of students that attended a certain lecture and methods to manage that list.

Security. Invasive aspect that assures that the passwords are hashed using a secure hashing algorithm. For this, it advises the methods that set and verify passwords of the Authentication module.

Permission. Invasive aspect that verifies that the logged in user has permissions to execute the command being executed. Advises almost every method in the code in order to do this verification.

Logging. Spectative aspect that logs to a file important information. At the moment only the creation of new objects and login attempts are logged. To do this, it advises the object creation methods but does not change their behavior.

Minimum Grade. Invasive aspect that adds the possibility of a course evaluation having a minimum grade that the student must attain to pass the course. Adds methods to define this minimum grade and advises the methods that calculate the student final grade.

Each one of the packages in the system was thoroughly tested. The total number of tests amounts to 55 with most of them belonging to the *Permission* package. This happens as this package crosscuts the entire application and modifies the behavior of almost all methods by adding a permission system. This makes it important to test if those methods are still working when the user has permission to use them, and also if access is denied when the user has no permission to use them.

By using *Aida*, interferences were easily spotted. Each time an invasive aspect was added, a test broke somewhere. In the rare event where that did not happen, it was due to an error in the implementation of the new aspect or a poorly written test. By using the technique described in this document, we were able to test all the packages of the system in isolation, without compromising modularity.

After testing the complete system, we tried to test smaller subsets of the system where some packages were not considered. We counted 77 different possible valid configurations with only some of the non-aspectual packages being used. If we add the other four invasive packages, in any possible combination, we get eight times more possibilities. Or a grand total of 616 configurations. We were able to test all of these successfully, using *Aida* without having to add, remove or change any of the tests.

7   Related Work

Katz [10] proposed the use of regression testing and regression verification as tools that could help identifying harmful *aspects*. The idea behind this technique is to use regression testing as normally and then weave each *aspect* into the system and rerun all regression tests to see if they still pass. If an error is found, either the error is corrected or the failing tests have to be replaced by new ones specific for that particular *aspect*. This approach is similar to the one presented in this paper but does not explore the possibility of adding the aspects in an automatic and controled order or the extra information that can be extracted by compiling the aspects in different orders. It also does not propose a wat of dealing with intended interactions.

Ceccato et al. [4] proposed a technique to establish which tests had to be rerun when incrementally adding *aspects* to a system. Combining this technique with our approach could reduce the ammount of time needed to run the tests as some tests would not have to be run twice if it can be proved that they will yield the same result.

Balzarotti and Monga [2] claims that the interaction detection problem can be solved by using a technique proposed in the early 80s, called program slicing. Although totally automatic, this technique does not account for intended interactions.

Havinga et al. [9] proposed a method based on modeling programs as graphs and *aspect* introductions as graph transformation rules. Using these two models it is then possible to detect conflicts caused by *aspect* introductions. Both graphs, representing programs, and transformation rules, representing introductions, can be automatically generated from source code. Although interesting, this approach suffers the same problem of other automatic approaches to this problem, as intentional interactions cannot be differentiated from unintentional ones.

Lagaisse et al. [12] proposed an extension to the Design by Contract paradigm by allowing *aspects* to define what they expect of the system and how they will change it. This will allow the detection of interactions by other *aspects* that were weaved before, as well as the detection of interactions by *aspects* that are bounded to be weaved later in the process.

It has been noticed by Kienzle et al. [11] that *aspects* can be defined as entities that require services from a system, provide new services to that same system and removes others. If there is some way of explicitly describing what services are required by each *aspect* it would be possible to detect interactions (for example, an *aspect* that removes a service needed by another *aspect*) and to choose better weaving orders.

A state-based testing method for aspect-oriented software has been developed by Silveira et al. [22]. According to the authors, this method provides class–aspect and aspect–aspect faults detecting capabilities.

Assunção et al. [1] explored different ways to determine the order for integration and testing of aspects and classes. Two different strategies, incremental and combined, for integration testing were evaluated.

8   Future Work and Conclusions

As with all research projects, a lot of possible ramifications of the work being done have been collected. We will now present some of them as pointers as a reference for future work.

The approach has been tested on several small projects created just for the effect. These case studies are no substitute for testing on a full-fledged project. Unfortunately, there was no opportunity for this to happen during the time frame of this work but it would be interesting to see this work applied in the real world.

The plugin developed during this work is nothing more than a crude prototype. We feel that it could be much improved by way of better auto-complete, auto-correct and automatic suggestions.

We have shown that the approach has several performance issues that might hinder its usage in larger projects. Using a smarter strategy to select the tests that are needed to run after a certain code is modified, or even to select which tests must be run after a certain aspect has been applied, would go a long way into making the process faster. We argue that this could be accomplished, in a future work, using *code slicing*.

As we argued before, this approach is very useful in situations where large repositories of modules exist. SPLs are one such case. Introducing this idea into the software product line research field would also be an interesting continuation of this work.

The only problem addressed was that of unit tests and AOP, but there are several other artifacts that suffer from the same problem. One example is documentation. Be it technical documentation or user manuals, AOP still has to address the issue of their modularity. We think the presented approach could be easily ported to these other artifacts.

The only language in which this approach was tested was *AspectJ*. Other aspect oriented programming languages exist, some of them with radically different approaches. It would be interesting to study how incremental compilation could be used in those.

Testing is an important and integral part of the development process. Any technique that hinders it or forces developers to write convoluted code to go around the problem, will have an hard time being accepted by the community.

The main advantage of using AOP is that we can maintain our concerns neatly inside their own units of modularity. This allows us to create beautiful code where each module is auto-contained and can be easily reused. However, in this paper, we have shown that tests will easily break this modularity when invasive aspects are used. So we are faced with a dilemma: we can either have a poorer testing process where some concerns are not tested in isolation, or we can have modules that are harder to reuse because they are testing code that pertains to other modules.

The proposed solution uses annotations so that developers can clearly mark the changes introduced by their invasive aspects. With these annotations in place, the whole project can be tested in an incremental process where modules are added following a topological order based on their dependencies.

We do not argue that the proposed solution is usable in every situation, but we have shown that it can be used in several different scenarios. We envision it being used in software houses that have a large repository of modules that can be combined in different ways in order to compose different software solutions. Anyone that has tried to create such a system knows that crosscutting concerns are a big issue.

Acknowledgements. We would like to thank FCT for the support provided through scholarship SFRH/BD/32730/2006.

References

1. Assunção, W.K.G., Colanzi, T.E., Vergilio, S.R., Pozo, A.T.R.: Evaluating different strategies for integration testing of aspect-oriented programs. J. Braz. Comput. Soc. **20**(1), 9 (2014). doi:10.1186/1678-4804-20-9
2. Balzarotti, D., Monga, M.: Using program slicing to analyze aspect-oriented composition. In: Proceedings of Foundations of Aspect-Oriented Languages Workshop at AOSD (2004)
3. Baniassad, E., Clarke, S.: Finding aspects in requirements with theme/doc. In: Tekinerdou gan, B., Moreira, A., Araújo, J., Clements, P. (eds.) Proceedings of Early Aspects 2004 Workshop, March 2004
4. Ceccato, M., Tonella, P., Ricca, F.: Is AOP code easier to test than OOP code? In: Workshop on Testing Aspect-Oriented Programs, International Conference on Aspect-Oriented Software Development, Chicago, Illinois, March 2005
5. Eclipse Foundation: The eclipse foundation open source community website, December 2010. http://www.eclipse.org/

6. Fowler, M.: Mocks aren't stubs (2007). http://martinfowler.com/articles/mocksArentStubs.html
7. Greenwood, P., Garcia, A.F., Bartolomei, T., Soares, S., Borba, P., Rashid, A.: On the design of an end-to-end aosd testbed for software stability. In: Proceedings of the 1st International Workshop on Assessment of Aspect-Oriented Technologies (ASAT 2007), Vancouver, Canada, Citeseer (2007)
8. Kiczales, G., Lamping, J., Mendhekar, A., Maeda, C., Lopes, C., Loingtier, J.-M., Irwin, J.: Aspect-oriented programming. In: Akşit, M., Matsuoka, S. (eds.) ECOOP 1997. LNCS, vol. 1241, pp. 220–242. Springer, Heidelberg (1997). doi:10.1007/BFb0053381
9. Havinga, W., Nagy, I., Bergmans, L., Aksit, M.: A graph-based approach to modeling and detecting composition conflicts related to introductions. In: AOSD 2007: Proceedings of the 6th International Conference on Aspect-Oriented Software Development, pp. 85–95. ACM Press, New York (2007)
10. Katz, S., Israel, H.: Diagnosis of harmful aspects using regression verification. In: FOAL: Foundations of Aspect-Oriented Languages, pp. 1–6 (2004)
11. Kienzle, J., Yu, Y., Xiong, J.: On composition and reuse of aspects. In: Software Engineering Properties of Languages for Aspect Technologies (2003)
12. Lagaisse, B., Joosen, W., De Win, B.: Managing semantic interference with aspect integration contracts. In: Software Engineering Properties of Languages and Aspect Technologies (2004)
13. Marin, M., Moonen, L., van Deursen, A.: An integrated crosscutting concern migration strategy and its application to jhotdraw. Technical report., Delft University of Technology Software Engineering Research Group (2007)
14. Tarr, P., Ossher, H., Harrison, W., Sutton, J.S.M.: N degrees of separation: multidimensional separation of concerns. In: Proceedings of the 21st International Conference on Software Engineering, ICSE 1999 (1999)
15. Rashid, A., Moreira, A., Araújo, J.: Modularization and composition of aspectual requirements. In: Proceeding 2nd International Conference on Aspect-Oriented Software Development (AOSD 2003) (2003)
16. Restivo, A., Aguiar, A., Moreira, A.: Incremental modular testing for AOP. In: Proceedings of the 11th International Joint Conference on Software Technologies (ICSOFT 2016): ICSOFT-PT. Lisbon, Portugal, 24–26 July 2016, vol. 2, pp. 50–59 (2016). http://dx.doi.org/10.5220/0005986600500059
17. Restivo, A.: DrUID: Unexpected interactions detection (2009). https://github.com/arestivo/druid
18. Restivo, A.: Aida: Automatic interference detection for aspectj (2010). https://github.com/arestivo/aida
19. Restivo, A.: School-aspectj-testbed (2014). https://github.com/arestivo/School-AspectJ-Testbed
20. Restivo, A., Aguiar, A.: Disciplined composition of aspects using tests. In: Proceedings of the 2008 AOSD Workshop on Linking Aspect Technology and Evolution, LATE 2008, New York, USA, pp. 8:1–8:5 (2008). http://doi.acm.org/10.1145/1404953.1404961
21. Restivo, A., Aguiar, A.: DrUID – unexpected interactions detection. In: Demonstration at the Aspect Oriented Software Development Conference (AOSD 2009) (2009)
22. Silveira, F.F., da Cunha, A.M., Lisbôa, M.L.: A state-based testing method for detecting aspect composition faults. In: Murgante, B., et al. (eds.) ICCSA 2014. LNCS, vol. 8583, pp. 418–433. Springer, Cham (2014). doi:10.1007/978-3-319-09156-3_30

Facilitating Reuse of Control Software Through Context Modelling Based on the Six-Variable Model

Nelufar Ulfat-Bunyadi[✉], Rene Meis, and Maritta Heisel

University of Duisburg-Essen, Duisburg, Germany
{nelufar.ulfat-bunyadi,rene.meis,maritta.heisel}@uni-due.de

Abstract. When control software is developed, the context of the software is not predefined or given. At first, certain properties of objects in the real world need to be monitored/controlled and developers decide which sensors, actuators, other systems to use to monitor/control them, i.e. they make contextual decisions. Frequently, it is not possible to monitor/control exactly these real world properties. Instead, a different set of properties is monitored/controlled whose values are related to the real world properties. Existing approaches like the famous Four-Variable Model call for documenting the monitored, controlled, input, and output variables for a control software. Yet, they do not ask for documenting the properties that have been of interest at first, before deciding which sensors, actuators, other systems to use, i.e. the real world properties. This results in problems when the control software shall later on be reused in another context. The new context may, for example, comprise additional sensors. In this situation, it is hard for developers to decide which input variables are still necessary and should somehow be monitored and which ones not. To avoid such problems, we suggest a context modelling method which is based on our extension of the Four-Variable Model, the Six-Variable Model, and needs to be applied during requirements engineering.

Keywords: Four-Variable Model · Context · Context modelling · Contextual decision · Satisfaction argument · Domain knowledge · Requirement · Specification

1   Introduction

Control software is typically connected to sensors and actuators in order to monitor/control the environment [9]. The *context* of the control software comprises the sensors and actuators it uses as well as the environment it monitors/controls [6]. *Context modelling* refers to modelling/documenting this context.

When starting development of a control software, its context is not predefined or given. At first, there are some objects in the real world which are relevant for the control software because it needs to monitor/control certain properties

© Springer International Publishing AG 2017
E. Cabello et al. (Eds.): ICSOFT 2016, CCIS 743, pp. 332–358, 2017.
DOI: 10.1007/978-3-319-62569-0_16

of them. Consider, for example, Adaptive Cruise Control (ACC) software [13]. The main goal of an ACC is to maintain the driver's desired speed while keeping the safety distance to vehicles ahead. So, for the ACC software, the following objects in the real world are relevant (among others). First, vehicles ahead are relevant, because the ACC software needs to know their speed, distance, and lane. Second, the ACC vehicle itself is relevant, because the ACC software needs to know the ACC vehicle's current speed and lane. Furthermore, the ACC software controls/adapts the speed of the ACC vehicle. We call these properties that are relevant for the control software in the real world the *real world properties*.

The developers of the control software then decide which sensors, actuators, or other systems to use in order to monitor/control the real world properties. Yet, frequently, it is not possible to monitor/control exactly those properties one is interested in. Instead, other properties are monitored/controlled whose values are related to the real world properties. For example, in case of the ACC software, the lane of vehicles ahead is not directly monitored. Instead, the relative position of vehicles ahead is determined. The calculation is done by the ACC software based on the data provided by the long range radar (LRR) sensor and ESP (Electronic Stability Program) sensors. The LRR sensor measures the speed, distance, and lateral offset of vehicles ahead. The ESP sensors measure wheel speed, yaw rate, lateral acceleration, and steering wheel angle of the ACC vehicle. Based on the data from the ESP sensors, the ACC software calculates the yaw rate corrected for offset. This value enables the ACC software to predict the course (driving direction) of the ACC vehicle. Based on the lateral offset of vehicles ahead (provided by the LRR sensor) and the predicted course of the ACC vehicle, the ACC software calculates the course offset of vehicles ahead. The course offset is the relative position of the vehicle ahead.

The Four-Variable Model [9] is a famous context modelling approach and focusses on control systems. It was suggested in 1995 by Parnas and Madey. It defines the content of software documentation (e.g. of a System Design Document, of a Software Requirements Document). These documents are representations of certain mathematical relations among the following four types of variables: monitored, controlled, input, and ouput variables. Monitored variables m are environmental quantities the control software monitors through input devices (e.g. sensors). Controlled variables c are environmental quantities the software controls through output devices (e.g. actuators). Input variables i are data items that the software needs as input and output variables o are quantities that the software produces as output.

Existing approaches like the Four-Variable Model but also others (see Sect. 5), mainly call for documenting these four variables (and the mathematical relations among them). However, documenting these four variables is not sufficient if software reuse is an issue, because then the real world properties which have been relevant at first (before deciding which sensors, actuators, other systems to use) are not documented. And this results in problems when the software shall later on be reused in another slightly different context. Imagine, the ACC software shall later be reused in another vehicle which is additionally equipped with a

Table 1. Input and monitored variables for ACC example (taken from [14]).

Sensor	Input variable	Monitored variable
LRR	Speed, distance, lateral offset of vehicles ahead	Speed, distance, relative position of vehicles ahead
ESP	Wheel speed, lateral acceleration, yaw rate, steering wheel angle of ACC vehicle	Course of ACC vehicle

stereo video sensor. This sensor provides information about the lane of vehicles ahead and the lane of the ACC vehicle. The input and monitored variables of the ACC software in its former context are given in Table 1. Yet, based on this information, it is quite hard for developers to decide, which of these variables still need to be monitored in the new context (i.e. with the additional sensor) and which ones not.

Reuse of control software would be facilitated, if (i) input and output variables of the software were not only traceable to monitored/controlled variables but also to the real world properties, i.e. the properties that were originally relevant in the real world before the developers decided to constrain themselves to certain sensors, actuators, other systems and (ii) if contextual decisions once made by developers were traceable together with the options they had. We make two contributions in this paper to achieve these two goals. First, we extend the Four-Variable Model with two additional variables (to cover the real world properties) as well as further mathematical relations which need to be documented among the resulting six variables. We call our model the Six-Variable Model. Second, we suggest a context modelling method that is based on the Six-Variable Model and ensures traceability of contextual decisions and the impact they have on the context and the requirements of the control software that is developed.

The paper we present here is an extended version of our paper published in [14] and is structured as follows. In Sect. 2, we describe some fundamentals which provide the basis of our work. In Sect. 3, we introduce our Six-Variable Model. Section 4 contains a description of our context modelling method which is based on the Six-Variable Model and combines existing approaches. We discuss related work in Sect. 5 and finally conclude our paper in Sect. 6.

2   Fundamentals

Satisfaction Argument. We use the terminology defined by Zave and Jackson [15] and differentiate between system, machine, and environment. A system consists of manual and automatic components. The machine is the computer-based artefact of the system that is the target of software development. The environment is a portion of the real world that is becoming the environment of the development project because its current behaviour is unsatisfactory in some way. The machine will be inserted into the environment so that the behaviour of the environment becomes satisfactory. The main issue of this distinction is that the problem to be solved by software development is not about the machine. Rather, it is about the effects that the machine produces in the environment.

There are indicative and optative statements about the environment. Indicative statements describe the environment as it is without or in spite of the machine. Optative statements describe the environment as we would like it to be because of the machine. Based on this differentiation, requirements, domain knowledge, and specification are defined as follows. A requirement is an optative statement, intended to express the desires of the customer concerning the software development project. Domain knowledge or domain assumptions represent indicative statements intended to be relevant to the software development project. The specification is an optative statement, intended to be directly implementable and to support satisfaction of the requirements. The relation between the set of requirements (R), the set of domain knowledge/assumptions (K), and the set of specifications (S) is defined by means of the satisfaction argument given in Eq. 1. The satisfaction argument says that if a machine is developed that satisfies S and is inserted into the environment as described by K, then the set of requirements R is satisfied.

$$S, K \vdash R \tag{1}$$

Three Types of Domain Knowledge. Van Lamsweerde [7] considers three types of domain knowledge: domain properties, domain hypotheses, and expectations. Domain properties are descriptive statements about the environment and are facts (e.g. physical laws). Domain hypotheses are also descriptive statements about the environment, but are assumptions. Expectations are assumptions, but they are prescriptive statements to be satisfied by environmental agents like persons, sensors, actuators in the environment.

Problem Diagrams. Problem diagrams have been suggested by Jackson [6]. A problem diagram shows the machine, its environment, and the requirement to be satisfied in the environment. The notation and an example are given in Fig. 1. The machine is shown as machine domain on the left-hand side (here: ACC software). The environment is shown in terms of so called problem domains (here: ACC vehicle and driver). A problem domain represents any material or immaterial object in the environment, e.g. people, other systems, a physical representation of data. The machine domain and the problem domains are connected by means of interfaces. At these interfaces, phenomena (e.g. events, states, values) are shared. Sharing means that one domain participating in the interface controls the phenomena while the other one observes them. Therefore, not only the phenomena are annotated at an interface but also the abbreviation of the domain controlling the phenomena followed by an exclamation mark (e.g. ACCV!{current speed}). On the right-hand side of the problem diagram, the requirement is shown (here: "drive at desired speed"). It is connected to the problem domains by means of two types of connections: a requirement reference and a constraining reference.

A requirement reference is used to express that the requirement refers somehow to phenomena of the problem domain. The corresponding phenomena are annotated at the requirement reference (e.g. D!{desired speed}). A constraining reference is used to express that the requirement not only refers to but even constrains the phenomena of the problem domain. These phenomena are annotated at the constraining reference (e.g. ACCV!{speed adapted}).

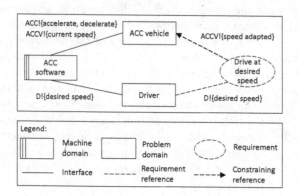

Fig. 1. Example of a problem diagram.

3   Our Six-Variable Model

As explained in the introduction, we argue that documenting only the classical four variables is insufficient if software reuse is an issue. The real world properties need to be documented as well. Therefore, we extend the Four-Variable Model with the following two variables:

- *referenced variable r*: environmental quantities that should originally be observed or monitored in the real world and were therefore referenced in the requirement
- *desired variable d*: environmental quantities that should originally be influenced in the real world and that shall be as desired by the requirement

In Fig. 2, we have depicted the Six-Variable Model as a problem diagram. The machine is a control machine. Sensors and actuators are used by the machine to monitor/control the environmental domains W and Z. Jackson [6] calls the sensors and actuators connection domains. A connection domain is a domain that is interposed between the machine and a problem domain (the remote problem domain then). There are reliable and unreliable connection domains. According to Jackson, they shall only be modelled if they are unreliable. If they are reliable, they can be omitted in the problem diagram. We will use the term connection domain in the following as well.

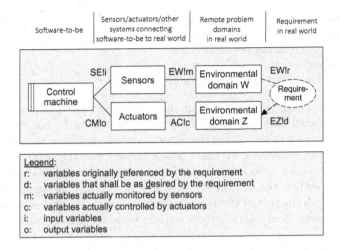

Fig. 2. Our Six-Variable Model (taken from [14]).

As regards the Six-Variable Model, there may be several connection domains (i.e. a chain of sensors or a chain of actuators) between the machine and the environmental domains W and Z, especially in embedded systems (see Fig. 3). For an example, consider again the ACC system described above. The driver may press the brake pedal to deactivate ACC. Yet the brake pedal is not directly connected to the ACC. The brake pedal is connected to two sensors: a travel sensor and a pressure sensor to measure the speed and force of the driver's command. These sensors are connected to the ESP and the ESP is connected to the ACC. The existence of connection domains means that there are not only six variables to be documented but even $6 + n$ variables. However, the method we present in this paper is already designed to consider the case that there may be more connection domains (see Sect. 4).

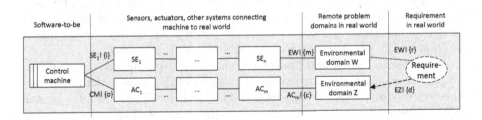

Fig. 3. Six-Variable Model with several connection domains.

As explained in the introduction, Parnas and Madey [9] define not only the four variables (monitored, controlled, input, and output) but also the following mathematical relations between them:

- NAT: indicative relation between m and c
- REQ: optative relation between m and c
- IN: indicative relation between m and i
- OUT: indicative relation between o and c
- SOF: optative relation between i and o.

On the one hand, the environment (i.e. nature and previously installed systems) places constraints on the values of the environmental quantities m and c. These are described by NAT. On the other hand, the software-to-be is expected to impose further constraints on them. These are described by REQ. IN describes how sensors translate m to i. OUT describes how actuators translate o to c. SOF, finally, describes how the software-to-be will/shall produce its output o from the input i. The introduction of the two new variables r and d necessitates that the following mathematical relations between the variables are described as well:

- IN_{RW}: indicative relation between r and m
- OUT_{RW}: indicative relation between c and d
- NAT_{RW}: indicative relation between r and d
- REQ_{RW}: optative relation between r and d.

IN_{RW} describes how a referenced variable is related to a monitored one (e.g. how lane of vehicles ahead is related to relative position of vehicles ahead). Note that there does not necessarily need to be a 1-to-1 mapping between the variables. Actually, lane of vehicles ahead is not only related to relative position of vehicles ahead but also to course of the ACC vehicle, since both are used to estimate the lane of vehicles ahead. So, there may be a 1-to-n, n-to-1, or n-to-m mapping between r and m variables. Similarly, OUT_{RW} describes how controlled variables are related to desired variables. Beyond that, there is an indicative and an optative relation between the newly introduced r and d variables. These are documented by means of the relations NAT_{RW} and REQ_{RW}. The mathematical relations between the six variables are depicted in Fig. 4. In the Four-Variable Model, the variable at the requirement reference is m, the variable at the constraining reference is c, and the set of requirements REQ refers to m and constrains c. Yet, in our Six-Variable Model, the set of requirements refers to r and constrains d. Instead of REQ and NAT, we need to document REQ_{RW} and NAT_{RW} beside IN_{RW}, IN, SOF, OUT, and OUT_{RW}.

According to Parnas and Madey, IN and OUT are indicative relations [9]. Yet, in our case, since we are not the developers of the sensors, actuators, and other systems connecting the machine and the real world, IN and OUT as well as IN_{RW} and OUT_{RW} are optative. We want these relations to be true, but they are not really facts. Rather, they are assumptions. In distributed development, it is beneficial to make these assumptions explicit, because (i) we as the developers of the machine become aware of them and (ii) we can discuss them with the developers of the sensors, actuators, and other systems and, thus, let them review our assumptions. Figure 5 makes the assumptions explicit. We adopt van Lamsweerde's differentiation between expectations and domain hypotheses (introduced in Sect. 2).

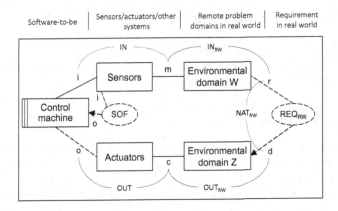

Fig. 4. Relations among the six variables (based on [14]).

First, there is a domain hypothesis *DH* about the domain W which says that *m* actually reflects *r*. This is a hypothesis made by us (as the developers of the machine) and it is a hypothesis because it has a descriptive statement. It has to be valid but there is no environmental domain that we could make responsible of satisfying this assumption. Therefore, it is no expectation. However, we have expectations regarding the sensors (*Exp-SE*), actuators (*Exp-AC*), and controlled domains (*Exp-CD*). The sensors have to ensure that *i* actually corresponds to *m*. The actuators have to ensure that *o* actually results in *c*. And, the controlled domains are responsible for ensuring that *d* is actually achieved by *c*. Beside these assumptions, the machine has to satisfy *SOF*, i.e. it has to produce *o* from *i*. If all the assumptions are valid and *SOF* is satisfied by the machine, the real world requirement REQ_{RW} is satisfied (see satisfaction argument at the bottom of Fig. 5).

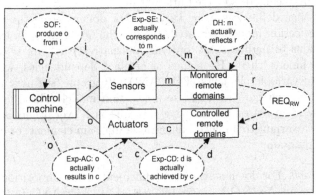

Satisfaction argument: *DH, Exp-SE, SOF, Exp-AC, Exp-CD* ⊢ REQ_{RW}

Fig. 5. Explicit assumptions (taken from [14]).

4 Our Context Modelling Method

In this section, we present our method that is based on the Six-Variable Model. Since we use existing techniques in our method, we first introduce them. Afterwards, we present the method and explain its benefit.

4.1 Used Techniques

Problem Diagrams. For documenting the six variables, Jackson's problem diagrams [6] are well suited because they allow for modelling the machine, the environment, and the requirement in the real world. Furthermore, the six variables can also be modelled as phenomena at the different types of connections between the domains. So, problem diagrams are a good means for modelling the six variables. However, Jackson provides no guidance in documenting the "right" six variables. This guidance is provided by our method (see Sect. 4.2). Although we use problem diagrams, we do not proceed in the way suggested by Jackson in his book [6]. Our method proceeds in another way.

For creating the problem diagrams, we used the UML4PF tool [4]. The benefit of using this tool is that different other analyses can be performed on the models that are created with this tool. In UML4PF, problem diagrams are shown as UML class diagrams with corresponding stereotypes to express the semantics of problem diagram model elements. For more details regarding the mapping of the notations, see [4].

OVM and Selection Model. To document contextual decisions and options/alternatives, we use the OVM (Orthogonal Variability Model) [11]. The OVM was originally developed to capture the variation points and variants of a product line together with their variability dependencies (mandatory, optional, alternative choice) as well as constraint dependencies (requires, excludes). The variants can be related to a development artefact like a requirement or a diagram (or a part of it) by means of so called artefact dependencies. The artefact (or the part of it) is then defined as being variable. For documenting the choices that are made, a selection model is created. We use the OVM to document the contextual decisions to be made, the options/alternatives that are selectable, and dependencies among them. By means of artefact dependencies, we relate the alternatives to variable elements of the AND/OR graph (see next paragraph). To document the choices, we also use a selection model. The strength of the OVM and the main reason for choosing this approach over others is that one is able to relate a variant to an entire diagram, a diagram element, or even certain sections of a diagram.

AND/OR Graph. For documenting the refinement or decomposition of requirements, we use an AND/OR graph (cf. e.g. [11]). The AND/OR graph is a directed, acyclic graph. Its nodes represent requirements and the edges represent AND/OR-decomposition relationships. A decomposition of a requirement into a set of subrequirements is an AND-decomposition iff all subrequirements must be satisfied to satisfy the requirement. A decomposition of a requirement into a set of subrequirements is an OR-decomposition iff satisfying one of the subrequirements is sufficient for satisfying the requirement. What needs to be documented in addition to the AND/OR graph, is the reasoning why each AND/OR-decomposition is sufficient. We suggest documenting this information at least informally in natural language.

Inter-model Relationships. The application of our method results in a number of models which are interrelated. The variants in the OVM and in the selection model need to be related to requirements in the AND/OR graph by means of artefact dependencies. The relationships between requirements in the two AND/OR graphs (the one containing all alternatives/options as well as the one containing only the selected alternatives/options) and the problem diagrams or domain knowledge diagrams (see next section) which show the corresponding requirements/domain hypotheses/expectation need to be documented by means of traceability relationships.

4.2 Method Steps

We applied our method to a real example, the ACC described in [13], and use this example to illustrate the application of our method in the following. Furthermore, we present validation conditions for each step of our method. These conditions are supportive when applying our method. On the one hand, they are rules that should be followed during creation of the documentation. On the other hand, they can be checked after each step to validate whether the step has been performed correctly. Figure 6 provides an overview of the method steps as well as the input and output of each step.

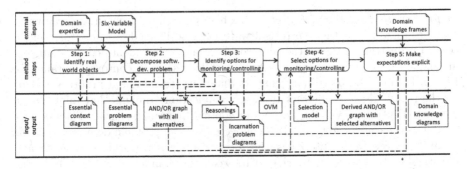

Fig. 6. Overview of our context modelling method (based on [14]).

The method needs to be applied when starting development of a control software, i.e. during requirements engineering. It supports documentation of the requirements and the domain knowledge (i.e. information about the context). We start in the real world and identify and document the real world variables

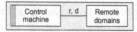

Fig. 7. Information to be documented in an essential context diagram (taken from [14]).

Table 2. Validation conditions for Step 1.

No.	Validation condition
1-1	The essential context diagram (CD) contains one machine domain
1-2	It contains at least one problem domain
1-3	It contains no designed domains
1-4	Problem domains in the essential CD are real world (RW) problem domains, i.e. they are objects in the real world that need to be monitored/controlled, provide input or receive output
1-5	The essential CD contains no connection domains, i.e. each RW problem domain is connected to the machine domain by means of an interface
1-6	At the interfaces in the essential CD only r and d variables are annotated, i.e. properties of the RW objects that are monitored/controlled or input from/output to the RW objects
1-7	In at least one interface, there are phenomena controlled by the machine

(right-hand side in Fig. 3). From there, we progress towards the machine (left-hand side in Fig. 3).

Step1: Identify Real World Objects. As a first step, the objects in the real world that are relevant for the control software because it needs to monitor/control certain properties of them (the real world variables) are identified. The objects are modelled as problem domains in a so called essential context diagram (see Fig. 7). In contrast to ordinary context diagrams (to be found in [6]), we focus on the real world and abstract from any connection domains that might be in between. Due to this reason, we call our context diagram essential. The machine therein is the control software. It is connected to each problem domain by means of an interface. At the interfaces, the corresponding real world variables (r and d variables) that need to be shared between the domains are annotated. The validation conditions for this step are given in Table 2.

Application Example. An essential context diagram for the ACC software is given in Fig. 8. It shows three problem domains in the real world: the driver, vehicles ahead, and the ACC vehicle. The driver is relevant in the real world because the ACC software needs to know his/her desired speed as well as his/her desire to (de-)activate the ACC. Vehicles ahead are relevant because the ACC software

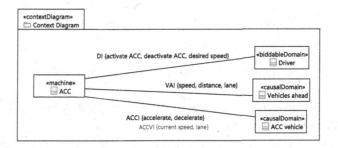

Fig. 8. Essential context diagram for the ACC software (based on [14]).

needs to know their speed, distance, and lane. Finally, the ACC vehicle is relevant because its speed is controlled by the ACC software. So, shared phenomena are accelerate and decelerate.

Step 2: Decompose the Software Development Problem. During this step, the overall software development problem is decomposed into subproblems and, for each subproblem, a problem diagram is created. The information to be documented in such a problem diagram is given in Fig. 9. We call these problem diagrams essential problem diagrams, since we still focus on the real world and abstract from any connection domains between machine and real world. An essential problem diagram shows the machine (or more precisely the subma-chine), the real world problem domains, the requirement, interfaces, requirement references, and constraining references. Interfaces and references are annotated with r and d variables.

Note that, during this step, the subrequirements are also formulated in a solution-neutral way, i.e. without considering any sensors, actuators, or other systems that could be used for monitoring/controlling. They focus on the real world and the effects the software should have there. The decomposition of the overall problem may be done in several steps, if necessary. The decomposition relationships of the problems and thus the corresponding requirements are documented as an AND/OR graph. For each AND/OR decomposition of a requirement, the reasoning why the decomposition is sufficient is documented too. The validation conditions for this step are given in Table 3.

Application Example. For the ACC software, the overall problem or requirement to be satisfied is R-0: "Maintain desired speed keeping safety distance to vehicles ahead". We decompose it into the following subrequirements. The reasoning explaining why this decomposition is sufficient is given as well.

Fig. 9. Information to be documented in an essential problem diagram (taken from [14]).

Table 3. Validation conditions for Step 2.

No.	Validation condition
2-1	An essential problem diagram (PD) contains one machine domain
2-2	It may contain designed domains
2-3	Problem domains in an essential PD are RW problem domains
2-4	An essential PD contains no connection domains
2-5	At the connections (interfaces and references), only r and d variables are annotated
2-6	An essential PD contains one requirement
2-7	The requirement shown in an essential PD is an essential requirement, i.e. it is defined in a solution-neutral way and, thus, contains no details regarding the solutions used for monitored/controlling of RW problem domains
2-8	A problem domain in an essential PD is either also shown in the essential CD, or it is part of a problem domain shown in the essential CD, or it is a combination of several problem domains shown in the essential CD
2-9	Each problem domain from the essential CD is either shown in at least one essential PD, or it has been splitted and each part of it is shown in at least one essential PD, or it has been combined with other problem domains and the composite is shown in at least one essential PD
2-10	Each phenomenon from the essential CD is either shown in at least one essential PD or its concretization is shown in an essential PD, or it is splitted and each part of it is shown in at least one essential PD, or it is combined with other phenomena and the composite is shown in at least one essential PD
2-11	An interface in an essential PD is either also shown in the essential CD, or it represents part of an interface shown in the essential CD, or it represents a combination of interfaces shown in the essential CD, or it represents a concretization of an interface shown in the essential CD
2-12	An interface in an essential CD is either also shown in at least one essential PD, or it has been splitted and each part of it is shown in at least one essential PD, or it has been combined with other interfaces and the composite is shown in the essential PD, or it has been concretized and its concretization is shown in at least one essential PD
2-13	The machines shown in all essential PDs are submachines of the machine shown in the essential CD
2-14	An essential PD contains at least one constraining reference
2-15	In an essential PD, biddable domains may also be constrained by the requirement. Causal domains, machine domain, and designed domains may also be constrained
2-16	In at least one connection (interface or reference), there are phenomena controlled by the machine

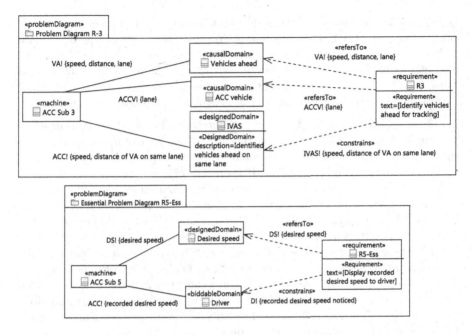

Fig. 10. Essential problem diagrams for R-3 and R-5 (based on [14]).

R-1: Enable driver to activate ACC.

R-2: Enable driver to enter desired speed.

R-3: Identify vehicles ahead for tracking.

R-4: Adapt speed to desired speed keeping safety distance to vehicles ahead.

R-5: Display recorded desired speed to driver.

R-6: Enable driver to deactivate ACC.

The decomposition into R-1 to R-6 is sufficient because: R-1 ensures that the ACC machine enters the "activated" state while R-6 ensures that the ACC machine leaves this state. In the "activated" state, the machine is able to satisfy R-2 to R-5 as follows. R-2 ensures that the driver may enter a new desired speed if he wants to. Otherwise, the ACC machine uses the currently stored desired speed. R-3 ensures that the ACC machine detects vehicles ahead driving on the same lane. R-4 ensures that the ACC machine not only drives at the desired speed but adapts the speed, if it detects vehicles ahead. R-5 ensures that the driver is always informed about the desired speed that is currently stored and used by the ACC machine.

In Fig. 10, the essential problem diagrams for R-3 and R-5 are shown. One peculiarity in the problem diagram for R-3 is that we introduced a designed domain called IVAS (identified vehicles ahead on same lane). IVAS is a so called designed domain, i.e. a data store which is actually part of the machine. It is modelled when a data store is shared by different problem diagrams. Based on the information the machine gets, it decides whether detected vehicles ahead are on the same lane or not. The ones that are on the same lane are stored in IVAS.

In the problem diagram for R-5, the real world domain is the driver. Here, we have again a designed domain called desired speed. The recorded desired speed is displayed to the driver so that s/he is informed about it. Therefore, the driver is constrained – s/he needs to notice the information displayed to him/her.

Step 3: Identify Options for Monitoring/Controlling. For each essential problem diagram from Step 2, connection domains are added. We call the resulting problem diagrams incarnation problem diagrams because they comprise a concrete solution for monitoring/controlling. If there are different options for monitoring/controlling a real world variable, separate incarnation problem diagrams for each option need to be created. Figure 11 shows which information needs to be documented in an incarnation problem diagram. The main difference is that sensors and actuators are considered and, thus, the m, c, i, o variables are introduced. If there are options for monitoring/controlling, a decision point with the corresponding alternatives is also created in an OVM. Due to the new requirement decompositions, the AND/OR graph from Step 2 needs to be extended and corresponding reasonings need to be created. The decision points and alternatives in the OVM are related to the corresponding variable elements of the AND/OR graph by means of artefact dependencies. The validation conditions for this step are given in Table 4.

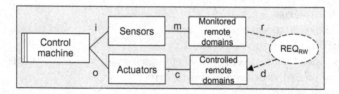

Fig. 11. Information to be documented in an incarnation problem diagram (taken from [14]).

Application Example. Examples of incarnation problem diagrams for R-3 are given in Fig. 12. These are two possible incarnations for the essential requirement R-3 (shown in Fig. 10). Alternative 2 represents the ACC system as described in the introduction using ESP sensors and the long range radar to identify vehicles ahead for tracking. In Alternative 1, in contrast, the long range radar is used together with a stereo video sensor for the same purpose. In case of Alternative 1, the lane of vehicles ahead is identified precisely, while it is only estimated in case of Alternative 2. The r and d variables (at the requirement reference and the constraining reference) in the two incarnation diagrams are the same, while the m, i, c, o variables at the interfaces are different.

Incarnation problem diagrams for R-5 are given in Fig. 13. There are two alternatives for displaying the recorded desired speed: on the display in the

Table 4. Validation conditions for Step 3.

No.	Validation condition
3-1	An incarnation PD contains connection domains due to the considered solutions for monitoring/controlling
3-2	An incarnation PD contains one machine domain and may contain designed domains
3-3	Due to a considered solution, new RW problem domains and phenomena may be introduced in an incarnation PD. They are new, since they have not been part of the corresponding essential PD. This is allowed, since the selection of a certain solution may necessitate the consideration of RW problem domains that have not been relevant so far, but whose properties need to be monitored/controlled if the solution is selected
3-4	At the interfaces between machine and connection domains, only i and o variables are annotated
3-5	At the interfaces between connection domains and RW problem domains, only m and c variables are annotated
3-6	At the references between RW problem domains and requirement, only r and d variables are annotated
3-7	The i variables in an incarnation PD must reflect the m variables given therein
3-8	The m variables in an incarnation PD must reflect the r variables given therein
3-9	The o variables in an incarnation PD must result in the c variables given therein
3-10	The c variables in an incarnation PD must effect the d variables given therein
3-11	An incarnation PD contains one requirement
3-12	For each essential requirement/PD, there is a at least one incarnation requirement/PD. An incarnation requirement contributes to the satisfaction of the corresponding essential requirement and is its subrequirement
3-13	The requirement in an incarnation PD may be renamed (compared to the corresponding essential requirement) to reflect the solution details but it does not need to. The ID of an incarnation requirement (e.g. R1-Alt1) is different than the ID of the essential requirement (e.g. R1)
3-14	All problem domains from the corresponding essential PD must be present in the incarnation PD. A problem domain from the essential PD may also be decomposed in the incarnation PD
3-15	Each problem domain from the essential PD is either shown in at least one incarnation PD, or it has been splitted and each part of it is shown in at least one incarnation PD, or it has been combined with other problem domains and the composite is shown in at least one incarnation PD

(continued)

Table 4. (*continued*)

No.	Validation condition
3-16	Each phenomenon from the essential PD is either shown in at least one incarnation PD, or its concretization is shown in an incarnation PD, or it is splitted and each part of it is shown in at least one incarnation PD, or it is combined with other phenomena and the composite is shown in at least one incarnation PD
3-17	An interface in an essential PD is either also shown in at least one incarnation PD, or it has been splitted and each part of it is shown in at least one incarnation PD, or it has been combined with other interfaces and the composite is shown in the incarnation PD, or it has been concretized and its concretization is shown in at least one essential PD
3-18	The machine shown in an incarnation PD is the same as the one that is shown in the corresponding essential PD
3-19	An incarnation PD may contain designed domains
3-20	In an incarnation PD, there must be at least one constraining reference
3-21	Biddable domains may be constrained in an incarnation PD, just as causal domains, machine domain, designed domains
3-22	In at least one interface/reference, there must be phenomena controlled by the machine

centre console and on the head-up display. In both cases, the recorded desired speed must first be transferred to the instrument cluster, because it is not only responsible for displaying all hints, warning messages, and error messages on the displays in the vehicle but also for prioritizing them. Therefore, the machine is not directly connected to the two displays.

Step 4: Select Options for Monitoring/Controlling. For each decision point in the OVM, one or (if possible and appropriate) several options are selected. The choices are documented in a selection model. Based on the selection model, a concrete model of the requirement decomposition is derived from the AND/OR graph. The validation conditions for this step are given in Table 5.

Application Example. Figure 14 depicts the OVM for the ACC software with the artefact dependencies (shown as dashed arrows) to the AND/OR graph. At the first decision point in the OVM, one of the options must be selected. At the second decision point, at most two options can be selected while at least one must be selected. And at the third decision point, at most three options can be selected while at least one must be selected. We do not show the selection model here because it is similar to Fig. 14 except that in the selection model the alternatives that are not selected are shown in grey while the selections are emphasized. The following options are selected: R3-Alt2, R5-Alt1, R5-Alt2, R6-Alt1, R6-Alt2, and R6-Alt3.

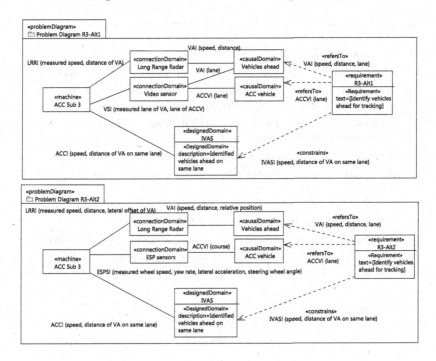

Fig. 12. Incarnation problem diagrams for R-3 (taken from [14]).

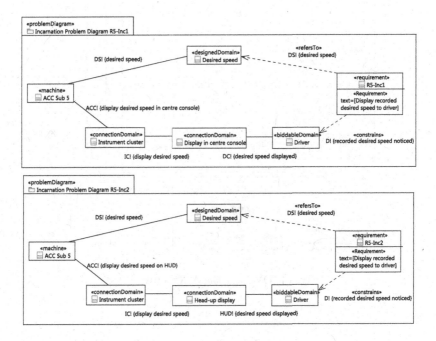

Fig. 13. Incarnation problem diagrams for R-5.

Table 5. Validation conditions for Step 4.

No.	Validation condition
4-1	All requirements shown in PDs are present in the AND/OR graph
4-2	Each PD is related by means of a traceability relationship to the corresponding requirement in the AND/OR graph
4-3	At an OR-decomposition in the AND/OR graph, at least two subrequirements must be existent
4-4	To each decomposition in the AND/OR graph, there is a reasoning
4-5	At each decision point in the OVM, at least one option must be selectable
4-6	To each variant in the OVM, there must be an artefact dependency to the corresponding requirement in the AND/OR graph
4-7	At each decision point in the selection model, there must be a selection
4-8	There is a derived AND/OR graph which is consistent with the selections in the selection model

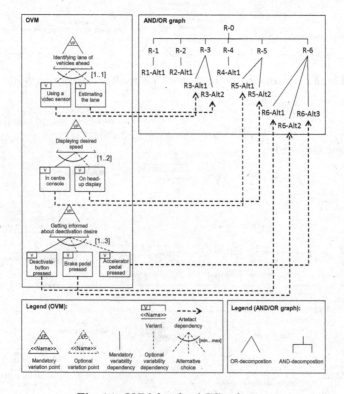

Fig. 14. OVM for the ACC software.

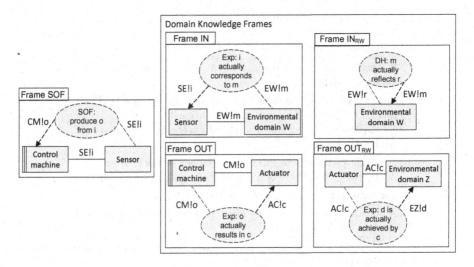

Fig. 15. Domain knowledge frames and Frame SOF (based on [14]).

Step 5: Make Expectations Explicit. During this step, we make the expectations and domain hypotheses explicit. This is necessary, since the real world requirements REQ_{RW} are not solely satisfied by the control software. We need to make the expectations and domain hypotheses explicit which need to be valid as well in order to satisfy the real world requirements (see Sect. 3). Therefore, to each incarnation problem diagram that has been selected in Step 4, the four domain knowledge frames given in Fig. 15 are applied to make the domain hypotheses and expectations explicit in so called domain knowledge diagrams. Domain knowledge diagrams have already been introduced in [1]. However, the four domain knowledge frames we present here are new.

Frame IN_{RW} is used to make domain hypotheses explicit (see also DH in Fig. 5). Frame *IN* is used to make expectations to be satisfied by the sensors/other systems explicit (see also Exp-SE in Fig. 5). Frame *OUT* is used to make expectations to be satisfied by actuators/other systems explicit (see also Exp-AC in Fig. 5). Frame OUT_{RW} is used to make expectations to be satisfied by controlled domains explicit (see also Exp-CD in Fig. 5). To make the software requirements (*SOF* in Fig. 5) explicit which need to be satisfied by the machine, Frame *SOF* given in Fig. 15 can be instantiated. In this way, a decomposition of REQ_{RW} is achieved. Therefore, the derived AND/OR graph from Step 4 needs to be extended with the requirement decompositions made in this step. Thus, the satisfaction argument is also reflected in the AND/OR graph. The reasoning for these decompositions need to be documented as well. The validation conditions for this step are given in Table 6.

Application example. In Fig. 16, the diagrams are shown that are created during decomposition of R3-Alt2. R3-Alt2 is satisfied, if D5, D6, D7, D8, and SofReq3 are satisfied (see satisfaction argument at the top of Fig. 16). Each one of these

Table 6. Validation conditions for Step 5.

No.	Validation condition
5-1	For each connection domain, there is a domain knowledge diagram (DKD)
5-2	Each expectation and domain hypothesis shown in a DKD is also related by means of a traceability relationship to the corresponding expectation/domain hypothesis in the derived AND/OR graph
5-3	For each selected incarnation requirement in the derived AND/OR graph, there is a corresponding software requirement
5-4	For each software requirement, there is a PD
5-5	A software requirement may directly refer to phenomena of the machine or constrain them
5-6	To each decomposition in the derived AND/OR graph, there is a reasoning

statements is shown in a separate diagram. The two domain knowledge diagrams for D5 and D7 (domain hypotheses) have been created by instantiating Frame IN_{RW}, while the diagrams for D6 and D8 (expectations) were created by instantiating Frame IN. D6 is to be satisfied by the ESP sensors. D8 is to be satisfied by the long range radar sensor. The problem diagram for SofReq3 results from instantiating Frame SOF. SofReq3 is to be satisfied by the ACC machine Sub 3.

We applied Frame OUT, OUT_{RW}, and SOF during decomposition of R5-Alt1. R5-Alt1 is satisfied, if D13, D14, D15, and SofReq5 are satisfied (see satisfaction argument at the top of Fig. 17). The two domain knowledge diagrams for D13 and D14 have been created by instantiating Frame OUT, while the diagram for D15 was created by instantiating Frame OUT_{RW}. D13 is to be satisfied by the instrument cluster, D14 by the display in the centre console, D15 by the driver, and SofReq5 by the ACC machine Sub 5. Once that all expectations have been made explicit, lists of expectations for each sensor, actuator, and other system can be created in order to discuss them with the corresponding developers. The decomposition of R3-Alt2 and R5-Alt1 is also reflected in the AND/OR graph in Fig. 18.

4.3 Benefit

The documentation that is created when applying our method enables developers to analyse the impact of contextual changes systematically and to integrate changes in a consistent manner. Assume, for example, that the ACC software is actually reused later on in another vehicle that is additionally equipped with a video sensor. The starting point for the analysis is SofReq3: "Identify vehicles ahead on the same lane". In the AND/OR graph shown in Fig. 18, we see that SofReq3 is a subrequirement of the real world requirement R3-Alt2. In the selection model we would see that R3-Alt2 is related to a variant. There was a decision point for identifying vehicles ahead and that a video sensor was even considered as an alternative for realizing R3. As another example consider the case in which other developers tell us that they are not able to provide an input variable that we expected from them but a slightly different one. Based on the documentation we have, we are able to trace back to which r this input variable contributed and whether there are other alternatives to achieve r.

5   Related Work

Gunter et al. [5] differentiate between four types of phenomena: e_h are environmental phenomena hidden from the system, e_v are environmental phenomena visible to the system, s_v are system phenomena visible to the environment, and s_h are system phenomena hidden from the environment. According to Gunter et al., e_v correspond to the monitored variables in the Four-Variable Model and s_v to the controlled variables. The s_h phenomena contain the input and output variables. However, according to Gunter et al., there are no e_h phenomena in the Four-Variable Model. e_h corresponds to the r and d variables in our Six-Variable Model. Yet, the benefit of our method is that we differentiate between the r and d variables and provide guidance in identifying them.

There are three further approaches that extend the Four-Variable Model. Yet, their extensions are directed towards the machine, while our extension is directed towards the environment/real world (i.e. the opposite direction). Nevertheless, we explain them shortly. First, Bharadwaj and Heitmeyer [2] suggest to specify the required behaviour of the machine in terms of the following three modules: an input device interface module, a device-independent module, and an output device interface module. The input device interface module specifies how the input variables provided by the sensors are to be used to compute estimates of the monitored variables. The device-independent module specifies how the estimated monitored variables are to be used to compute estimates of the controlled variables. The output device interface module finally specifies how the estimates of the controlled variables are used to compute the output variables that drive the actuators. Thus, the focus of this approach is mainly on the machine and its input and output variables. The second approach is the one of Miller and Tribble [8]. They propose an extension of the Four-Variable Model that clarifies how system requirements can be allocated between hardware and software. So, the focus of their extension is on the machine. The third approach is the one of Patcas et al. [10]. They criticise that the Four-Variable Model does not specify the software requirements, but bounds them by specifying the system requirements and the input and output hardware interfaces of the system. It is the software engineers task to develop a software that satisfies the system requirements and hardware interfacing constraints. To ameliorate this situation, the authors formalize the properties of acceptable system and software implementations and provide a necessary and sufficient condition for the existence of an acceptable software implementation. Beyond that, the authors provide a

$SofReq3, D5, D6, D7, D8 \vdash R3 - Alt2$

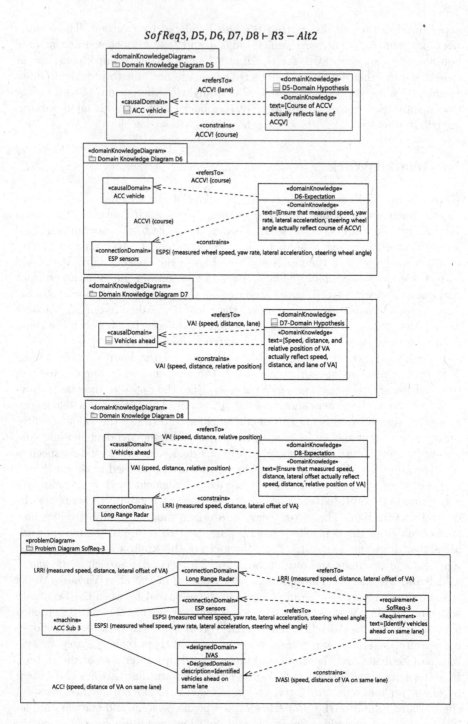

Fig. 16. Further decomposition of R3-Alt2.

$SofReq5, D13, D14, D15 \vdash R5 - Alt1$

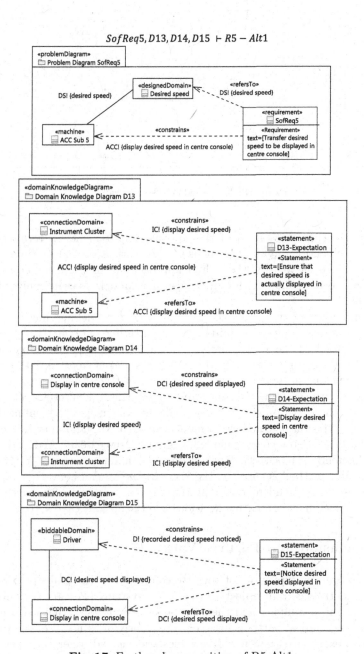

Fig. 17. Further decomposition of R5-Alt1.

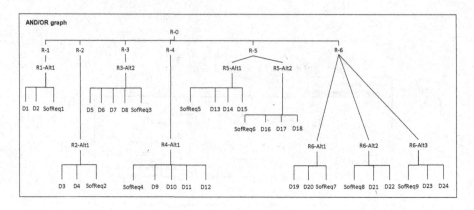

Fig. 18. Extended AND/OR graph.

mathematical characterization of the software requirements in terms of their weakest specification. Again, the focus of this work is on the machine and its interfaces. Since the focus of these three approaches is on the machine, they can theoretically be combined with our Six-Variable Model. We will analyse that in future work.

Another work that is related to our context modelling method is van Lamsweerde's goal-oriented requirements engineering method [7]. He assumes Jackson's model of the world and the machine and suggests a goal-oriented method. Multi-agent goals are refined (in AND-refinement trees) until the subgoals can be assigned to single agents in the environment (then they are expectations) or to agents in the system (then they are requirements). Leaf nodes may also be domain hypotheses or domain properties. For the system agents, agent models are created. For expectations, no further models are created. Van Lamsweerde's work has similarities with our context modelling method, since we use AND/OR graphs and his differentiation between expectation and domain hypotheses. Yet, our context modelling method is based on the Six-Variable Model, i.e. we document the six variables, while he documents only the classical four variables. Furthermore, he does not document contextual decisions and the options that were selectable.

6   Conclusion and Future Work

Control software is typically not directly connected to the real world where it monitors/controls certain objects. In complex systems like cars and airplanes, the connection is complex and there are a lot of sensors, actuators, other systems, and mechanical parts in between. Frequently, it is not possible to monitor/control exactly the real world variables and instead other variables, whose values are related to them, are monitored/controlled. Documenting only the classical four variables for such a control software results in problems when the software shall later on be reused in another, slightly different context, because it is no more clear why each variable was relevant for the software, which variables can be replaced, and which ones need to remain as they are. The traceability to the real world variables is missing. Furthermore, the contextual decisions once made, i.e. the decision, which sensors, actuators, other systems to use for monitoring/controlling, are also not traceable any more. As a result, it is very hard for developers to decide which variables are still necessary and which ones not in the new context. To overcome these problems, we presented a context modelling method that supports the documentation of the classical four variables and the real world variables as well as the mathematical relations among them. Furthermore, our method supports documentation of contextual decisions and options that were selectable so that decisions can be traced back and even considered options can be reconsidered. This is especially important when the software shall later be reused.

In future work, we plan to apply our method to further, more complex examples, also in other domains (e.g. a patient monitoring system as part of ambient assisted living in the health domain). We also consider a comparative evaluation with student groups to compare our Six-Variable Model with the approach suggested by Gunter et al. [5].

References

1. Alebrahim, A., Heisel, M., Meis, R.: A structured approach for eliciting, modeling, and using quality-related domain knowledge. In: Murgante, B., et al. (eds.) ICCSA 2014. LNCS, vol. 8583, pp. 370–386. Springer, Cham (2014). doi:10.1007/978-3-319-09156-3_27
2. Bharadwaj, R., Heitmeyer, C.: Hardware/software co-design and co-validation using the SCR method. IEEE International High Level Design Validation and Test Workshop (1999)
3. Broy, M.: Challenges in automotive software engineering. In: Proceedings of the 28th International Conference on Software Engineering (ICSE 2006), pp. 33–42. ACM (2006)
4. Cote, I., Hatebur, D., Heisel, M., Schmidt, H.: UML4PF – a tool for problem-oriented requirements analysis. In: Proceedings of RE 2011, pp. 349–350. IEEE Computer Society (2011)
5. Gunter, C., Gunter, E., Jackson, M., Zave, P.: A reference model for requirements and specifications. IEEE Softw. **17**(3), 37–43 (2000)
6. Jackson, M.: Problem Frames - Analyzing and Structuring Software Development Problems. ACM Press, New York (2001)
7. van Lamsweerde, A.: Requirements Engineering - From System Goals to UML Models to Software Specifications. Wiley, Hoboken (2009)
8. Miller, S.P., Tribble, A.C.: Extending the four-variable model to bridge the system-software gap. In: Proceedings of DASC 2001 (Digital Avionics Systems Conference) (2001)
9. Parnas, D., Madey, J.: Functional documents for computer systems. Sci. Comput. Program. **25**(1), 41–61 (1995)
10. Patcas, L., Lawford, M., Maibaum, T.: From system requirements to software requirements in the four-variable model. In: Proceedings of AVoCS 2013 (Automated Verification of Critical Systems) (2013)

11. Pohl, K.: Requirements Engineering - Fundamentals, Principles, and Techniques. Springer, Heidelberg (2010)
12. Pretschner, A., Broy, M., Krueger, I., Stauner, T.: Software Engineering for Automotive Systems: a roadmap. In: Proceedings of Future of Software Engineering, pp. 55–71. IEEE Compurter Society (2007)
13. Robert Bosch GmbH: ACC Adaptive Cruise Control. The Bosch Yellow Jackets (2003)
14. Ulfat-Bunyadi, N., Meis, R., Heisel, M.: The six-variable model - context modelling enabling systematic reuse of control software. In: Proceedings of ICSOFT-PT 2016 (11th International Joint Conference on Software Technologies), pp. 15–26. SciTePress (2016)
15. Zave, P., Jackson, M.: Four dark corners of requirements engineering. ACM Trans. Softw. Eng. Methodol. **6**(1), 1–30 (1997)

Author Index

Printed in the United States
By Bookmasters